Other works by this book's editors are listed on page ii. The editing of this edition was facilitated by the Graduate School of Management at Griffith University and the Department of Industrial Relations at the University of Sydney.

The Griffith University Graduate School of Management (GSM), drawing on a staff of more than 200, offers management education, research and consultancy services. The GSM's courses are conducted by leading academics who have strong international connections with businesses, unions, governments and other enterprises, and who are complemented by prominent adjunct professors. Its classic Master of Business Administration (MBA) course is designed to provide graduates from any background, who have some relevant experience, with a fine appreciation of management and business. The School's MBA (International) is designed primarily for academically well qualified young people who may not have the work experience required for entry into the classic MBA. The GSM also gives high priority to research by staff and students. Its staff are at the forefront of their fields, win national and international research grants and publish widely. The GSM is attracting an increasing number of research students from Australia and overseas. The current Director of the School is Professor Greg Bamber. For more details of the school, see internet site <http://www.gu.edu.au/gwis/gsm/home.html>.

The Department of Industrial Relations at the University of Sydney was established in 1976, although Industrial Relations has been taught as a subject within the Faculty of Economics since 1953. The Department offers a wide range of courses at both undergraduate and graduate levels, including Masters degree programs in Industrial Relations, Human Resource Management and Industrial Law. In 1989, the Department established the **Australian Centre for Industrial Relations Research and Training (ACIRRT)** as a national key centre with a nine-year grant from the Australian Research Council. The Foundation Director of ACIRRT and current Head of the Department of Industrial Relations is Professor Russell Lansbury. For more details of the Department, see internet site <http://www.econ.su.oz.au/ir/index.htm>.

A selection of other works by this book's editors

Changing Approaches to Industrial Relations in the Asia-Pacific (Bamber, Park, Lee & Ross) Allen & Unwin (forthcoming)

Changing Employment Relations in Australia (Kitay & Lansbury) Oxford University Press

After Lean Production: Evolving Employment Practices in the World Auto Industry (Kochan, Lansbury & MacDuffie) Cornell University Press

'HRM in the Asia-Pacific Region', Special Issue, *Human Resource Management Journal* (Bamber & Leggett)

Managing Together: Consultation and Participation in the Workplace (Davis & Lansbury) Addison Wesley Longman

Employment Relations in the Changing Asian Economies (Verma, Kochan & Lansbury) Routledge

Strategic Management of Organisational and Industrial Change (Patrickson, Bamber & Bamber) Longman

The Future of Industrial Relations: Global Change and Challenges (Niland, Lansbury & Verevis) Sage

Managing Managers (Snape, Redman & Bamber) Blackwell

New Technology: International Perspectives on Human Resources and Industrial Relations (Bamber & Lansbury) Unwin Hyman (Routledge)/Allen & Unwin

Workplace Industrial Relations (Lansbury & MacDonald) Oxford University Press

Militant Managers? (Bamber) Gower

International and Comparative Employment Relations

A Study of Industrialised Market Economies

New fully-revised edition

Edited by Greg J. Bamber and
Russell D. Lansbury

SAGE Publications

London • Thousand Oaks • New Delhi

*To Betty, Gwen, Owen, Nina, Alex and Kate, and
in loving memory of Freda and Doug*

Copyright © Selection and editorial material, Greg J. Bamber
and Russell D. Lansbury, 1998
© Individual chapters to their authors, 1998
Index by Russell Brooks

Royalties from this book will contribute to cancer research

First published in Australia in 1998 by
Allen & Unwin

 SAGE Publications Ltd
6 Bonhill Street
London EC2A 4PU

SAGE Publications Inc
2455 Teller Road
Thousand Oaks, California 91320

SAGE Publications India Pvt Ltd
32, M-Block Market
Greater Kailash – I
New Delhi 110 048

British Library Cataloguing in Publication Data

A catalogue record of this book is available from
the British Library.

   ISBN 0 7619 5592 5 (hbk)
   ISBN 0 7619 5591 7 (pbk)

Library of Congress catalog record available

Set in 10/11pt Times by DOCUPRO, Sydney
Printed and bound by KHL Printing, Singapore

Foreword

The third English-language edition of *International and Comparative Employment Relations* is a welcome contribution to and timely update of the literature in this growing field of study and teaching. The book embodies the best principles of international scholarship. By assembling a premier group of experts from different countries to address a similar set of issues, Greg Bamber and Russell Lansbury have produced a book that provides rich and detailed country-specific knowledge and information from which readers can make informed comparisons.

The field of international employment relations has come alive again after a period when most researchers focused on developments within their national systems. There is now a consensus that we have more to learn from each other than we do from further self-examination. This is understandable given the growing importance of world markets and regional trading blocs, the remarkable political transformations in Eastern Europe and the former Soviet Union, the advancing Asian economies, and the speed with which organisational and technological innovations cross national boundaries.

All these developments increase the range of options from which managers, union leaders and government policy makers can choose in shaping their own employment practices. Our challenge as teachers, researchers, students and practitioners is to determine which employment relations institutions and practices can be effectively transferred across international borders and can be adapted satisfactorily to different local settings. Yet, as the material in this book attests, there are significant limitations to this transfer process, given the desire by most parties to maintain well-established traditions and the fear of changing existing power relationships. Debates over these issues are likely to be at the forefront of employment relations in many countries, firms, unions and policy-making bodies well into the next century.

Professors Bamber and Lansbury provide a useful guide to how we might go about this cross-national learning. They point out that a variety of different analytical frameworks exist to support international comparisons. I believe these frameworks will become the focal points of important debates in our field in the years ahead. This book should serve as a valuable empirical point of reference in those debates.

I am delighted that in producing this book the authors continued to use to good avail the meetings and members of the International Industrial Relations Association, and to draw on the results of the cross-national research teams and projects promoted by our Association. My hope is that the Association will continue to serve as host to similar international and comparative projects in the future.

Thomas A. Kochan
Sloan School of Management
Massachusetts Institute of Technology

Contents

Figures and tables

Figures

Tables

Preface

This book summarises traditions and issues in employment relations in ten significant industrialised market economies (IMEs)—Britain, the United States (USA), Canada, Australia, Italy, France, Germany, Sweden, Japan and Korea. We discovered the need for this book while researching, consulting and trying to encourage people to understand international and comparative industrial relations (IR) and human resources (HR) in Australia, Britain, the USA and elsewhere.

In this fully revised edition of the book, the introductory and concluding chapters explore trends across IMEs in general. The book begins by showing why international and comparative employment relations is an important area of study. It goes on to consider some of the relevant methodological problems and to evaluate some of the most influential theories in this field. (Some may prefer to defer reading these two general chapters until after they have read the more specific country chapters.)

A chapter is devoted to each of the countries, which all belong to the 'rich countries club': the Organisation for Economic Co-operation and Development (OECD). The first four of these countries have comparable adversarial traditions: Britain, the USA, Canada and Australia. The next four are from the European continent. Two are Latin countries, with strong post-war traditions of communist and Catholic unionism: Italy and France. The next two are from North-Western Europe and have developed distinctive approaches to industrial democracy and skill formation: Germany and Sweden. The remaining two countries are from North-East Asia and have tended since 1945 to develop alternative employment relations to those in the West: Japan and Korea. The narrative starts with the country where industrialisation began (Britain) and finishes with a newly industrialising economy (NIE) that has moved from being an agrarian to an industrialised economy in less than 50 years (Korea). To aid comparisons, countries that display some similarities are considered in adjacent chapters. For example, the neighbouring chapters on Canada and Australia, France and Italy, Germany and Sweden, and Japan and Korea can fruitfully be read alongside each other.

Each country is analysed according to a similar format, with an examination of the context—economic, historical, political, legal and social—and the characteristics of the major interest groups—employers, unions and governments. Then follow concise analyses of the main processes of employment relations, such as legislation, plant or enterprise bargaining, centralised bargaining, arbitration and joint consultation. Important and topical issues are discussed, such as novel forms of human resource management (HRM), labour law reform, technological change, employee participation, labour market flexibility and incomes policy. Periodically, these issues are controversial in most economies and valuable lessons can be learnt—and anticipated—from the experience of others. For each country there is a list of references and a historical chronology of major relevant developments, which is a helpful way of putting current events into perspective. The chapters also comment on prominent disputes and controversies (e.g. the 1992 German public sector pay dispute in ch. 8 and the 1996–97 union protests against Korea's new labour laws in ch. 11). Chapter 9 describes the altercations about the wage-earner funds in Sweden, while chapter 10 illustrates how Japanese enterprises may differ fundamentally from those of most other countries. The Appendix includes a useful collection of comparative international economic and labour market data on these ten countries.

The first and second English-language editions and the subsequent Japanese and Korean editions of this book were reprinted and have been read in many countries; Chinese and Indonesian editions are currently in preparation. According to an international survey of comparative courses, this book is one of the two most widely prescribed texts in its field around the world (Adams 1991:49). This success is a tribute to the perseverance and skill of all those who have helped. We greatly appreciate the constructive comments that readers have passed on. As we are already planning to improve the next edition, we would be glad to receive any suggestions or corrections to any of our inevitable errors (which have occurred in spite of all the people who have cooperated). Correspondence can be sent to the addresses given below.

Despite the difficulties of working across different languages, cultures and disciplines, the contributors have patiently met our requests for their original material to be updated and redrafted and, sometimes, to be reinterpreted by the editors. We are grateful that the contributors to this new edition include all of the team that compiled the 1993 edition. We thank eight new contributors, who are listed on the Contents page. Oliver Clarke has as usual been an indefatigable help. Peter Ross not only co-authored the revised Appendix, but has also done a great job coordinating the publication of this new edition, corresponding with all of the contributors and reviewers. We appreciate assistance with the

Appendix from the Australian Bureau of Statistics; Office for National Statistics, UK; International Labour Organisation (ILO); Korea Labor Institute; OECD; and the US Bureau of Labor Statistics (BLS). Unless otherwise specified, currencies cited throughout the book are in US dollars at current exchange rates, as in Appendix Table A.8.

We are indebted to all those who have facilitated this project, including Tom Kochan, who wrote the Foreword to the new edition. Many people have commented on parts of the draft manuscript of this edition and/or helped in other ways, including Cameron Allan, Marco Biagi, Kaye Broadbent, Jeff Bridgeford, Oliver Clarke, John Crittall, Jackie Davies, Geoff Dow, Michael Hasse, Winton Higgins, Richard Hyman, Karl Koch, Soh Pheck Kuah, Lionel Ledlie, Chang-hee Lee, Changwon Lee, Sol Levine, Leong Liew, David Marsden, Adriana Mata-Greenwood, Jan Nixon, Denis Nolan, Gerry Phelan, Jacques Rojot, Peter Sheldon, Bill Simpson, Bob Stern, George Strauss, Mike Terry and Nils Timo.

The Industrial Relations Research Centre, University of New South Wales, originally commissioned this book in their series with Allen & Unwin. We thank the chief executives of the university and the publisher for their longstanding personal interest and encouragement: John Niland and Patrick Gallagher.

We much appreciate the support of our colleagues (not least the library staff) in Australia at Griffith University and the University of Sydney. Institutions in several other countries have also augmented our efforts over several years, including, in Japan, Dokkyo University and the Japan Institute of Labour; in Korea, the Korea Labor Institute; in Sweden, the *Arbetslivsinstitutet*; in Britain, the University of Durham; in the USA, Harvard University and the Massachusetts Institute of Technology.

Our debts extend to other friends too numerous to mention, including all those who were associated with the first edition. But our greatest debt is to our families, to whom this book is dedicated.

Greg Bamber and Russell Lansbury
Graduate School of Department of Industrial
Management, Relations,
Griffith University University of Sydney
Brisbane Queensland 4111, Sydney NSW 2006
Australia Australia
Fax: +61 7 3875 3900 *Fax*: +61 2 9351 4729
Email: *Email*:
g.bamber@gsm.gu.edu.au lansbury@sue.econ.usyd.edu.au

Note: We acknowledge that parts of this Preface draw on Roger Blanpain's Foreword to this book's first edition.

1 An introduction to international and comparative employment relations

Greg J. Bamber and Russell D. Lansbury

Most studies of industrial relations (IR) have focused on the *institutions* involved with collective bargaining, arbitration and other forms of job regulation. However, the editors and authors of this book see industrial relations as dealing with all aspects of the employment relationship, including human resource management (HRM).[1] Hence the term *employment relations* is used in this book to encompass aspects of industrial relations and HRM. On some occasions, where appropriate, the terms industrial relations and HRM are also used.[2]

Although the study of employment relations focuses on the regulation of jobs, it must also take account of the wider economic and social influences on the relative power of capital and labour, and the interactions between employers, workers, their collective organisations and the state. A full understanding of employment relations requires an interdisciplinary approach that uses analytical tools drawn from several academic fields including history, sociology, psychology, politics, law, economics, accounting and other elements of management studies. Adams (1988) sees this field as having a dual character: 'it is both an interdisciplinary field and a separate discipline in its own right'.

Adopting an internationally comparative approach to employment relations requires not only insights from several disciplines, but also knowledge of different national contexts. Some scholars distinguish between *comparative* and *international* studies in this field. Comparative employment relations may involve describing and systematically analysing two or more countries. By contrast, international employment relations involves exploring institutions and phenomena that cross national boundaries, such as the labour market roles and behaviour of intergovernmental organisations, multinational enterprises and unions

1

(cf. Bean 1994). This is a useful distinction but, again, we veer towards a broader perspective, whereby *international* and *comparative* employment relations includes a range of studies that traverse boundaries between countries.[3]

This book emphasises an *internationally comparative* approach, then, by analysing ten different countries that could all be categorised as industrialised market economies (IMEs). In other words, it combines comparative and international approaches to the subject. In this introductory chapter we begin by examining the important reasons for studying comparative and international employment relations; we then go on to discuss the difficulties and problems in this field, highlight some of the major issues and review several theories that can help to explain different national patterns of industrial relations. There are aspects of international employment relations issues in the country chapters. However, such issues are discussed more explicitly in the introductory chapter and, in particular, in the concluding chapter.

Why study internationally comparative employment relations?

There are many ways in which comparative studies can contribute to knowledge about employment relations. One of the main reasons for studying the experiences of other societies is to gain a better insight into our own country's institutions and practices. 'If one's environment never changes', argues Kahn-Freund, 'one tends to assume that an institution, a doctrine, a practice, a tradition, is inevitable and universal, while in fact it may be the outcome of specific social, historical or geographical conditions of the country' (1979:3). The reasons for studying internationally comparative employment relations include the need to understand the relative significance of various factors such as technology, economic policies, laws and culture in determining the type of employment relations system adopted by different countries.

Employment issues are important in all countries. The growth of international commercial and industrial links has made it imperative for governments, employers and unions to be aware of the patterns and idiosyncrasies of labour markets in other countries. For example, certain governments try to maintain up-to-date analyses of employment relations in other countries, particularly major trading partners. Countries send labour *attachés* to their most important foreign embassies. To be sure of obtaining appropriate supplies, Japanese and Korean steel companies monitor employment relations in the Australian mining and maritime industries, and have exploited industrial disputes there to advantage; for example, when negotiating to buy coal and other raw materials. The realisation that employment standards are important in determining fair international trade between states has further heightened the need for the comparative study of labour relations and its role in export competitiveness (Servais 1989; Van Liemt 1989). Within the World Trade Organisation (WTO), for example, many IMEs have pressed for the inclusion of a 'social clause' in bilateral and multilateral trade agreements. The United States (USA) and China have repeatedly clashed over the linking of trade to notions of human rights.

The study of employment relations practices in other countries can provide the basis for reforms in our own country and has important implications for public policy. Most countries are confronting social change, whereby there are proposals to adapt employment relations institutions to new circumstances. An internationally comparative approach can facilitate reform by indicating alternative institutions or procedures that other countries have used in an attempt to solve particular problems. However, programs of reform based on the experience derived from another context can also have unanticipated consequences. A British Conservative government introduced an Industrial Relations Act in 1971 based partly on US and Australian experiences to constrain unions and thereby reduce industrial disputes (see ch. 2). Nonetheless, this Act induced a great deal of industrial conflict. Following a change of government, the Act was repealed in 1974. It was seen as a failure by employers as well as by unions, thereby demonstrating the difficulty of attempting to initiate fundamental change by grafting regulations and practices derived from one country onto another. Hence Kahn-Freund argues:

> We cannot take for granted that rules or institutions are transplantable . . . any attempt to use a pattern of law outside the environment of its origin continues to entail the risk of rejection . . . Labour law is part of a system, and the consequences of change in one aspect of the system depends upon the relationship between all elements of the system. Since the relationships may not be similar between the two societies, the effects of similar legislation may differ significantly as between the two differing settings. (1974:27)

Another reason for studying internationally comparative employment relations is to assist with the construction of theories. Such an approach can be a useful way of verifying hypotheses or of producing generalisations derived from research findings from different national contexts. Many researchers have criticised the relative lack of theory in the study of IR and HRM in general (Barbash & Barbash 1989; Sisson 1994). This deficiency reflects the contributions by policy makers and practitioners, as well as academics; many of their studies are directed towards settling a particular dispute or issue and tend to be predominantly descriptive, without much of an analytical framework (see Giles 1989).

A further factor adds to the complexity of this field: analysts have to collect much information about more than one country before being able to make generalisations. There is also a tendency to focus on the formal institutional and legal structures as a basis for comparison, rather than on the more complex informal practices and processes. Strauss (1992) advances the interesting proposition that it is fruitless to seek to design a complete full-grown comparative theory at this stage of the field's development. Rather, he suggests, it is more appropriate to 'creep towards a field of comparative industrial relations' by developing generalisations and testable hypotheses that explain differences among countries, and which may subsequently provide the basis for developing useful theories. He draws attention to advantages to be gained from studying close pairs of countries with somewhat similar economies, cultures and historic traditions. This permits the researcher to hold many characteristics constant and to examine those that vary between each country. 'By looking at differences we seek uniformities, universal rules which explain these differences' (Strauss 1992:1).

As an illustration of such a comparative approach, Lansbury et al. (1992) matched Swedish and Australian plants in the automotive components industry. They examined productivity levels in each of the plants and sought to determine which variables explained differences in performance. The superior levels of productivity achieved by the Swedish plant appeared to be related not only to levels of investment but also to employment relations in the broadest sense, including the degree of consultation between management and the workforce, type of work organisation and degree of teamwork. However, the study also demonstrated the difficulty of seeking to hold all characteristics constant, even when the products being manufactured and the processes used are identical.

What and how to compare?

One of the challenges of comparative studies is the choice of 'what' and 'how' to compare. As Schregle (1981:16) argues: 'international comparison . . . requires the acceptance of a reference point, a scale of values . . . a third factor to which the industrial relations systems or phenomena of the countries being compared can be related'. He illustrates his argument by considering three examples: labour courts and labour disputes; collective agreements; and collective bargaining. In each case there are problems of distinguishing the formal institutions themselves from the functions that they perform. Thus, a comparative study of labour courts in Western Europe immediately encounters the difficulty that the functions of these institutions differ so markedly. In France, for example, the labour courts deal with individual as distinct from collective disputes, while the Swedish labour court is competent to deal with little more than disputes arising out of the interpretation of collective agreements.

Employment discipline or industrial justice is an issue in all countries, and therefore is an especially appropriate focus for comparative analysis (see ch. 3), even though there are many international differences in terminology. There are challenges in communicating even between English-speaking countries; for instance, there are significant differences in the style and legal status of a British *collective agreement*, an American *labor contract* and an Australian *industrial award*. Nevertheless, each of these instruments has a broadly similar role. Hence, it is important to compare the role of particular institutions, irrespective of the terminology used.

The lack of a common language and terminology may create confusion. As Blanpain (1998) points out: 'identical words in different languages may have different meanings, while corresponding terms may embrace wholly different realities'. He notes that the term 'arbitration' (or '*arbitrage*' in French), which usually means a binding decision by an impartial third party, can also signify a recommendation by a government conciliator to the conflicting parties. There can also be difficulties in distinguishing between the law and the actual practice. For example, while Australia formally practised 'compulsory arbitration' from the beginning of the twentieth century at least until the mid-1990s, there was relatively little 'compulsion' in practice and the arbitration tribunals have relied mainly on advice and persuasion (see ch. 5).

An example of how similar institutions may be applied in different ways is provided by works councils. Despite the adoption of the European Works Council by the Council of Ministers in 1994, there remain a variety of different approaches to works councils at a national level in Europe. This is due to differences in history, legal frameworks and in relationships between unions, employers and the state in various European countries where similar concepts of works councils have been introduced (Rogers & Streeck 1995). In other regions of the world, where works councils are being introduced, the differences are even greater. In Korea and Taiwan (where a process of democratisation was introduced after 1987) works councils have been introduced with very different consequences (Kim 1997). Yet it is possible that over time, as more experience is gained with the operations of works councils, they tend to become more similar. Streeck (1997) argues that European works councils are not truly 'European'; nor should they be described as 'works councils'. The same terms do not always have the same meaning in different contexts.

The collection of comparative data also poses challenges for those studying this field; for example, the definition of industrial disputes differs between countries (see Appendix). In Australia and Britain, generally there is no explicit distinction between conflicts of *right* and of *interest*, though in one Australian State (New South Wales) and also in New Zealand, a legal distinction between rights and interests was proposed in the early 1990s as part of wide-ranging reforms of labour law. These innovations received a mixed reception by the parties there. However, in the USA, Sweden and many other countries, this distinction is important. Conflicts of right concern the interpretation of an *existing* contract or award, such as which pay grade applies to a particular individual or group of workers. However, conflicts of interest arise during collective bargaining about a new demand or claim, such as for a general pay increase or a reduction in working hours. In practice, conflicts of interest are usually collective disputes. In France, Italy and many other countries, conflicts of right are further divided into individual and collective disputes. The general intention is that different settlement procedures will apply to the different types of dispute. In some countries only conflicts of interest can lead to lawful strikes or other forms of sanction, while conflicts of right should be settled by a binding decision of a labour court or similar body.

An illustration of the way in which institutions are reshaped by different environments may be seen in the former British colonies. Although many of these countries inherited the English legal system and other institutions from Britain, most of them have subsequently modified or transformed this legacy. Many of the American (ch. 3), Canadian (ch. 4) and Australian (ch. 5) approaches to employment relations are as different from each other as they are from that of Britain (ch. 2). In Japan (ch. 10), following the Second World War, the occupying forces imposed American-style labour laws and managerial techniques. These were not completely rejected, but were subsequently reshaped by the Japanese to suit their particular circumstances (Shirai 1983; Gould 1984). In practice, much of the Japanese industrial relations legislation was reinterpreted by Japanese courts.

Comparative approaches

It is important to bear in mind that ideology is a significant issue and sometimes a problem in shaping the framework within which research questions are formulated (Korpi 1981:186–7). Employment relations research in the English-speaking countries, for example, tends to focus on procedural and institutional approaches to problem solving, predominantly within a *pluralist* framework (discussed later). Some writers have also tried to formulate broader theories to explain similarities and differences between countries. From a radical Left perspective, employment relations issues tend to be seen as only one component of a larger concern with economic and social change and relationships between classes. In some countries, such as Sweden and France, there is a combination of approaches so that Leftist-oriented research is tempered by a pragmatic orientation towards public policy (Doeringer et al. 1981). Another approach has been developed in the USA by political economists (see Gourevitch et al. 1984). In the next part of this chapter we examine these approaches and indicate their strengths and weaknesses.

The way in which different countries handle similar employment relations issues can be illustrated in terms of technological change. We suggest that in societies which have had an adversarial approach to industrial relations such as Britain, Australia, the USA and Canada the parties tend to find it more difficult to cope with technological change than do those that appear to have more of a social partnership approach to industrial relations, such as the Nordic countries and Germany. Based on observation of the way in which new technology has been introduced in these countries and the degree to which conflict is engendered between the parties during this process, hypotheses can be developed to begin to explain different approaches (Bamber & Lansbury 1989). Hence, countries that share an inheritance of occupationally based unionism, relatively weak unions and employers' associations, an inconsistent government role in industrial relations (depending upon which political party holds office) and adversarial traditions of employment relations, tend to take a 'distributive bargaining' approach to technological change (cf. Walton & McKersie 1991). By contrast, those countries with industry-wide unions, stronger employer associations and a more consensual tradition of industrial relations, tend to take a more 'integrative bargaining' approach to the issue. They also appear to be able to introduce technological and other forms of organisational change with greater cooperation from the workforce and their unions.

The bilateral distinction between adversarial and consensual industrial relations systems, outlined above, and the interrelationships with other aspects of labour market behaviour has been further developed by Campbell and Vickery (1991). As shown in Table 1.1, they argue that the systemic features of social partnership countries, such as union structure, the level of bargaining and degree of state involvement in employment relations, as well as the character of employment relations, are more compatible with the implementation of new technology than those of countries with a more adversarial approach. Campbell and Vickery also note that both types of systems are undergoing change and that systemic differences in employment relations across the two groups of countries appear to have created quite different patterns of adjustment. In countries with adversarial systems, the relatively decentralised system of employment relations and the relative absence of state intervention exacerbate the weakening of unionism; conversely, the changes facilitate the strengthening of management's role, so that changes are introduced in a more unilateral manner by management and with less involvement by employees and their unions.

Table 1.1   Generalised features of 'adversarial' versus 'social partnership' systems of employment relations

Feature	Adversarial	Social partnership
Internal labour market structures	Fragmented, narrow and numerous job classifications and boundaries	Broader job classifications and greater internal redeployment
	Occupationally based unions	Industry-wide unions
	Seniority rules applied to job assignments	Greater reliance on 'merit' for job assignments
	Focus on 'jobs'	Focus on 'employment security' rather than on individual 'jobs'
	Internal inflexibility	Internal flexibility
Decision making	Greater managerial controls over access to information	More statutory-based consultation and access to information; institutionalised cooperation
	Decentralised bargaining remote from key decision-making centres	Greater scope for settling substantive terms applicable to all employees, due to more centralised labour–management decision making
Other	Voluntaristic or market-based system	Statutory-based system, meaning greater state involvement in the maintenance of structures
	Weak vertical integration of labour organisations	Strong vertical integration of labour organisations (e.g. between trade unions and works councils)
	Gaps in external labour market organisation	More comprehensive external labour market organisations

Source: Adapted from Campbell & Vickery (1991).

Gill and Krieger's (1992) study of technological change in a comparative perspective draws similar conclusions. They conducted a survey of managers and employee representatives throughout the

European Union (EU) to explore the degree of participation exercised during the introduction of new technologies. Far from being 'harmonised', Gill and Krieger found that practices differ significantly between countries, and they concluded that the degree of employee involvement in decision making depends on several variables including the bargaining power of organised labour; managements' attitudes; legal regulation; and the degree of centralisation of the industrial relations system. The EU countries that were found to be most favourable on the majority of these variables were Germany, Denmark, the Netherlands and Belgium.

Japan, with the world's largest stock of industrial robots, generally has enterprise rather than industry-wide unions. Nevertheless, it is also generally seen as having a 'consensual' model of employment relations. While some observers argue that enterprise unions in Japan tend to be docile and powerless, Kume (1997) traces the achievements of enterprise unionism in private firms. Labour, he claims, has gained significant corporate influence by establishing joint institutions with management. Labour–management councils, supported by the unions, have become an important feature of Japanese industry. Unions have become regular participants in government councils and have gained access to important information as a result. Hence, despite the decline of unionisation, labour still exercises an important influence in decision making through its partnership with management in such councils.

These examples illustrate how we can draw on international studies to generate testable hypotheses. We must still be wary, however, of the pitfalls that confront those who seek to develop grand theories to apply to a wide range of countries.

Interpreting changing patterns of employment relations

In the following sections, various theoretical approaches to comparative employment relations are reviewed and debates about convergence and divergence between industrial relations systems are considered. Several alternative perspectives are discussed, including contributions from political economy and the concept of strategic choice. The emergence of a new paradigm for understanding comparative employment relations and the impact of globalisation on industrial relations are examined, as is the relationship between industrial relations and economic performance. Finally, the application of theory to practice is discussed.

Industrial relations systems

Dunlop (1958) developed an approach based on a notion of an 'industrial relations system'. This includes three sets of 'actors' and their representative organisations ('the three parties'): employers, workers and the state. (In some Western European countries, the parties are known as 'the social partners'.) These parties' relations are determined by three environmental contexts: the technology, market forces, and the relative power and status of the parties. Dunlop defined *the network of rules* that govern the workplace (e.g. the web of rules about pay and conditions) as the *output* of the industrial relations system. Dunlop's approach has been influential among a generation of scholars in the English-speaking countries and elsewhere; it was a notable attempt to identify a theoretical framework for industrial relations. Walker (1967) was influenced by Dunlop and went on to urge that we should transcend the dominant descriptive approaches to 'foreign industrial relations systems' and concentrate on identifying the role, importance and inter-action of different factors that shape and influence industrial relations in different national contexts. Others enlarged on Dunlop's approach (e.g. Blain & Gennard 1970; Craig 1975).

Various critics accept that Dunlop's framework is useful as 'a model within which facts may be organised, but stress that it must not be understood as having a predictive value in itself' (Gill 1969). Criticisms of the systems approach include its neglect of the importance of such behavioural variables as motivations, perceptions and attitudes (Bain & Clegg 1974). Dunlop ignores the insights about the importance of informal work groups that were developed by his Harvard colleagues, the 'human relations school' (e.g. Mayo 1949). Moreover, Dunlop's approach tends to concentrate on the rule-making institutions and the settlement of conflict rather than examining the causes of conflict and the role played by *people* in making decisions about the employment relationship (Hyman 1975). In spite of the many attempts to develop a systems approach, it is by no means a generally accepted theory.

Collective bargaining

Dunlop's approach has been a point of departure for subsequent re-searchers who have compared various systems of collective bargaining. Clegg draws on data from six countries to support his argument that:

> The extent and depth of collective bargaining and the degree of union security offered by collective bargaining are the three dimensions which influence trade union density. The level of bargaining accounts for the extent of decentralisation in union government, including the power and independence of workplace organisations, and decentralisation in turn helps to explain the degree of factionalism within unions . . . (1976:118)

Clegg argues that dimensions of collective bargaining are mainly determined by the structures of management and of employers' organisations. However, he also emphasises the importance of the law in shaping collective bargaining, especially when introduced in the early stages of the development of an industrial relations system.

Clegg's approach is narrower than Dunlop's in that he seems to ignore the importance of the economic, social and technological environment while concentrating on collective bargaining and the 'web of rules'. Clegg sees collective bargaining as the principal influence on union behaviour, yet unions are also part of the collective bargaining process. Clegg was writing during a period when centralised forms of collective bargaining, especially in Europe, were at their zenith. From 1945 until the late 1970s, collective bargaining expanded in most IMEs in terms of coverage of the workforce and the scope of issues. Elements of the employment relationship that had traditionally been regarded as the prerogative of management were drawn into the bargaining process. By the early 1980s, however, there was a change in bargaining relationships. Unions were losing power in the labour market as well as in the political arena; moreover, employers were demanding that labour markets should be deregulated. By the mid-1980s the movement towards deregulation and decentralised bargaining had gained momentum in Britain and many other European countries, though the trend was by no means uniform (Albeda 1984).

Adams (1981) and Sisson (1987) sought to develop the collective bargaining approach in an international context, but they both focus on the role of employers. Adams points out that employers' attitudes and behaviour towards unions differ significantly between Europe and North America. In the former, typically, employers are organised into strong associations that engage in collective bargaining with unions (and sometimes with the state). By contrast, in North America, employers have generally not formed strong associations and even where they have, it is much less usual for them to engage in collective bargaining. Adams holds that these differences are attributable to the differing early political or economic strategies of the various labour movements and the resulting differing degrees of state intervention in industrial relations arrangements.

Sisson argues that there could be no adequate theory of collective bargaining that overlooked the interests of management. Furthermore, there has been widespread failure to appreciate how the role of employers in collective bargaining varies from country to country. Sisson compares the role of employers and their organisations in the development of collective bargaining in seven IMEs. He also concludes that differences between the countries were rooted in historical experience, particularly flowing from the impact of industrialisation. Hence, in Western Europe, including Britain, multi-employer bargaining emerged as the predominant pattern largely because employers in the metalworking industries were confronted with the challenge of national unions organised along occupational or industrial lines. By contrast, single-employer bargaining emerged in the USA and Japan because the relatively large employers that had emerged at an early stage in both countries were able to exert pressure on unions to bargain at the enterprise or establishment level. When legislation was introduced requiring employers to recognise unions (in the 1930s and 1940s), such employers had already exerted a profound influence on the labour movement and were able to deny unions the platform from which to push for more effective national unionism, especially in Japan.

The key features of collective bargaining whether single-employer or multi-employer are not easily changed. Sisson instances the lack of success of attempts to extend the scope of collective bargaining at the workplace level in several Western European countries, excluding Britain. He also makes the important point that most attempts to change the collective bargaining system by legislation are unlikely to have the intended effect, unless they take into account the parties' wishes (as illustrated by the above-mentioned experience of the British 1971 Act). There are significant forces in most countries that tend to constrain major deviations from their industrial relations traditions. Nonetheless, in the 1979–97 period, following determined and continuing attempts by the Thatcher Conservative government, there were fundamental changes in British industrial relations (see ch. 2).

Decentralisation of bargaining

Since the mid-1980s there has been a trend towards less-centralised forms of collective bargaining in most IMEs. This has generally involved the locus of bargaining shifting downwards from a national or industry level, to the enterprise or workplace level. However, the degree of decentralisation and the means by which changes in bargaining structures occurred have varied between countries. Based on a comparison of experiences in six countries (Australia, Germany, Italy, Sweden, Britain and the USA), Katz (1993) reports many similarities in the process of decentralisation. In each country except Germany, there was a downward shift in the formal structure of bargaining initiated by employers, and a consequent reduction in the extent of multi-employer bargaining. With the exception of Australia (where there was an Accord between the unions and the then Labor government; see ch. 5) most central union organisations opposed decentralisation of bargaining.

Katz evaluates three hypotheses that have been advanced to explain the trend towards decentralised bargaining: shifts in bargaining power from unions to employers; the emergence of new forms of work organisation that put a premium on flexibility and employee participation; and the decentralisation of corporate structures and diversification of worker preferences. Katz concludes that the second hypothesis is the most convincing on the grounds that both labour and management appear to have gained distinct advantages from the work restructuring that accompanied decentralisation. However, shifts in bargaining power, as well as the diversification of corporate and worker interests, are also important contributing factors to the decentralisation process. Locke (1992) highlights the continuing wide variations in bargaining practices within particular countries.

Controversies about convergence

A focus for much of the theorising about comparative employment relations (and especially about industrialisation) has been the debate about whether there has been convergence or divergence between the different patterns of institutional behaviour in various countries, especially the IMEs. One of the most influential comparative books argues that industrial societies would gradually become more alike. Although their book was first published in 1960 and has often been misinterpreted, the arguments of Kerr, Dunlop, Harbison and Myers (1973) remain influential, especially in English-speaking countries. Their core proposition is that there is a global tendency for technological and market forces associated with industrialisation to push national industrial relations systems towards uniformity or 'convergence'. They argue that there is a *logic of industrialism*, even though the process has various patterns in different countries. Among the 'universals' of the logic are the development of a concentrated, disciplined workforce with new and changing skills, and a larger role for governments in providing the infrastructure required for industrialisation. An essential part of the logic of industrialism is the growth or imposition of a pluralistic consensus which provides an integrated body of ideas and beliefs. Each industrialising society develops an industrial relations system, which becomes increasingly tripartite as industrialisation proceeds.

Figure 1.1 illustrates schematically the logic of industrialism, showing how the various social changes are related to the prime cause: technology. Convergence between advanced industrial societies occurs most readily at the technological level, at workplace and industry levels, or at urban levels, and then at national levels. However, Kerr et al. do concede that total convergence is unlikely because of the persistence of political, social, cultural and ideological differences. Kerr later (1983) modified his views and argues that convergence is a *tendency* that is not likely to precipitate identical systems among industrialised countries. He also notes that while IMEs at the macro level might appear to be similar, differences at the micro level could be quite profound. Further, industrialisation on a world scale is never likely to be total because the barriers to it in many less-developed economies (LDEs) are insurmountable. Nevertheless, he still holds the central assumptions of the original study; namely, that the basic tensions inherent in the process of industrialisation had been overcome by modern industrial societies and that there would be a growing consensus around liberal–democratic institutions and the pluralist mixed economy. Relations between 'managers and the managed' would be increasingly embedded in a web of rules agreed to by both parties, so that industrial conflict would 'wither away' (Ross & Hartman 1960).

Modified convergence

Many writers criticise the 'liberal–pluralist' approach of Kerr et al. For example, Chamberlain (1961:480) sees their book as:

> . . . long on categories and classifications and impressionistic observations, but . . . short on analysis. It is perhaps best described as a latter-day descendant of the 19th century German school of economic history, whose hallmark was a literary exposition of the transition from one idealised state of economic development to another.

Other critics focus on the 'deterministic view of the future' represented by industrialisation as an 'invincible process' (Cochrane 1976). According to Bendix (1970:273), 'seldom has social change been interpreted in so *magisterial* a fashion, while all contingencies of action are treated as mere historical variations which cannot alter the logic of industrialism'. Arguably, Kerr et al. were too concerned with maintaining the *status quo*, controlling conflict, defending the existing institutions and imposing an ethnocentric, American, perspective on the rest of the world. It is relevant to note that they were writing against the background of the Cold War.

Doeringer (1981) is less critical, but argues that convergence should be seen in a different form compared with that envisaged by Kerr et al. Doeringer argues that countries develop alternative solutions to common industrial relations problems; thus all industrialised countries show a tendency to institutionalise their arrangements for rule making about employment, even though their particular approaches vary. Differences between countries, therefore, are by no means random, but are rooted in their individual responses to the underlying compulsions of industrialisation. He analyses convergence using a three-part framework: first, as the result of responses to problems common to all industrial relations systems; second, as the process by which gaps in areas in the institutional industrial relations arrangements are filled; and third, as the realisation that, over time, all industrial relations systems selectively respond to multiple and often incompatible goals. Hence, what may appear as differences between systems may be due

Figure 1.1   The logic of industrialism

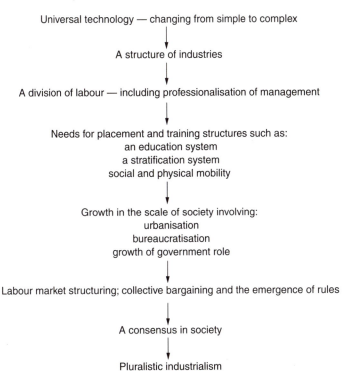

Universal technology — changing from simple to complex

A structure of industries

A division of labour — including professionalisation of management

Needs for placement and training structures such as:
an education system
a stratification system
social and physical mobility

Growth in the scale of society involving:
urbanisation
bureaucratisation
growth of government role

Labour market structuring; collective bargaining and the emergence of rules

A consensus in society

Pluralistic industrialism

Source: Reproduced with permission from Brown & Harrison (1978:129).

simply to differences in the goals that are being pursued at a particular point in time.

Piore (1981) also doubts that the convergence thesis is a general theory of comparative employment relations. He observes that certain aspects of industrial societies tend to converge while others diverge, depending upon time and circumstances. An alternative approach suggested by Piore is to focus on the role of regulatory institutions in the industrial relations of different societies. He argues that capitalist economies pass through a distinct series of regulatory systems in the course of their historical development. As technology and industry change, they outgrow the regulatory structures initially adopted, and the system has increasing difficulty maintaining itself in balance. The result is an economic and social crisis that can be resolved only by the development of a new set of institutions.

Industrialisation appears to be occurring more rapidly in some of the newly industrialising economies (NIEs) than has been the case in the past; therefore, industrial relations institutions in the NIEs have developed more quickly than in the IMEs. An example of this is the weak state of unions in most of the first four Asian 'tigers'—Hong Kong, Korea, Singapore and Taiwan—although the growth of unions (official and unofficial) in Korea since 1987 provides an exceptional case in the Asian region (see ch. 11; Verma et al. 1995).

Late development

In comparison with the work of Kerr et al. and that inspired by it, Dore (1973) has a more modest approach. He too aims to account for international differences, but he focuses on Japan and Britain. He places less emphasis on technology than Kerr et al., and highlights the importance of other factors: the emergence of giant corporations and the spread of democratic ideals of egalitarianism.

In examining Japanese industrial relations, Dore identifies a 'late-comer' effect. Since Japan began to industrialise relatively late (a century after Britain), it was able to learn from the experience of the countries that had already been through that process. He argues that late developers had been able to adopt organisational forms and institutions that were more suited to industrialisation than those of countries that industrialised relatively early. There have been general criticisms of Dore's thesis and specific criticisms of some of his detailed interpretation, including the narrow basis of his empirical research; however, his approach has considerable potential in this field. 'By concentrating on only two country cases and dealing with these cases in a consistently and systematically comparative fashion, Dore succeeded in minimising the danger of lapsing into either vacuous description or superficial comparison' (Shalev 1980:40).

Dore concludes that employment arrangements are becoming more alike, but Japan, rather than any Western country, is the model towards which other countries are converging. Support for this argument can be found in the number of so-called 'Japanese management practices' that have now been incorporated under the umbrella of 'world best practice' in manufacturing industry.

Since the 1970s, as they adopted more globally oriented strategies, Japanese transnational enterprises have been increasingly exporting their approaches to managing production, human resources (HR), work organisation and industrial relations. Although these approaches have been strongly criticised (e.g. Parker & Slaughter 1988), business leaders tend to see them as successful, especially in the manufacturing sector, so that many non-Japanese enterprises are trying to emulate Japanese role models. This is illustrated vividly in a best-selling book on the automobile industry, a study of 'Japan's revolutionary leap from mass production to lean production, and what industry everywhere can learn from it' (Womack et al. 1990; also see Fucini & Fucini 1990; Bamber et al. 1992). Yet a recent study of the application of the 'lean production' concept—derived from Toyota—by auto companies around the world, indicates that this has not resulted in exact duplication or imitation. Instead, there are important variations which reflect differences in strategies and power of the parties involved, as well as the effects of local institutional and cultural forces (Kochan et al. 1997). Hence, it may be more accurate to refer to 'Mediterranean' or 'Scandinavian' forms of lean production, which share certain common characteristics but also reflect important local differences (Camuffo & Micelli 1997; Brulin & Nilsson 1997). Furthermore, some companies have chosen not to adopt lean production in certain (or all) of their locations because its organisational and employment relations requirements are not consistent with their managerial values and traditions.

Towards divergence?

Poole (1986) and Streeck (1988) refuelled the earlier convergence debates. They outline several factors that operate in most IMEs to induce structural change, but hold that these are leading to diverse outcomes or 'divergent evolutionary trajectories'. Streeck likens this situation to the growing variety in the use of technology and in the structure of work organisation—whose present trend has been described as an 'explosion', with different strands of development moving away from one another in different directions; as opposed to 'implosive' convergence towards one central 'best practice'.

The changes in the structure of employment are causing unions to lose power. These changes include shifts in employment from the industrial to the service sector; the growth of a 'secondary sector' of small subcontracting firms and of a marginal workforce in unstable employment ('dualisation'); increases in part-time work and white-collar jobs; the increasing participation of women in the labour market; the growing use of HRM techniques, including worker-involvement schemes; and other individually oriented approaches. Although these changes are widespread, they are likely to have very different consequences for employers, governments and unions, depending on their organisational base. Thus, where union density is low, it is likely to decline further; whereas where density is high, it is more likely to remain stable.

Union strategies for coping with structural changes are also likely to vary in accordance with their current situation. Heterogeneity is increasing not only between, but also within, national industrial relations systems. A growing 'individualisation' within the workforce (which is promoted by many employers) is eroding the membership base of unions and resulting in three different responses. There is, first, de-unionisation; with unions organising fewer of the many groups with differing interests that form the labour force; second, the decomposition of the labour movement resulting from interorganisational fragmentation; third, the preservation of formal organisational unity at the national or sectoral level, but at the price of heightened internal policy conflict. Streeck warns that the ability of unions to manage internal heterogeneity (and thereby preserve a strategic continuity) will be put to severe test in the coming years in all IMEs. To maintain even a modicum of centralised decision making, unions will require major organisation and institutional change. Hence unions in Britain, the USA, Canada and Australia, and elsewhere, appear to be implementing significant innovations.

Divergence in unionism?

Based on data from the USA and other IMEs, Freeman argues that 'far from converging to some modal type, trade unionism . . . traditionally the principal worker institution under capitalism developed remarkably differently among Western countries in the 1970s and 1980s' (1989). While union density rose or at least was maintained at high levels in much of continental Europe and Canada, it declined significantly in the USA and, to a lesser extent, in Japan, the United Kingdom (UK), and Australia (see Appendix). This divergence in density occurred despite such common factors as increasing trade, technological transfer and capital flows between countries, which might have been expected to exert pressures for similarities.

The USA has adopted a different route from most other IMEs with regard to unionisation and employment relations in recent years (see ch. 3); no other country has gone as far towards 'the union-free nirvana of the rabid opponents of trade unionism' (Blanchflower & Freeman 1989). Yet the USA also exhibits a mixture of two contrasting trends: a near collapse of unionism in the private sector, but a relatively stable level of unionisation in the public sector. One of the main causes of decline in private sector unionism in the USA is that unions there have significantly greater effects on wages than do unions in other countries, which gives US employers a significant financial incentive to oppose them. Blanchflower and Freeman forecast that unless the decline can be arrested, unions in the USA will be 'relegated to a few aged industrial sectors and to public and some non-profit sectors, producing what can be called ghetto unionism'. To recover their position, unions, they argue, will have to emphasise their 'collective voice' role, drawing on international experience and experimenting with new initiatives. The re-election of a Democratic Party candidate, President Clinton, in 1996, renewed some hopes of a revival in unions' fortunes.

We should not be surprised to see conflicting perspectives emerge in parallel debates and controversies that are taking place in Europe and the USA. As Streeck argues in relation to European developments, unionists are faced with a choice of strategy between 'optimistic conservatism' and a 'productionist strategy' (1987). The former strategy assumes that the economic and industrial environment has not undergone a permanent change and that economic cycles will allow unions to resume their traditional roles and functions involving a predominant concern for wage bargaining and securing non-wage benefits for their members. Alternatively, unions can adopt a 'productionist strategy' in which they assist employers to develop a cooperative and committed workforce that will comply with the new production systems, thereby avoiding the marginalisation of the unions and an associated decline of union membership.

The diversity of responses by unions, employers and governments to changing conditions in Western Europe is emphasised by Clarke (1990), who notes that when 'surveying the European scene today it is difficult to see much of a convergence of industrial relations systems'. Nevertheless, there is a conspicuous difference between, on the one hand, Norway, Sweden and Austria and, on the other hand, most other countries. In the first group unions have not had to face substantial membership loss and they continue to have a strong influence on (mainly) social democratic governments.

Flexibility

Changes in markets and production methods are precipitating strong pressures for the decentralisation of employment relations and for custom-made rules for particular workplaces or enterprises, even within the most centralised systems of employment relations. In recent years, 'flexibility' has been seen as an important issue (Bamber, Boreham & Harley 1992), though its meaning and application have varied widely. Streeck argues that industrial relations systems are polarising around three types of flexibility as a response to the changing economic environment. First, there is the 'neo-liberal model' of flexibility through recourse to the external labour market (or a 'return to the market'), especially where there are weak unions and few legal provisions for employment protection. This response is most likely in relatively low-wage, mass-production sectors or economies (e.g. Britain; see ch. 2). Second, there is the 'dualistic model' that combines internal flexibility and external employment rigidity for the core workforce, on the one hand, with external flexibility in the employment of a sizeable marginal workforce, on the other (e.g. Japan; see ch. 10 and Chalmers 1989). Third, there is a 'quasi-corporatist model' that involves high internal flexibility as a compensation for continuing external rigidities (or 'flexibility within centralism'). This occurs mainly where there is a strong labour movement that is able to intervene in political decision making. Internal flexibility, in this case, is accomplished and mediated through institutions that provide for union–management cooperation (e.g. systems of co-determination as in Germany and Sweden; see chs 8 and 9). The economic viability of this form of flexibility depends on whether the predominant product markets will continue to sustain a premium on high skills and worker commitment, and thereby still have the potential to underwrite the costs of joint regulation.

A conclusion from such analyses is that employment relations should not be treated as distinct from the rest of the economy (as it was by writers such as Clegg and Flanders, who focused on collective bargaining). Rather, the terms of employment relationships are becoming increasingly sensitive to changes in economic conditions. The influence that unions are able to wield depends upon their strategic choices, institutional opportunities and the historical, political, social and economic context. Hence, the introduction of flexibility can be achieved against union opposition through the restoration of managerial prerogatives (the 'neo-liberal model') or without union participation but through enlightened HRM policies (the 'dualistic model'). Alternatively, unions may participate in decisions and operations of integrated flexible production systems (the 'quasi-corporatist' model).

Alternative approaches

Most of the writers in the orthodox industrial relations tradition could be described as liberal–pluralists in terms of their ideological perspectives. Critiques of such perspectives argue that the orthodox approaches are parochial and generally ignore the world outside a narrow definition of industrial relations (e.g. Mills 1959; Mandel 1969). They hold that, at most, the wider society is included in the pluralists' models only through narrowly circumscribed channels of 'adjustment' and 'feedback' (Hyman 1980). Most Marxists, for example, generally see industrial relations merely as a derivative of the patterns of economic ownership, political domination and of relations of production. Therefore, much of their analysis has been concerned with examining such broader issues as capital accumulation and class struggle. However, from their writing, which focuses mainly on other issues, we generally have to infer the radical interpretations of industrial relations.

Goldthorpe (1984), for instance, argues that in confronting macro-economic problems, societies have diverged from the pluralistic mould that hitherto held sway; hence the convergence thesis should no longer be seen as appropriate. On the one hand, there are countries like Norway, Austria, Germany and Sweden (see chs 8 and 9) where inequalities between capital and labour have been mitigated by corporatist state policies; these seek to balance, to an extent, the interests of employers, unions and the state. By contrast, in countries like Britain and the USA (see chs 2 and 3), traditional labour market institutions (e.g. collective bargaining) have been undermined by market forces that have operated to overcome perceived rigidities. This has resulted in a tendency towards dualism in which the workforce is separated into core and peripheral employees. The former may remain unionised and within the collective bargaining framework, albeit in a more decentralised mode, while the latter are employed under more individualistic work arrangements characterised by contractual forms of control (see ch. 12).

Goldthorpe is pessimistic about the long-term likelihood that such corporatist and dualist structures could continue to coexist within the same society. Rather, the logical and political implications of each approach were so dramatically opposed that this would lead to increasing tension between them, resulting in the ultimate dominance of one structure over another. In other words, any compromise would be unstable and ineffective in resolving macro-economic problems. Thus, either the corporatist system would triumph or the more market-based, dualistic industrial relations system would become the norm. However, different societies find their own solutions depending upon social, economic and political pressures.

Political economy

Certain political economists have drawn upon social, political and economic theory in an attempt to compare some aspects of industrial relations. They have argued that the pluralists have either ignored or denied the interaction between politics (or power relations) and industrial relations, while Marxists have not provided a satisfactory framework for analysing the labour markets and associated political processes.

In an analysis of union strategy and political economy in five Western European countries (Lange et al. 1982; Gourevitch et al. 1984b), this Harvard group supports a 'divergence thesis', arguing that in those sectors where they have representation, the unions have responded to the economic crisis in Europe in quite different ways (also see Goldthorpe 1984).

Four broad approaches are identified in the responses of Western European unions. First, a *maximalist* response has been associated with some of the French unions, especially those on the Left, as demonstrated by their refusal to play any role in the 'management of the crisis' at the firm, sectoral or national levels. Second, an *interventionist* approach has been followed by some of the Italian unions, which have sought to intervene at the firm, sectoral and national levels in order to develop incremental policies to relieve the economic crisis (see ch. 6).

Third, a *defensive–particularistic* strategy has occurred where groups of workers have sought to protect themselves in the face of income and job insecurity, using rank-and-file power bases to veto changes with which they disagree. This has been characteristic of some British unions (see ch. 2). Fourth, a *corporatist* strategy has been associated with unions that collaborated with the state and employers in areas such as incomes policies and broader economic and social programs. This approach has been epitomised by unions in Sweden and, to some extent, in Germany, especially during periods of social democratic government (see chs 8 and 9). These categories are not intended to fit different national union movements precisely, but are merely intended as ideal–typical illustrations of how unions differ both within and between the countries of Western Europe.

Lange et al. also outline four different characteristics that have distinguished these union movements: market strength, political influence, inter-union relationships and expectations. While these writers are able to demonstrate the existence of important differences between the union movements of Western Europe, they rather neglect such areas of common interest as confronting multinationals and defending members' job security. Events since the publication of the first volume of their work (e.g. renewed activity by the French unions in leading a general strike against the Juppé government in 1996) illustrate the current difficulty of predicting even a few years ahead. A more important limitation of such approaches, however, is the focus on the macro level and the neglect of rank-and-file perspectives. For this reason, they emphasise the role of the state and the role of union confederations, which, although important, are only two elements in the wider spectrum of industrial relations.

A broad political economy perspective on internationally comparative employment relations, however, emphasises the importance of understanding the interaction between systems of production, the role of government, the broader socio-economic environment and employment relations policies at the enterprise, industry and national levels. This perspective is particularly important with regard to NIEs such as Korea in which the role of the state is more important than in many advanced industrialised countries where the patterns of relationships and social partnerships between employers, unions and government are more established (see ch. 11). Yet most countries covered in this volume are experiencing dynamic changes in their broader political and economic environments which are, in turn, impacting on patterns of employment relations.

Employment relations and economic performance

There is considerable debate about the links between industrial relations systems and economic performance at the national level (unemployment, inflation, economic growth) and those at the level of the firm (labour turnover, productivity, profitability). Most of the studies published in the late 1980s and early 1990s (e.g. Freeman 1988; Calmfors & Driffill 1988; Layard et al. 1992) suggest that economies in which the degree of corporatism, centralisation or coordination of employment relations was highest (e.g. Austria and the Nordic countries) or lowest (e.g. the USA) achieved employment and economic performance records superior to those of intermediate cases (e.g. France and Italy). The explanation of this 'hump-shaped' relationship is that in corporatist, centralised or coordinated systems, the bargaining parties would aim at achieving low unemployment through wage restraint because they covered the whole economy and would take into account the interests of all constituencies. Similarly, in non-corporatist, decentralised or non-coordinated systems, the parties would be forced by market constraints to act in a way that was conducive to real wage moderation and low unemployment. By contrast, in the intermediate systems, pressures similar to those in the other two systems would be too weak to secure aggregate wage restraint and low unemployment.

However, support for the 'hump-shape' hypothesis has considerably weakened in the 1990s as the result of deteriorating economic performance among some countries whose systems were formerly seen as corporatist or centralised (Dell'Aringa & Lodovici 1992; Calmfors 1993). Furthermore, it is argued that decentralised industrial relations systems might yield the best economic outcomes (OECD 1994). In a modification of the earlier thesis, Soskice (1990) suggests that those economies with centralised bargaining, or with decentralised but coordinated industrial relations systems, achieve superior wage/employment trade-offs. However, it is not easy to identify broad correlations between industrial relations systems and economic outcomes. The difficulties of measurement, especially over time, are simply too great. While employment relations certainly has an influence on economic performance it is difficult to isolate this from other interrelated factors (Bean 1994).

One of the challenges is the way in which various industrial relations systems are classified. While many countries receive similar ratings under various classification systems, certain countries (such as Japan and Switzerland) receive divergent ratings. The variables that are used to assess the economic performance of various countries suffer from similar weaknesses in that they provide, at best, only a partial view of the total situation. Other problems stem from inadequate geographical and time coverage in many studies, which usually provide data only for certain countries in specific years. The employment and economic outcomes of various countries constitute a specific combination of many components and judgments about these outcomes, which depend largely on underlying value systems.

Thus, evaluation of the merits of the US system, which has achieved low unemployment combined with a large amount of low-skilled and low-paid work, compared with the high-wage and high-unemployment experience of many European countries, involves value-laden choices (Nevile 1996). Yet the quest for classification continues as a way of developing meaningful comparisons.

While not seeking to demonstrate the superiority of one particular employment relations system over any other, Jacoby (1995) has constructed various 'ideal types' on the basis of two dimensions: the role of government and the degree of centralised wage bargaining. Jacoby claims that while most industrial relations systems aim to achieve social integration between the key social actors, they take different paths to achieve this objective. Hence, while macro-corporatist economies seek nation-wide consensus, voluntarist economies focus on enterprise-level cooperation. Jacoby further argues that centralised systems tend to produce better macro-economic than micro-economic results, while the opposite is the case for decentralised systems.

The categories shown in Figure 1.2 can be briefly outlined as follows. *Macro-corporatist* approaches enjoyed success in the 1970s and early 1980s when centralised bargaining, wage synchronisation and government coordination of wage norms were achieved. However, corporatism has faced many difficulties in recent years as bargaining has become less centralised and welfare expenditure levels have been more difficult to maintain than real wages. *Statist micro-corporatism*, which is exemplified by Japan, is increasingly prevalent among the 'tiger economies' of Asia. Yet some countries, such as Korea, are exhibiting social tensions as they confront economic crises while organised labour seeks to achieve a greater role in wage bargaining and other areas of economic and political activity. *Voluntarism* has been followed by the USA and UK. Both countries have some ideological antipathy to the notion of government involvement (and to strong corporatist institutions) in the formation and implementation of industrial policy. While declining unionisation has depressed wages in the USA and UK, some employers in both countries are looking towards micro-corporatism as an alternative model based on the superior economic performance of the Japanese.

Regionalism is typified by the success of industrial districts in France and Italy where agglomerations of small firms, often family-owned, have been successful in developing niche markets for high-value-added products (Piore & Sabel 1984; Storper 1995). The prosperity of these districts has accelerated the decline of national unions and shifted the locus of bargaining to regional and local levels. There is a high degree of cooperation between many of the firms and unions in regional districts to support common institutions for supplying skilled labour. Support for regional approaches is spreading to other countries, particularly in Europe. Jacoby argues that cooperation at

Figure 1.2   Employment relations systems

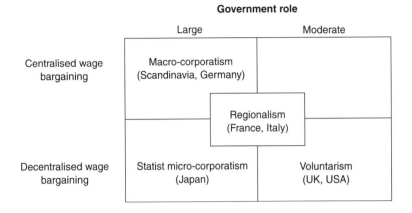

Government role

	Large	Moderate
Centralised wage bargaining	Macro-corporatism (Scandinavia, Germany)	
	Regionalism (France, Italy)	
Decentralised wage bargaining	Statist micro-corporatism (Japan)	Voluntarism (UK, USA)

Source: Adapted from Jacoby (1995).

municipal and regional levels, with the participation of employers, unions and local government, may have wider applicability to other countries including the USA. However, more research is needed to gain a greater understanding of precisely how industrial relations systems are related to economic outcomes.

Strategic choice

Collective bargaining specialists Kochan et al. (1984) offer another perspective. Although this perspective focused on the changing patterns of American employment relations, Kochan et al. take an interdisciplinary approach and their work has a comparative application. They seek to add a dynamic component, which they call 'strategic choice', to Dunlop's analysis. They propose a framework that differentiates between three levels of decision making (macro, industrial relations system and the workplace) and three parties (employers, unions and governments) and which identifies the relatively independent effects of the levels on employment relations.

The concept of strategic choice is not new and has previously been used in economics and organisational behaviour, but there are differences in the way this concept is considered by Kochan et al. They use a matrix to encompass the three levels of strategic decision making. As shown in Table 1.2, the columns of the matrix represent the three key parties who make strategic decisions. The rows represent three levels at which these decisions can be made. The effects of particular decisions, however, may appear at levels other than those where the decisions are made.

Examples of strategic decisions made at different levels are illustrated in Table 1.2. Strategic choices in the bottom row are those associated with individual workers or work groups and their relations with the immediate work environment. In the middle row are decisions associated with the practice of collective bargaining and the implications of HRM. Strategic choice in the top row is concerned with macro or organisation-wide matters. As discussed in chapter 3, due to their 'job-control' traditions US unions have not generally emphasised decisions at this highest level. By contrast, Western European and Australian unions have been more involved in the decisions at the highest level, within the tradition of tripartite discussions between governments, unions and employers. The emphasis given by the different parties to decisions at various levels tends to change according to circumstances.

However, a strategic approach does not dispense with the need for institutional analysis (Thurley & Wood 1983:2). Other writers criticise the use of strategic choice as a concept. Although Hyman (1987) is explicitly concerned with how Marxist analysis can relate to strategic matters, he raises some significant questions. For example: 'If capitalist production is subject to the determinism of economic forces or laws external to the individual enterprise, what latitude is there for strategic choice?' In other words, are choices in employment relations made by individual managers (or unions, for that matter) constrained by their external environment over which they have little control? If so, how credible is it to describe the parties as acting 'strategically' in employment relations? A thorough treatment of strategic choice must emphasise the contradictions of capitalism, so Hyman redefines management strategy as 'the programmatic choice among alternatives none of which can prove satisfactory'. He reminds us that we are glossing over the complex realities of organisational power if we assume that management as a whole has a unified 'strategic choice'.

Reconceptualising comparative employment relations

Notwithstanding criticisms of the strategic choice approach, a series of comparative studies has been undertaken by a consortium of researchers coordinated by Kochan et al. at the Massachusetts Institute of Technology (MIT) (see Locke et al. 1995a, b). This research has sought to understand the impact on employment relations of increasing international competition and of new production technologies. It has focused, in particular, on the effects of different competitive strategies on firm-level employment strategies. Key questions have driven the research, including: Are changes in employment relations in IMEs being driven by differences in the competitive strategies of firms or by differences in national institutional arrangements and public policies? Who are the relevant actors driving this process and at what level of

Table 1.2   Employment relations strategy matrix

Decision level	Nature of decisions		
	Employers	Unions	Government
1. Macro or global level for key institution	The strategic role of human resources; policies on unions; investments; plant location; new technology; and out-sourcing	Political roles (e.g. relations with political parties and other interest groups); union organising (e.g. neutrality and corporate campaigns); public policy objectives (e.g. labour law reform); and economic policies (e.g. full employment)	Macro-economic and social policies; industrial policy (protection vs free trade)
2. Employment relationship and industrial relations system	Personnel policies and negotiations and strategies	Collective bargaining policies and negotiations strategies (employment vs income)	Labour and employment standards law; direct involvement via incomes policies or dispute settlement
3. Workplace individuals and groups	Contractual or bureaucratic; and individual employee/workgroup participation	Policies on employee participation; introduction of new technology; work organisation design	Regulation of worker rights and/or employee participation

Source: Reproduced with permission from Kochan, McKersie & Cappelli (1984:23).

the political economy and the industrial relations system do they interact? What role do national institutions play in an increasingly global economy? How do they interact with micro-level actors so as to shape and/or restrict the range of strategic choices of individual firms and unions? Perhaps the most challenging question raised by the research, however, is whether it still makes sense to try to conceptualise distinct national systems of industrial relations when there appears to be almost as much variation in employment relations practices within countries as between them (Locke et al. 1995a, b).

The research project began in the early 1990s with the development of an agreed analytical framework between a group of researchers, mainly from IMEs. The group was subsequently enlarged to include researchers from NIEs in Asia (Verma et al. 1995). The first phase was to describe developments in the various countries and to compare them. The second phase was to examine employment relations within specific industries in these countries, including airlines, automobiles, banking, electronics, steel and telecommunications (e.g. Darbishire & Katz 1997; Kochan et al. 1997). The analytical framework guiding the research is summarised in Figure 1.3. At the core of the framework are four important firm-level employment practices:

1 Changes in work organisation due to the introduction of new technologies and the adoption of new competitive strategies (such as decentralisation or team systems); linked to these changes are new work rules and patterns of employee participation within the firm.
2 Changing patterns of skill acquisition and training to match the needs of firms; this takes account of the shifting balance between the public and private provision of education and training.
3 New compensation or remuneration systems which affect employees within the firm.
4 Staffing, employment security and recruitment policies which affect the way in which firms adjust their workforce when faced with cyclical or long-term structural changes in demand for their output.

The framework used to explain variations in these employment practices includes two competing explanations for the degree of transformation in industrial relations and HRM. One explanation stresses the importance of institutional structures (at the national, industry and firm levels) that limit the discretion of firms and other actors in industrial relations. The alternative explanation emphasises the range of strategic choices available to firms. In each country and for each industry, data are analysed to compare the explanatory power of these two hypotheses in relation to contemporary workplace developments.

The evidence of changing employment practices in the various industries and countries suggests that several emergent patterns can be discerned. First, the enterprise emerges as an increasingly important locus for strategy and decision making on employment relations. Management is generally the driving force for change albeit sometimes in collaboration with unions or works councils. Second, decentralisation of firm-level structures is accompanied by the search for greater flexibility in work organisation and the deployment of labour. Third, many firms and governments in most countries appear to be increasing their investment in training and skill development, which is often associated with a trend towards skill-related pay systems. Also, unions are experiencing major challenges in most countries as the pace of restructuring intensifies, the workplace becomes more diverse and the average size of enterprises decreases.

Three types of tension are observed in patterns of adjustment to changing patterns of employment relations. First, in all the countries studied, cost cutting and high-value-added competitive strategies coexist uneasily. Second, the drive for increased flexibility in work organisation and related employment practices has the potential to create polarisation between workers with access to jobs and those without. Third, while unions in many countries are experiencing declining influence and membership, arguably the need is growing for a stronger employee voice in corporate decision making as well as in industry-level interactions and national policy making. Yet there is little evidence that HR issues are consistently attracting much greater attention in corporate decision making. A simple reconstruction of union membership and power along traditional lines appears unlikely in the foreseeable future, although new forms and approaches to employee representation might emerge.

The MIT-initiated comparative research has fuelled debate about appropriate analytical frameworks for interpreting and guiding the study

Figure 1.3   Framework for analysing comparative employment relations and human resource issues

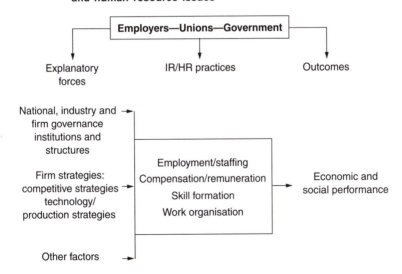

Note: Within any single country industrial relations/human resources (IR/HR) practices vary across industries, firms and over time, and all the variables in the model may be shaped by different combinations of employer, union and government influence.

Source: Adapted with permission from an original in Kochan, Locke & Piore (1992).

of employment relations across countries and at the global level. Two lessons can be drawn (see Locke et al. 1995a, b). First, the variations in employment practices and outcomes identified by the research demonstrate that there is no single response to increased market competition. However, in contrast to the neo-liberal models of IMEs and economic restructuring that have dominated recent political and economic debate, the research shows that labour market institutions are important in shaping outcomes. Employment relations are shaped in systematic ways by institutions that filter external pressures and influence the strategies adopted by the key actors. Hence, countries with a history of strong centralised industrial relations institutions have tended to follow an incremental, negotiated pattern of changes and aim to achieve results that balance the interests of different social groups and economic interests. By contrast, those countries with a relatively decentralised tradition have adopted a more dramatic and unilateral approach to change. However, even in these latter countries, there have been social strains arising from increased wage inequality and a widening gap between the winners and losers from radical economic changes. These have led to a search for new ways to ensure greater representation for workers' interests at the workplace level, as well as in broader economic policy making.

Second, it is apparent that there is a need for more comparative research at the micro or workplace level. Much of the previous research in this field has focused on the macro level and role of national institutions. Yet the implementation of strategies at the level of the enterprise is increasingly important. Much can be learnt from comparative research at the enterprise and industry level. Hence, explaining why flexible work systems and various forms of teamwork in internationally competitive industries (such as car manufacturing and telecommunications) have emerged requires detailed research at the micro level. However, it is also important to understand how concepts like teamwork vary as a result of local customs, union traditions and social norms. This requires an understanding of the national context as well as knowledge of internationally comparative dimensions.

In an extension of the MIT project, Darbishire and Katz (1997) coined the phrase 'converging divergences' to describe commonalities in the changes underway in employment relations across countries. Yet there is little evidence of a simple new international convergence in employment relations. Indeed, rather than convergence, Darbishire and Katz report increasing variation in employment relations within countries through the expansion of various patterns of workplace practices. Darbishire and Katz base their findings on studies of the car and telecommunications industries across seven IMEs. They categorise emerging patterns of workplace practices into four types: low wage, HRM, Japanese-oriented and joint team-based. As shown in Table 1.3,

Table 1.3   Emerging patterns of workplace practices

Patterns of workplace practices			
Low wage	HRM	Japanese-oriented	Joint team-based
Managerial discretion with informal procedures	Corporate culture and extensive communication	Standardised procedures	Joint decision making
Hierarchical work relations	Directed teams	Problem-solving teams	Semi-autonomous work groups
Low wages with piece rates	Above-average wages with contingent pay	High pay linked to seniority and performance appraisals	High pay with pay-for-knowledge
High labour turnover	Individualised career development	Employment stabilisation	Career development
Anti-union ideologies	Union substitution	Enterprise unionism	Union and employee involvement

Source: Adapted with permission from Darbishire & Katz (1997).

five clusters of workplace practices appear across firms in part because the various practices that make up each pattern reinforce one another. Like Locke et al. (1995a, b), Darbishire and Katz argue that institutional influences remain important in shaping employment relationships. For example, institutions affect the mix and/or spread of various employment patterns and the degree to which these patterns operate on a union or non-union basis.

Conclusions: applying theory to practice

In a period of apparently declining union power when there is a transformation of employment relations, traditional approaches to the analysis of labour and management issues are being challenged. However, as we try to develop fuller and more satisfactory explanations, it becomes more important to draw on insights from several disciplines rather than relying only on one.

Even though the role of the state may appear to be declining, following the deregulation of the economy in many IMEs and Eastern European countries, the insights from political economy are still useful. As there is an increased role for markets in determining employment relations outcomes, a micro-economics paradigm is also relevant, especially as micro-economic labour market reform is high on the agenda of many governments, employers and unions around the world. Moreover, a significant number of economic policy makers are realising the desirability of attempting to incorporate into their analyses institutional concerns and insights from industrial relations (cf. Oswald 1985; 1987).

Innovative approaches are needed to interpret increasingly complex and seemingly contradictory developments. There is increasing globalisation of capital and greater international competition. Changes in the nature of production, such as the advent of flexible specialisation (Piore & Sabel 1984), mean that the search for improved labour and capital flexibility is international in its extent and influence. Yet given the different institutional bases of national industrial relations systems, the manner in which changes are introduced, mediated and handled can lead to different outcomes. Thus, in a sense, convergence at the global level in terms of economic forces and production technologies may result in divergence at the national and intranational level, as these forces are mediated by different institutions with their own traditions and cultures (cf. Poole 1992). This provides further support for the arguments advanced above for paying close attention to the linkages between historical, political, social and economic factors and employment relations outcomes.

The differences between employment relations in economies that are at different stages of industrialisation (let alone those at similar stages) are so vast as to defy a single theoretical explanation. Yet the quest continues for conceptual approaches that will help to explain why particular systems develop and change. Various writers in the pluralist tradition provide some categories that are useful for analysing developments in employment relations, but they tend to have a restricted focus and some make naive assumptions about the maintenance of consensus. Certain radical writers usefully focus on critical issues and on rank-and-file workers themselves, but some tend to dwell unduly on a presumed inevitability of increasing class conflict. They also tend to deny any autonomy to employment relations processes, while pluralists tend to exaggerate such autonomy. The reality is that class and employment relations issues are both important, as shown by some sociologists and political economists.

Each approach is partial. Political economists show how there has been a growing divergence, even between Western European nations. They provide convincing explanations of national union strategies in the polity, but neglect the increasing initiating role played by employers. On the other hand, the importance of managerial strategies is highlighted by Kochan and his colleagues.

When analysing patterns of employment relations in their own countries, the contributors to the present book have been most influenced by pluralist approaches. But readers should draw selectively from other approaches in an attempt to make sense of the various aspects of the complex realities of the real world. The development of international and comparative employment relations as a viable and robust field is still in its early stages and as yet we do not have a comprehensive analytical approach to the field. We agree with Strauss, who concludes that 'eventually perhaps the work of model builders and systems theorists may fruitfully interact and the field may flourish at the intersection of these seemingly disparate approaches. But much creeping will be required before we can run' (1992:6). This is an exciting challenge for practitioners and students of international and comparative employment relations, and we hope that this book may help with the necessary pathfinding and mapping of the terrain.

2 Employment relations in Britain

John Goodman, Mick Marchington, John Berridge, Ed Snape and Greg J. Bamber

The United Kingdom (UK)[1] has a total population of 59 million people and a labour force participation rate of 74 per cent. While the participation rate for women continues to rise, the rate for men dropped markedly over the decade 1985–95. (Such statistical data cited in each chapter are elaborated and discussed in more detail in the Appendix.) The UK has relatively fewer people employed in agriculture (2 per cent of civilian employees) than any other Organisation for Economic Co-operation and Development (OECD) country. About 27 per cent of its civilian employees work in industry; the remaining 70 per cent work in services (according to OECD definitions). There has been a greater decline in its 'industry' category since 1970 than in any other OECD country. In spite of the relative growth of services, there was a steep rise in unemployment, from 1.2 per cent of the working population in 1965 to nearly 12 per cent by 1986, by which time the UK had a higher unemployment rate than any of the other countries discussed in this book. The unemployment-benefits claimant rate, much redefined, fell in the late 1980s, but rose again in the early 1990s before subsequently falling to around 6 per cent in the late 1990s. In terms of gross domestic product (GDP) per capita—an approximate indicator of labour output—the UK ranks in the lower half of the ten countries (see Appendix). The rate of inflation declined during the 1990s, with the UK rate being around the average for the ten countries during the 1990–96 period.

There has been much change in employment relations in recent years in Britain. Successive Conservative governments over the period 1979–97 set the tone with their radical step-by-step reform of industrial relations law; labour market deregulation; and attempts to foster a

competitive 'enterprise culture', not simply in the smaller and transformed public sector, but throughout the British economy. After the
post-war period of general labour scarcity, employers have cut workforces, often substantially. With union membership having fallen by
well over a third since 1979, employers have held the initiative. Overall,
if there has been a single dominant thrust in employer strategies and
policies in what is a diverse picture, it might be summarised as the
promotion of the decentralisation and individualisation of the employment relationship, aimed at greater flexibility but often also bringing
perceived (and actual) job insecurity. In a few well-publicised cases,
'personal contracts' have been substituted for collectively negotiated
conditions. More generally 'individualisation' has been pursued less
abrasively, for example through individual performance-related pay, and
managerially initiated employee-involvement (EI) and other techniques.
These are targeted at winning employee commitment to organisational
goals, and at trying to redefine 'them and us' away from its traditional
adversarial meaning to a more unitarist perspective focused on the
external relationship between the employing company and its rivals in
product markets. Some writers have highlighted an increased distinction
between the treatment of core and peripheral workers and the growth
in the proportion of the latter relative to the former (Atkinson 1984;
Casey 1991).

Some commentators argue that there has been a fundamental *change*
towards a 'new industrial relations' (e.g. Bassett 1986), but several
scholars counter that the general pattern is of *continuity*, especially if
we take a historical perspective and avoid focusing only on a few highly
publicised cases (e.g. MacInnes 1987; Sisson 1992). This debate continues, but it is beyond doubt that unionised employment has greatly
diminished, and that—whatever its present character—collective bargaining now covers less than half of all employees.

British politics have been dominated by two political parties since
1945 (see the chronology at the end of this chapter). The Conservative
Party's support is strongest in the more prosperous south of England,
and more generally among the business and rural communities. In the
general election of 1997, it had no MPs elected in either Scotland or
Wales. The Labour Party's support is traditionally strongest in the
north of England, and in Scotland and Wales, particularly in urban
working-class communities. There are several other political parties,
including the Liberal Democrats and the nationalist parties in Scotland
and Wales, all of which increased their representation in the 1997
election. The majority of seats in Northern Ireland are held by Ulster
Unionists, who tend to support the Conservatives, though not consistently so.

The fragmentation of the parliamentary opposition helped the Conservatives to retain political power through four general elections after

1979, up to the landslide Labour victory in May 1997, which led to Tony Blair becoming Prime Minister. Parliament is elected on the basis of 'first past the post' in each constituency and the smaller parties find it difficult to win many parliamentary seats. The stark contrast between the Conservative south and Labour-held Scotland was a major factor behind the high level of support for greater political devolution for Scotland.

The employment relations parties

Unions

Britain was the cradle of industrialisation, with the 'industrial revolution' taking place long before adult electoral suffrage. Workers were seen as 'hands', as expendable resources for whom the employer had no responsibility beyond the minimal legal obligations of contract (Fox 1985). The law and the reality of master and servant were deeply embedded.

Many present British unions can trace their roots back to this mid-nineteenth-century period or before, the earliest enduring unions being formed by skilled craftsworkers. Widespread and durable unionisation of semi-skilled and unskilled manual workers began in the late nineteenth century, while relatively few white-collar workers joined unions until after the Second World War. For a period, British unions could be classified as craft, general, industrial or white-collar, but this categorisation was only approximate and has become more blurred as unions merged and/or broadened their membership. It is more useful to see unions as either 'closed' or 'open', according to whether or not they restrict recruitment to particular industries, sectors or occupational categories (Turner 1962). Although there were 1384 UK unions recorded in 1920, by the end of 1995 there were only 238. However, membership is highly concentrated, with the 23 unions that have over 50 000 members accounting for 85 per cent of the total membership.[2]

Multi-unionism is widespread, being a legacy of the mode of union development in the late nineteenth and early twentieth centuries. According to the 1990 Workplace Industrial Relations Survey (WIRS) of a large sample of workplaces with at least 25 employees, there is an average of 2.5 unions among the WIRS workplaces that recognise unions (Millward et al. 1992). Union mergers have added to their internal heterogeneity, often bringing together disparate occupational and industrial groups (as illustrated in Table 2.1).

The level and density of union membership have varied since the Second World War. Bain and Price (1983) identify three broad post-war phases. First, between 1948 and 1968 membership grew—from 9.3 million to 10.2 million—but lagged behind employment growth. This led to a 15-year union density plateau at around 43 per cent. Second, the level and density of membership grew markedly in the 1970s as (particularly white-collar) workers were attracted into unions, in part by the 'threat' effect of rapidly rising prices and the 'credit' effect of big pay increases in a period of high inflation. Membership grew from 10.2 million in 1968, to an all-time peak of 13.4 million in 1979— density increased to an all-time high of 55 per cent. The period 1974–79 was notable for a legal and political climate generally favourable to union growth, under the Wilson–Callaghan Labour governments. At that time union density in Britain was around the middle of the range for the OECD countries (see Appendix and OECD 1991).

The beginning of the third phase in 1979 coincided with the return of a radical Conservative government led by Margaret Thatcher, the acceleration of the decline in manufacturing employment (to around 20 per cent), and the onset of the deepest post-war economic recession (in the early 1980s). The sharp rise in unemployment reduced union membership, partly because most of the unemployed allowed their membership to lapse. However, union membership continued to decline in periods of employment growth, largely because many new jobs were part-time or atypical, and were concentrated in private sector services where unions had long found it difficult to recruit. Union density declined continuously during the 1980s and 1990s, as in most OECD countries. Between 1979 and 1995 union membership fell by well over one-third (5.2 million) to 8 million, and density fell from 55 per cent to around 29 per cent. It is estimated that structural and labour force compositional effects such as the decline of manual work, manufacturing, public sector employment and large workplaces, plus the rise of service sector employment, part-time work and self-employment, are important factors in the reduction (Green 1992), although they are not the only influences. Perhaps a fourth phase will begin in the late 1990s, following the election of the new Labour government in 1997, with a different reform agenda in industrial relations and labour markets.

There are marked variations in union density. Non-manual workers have constituted an increasing proportion of total union membership. Unlike earlier periods, in the 1990s manual workers are no more likely to be unionised than are non-manual staff.[3] According to the 1996 Labour Force Survey, union density is higher among men (33 per cent) than women (about 29 per cent), and is higher among full-time workers (35 per cent) than part-timers (21 per cent). There are significant differences in density between industries. Private sector services have lower union density—for example, only 11 per cent in retailing and 8 per cent in hotels and restaurants, compared with 31 per cent in manufacturing. There is also a wide differential in union density between the public sector (61 per cent) and the private sector (21 per cent). According to WIRS, the number of workplaces that recognised union(s) for collective bargaining declined from 66 per cent in 1984 to 53 per cent in 1990. However, in manufacturing, unions were recognised at approximately 80 per cent of workplaces employing more than 200 people, with only a slight decline during the latter half of the 1980s (Millward et al. 1992).

The closed shop, under which workers must join a union either before (pre-entry) or soon after (post-entry) starting a job was an important factor in union membership and union security. Most manual unions have preferred closed shops wherever possible—and many employers also welcomed this arrangement, to ensure that union shop stewards[4] speak for the whole workforce, and as a means of stabilising union structure in the workplace (McCarthy 1964). The extent of the closed shop increased significantly during the 1970s, covering around 23 per cent of all employees by 1978, the majority by post-entry closed shops (Dunn & Gennard 1984). However, the closed shop declined from a coverage of nearly 5 million employees in 1980 to only half a million employees by 1990 (Millward et al. 1992; cf. Stevens et al. 1989). In part, this decline reflected structural change in industry and employment, but it also reflected the removal of earlier legal protection for closed shops, a process completed in 1990.

Unlike most other Western European countries, Britain has only one main union confederation: the Trades Union Congress (TUC). In 1996, 74 unions representing around 80 per cent of British union members were affiliated to the TUC. In contrast with its counterparts in many other countries, the TUC has no direct role in collective bargaining and cannot itself implement industrial action. British unions have generally been too jealous of their own autonomy to allow the TUC such powers. It has a longer continuous history than most central confederations in other countries. Established in 1868 to lobby government, this has remained a primary role. During and after the Second World War the TUC's political influence increased, and it participated in many tripartite bodies and quasi-governmental agencies (Goodman 1994), a role that peaked under the 1974–79 Labour government. The TUC has also long played an important role in regulating inter-union relations. However, membership decline among affiliates has reduced TUC income, necessitating cost cutting, while its virtual exclusion from the 'corridors of power' during the 1979–97 Conservative governments reduced its lobbying effectiveness with government to a lower level than it had experienced since the 1930s. This major turnaround induced some heated debates about future policy and direction, exacerbated by successive election defeats for the Labour Party. In the 1990s the TUC placed a greater emphasis on building constructive partnerships with 'good' employers, and embracing a more

Table 2.1 The largest British unions

	Membership ('000)		% change	Summary description
	1980	1995	1980–95	
UNISON—The Public Service Union[a, b]	1697	1355	−20	Public services; white-collar and manual
Transport and General Workers' Union	1887	897	−52	General/open; has white-collar section
GMB (General, Municipal & Boilermakers' Union)[a]	1180	740	−37	General/open; has white-collar section
Amalgamated Engineering and Electrical Union[a]	1690	726	−57	Ex-craft; now fairly open
Manufacturing Science and Finance Union[a]	683	446	−35	White-collar, technicians and supervisors
Royal College of Nursing	181	303	+67	'Professional union', largest union not in TUC
Union of Shop Distributive and Allied Workers	450	283	−37	Based in retailing, but wider
Communication Workers Union[a,c]	334	275	−18	The 'industry' union for post and telecommunications
National Union of Teachers	273	248	− 9	School teachers
National Assoc. of School Masters & Union of Women Teachers[a]	156	234	+50	School teachers
Graphical Paper and Media Union	286	217	−24	Ex-craft, printing/paper industries
Association of Teachers and Lecturers	90	171	+90	School and some college teachers, second-largest non-TUC union
Banking Insurance and Finance Union	141	124	−12	Financial services union, competes with non-TUC staff associations

Notes: a The 1980 membership figures for these unions have been adjusted to take account of amalgamations.

b Formed by the merger in July 1993 of three of the largest unions, namely the National and Local Government Officers Association, the National Union of Public Employees, and the Confederation of Health Service Employees.

c Formed by the merger of the Union of Communication Workers and the National Communication Union in 1995.

Source: Certification Office Annual Report (1996).

continental-European-style approach based on broader statutory rights for *all* employees (i.e. embracing the non-unionised), including a right to representation (TUC 1995). The return of Labour in 1997 presaged a more fruitful role for the TUC as a valued social partner with government, though this will be less close than under previous Labour governments.

Besides establishing the TUC to lobby governments, the unions were instrumental in the establishment of the Labour Party in 1906. This was seen as a necessary complement to the industrial activities of the unions, particularly after a series of adverse legal judgments meant that new legislation was required to re-establish union rights. Individual unions may affiliate to the Labour Party, contributing to its funds through a 'political levy' on members, from which individuals may 'opt out' if they wish. Unions also sponsor individual candidates, usually Labour, in parliamentary and local government elections. Most of the major unions are affiliated to the Labour Party, historically providing the largest component of the party's income. Nearly half its funds still come from affiliated unions. Since the mid-1980s, however, the Labour Party leadership has attempted to distance the party from the unions. Individual membership of the Labour Party has grown rapidly in recent years, and the unions' voting power at its policy-making annual conference has been reduced.

Employers and their organisations

The Confederation of British Industry (CBI), formed in 1965 following a merger of three separate employers' confederations, is the peak employer body in Britain. It is an important lobbyist in relation to the British government and European Union (EU) agencies but, like the TUC, it does not participate in collective bargaining. After 1979 the Institute of Directors[5] became influential, being closer in ideological terms to the Thatcher and Major governments.

Historically, industrial associations of employers that were created mainly in the late nineteenth and early twentieth centuries—largely in reaction to the growth of unionism—played an important part in shaping the British system of industrial relations (Gospel & Littler 1983). Initially at local level and then (more importantly) at national level they brought together, and acted as representatives for, employers in each industry, reaching agreements with unions over recognition, disputes procedures and the substantive terms and conditions to apply in member companies. They tended to remove the responsibility for determining wages, hours and other employment conditions beyond the level of individual companies. They offered forms of mutual defence against union campaigns and to some extent took wages 'out of competition' among British employers participating in the same product market. Occasionally they took the offensive, as in 1896 when the Engineering Employers' Federation led a national 'lockout' of workers in opposition to union pressure for an eight-hour day. With the extensive establishment of multi-employer, industry-level collective bargaining in the first three decades of the twentieth century, the numerous industry employers' associations were crucial actors in what the Donovan Commission (1968) characterised as the formal system of industrial relations (see below).

There were many signs in the 1950s and 1960s, especially in engineering and related industries, that the agreements to which employers' associations were signatories were losing their regulative effectiveness. The growth of establishment-based incentive payment and job evaluation systems, the escalation of overtime working, and the broadened scope of joint regulation into what were notionally areas of management prerogative, were being led by workplace-based union shop stewards. A few major companies (e.g. Ford) had never joined employers' associations, and others began to leave them to allow greater flexibility to tailor their collective agreements more precisely to their specific needs, particularly through agreements that directly addressed workplace productivity issues (Sisson 1987). Moves away from multi-employer bargaining in the private sector have accelerated since 1979. Between 1980 and 1990 private sector firms' membership of employers' associations fell from 29 to 13 per cent (Millward et al. 1992). Although there are some exceptions, such as in footwear, and although in some sectors they still operate dispute resolution procedures, employers' associations have moved to the periphery of industrial relations, offering legal, advisory, training and other services, and are generally shadows of their former selves. A number have been wound up.

Since the 1960s formal collective bargaining in the private sector has increasingly decentralised to company, division or establishment level, reflecting the strong trend in corporate organisation to decentralised profit centres and business units with devolved budget and personnel responsibilities. While head offices retain a strong (though often less than fully overt) influence over key decisions (e.g. annual pay negotiations), operational performance issues are usually delegated.

The steep rise in unemployment in the early 1980s and its continuing high level relative to earlier post-war decades, combined with sharper international competition in product markets and reductions in unionism, have greatly enhanced employer power and freedom of action. While employer objectives in the labour field continue to focus on control, productivity improvement and cost reduction, their methods are diverse. Analysts (e.g. Purcell 1987) have offered various typologies of the management styles adopted by employers. These distinguish between traditionalist, sophisticated paternalist, consultative and constitutional management styles, though many employers appear to fit the residual pragmatic/opportunist category.

Despite a few well-publicised and dramatic examples of union derecognition (e.g. News International at Wapping in 1986), few employers have sought to exploit the changed industrial relations climate in such a confrontational way. Rather, the recurrent managerial aims have been to seek more flexibility and employee commitment, with many employers retaining collective bargaining arrangements, but also initiating improved direct employee communications arrangements, total quality management (TQM), teamworking and other techniques associated with human resource management (HRM). They have also unilaterally introduced performance-related elements into pay, sometimes linked to individual performance appraisals. Encouraged by tax incentives, there has been a growth in the use of variable profit-related elements in pay. Experience of redundancy was widespread during the 1980s and 1990s, and self-employment, part-time and limited-term employment contracts have expanded in a relatively deregulated labour market. There has been a growth in direct investment in manufacturing and financial services by Japanese and other East Asian companies. Given their association with international competitive success, the employment practices of these multinational enterprises (MNEs) have had disproportionate influence on the policies of indigenous British firms, and there has been much talk of the 'Japanisation' of British industry (e.g. Oliver & Wilkinson 1992).

The role of the state

The state (including national and local government and their various agencies) plays a crucial role in industrial relations, both directly and indirectly. Perhaps the most prominent role of the state is its association with the broad working of the law, but the contemporary state has many other roles, including that of 'manager' of the economy.

During much of the nineteenth century the law was hostile to trade unionism. When this stance was modified towards the end of the century the route chosen was not that of positively stated rights for either employees or unions (as in many other countries), but rather a system of immunities for unions from various areas of criminal and civil law. This process was completed by the 1906 Trade Disputes Act, which provided the main principles of union law until the 1980s. This peculiar legal framework was supplemented by a number of features accepted by peace-time governments of different political complexions, giving rise to what became known as 'voluntarism'. This notion minimised the intervention of the state and of the law and lawyers, being varied only by the imposition of some compulsory arbitration processes during and briefly after the two world wars. Despite short-lived legislative attempts to change them in the 1970s, three principal features of voluntarism remain:

1   Collective agreements are not legally binding on the parties.

2   Union recognition by employers is voluntary, there being no general administrative or judicial route for unions to secure recognition.

3   A light, essentially voluntary, framework of state-provided supplementary dispute resolution facilities, with no governmental powers to order suspension of industrial action or impose cooling-off periods.

These longstanding features have not been directly changed by the substantial Conservative legislation over the period 1979–97 (see below).

A further characteristic of the British system up to the 1960s was that in remarkably few areas, outside the health and safety field, were minimum labour standards established by statute. The main exception was in relation to low pay (see below). For most of the twentieth century governments encouraged the parties to develop voluntary collective bargaining arrangements, though post-1979 Conservative governments abandoned this longstanding official support for collective bargaining, and pursued labour market policies targeted at reducing collectivism and regulation. Use of statutory measures to establish a broader platform of minimum employee rights on a universal basis (some subject to length-of-service qualifications) began in the 1960s and encompass redundancy payments; written statements of terms of employment; remedies for unfair dismissal; protection from victimisation for union activity; continuity of employment following a change of ownership; sex and race discrimination; and maternity arrangements. Many of these rights were established by Labour governments after 1964; Conservative legislation post-1979 tended to dilute certain details while European legislation has tended to extend and enhance such provisions incrementally. It is expected that legislation introduced by the post-1997 Labour government will strengthen such rights, particularly in the areas of representation and union recognition, works councils, a national minimum wage and individuals' employment rights.

Economic policies and incomes policies

Over the post-war period from 1945 to the late 1970s, British governments followed Keynesian economic policies aimed at achieving full employment, economic growth and low inflation, the principal constraint being the balance of payments in a period of fixed exchange rates. The employment goal was more or less accomplished, with average unemployment levels often below 3 per cent. Although economic growth was high by historical standards, it was significantly lower than in other industrialised market economies (IMEs), and Britain suffered from substantially higher rates of inflation and experienced currency devaluations.

During the 1960s and 1970s, British governments repeatedly used prices and incomes policies in seeking to control inflation and offset balance of payments difficulties while maintaining full employment. Some governments opted for a statutory policy, often with a quasi-independent agency to adjudicate on proposed pay and price increases with penalties for those breaking the norms; while other governments followed a voluntary approach, seeking to win the support and compliance of unions and employers by persuasion. The 1974–79 Labour government, for example, introduced a 'Social Contract', offering pro-union legislation and continued Keynesian economic policies in exchange for voluntary pay restraint, in an accord with the TUC. This was effective initially, yielding substantial reductions in the rates of pay and price inflation, and in stoppages. But the Social Contract had collapsed by 1978–79, with widespread industrial action in a 'winter of discontent'. The incomes policies of the 1960s and 1970s were not successful in constraining pay increases over the longer term. Typically, periods of restraint were followed by periods of 'catching up' as unions, especially those in the public sector, sought additional pay increases to compensate for what they perceived to be differential compliance with the various norms and restraints.

The post-1979 Conservative governments took a radically different approach, adopting monetarist policies and fiscal restraint as a way of dealing with inflation, with direct controls and 'cash limits' in the public sector. This strategy amounted to a rejection of the Keynesian consensus. The defeat of inflation became the dominant priority, and the commitment to full employment (or indeed any specific employment target) was abandoned. During the mid/late 1980s, and again after 1992, the government had some success in restraining inflation, although an economic boom at the end of the 1980s saw a temporary rise to over 7 per cent. This brought renewed concern about inflation and the consequential loss of international competitiveness, which was offset only by a depreciation of sterling.

In 1990 the UK joined the European exchange rate mechanism (ERM), whereby the British pound was linked to the value of other European currencies, but its membership was short-lived due to the inability of the pound to remain within the agreed broad exchange-rate band. The UK withdrew from the ERM in 1992 as sterling continued to depreciate. Mrs Thatcher's replacement as Prime Minister by John Major in 1990 led to little change in the government's broad economic strategy. Corporatist approaches remained anathema, and the government opposed a range of EU social/employment legislation, securing an 'opt-out' from the Social Chapter of the 1991 Maastricht Treaty (see ch. 12). This opposition to many aspects of 'Social Europe', as distinct from the EU as a 'single market', was rooted in ideology. However, taken together with the government's concern to minimise wage costs

employers more than doubling to almost 100 000 in the decade to 1996. Approximately half of these were about alleged unfair dismissals.

Legal reforms of industrial relations

By the 1960s there was increasing concern at Britain's relatively poor economic performance, with slow growth, high inflation and recurrent balance of payments difficulties. Some commentators argued that Britain's old established industrial relations system was a major factor, with restrictive (or protective) working practices and unofficial strikes[6] making industry uncompetitive. Accordingly, after the late 1960s industrial relations reform was high on the political agenda.

Although the Donovan Commission (1968) had argued for *voluntary* reform to formalise workplace bargaining, in subsequent years successive governments have also resorted to legislation. The Conservatives' 1971 Industrial Relations Act sought to legislate for rapid and fundamental reform. Following the US example, this ill-fated Act aimed *inter alia* to make collective agreements into legally enforceable contracts. The unions boycotted much of the Act and few employers used it, thereby rendering it largely ineffective. Most of the Act was repealed by Labour in 1974 (see ch. 1).

Between 1979 and 1997, Conservative governments successfully adopted a more gradualist approach. They enacted important new laws at roughly two-yearly intervals through the 1980s and early 1990s (see Goodman & Earnshaw 1995). The legislation limited the ability of unions to organise lawful industrial action; it narrowed union immunities from legal action (principally injunctions) by employers and others through the courts; outlawed secondary industrial action; and restrained picketing. Workers are allowed to picket only in small numbers and only at their own place of work. Since 1984, to be lawful, industrial action has to be preceded by a secret ballot of the workers concerned, with a requirement since 1993 that ballots be fully postal. A union cannot lawfully discipline a member who refuses to support industrial action, even where the majority have voted in favour. In 1990 the complex issue of the vicarious liability of unions for unauthorised or unofficial industrial action was tackled by making unions responsible at law if any official (including workplace representatives) called such action. Union liability could be avoided only if senior officers or committees repudiated the action without delay and in written notice to members.

Legislation effectively 'outlawed' the closed shop and made it more difficult for unions to consolidate and extend union membership by removing the statutory procedures to facilitate union recognition introduced by the 1974–79 Labour government. Furthermore the widespread practice of deducting union dues directly from pay was made subject to reaffirmation by members every three years.

In addition, the post-1979 laws intervened prescriptively in internal union governance; for example, requiring secret membership ballots both to elect union executive committees and national leaders directly rather than indirectly via delegates, and to approve the continuation of a 'political fund'. Union members were given new rights to bring legal actions against their unions. The espoused aim was to ensure that unions were responsive to the wishes of their members on the assumption that ballots would moderate the influence of militant activists. One implicit aim was to reduce the number of union political funds and thereby erode financial support for the Labour Party. Paradoxically this law prompted unions to improve their communications with their members. Not only were no political fund ballots lost, but several public sector unions, concerned that campaigns aimed at resisting government policies on the public services would be seen as 'political', established political funds for the first time. Compulsory pre-strike ballots have also proved double-edged, with the great majority of such ballots apparently supporting industrial action (ACAS 1991). In practice the ballots are widely seen as an additional element in the bargaining game, aimed at securing improved offers. The huge decline in strikes since the 1970s (see Appendix), although influenced by many other factors (Edwards 1995), adds credence to this view.

The post-1997 Labour government has promised that it will not change the broad framework of industrial relations law introduced by the Conservatives, though it may amend some details, such as check-off arrangements (whereby union subscriptions are deducted directly from members' pay), and provide a mechanism for unions to secure recognition from employers.

The public sector

The state has an important role to play—as an employer for a substantial proportion of the labour force, and indirectly through its influence as an exemplar to other employers. For much of the twentieth century the government aimed to be a 'good' employer, encouraging union membership, and offering broadly comparable terms and conditions and generally more secure employment than the private sector.

Over the 1979–97 period many of these traditions were rejected, as Conservative governments sought a transformation in the public sector, seeking to limit and reduce public expenditure and to reduce the role of the state. Most dramatic was the process of privatisation, with the sale of publicly owned corporations (e.g. telecommunications, airways, coal, steel and railways) and utilities (e.g. gas, electricity and water) to the private sector. Public sector employment fell from around 30 per cent to 22 per cent of the labour force (Winchester & Bach 1995). Secondly, strict controls, in the form of cash limits and projected 'efficiency gains' built into forward budgets, were used to restrain public sector pay settlements to less than inflation rates in most areas (Beaumont 1992). Public sector strikes were resisted, generally successfully: most notably the year-long miners' strike in 1984–85. Access to arbitration was withdrawn or restrained. At the Government Communications Headquarters (GCHQ) union membership rights and recognition were withdrawn in 1984, on the grounds of 'national security', leading to (ineffectual) union complaints to the ILO and the European Commission on Human Rights. Collective bargaining rights for teachers were withdrawn following lengthy industrial disputes, with pay and conditions in schools subsequently being set by Cabinet approval of recommendations from a Pay Review Body. Similar arrangements cover around a third of public sector workers.

Where collective bargaining survived, the Conservative government generally pressed for its decentralisation to local level, aiming to break up large bargaining units and to relate pay and conditions more closely to specific employer needs, to local labour market conditions and to assessed employee performance. Progress was patchy and uneven, with unions fighting to limit such moves—as in a protracted dispute in the National Health Service (NHS) in 1995. Local government was made subject to tight limits on expenditure and revenue raising through local taxes.

Deregulation was introduced in many areas (e.g. local bus passenger transport, local authorities and the NHS). Many civil service functions were reorganised into more autonomous executive agencies and other areas were subjected to substantial reductions in employment and to 'market testing' (Stewart & Walsh 1992). The process introduced private sector values and practices into what became a smaller and more fragmented public sector, which generally experienced increases in pay and conditions at a lower rate than those in the private sector. Union density, however, remained high, with some of the traditionally moderate unions experiencing sharp increases in membership (see Table 2.1).

One of the first symbolic actions of the Labour government in 1997 was to revoke the ban on unions at GCHQ (see above). Otherwise, many of the Conservative reforms of public sector industrial relations looked set to remain, in view of the tight monetary and fiscal policies adopted by this government, and given that re-nationalisations were not envisaged.

Employment relations processes

The terms and conditions under which employees work—and that regulate their levels of pay, working hours, methods of working, procedures for settling differences with employers, and so on—are central to the employment contract and industrial relations. These terms and conditions can be established in a number of ways, including legal enactment, unilateral management or union imposition, managers communicating and consulting with employees, and collective bargaining between unions and employers. While there has been an increasing tendency since the early 1980s for managements to communicate and consult with employees rather than bargain with unions about employment terms and conditions, collective bargaining remains prominent in most unionised establishments. In non-union firms, however, employment relations processes are likely to be characterised by unilateral management imposition or, at best, communication and consultation with employees.

Collective bargaining

Collective bargaining has a long history in Britain, developing in the engineering industry in the late nineteenth century and in other industries through 'joint industrial councils' soon after the First World War. By the early 1920s, multi-employer bargaining was well established in Britain, and industry-level negotiations were encouraged by the government as a way of establishing orderly relations between the parties. Though there were some exceptions, centralised negotiations across whole industries generally left little room for workplace bargaining, and it was rare for shop stewards to be mentioned in union rules, except as collectors of union subscriptions.

After the Second World War, stewards increasingly became involved in bargaining with employers, as a supplement to industry-wide negotiations conducted between national union officials and representatives of employers' associations. This was partly due to the inability of centralised agreements to specify workplace rules in sufficient detail, but was also due to the increasing power of stewards brought about by tight labour markets. By the mid-1960s, an upward trend in unofficial strikes, especially in manufacturing, led to a clamour of public opinion to 'sort out industrial relations problems'. The Donovan Commission (1968), set up in 1965 to examine this issue, concluded that Britain had two systems of industrial relations: on the one hand, there was industry-level bargaining, which set a framework and provided a floor of terms and conditions; while on the other, workplace negotiations not only supplemented these formal arrangements but also led to deals between local managers and shop stewards, which put a strain on the formal system. As the two systems were seen to be in conflict, Donovan argued for workplace bargaining to be formalised, as this would weaken the influence of multi-employer, national negotiations but at the same time remove the disorder created by uncoordinated sectional agreements. To the extent that employers and unions took this advice, and there is some disagreement about this (Purcell 1981), single-employer bargaining received a significant boost.

By 1970, collective bargaining covered approximately 70 per cent of the workforce, but since then it has declined to less than half of all employees (Brown et al. 1995). There are sizeable variations between sectors, with the public sector showing the highest coverage and private sector services the lowest. The shape and character of collective bargaining also varies considerably between workplaces, in relation to the *level* at which bargaining takes place, the size/structure of the *unit* of employees who are covered by any agreement, and the *scope* of the subjects that are determined by joint regulation.

There have been changes in the level at which bargaining takes place, especially in the private sector, with a continuing shift away from multi-employer negotiations. Several major multi-employer deals have been terminated since the early 1980s, for example in engineering, national newspapers, multiple food retailing, and bus and coach operators (Jackson et al. 1992). It is important, however, to place the decline in multi-employer bargaining in perspective (Walsh 1993). According to Millward et al. (1992:218), even though there was a sizeable reduction in the importance of multi-employer bargaining during the latter part of the 1980s, it still formed the basis for the most recent pay increase in more workplaces than did single-employer bargaining. While there are signs that multi-employer bargaining is weakening in the public sector, it is still four or five times as important as single-employer bargaining. Within the private sector, the decline has been much more pronounced, with single-employer bargaining now four times as likely as its multi-employer equivalent.

Bargaining units at workplace and company level have become wider since 1980. The move to single-table bargaining (STB) has accelerated since 1990, with an estimated doubling in the number of employers using/introducing this form of bargaining during the early part of the decade (Gall 1993). The number of employees whose terms and conditions of employment are negotiated via STB increased over the same period from 30 000 to nearly 250 000, with examples in manufacturing, newly privatised firms and the NHS. Despite media interest, one survey (IRS 1995:10) suggests that STB might be 'an idea whose time has yet to come', a feeling reinforced by the fact that these deals still cover a very small proportion of the workforce. Some employers have compromised by introducing two-table bargaining, which keeps bargaining for supervisors and professional staff separate from that for other workers. The simplest bargaining structures are generally in foreign-owned and newer firms in the private sector.

The scope of collective bargaining has shrunk since the early 1980s, leading Marchington and Parker (1990:228) to suggest that union involvement in the regulation of workplace industrial relations has been 'marginalised'. Under this scenario, the institutions of collective bargaining remain intact but steward involvement is reduced as managers refuse to discuss some issues with them and also place restrictions on the time allowed for union duties (Marchington 1995a). Rather than bargaining about a wide range of issues at the negotiating table, union representatives find that they are presented with a 'take-it-or-leave-it' offer or merely provided with information about the parlous state of company finances (Kessler & Bayliss 1995). This has led some commentators to suggest that, in some instances, collective bargaining may be little more than an 'empty shell' or 'form without substance' (Storey 1992; Guest 1995).

Employee involvement

Interest in participation and employee involvement (EI) has waxed and waned over the past century, with surges of activity at times when employers felt they were under threat from labour and a loss of impetus when this threat receded (Ramsay 1977). This is illustrated by a growth in participation through profit sharing in the late nineteenth century; joint consultation during and just after the two world wars (1917–20; 1940s); and worker directors through the TUC and the Bullock Committee of Inquiry during the 1970s. The most recent growth of interest and activity has occurred under the heading of EI during and since the 1980s, and differs substantially from earlier variants. It tends to be individualist and direct (as opposed to collective and conducted via representatives), is initiated by managements unilaterally, and is aimed at securing greater employee commitment to and identification with the employing organisation. Whether these aims have been successful is open to doubt (Marchington 1995b). Since the 1980s EI has grown without much pressure from employees or unions, but with some legislative support (for employee share ownership, profit-related pay, and statements in annual reports). It has been pursued with a voluntarist tenor.

Millward et al. (1992:166) note that 'management initiatives to increase EI were made with rising frequency throughout the 1980s', a trend that seems to have continued into the 1990s. The 'systematic use of the management chain' was described by WIRS respondents as the most extensively used method of communication. Regular meetings between managers and employees also grew, as did suggestion schemes and newsletters, but each was from a low base. There were variations between sectors, the highest level of activity being in the public sector and the lowest in manufacturing, with some growth in private services. Research by Marchington et al. (1992) shows that many organisations practised multiple forms of EI, and if anything a wider range of techniques were employed in unionised firms than in their non-union counterparts.

Direct EI takes several distinct forms in practice. Firstly, there is downward communication from managers to employees, the principal purpose of which is to inform and 'educate' staff so that they accept management plans; this includes techniques such as team briefing, informal talks between managers and their staff, employee reports, house journals, email and company videos. Secondly, there is problem solving, which is designed to tap into employee knowledge and opinion, either at an individual level or through small groups; the best known of these techniques are quality circles and suggestion schemes. The third category of EI initiatives is task participation, in which employees are encouraged or expected to extend the range and type of tasks undertaken at work. They are a form of direct EI of an individualist nature, some of which have their roots in earlier quality of working life experiments (Kelly 1982). Examples of task-based participation are job rotation, job enrichment and teamworking. Fourth, there is financial involvement, with schemes designed to link part of an individual's rewards to his or her own performance and/or that of the unit or enterprise as a whole. These take a variety of forms in practice, including profit sharing and various employee share ownership schemes. There has been a growth of interest in profit-related pay, which allows employees to gain tax relief from a small proportion of their pay if it is linked directly to profitability; in return, employers either pay a lower base wage rate to employees or build on an extra incentive element.

Even though direct EI has become more pronounced in recent years, representative participation has not disappeared. Joint consultative committees (JCCs) are the best-known example of this form of EI in Britain, having had a long and somewhat chequered history comprising various periods of growth and decline; JCCs were written off by observers in the 1960s, being viewed as unlikely to survive the development of strong shop steward workplace organisation, only to re-emerge during the 1970s before declining slightly during the 1980s (Millward et al. 1992). JCCs are likely to be present in about one-quarter of all workplaces that have at least 25 employees in the late 1990s compared with one-third in the mid-1980s. The decline is due to the changing structural and sectoral composition of workplaces (in particular the falling number of larger establishments) rather than to any concerted attempt by employers to terminate existing arrangements or by unions to boycott committees (Millward et al. 1992).

Non-unionism

The issue of non-union firms has received little attention in the literature until recently, even though large numbers of small companies did not deal with unions. Despite a few well-publicised and dramatic examples of union derecognition (e.g. News International at Wapping in 1986) most employers have not sought to exploit the changed industrial relations climate in this way. It was only with the growing awareness of what Beaumont (1987) refers to as the 'household name' group—companies such as IBM, Marks and Spencer, and Hewlett Packard—that academic interest started to blossom. These companies were praised for HRM policies designed to offer employees better terms and conditions than were generally achieved by unions through negotiations. However, it is misleading to assume all non-union enterprises are similar. Guest and Hoque (1994) propose a fourfold categorisation of non-union firms—the good, the bad, the ugly and the lucky.

The 'good' non-union firms are employers that have a clear strategy for managing people and use a wide range of human resource policies. These employers have tended to offer a complete employment package which can be seen by employees as an attractive alternative to union membership. According to Foulkes (1980), Beaumont (1987), McLoughlin and Gourlay (1994), this may include some or all of the following:

1 A highly competitive pay, fringe benefits and employee welfare package which is typically in excess of others recruiting from the same labour market.
2 A focus on employee communications and information sharing within the enterprise.
3 A 'voice' system (such as 'speak-up') enabling employee concerns and anxieties to be expressed to and dealt with by management.
4 A commitment to providing employees with secure and satisfying work while employed by the organisation, often involving regular moves to different types of job.
5 Single status and harmonised employment policies between blue-collar and white-collar employees.
6 An individualised pay and appraisal system to reward those who contribute most to organisational success.

The 'bad' or 'ugly' non-union firm is the traditional, sweatshop employer—often a small independent single-site company operating as a supplier to the large non-union enterprises analysed above. Managements that deliberately deprive workers of their rights would be categorised as 'ugly' whereas those that offer poor terms and conditions without such a manipulative intent are referred to as 'bad'. These employers are prone to believe that business success is only achievable without 'interference' from unions; thus the high likelihood of these firms remaining non-union by a strategy of 'union suppression' (Beaumont 1987). Their employment practices contrast sharply with those outlined above: pay rates are likely to be low, fringe benefits may be non-existent, and the absence of formal grievance and disciplinary procedures means that employees typically lack any form of effective 'voice'.

The stock of non-union firms has also been increased due to the derecognition of unions at some workplaces where they were recognised previously for collective bargaining or representation. Despite their media coverage, the impact of derecognitions on union membership in general has so far been slight. The complete withdrawal of collective bargaining rights for all employees has been rare, although derecognition of specific groups of employees has been rather more common, as has the removal of bargaining rights but the retention of union representation in the event of grievance or disciplinary cases (Claydon 1989; Millward et al. 1992). Although the survey by Gall and McKay (1994:434) points to an increasing rate of derecognitions during the 1990s, they conclude that 'the scale of derecognitions to date is still fairly small. As yet, there is no stampede towards union derecognitions, though it is more prominent in some sectors'.

Current and future issues

The pattern of employment relations in Britain has been reshaped by structural changes in labour markets since 1979. Many of these are similar to trends in IMEs elsewhere; others were brought about or accentuated by policies pursued by the four successive Conservative governments 1979–97 (Booth 1995:29–30).

Changing labour markets

The period of the 1980s was one of industrial restructuring, with a sharp contraction of employment in manufacturing, offset by some growth in the service sector. Official (claimant) unemployment rose to a peak of more than 12 per cent in 1983–84, falling subsequently to around 6 per cent in 1997. Unemployment has particularly affected new entrants, less-skilled workers and older men. Government policy throughout the 1980s and 1990s was characterised by attempts to promote the 'enterprise culture', labour market flexibility, self-employment, or the creation and growth of small firms. Most of the new jobs were in the less unionised service sectors (Kessler & Bayliss 1995:52–66). The privatisation of state-owned industries and commercialisation of large sectors of the civil and public service created new firms, autonomous agencies and health-care trusts. These new employers have often abandoned old public service traditions of being 'good employers', instead effecting change through unilateral managerial action (McIlroy 1995:123).

The employment of women grew disproportionately, but not many of the new jobs for women were in positions of authority. Many of the new jobs for women or men are based on atypical contracts—such as part-time, short-term, fixed contract, contracts subsidised by government training programs—or other forms of less-skilled, less-secure and poorly paid employment. Many such jobs are overshadowed by uncertainty, reorganisation, re-engineering, relocation, de-layering or redundancy. For such employees, feeling powerless, the weakened coverage of collective bargaining offers reduced protection (Millward 1994:14–34).

There are other qualitative aspects to such changing labour market trends. Gender and ethnic issues leading to employment discrimination, social exclusion and social inequality are seen by critics as being more acute than in comparable countries (e.g. Joseph Rowntree Foundation 1995). These contribute to social tensions, with around 30 per cent of total public expenditure being directed towards social welfare, thereby adding to the burden of social costs on employers and employees alike. The mounting evidence of stress and breakdown (mental health issues especially) occurring as a result of pressure within jobs (stress, overload, long hours, insecurity, intensification) are often blamed on aggressive managerial methods, such as 'hard' HRM. For unions, however, such individualised issues are not easy to tackle using their traditional collective methods.

The future nature of British labour markets points to continuing levels of unemployment above the 1945–70 average. Employment in manufacturing appears unlikely to rise, partly due to continuing productivity improvements. While service sector employment may rise numerically, the proportion of atypical jobs shows no tendency to diminish and the problem of unemployment among young people remains. The new Labour government, while aiming to move people off benefits into work, nevertheless has avoided setting a specific target for unemployment. It has had little option other than largely to accept the labour market configurations that it inherited, while concentrating initially on measures to enhance job training for unemployed youngsters.

Industrial relations and human resource management (HRM)

There has been much debate in Britain over the precise meaning of HRM and its compatibility with collective industrial relations. Practitioners and academics agree that a new HRM is developing in Britain, but there is a lack of representative surveys about its precise nature or the extent of its application. One British authority defines HRM as:

> . . . a distinctive approach to employment which seeks to achieve competitive advantage through the strategic deployment of a highly-committed

and capable workforce, using an integrated array of cultural, structural and personnel techniques. (Storey 1995:5)

The 'integrated array' includes the manipulation of corporate cultures through a calculated approach to recruitment, selection and deployment; performance measurement and reward; individualisation of contracts; reduction of stewards' and unions' influence; EI quality initiatives; narrowly specific training; teamworking; multi-skilling; flexibility; differential treatment of core and peripheral workers; and identification with the enterprise—according to the strategic and tactical needs of the employing organisation (Storey 1992:82). Where they adopt such an approach, employers in Britain are seeking to introduce a more-focused business logic into employment relations and to place greater individual emphasis on employees' work contracts (Tyson 1995:1–29).

Unions suggest that HRM is being used in some instances by employers to undermine the institutions of collective bargaining, assisted by anti-union legislation enacted after 1979. It is said to have become a tool to intensify work, demand excessive flexibility, reduce employment, marginalise stewards, weaken or eradicate unions and pursue competitive advantage to a socially irresponsible extent (Labour Research Department 1995). The uncomfortable message for unions is that HRM *can* be used thus in a concerted and effective way by employers (Ackers et al. 1996:13–27) and to individualise all or part of the employment relationship formerly based on collectivism (Bacon & Storey 1993). However, 'unions are not opposed to HRM strategies which respect their collective bargaining rights, and are consistent with the development of high-quality, well-paid employment' (TUC 1994). This wariness of HRM ('a slippery concept') displays the TUC's reluctance to make HRM the basis of any new partnership with employers, although it created a specific task force to investigate union responses to HRM.

What then are the potential outcomes in the interaction between industrial relations and HRM? Guest (1995) has suggested that four distinct patterns may emerge:

1   A new realism—a dual emphasis on HRM *and* industrial relations: as for example in the car industry, where industrial relations are kept 'ticking over' alongside HRM initiatives (Storey 1995).
2   Traditional collectivism—retaining industrial relations without HRM: the evidence from Millward et al. (1992) suggests that many managements in manufacturing are unwilling to take the risks or lack the skill to opt for HRM.
3   Individualised HRM—comprehensive HRM and no union recognition: supposedly adopted by some US-owned firms, much of the electronics industry and small owner-managed high-tech companies.

4 The black hole—no HRM *and* no industrial relations: for example, in small firms, and in new atypically structured enterprises, where unions may never have been recognised or may have disappeared by derecognition or disuse.

The capacity of HRM to replace industrial relations has been questioned also by academic commentators. Its critics argue that it is intellectually inconsistent (Legge 1995), lacks a moral foundation and represents unprincipled opportunism (Hart 1993), or that most practice displays little sustained strategic thinking (Sisson 1992:30). The resilience of union organisation seems to assure the continued existence of British collective bargaining in some form in the twenty-first century, as a key institution that performs a necessary regulatory function, with or without HRM. However, much will depend on managements' objectives and business strategies in future economic climates, and on the national and EU legislative frameworks.

British employment relations and the European dimension

Britain's relationship with the EU since the 1960s has been characterised by conflict, reversals of public and political opinion, renegotiation of terms, and battles over fundamental policies such as Britain opting out of the Social Chapter of the 1991 Treaty of Maastricht (see ch. 12). The adaptation of Britain's employment relations system to (non-Maastricht) EU directives, policy and legal judgments is contested. While convergence on some issues has occurred, the intensity of the debate among employers, unions and politicians has tended to increase (Berridge 1995:284–7).

The CBI's initial resolute opposition to the 'Europeanisation' of British employment relations reflected the arguments of Conservative politicians after 1979. It saw the increasing impact of European Court of Justice (ECJ) rulings (and the ensuing modifications required to statute law) as inimical to the restructuring of Britain into an 'enterprise society', with more job flexibility. Hence some judgments supporting workers' rights are argued to be against workers' interests as jobs may consequently be lost. The Social Chapter was described by the CBI as 'an employment-destroying disaster' (*Guardian* 1995). The Engineering Employers' Federation expressed similar opposition to EU proposals for statutory employee participation rights—preferring traditional informal, locally devised consultation (Kessler & Bayliss 1995:114–16). However, a challenge by the UK government to its being required to implement the Working Time Directive as a health and safety measure was lost at the ECJ in 1996.

At the level of the individual firm, however, many medium-sized and larger firms see economic and financial advantages in the EU. They

are willing to introduce procedural arrangements for employee information, and are not perturbed unduly by ECJ rulings on working time,
or gender and equality issues such as pensions and atypical workers'
rights, and redundancy procedures (James 1994). Even on European
Works Councils (EWCs), some firms can see benefits of increased
involvement without detriment to competitiveness (Welch 1994).

Initially, the TUC and most unions opposed membership of the EC,
but by 1983, along with the Labour Party, they had become supporters.
The address to the TUC in 1988 by Jacques Delors, then President of
the European Commission, prompted a fundamental review, and the
publication of a union 'charter' for Europe (TUC 1991). Despite some
former concerns that the Social Chapter would create only a complex
web of social dialogue (Tyson 1995:20), in 1995 the TUC endorsed
European-style statutory representation measures (TUC 1995). Collective bargaining in a European perspective at company level has been
little affected by the EU, since international businesses such as General
Motors, IBM, Kodak, Phillips and Peugeot have resisted union
attempts. Until the UK's membership of the Social Chapter takes effect,
employees in Britain are exempt from the European Works Council
(EWC) Directive. Nevertheless, some British MNEs decided to include
their workers at British plants in any pan-European committees, even
though the Conservative government and employers' organisations had
opposed the principle of statutory works councils (Hall et al. 1995).
Many commentators see the future European pattern in such consultation, rather than in integrated cross-border negotiation (e.g. Marginson 1992). The main EU impact on British employment relations under
Conservative governments was the incorporation of ECJ rulings on
employee rights into statute law (however reluctantly). The new Labour
government, in contrast, is more sympathetic to more aspects of the
EU social legislation, but does not completely accept all aspects. The
changed approach is illustrated by its signing the Social Chapter of the
1997 Treaty of Amsterdam.

Conclusions

The British employment relations system is complex, with a long
history, yet perhaps it is at a watershed. Union density in the late 1990s
is little more than half of its peak in 1979 and employers' associations
have largely lost their authority in employment relations. As a result
mainly of economic changes, British labour markets offer less job
security and are increasingly diverse, making prediction difficult. The
political system probably contains the key to the future. A fifth Conservative government following the election in 1997 would probably
have led to further labour market deregulation and a sharper antagonism

towards the EU, including its social/employee rights dimension. In the event, the new Labour government of 1997 presages a limited rapport with unions and their objectives. There is no intention on the part of the new government for a 'root and branch' repeal of union reform legislation, but what is envisaged includes a clear commitment to greater integration with Social Europe, additional employees' rights, and a social reconstruction of labour markets.

The peak organisations of employers and workers face challenges. The TUC's decision in 1995 to support a European-style regulatory and representational framework for Britain's future employment relations will require courageous leadership and run political risks. It also could portend new moral authority for the TUC, which employers' peak organisations may have to match.

The proponents of HRM still have much to prove—can it deliver economic results for employers, can it fully satisfy the newly individualised employee, and can it coexist with emerging concerns such as social exclusion and business responsibility? Survey data indicate that provisions for representation, information, participation and involvement are still finding resonance with many employees, whether union members or not (Towers 1997). However, union organisation—though weakened—remains remarkably intact, particularly in larger organisations, and is making itself more efficient under conditions of stringency (Willman, Morris & Aston 1992). Britain's employment relations system may prove to be at a watershed in the late 1990s, but the evidence is that most of its players seem ready and capable of adaptation—and hence survival.

A chronology of British employment relations

1349	Ordinance of Labourers set up pay determination machinery (the first recognisable labour legislation).
1563	Prohibition of workers' 'conspiracy' and 'combination' to raise wages.
1780–1840	Period of primary industrialisation.
1799–1800	Combination Acts provided additional penalties against workers' 'combinations'.
1811–14	'Luddites' began smashing machines.
1824–25	Repeal of Combination Acts.
1829	Grand General Union of Operative Spinners formed.
1834	'Tolpuddle martyrs' transported to Australia for taking a union oath.
1851	'New model unions' formed, mainly of skilled craftsworkers.
1868	First meeting of TUC.

1871	Trade Union Act gave unions legal status.
1880–99	Growth of militancy and development of 'new unionism' among unskilled workers.
1891	Fair Wages Resolution of the House of Commons.
1899	TUC set up Labour Representation Committee, which became the Labour Party in 1906.
1901	House of Lords' Taff Vale Judgement held that a union could be liable for employers' losses during a strike.
1906	Trade Disputes Act gave unions immunity from such liability, if acting 'in contemplation or furtherance of a trade dispute'.
1909	House of Lords' Osborne Judgment ruled that unions could not finance political activities.
1913	Trade Union Act legalised unions' political expenditure if they set up a separate fund, with individuals able to 'contract out'.
1917–18	Whitely Reports recommended joint industrial councils.
1926	General strike and nine-month miners' strike.
1927	Subsequent legislation restricted picketing and introduced criminal liabilities for political strikes.
1945	Election of Labour government.
1946–51	Repeal of 1927 Act. Nationalisation of the Bank of England, fuel, power, inland transport, health, steel etc.
1951	Election of Conservative government.
1962	National Economic Development Council established.
1964	Election of Labour government.
1968	Donovan Report advocated voluntary reform of industrial relations.
1969	Labour government proposed legal reforms, but was successfully opposed by the unions.
1970	Equal Pay Act. Election of Conservative government.
1971	Industrial Relations Act legislated for reform; most unions refused to comply with the Act, which also introduced the concept of 'unfair dismissal'.
1974	A miners' strike precipitated the fall of the Conservative government. Trade Union and Labour Relations Act replaced the 1971 Act, but retained the 'unfair dismissal' concept, set up ACAS and signalled a new Social Contract. Health and Safety at Work etc. Act.
1975	Employment Protection Act extended the rights of workers and unions. Equal Pay Act implemented.
1976	Race Relations Act.
1978–79	'Winter of discontent'.

1979	Election of Conservative government led by Mrs Thatcher.
1980	Employment Act restricted unions' rights to enforce closed shops, picket and invoke secondary action; it weakened individuals' rights (e.g. in relation to unfair dismissal, maternity leave).
1982	Employment Act restricted closed shops, strikes and union-only contracts.
1984	Trade Union Act required regular secret ballots for the election of officials, before strikes, and to approve the continuance of political funds.
1984–85	Miners' strike.
1986	Wages Act restricted the scope of wages councils.
1988	Employment Act removed all legal support for post-entry closed shops.
1990	Employment Act ended pre-entry closed shops and further restricted unions and their scope for invoking industrial action. Margaret Thatcher replaced as Prime Minister by John Major.
1991	UK opted out of the Social Chapter of the Treaty of Maastricht.
1992	Re-election of Conservative government (the fourth consecutive defeat for the Labour Party).
1993	EC established a single European market. Trade Union Reform and Employment Rights Act abolished wages councils, required more notice of strike ballots and action to employers and made industrial action ballots postal.
1994	Recorded stoppages due to labour disputes (205) and 'days lost' (280 000) at an all-time low since records began in 1891.
1995	EC became European Union (EU). Department of Employment merged into other departments, including Education.
1997	Labour government, led by Mr Tony Blair, elected with a large majority.

3 Employment relations in the United States

Hoyt N. Wheeler and John A. McClendon

The American workplace is undergoing dramatic change. American firms, in response to increased global and domestic competition, are undertaking numerous work systems innovations designed to increase productivity, reduce costs and improve quality. Most of these redesigned work systems involve changes in the nature of work and include various types of employee involvement programs and workplace innovations. Simultaneously, however, these changes in work design are occurring in a period of increased use of part-time and casual workers, declining real wages for many workers, downsizing and concerns about job security. In addition, this transformation in the organisation of work is occurring during a tumultuous period for organised labour.

The effects of these changes on the US workplace are profound, with employee influence through the process of collective bargaining becoming an increasingly elusive opportunity. As a result, one of the most successful industrial relations systems of the post-Second World War era, that of the United States (USA), is currently under siege.

The American context

As shown by its gross domestic product (GDP) of $7263 billion, population of 263 million and labour force of 134 million, the American economy is the largest of any reviewed in this book. Partly because of the size of its economy, America has traditionally played an important role in the development of other national systems.

History

Prior to industrialisation, beginning in the 1790s, American skilled craftsworkers formed unions. It is generally believed that the skilled trades' nature, practical goals and economic strategy of these early, pre-factory unions had a permanent influence on American unions (Sturmthal 1973). Yet, from the time of the American Revolution in 1776, there has also been a strong element of radical egalitarianism in the labour movement of this country. Also, in the early years of the nineteenth century many workers were attracted to various utopian schemes (Foner 1947).

The industrialisation of the USA, which took place somewhat later than that of Britain, began in the period 1810–40. From the mid-1820s to 1860 manufacturing developed in a broad range of industries, with textiles being among the most significant (Lebergott 1984:130–6). Prior to the 1850s, however, production occurred mainly in small shops and in workers' homes. This extensive use of part-time homeworking ameliorated the labour shortage that existed throughout this period (Taylor 1951:215).

The widespread establishment of the factory system in the 1850s and 1860s brought into the industrial system large numbers of American-born rural women and children, and eventually many immigrants from Ireland, Britain, Germany and other countries. These early factory workers did not unionise. This may have been partly because their pay was generally comparable to American farm earnings and higher than that of factory workers in Europe. It may also be that the high rate of worker mobility to other jobs, and the considerable degree of social mobility, hindered the development of worker solidarity that would have facilitated widespread organisation of unions (Lebergott 1984:373, 386–7; Wheeler 1985). In addition, as often occurred later in American history, vigorous repression of unionisation by employers, both directly and through government action, inhibited unionisation (Sexton 1991).

In spite of these difficulties, skilled craftsworkers did form national unions in the 1860s. Also, the social-reform-oriented Knights of Labor rose to prominence in the 1880s, and by 1886 they had organised 700 000 workers, many of them unskilled. Unlike the craft unions, which focused on the wages and working conditions of their members, the Knights aimed at reforming society as a whole by 'turning back the clock' to a better time before the rise of capitalism. Their strategy was 'cooperation', which meant forming worker cooperatives. The Knights had only a brief period of prominence. In the same year that their membership peaked, 1886, the craft unions organised on a national basis into the American Federation of Labor (AFL). These pragmatic 'business' unions quickly drove the Knights of Labor from the field, and by the turn of the century the Knights had ceased to be an important force. This experience of idealistic unionism rising for a time, only to fall before pragmatic economic unionism, has occurred on several occasions in the history of American labour (Taft 1964).

Around 1900, building on a large home market made accessible by an improved transportation system, large corporations achieved dominance in American industrial life. These complex, impersonal organisations required systematic strategies for managing their workers. Responding to this need Frederick Taylor, the father of 'scientific management', and his industrial engineer disciples gained a powerful influence on the ideology and practice of management in the USA (Hession & Sardy 1969:546–7). These ideas became widely accepted in this country before they became popular in Europe and other parts of the world. By declaring 'scientific' principles for the design of work and pay, the Taylorists undermined the rationale for determining these matters by power-based union bargaining. Added to this difficulty for the unions was the continuing vigorous opposition of the capitalists, who had both enormous power and high prestige (Sexton 1991).

Once again the unions were able to have some success in overcoming the difficulties posed by the American environment. The craft unions survived and prospered in the early part of the century, partly because of cooperative mechanisms put into place during the First World War and also because of their patriotic support of the war. During the pre-war period the craft unions were challenged by the rise of the first powerful American union of the Left, the Industrial Workers of the World (IWW). The IWW, or 'Wobblies' (a title allegedly derived from their drinking habits), combined philosophies of anarchism and syndicalism with tactics that included inspirational songs and the making of martyrs. They rose to prominence during the years before the First World War. Like the reformist Knights, they had a brief moment of glory. However, during the First World War (which they opposed) and in the post-war reaction to the Russian Revolution, they were brutally crushed by the forces of capitalism and patriotic fervour.

By the 1920s a combination of the influence of Taylorism, employer use of company-dominated unions as a union-substitution device, tough employer action in collective bargaining, widespread use of anti-union propaganda by employer groups and a hostile legal environment had reduced even the proud and once-powerful craft unions to a very weak position, although unions in a few industries such as railroads and printing continued to have some success. The unions were reduced to such a state that William Green, then President of the AFL, travelled around making speeches about how unions were in fact compatible with scientific management principles and could help management improve productivity. This bears an interesting resemblance to the current union interest in joint initiatives with employers.

It was not until the 1930s, during the Great Depression, that American unions first arose as a broadly influential and seemingly permanent force. Then, for the first time, they penetrated mass production industry, organising large numbers of factory workers. A fateful conjunction of circumstances led to this. Working conditions and pay had deteriorated. There was a changed political environment with the election of Franklin D. Roosevelt in 1932. A great wave of strikes, many of which were successful, broke out in 1933–34. The Wagner Act was passed in 1935, giving most workers a federally guaranteed right to organise and strike for the first time. Under these conditions, the strategy of mass campaigns by unions organised according to industry, rather than craft (United Automobile Workers, United Mine Workers, United Steel Workers), and united in a new labour movement—the Congress of Industrial Organizations (CIO)—led to unionisation of cars, steel, rubber, coal and other industries (Bernstein 1970; Wheeler 1985).

In the 1940s and 1950s the unions continued to grow, although federal legislation of this period restricted and regulated them. It was during this time that they developed the collective bargaining system. The post–Second World War period saw general prosperity and constantly improving standards of living accompanied by industrial peace. Union automatic wage increases (COLA clauses) in major industries contributed to the rise in living standards during this period.

Since the 1950s unions have organised large numbers of government employees. A massive wave of organising in the 1960s and 1970s, led by public school teachers, transformed government employment in many parts of the country into a sector with strong unions. However, organised labour has declined in strength overall during recent years. Currently, American unions cover less than 15 per cent of the workforce (US BLS 1997). In the private sector, union density has fallen to less than 11 per cent, a level approximating that of the 1920s. In recent years militancy has decreased significantly, with various measures of strike activity falling precipitously. During recent years the number of strikes, number of workers involved in strikes, and the number of days lost due to strikes have fallen to their lowest levels in decades (the apparent fall has been exaggerated by definition changes; see Appendix).

In the 1980s and mid-1990s there was a great deal of legislative activity in the broad field of employment relations. Legislative initiatives in the areas of minimum wages, termination of employment, race and sex discrimination in employment, pensions, health and safety, plant closing, drug testing, discrimination against disabled workers, polygraphs (lie detector machines), and family and medical leave have all drawn a great deal of attention and produced a plethora of new laws. Perhaps the most controversial issue in recent years has been the conservative attack on 'affirmative action' programs that are designed to deal with racial and gender discrimination.

The economy

Employment patterns in the USA are rather distinctive. Seventy-three per cent of civilian employees are employed by the services sector—along with Canada this is a higher percentage than in any other Organisation for Economic Co-operation and Development (OECD) country; 24 per cent are employed in manufacturing and transportation; and less than 3 per cent are employed in agriculture—less than in any of the other countries in this book, except Britain.

The level of unemployment in the USA historically tended to be higher than that in Australia, Japan and most of Western Europe, but this relationship reversed relative to Europe and Australia in the 1980s. In 1996 the USA had the third-lowest unemployment rate (5.4 per cent) of all the countries in this book (see Appendix). In contrast to the early 1980s, in the mid-1990s the consumer price index (CPI) has remained low with inflation increasing at about 3 to 4 per cent per year. Throughout the mid-1990s the US economy has recorded sustained growth and a rapidly rising stock market. This combination of low employment, low inflation, substantial growth and a booming stock market has indicated the presence of a robust economy. However, in contrast to higher income Americans, the strong economy has to date not produced the income growth for middle and lower paid workers typically associated with economic expansion. In fact, in the mid-1990s, the median household income has risen only slightly and the 'real' income of the lower 20 per cent of households has decreased. In addition, the poverty rate has increased since 1989.

Exports of goods constitute 11 per cent of the US GDP—a smaller percentage than for any other OECD country (US Chamber of Commerce–Bureau of Economic Analysis 1995). The relative unimportance of exports to the economy reflects the USA's large home market, which creates a considerable potential for self-sufficiency. However, exports have become increasingly important to the US economy in recent years. Free trade agreements and an increasingly globalised economy have led to a major expansion of international trade. The increased importance of international trade has, in turn, created greater pressures to control labour costs. The wage pressures resulting from this increased competition have led to more aggressive management behaviour towards unions.

International trade deficits continue to be a major problem for the economy. Imports exceeded exports by $102 billion in 1994 (US Department of Commerce–Bureau of Economic Analysis 1995), constituting a record-level trade imbalance. The 1993 adoption of the North American Free Trade Agreement (NAFTA), over the strong opposition of American unions, has opened the American economy to that of Mexico. Increased trade with Mexico has further contributed to the expanding pressure on American domestic employers to control labour costs. The current efforts to expand NAFTA-type trade liberalisation throughout the region, if successful, may further enhance the influence of greater international competition on US employment relations.

Nature of employment relations

The employment relations system in the USA consists of two distinct sectors: a non-union sector and a unionised sector. These two sectors interconnect in many ways, and share some common legal and social underpinnings, but nevertheless differ quite significantly.

The *non-union sector* is characterised by broad management discretion and control over the terms and conditions of employment. This is limited only by labour market constraints, protective labour legislation, the desire of managers to avoid unionisation and the strong influence of a 'positive' managerial outlook. This prevailing management ideology, which sometimes carries the label 'human resource management', holds that for various reasons firms 'should' offer favourable conditions of employment to employees.

The non-union sector includes most private white-collar employment, electronics, small firms, most of the textile industry, most of the service sector, and manufacturing employees in a variety of industries. The main threat to the stability of this sector in remaining non-union is the sporadic efforts of unions to organise it.

The *unionised sector* has historically been characterised by openly adversarial relations between labour and management (Barbash 1981: 1–7). For the most part Americans view unions and management as serving rather discrete and fundamentally opposed interests. The conflict between unions and management is circumscribed, however, by the limited goals of American unions. As the unions are still mainly concerned with the 'pure and simple' goals of the founders of the American labour movement—better wages, hours and conditions of work—and do not wish to be broadly involved in management, their challenge to management has been rather constrained. They have been willing to enter into what the old radical trade unionists called a 'treaty with the boss'—a collective bargaining agreement covering those matters that concern them—giving up the right to strike for the duration of this 'treaty'. Conflict in the unionised sector is further bounded by the recognition by managers and unions that there are some broad areas of mutual interest.

The end result in the unionised sector is a rather stable situation where conflict is legitimate but bounded as to grounds, timing and emotional intensity. The main threat to its stability is endemic managerial resistance to unions, which from time to time results in efforts to move establishments from the unionised sector to the non-union sector—either by disestablishing a union in an existing location or by moving the work to a southern or western location where unions are weak. There has always been wide variation among firms regarding the degree to which they are willing to work jointly with unions, ranging from real jointness to vicious union-busting antagonism.

In the late 1980s and 1990s a challenge to the basic adversarial nature of the American system developed from managers and unionists who were proponents of labour–management cooperation. There has been, however, considerable variation in these cooperative approaches. The key question is whether this represents a fundamental and permanent change or is merely a tactical expansion of traditionally recognised areas of common interest. Many unions, such as the United Steelworkers, have made a commitment to labour–management cooperation. Coupled with the decline of strikes in the USA, this trend may signal a fundamental change in the system.

The environment of employment relations

The economic environment has always had a powerful influence upon the American employment relations system. The predominant employers have, since the beginning of the twentieth century, been large private sector enterprises. American unions were created to deal with, and have adapted to operating in, a capitalist economy dominated by such firms. Government's role in the economic system, although it has fluctuated over the years, has largely remained more limited than in other countries. Economic growth has helped to produce relatively favourable terms and conditions of employment for the majority of workers in the USA since the Second World War.

A reduction in demand for American goods was part of the general decrease in demand during the post-1974 oil-shock recession, and was exacerbated by the competition from high-quality goods produced in other countries. In the home market, competition from higher quality or lower cost foreign goods has particularly affected major industries such as cars, textiles and steel. In these and other industries, improvements in technology, encouraged by this competition, have caused workers to be replaced by machines. To further complicate matters, the type of labour demanded has been changed by both new technology and the shift of the American economy from manufacturing to services. The workforce has become increasingly diverse in terms of gender, race and national origin (Johnston & Packer 1987). The increasingly competitive market environment and emphasis on cost reduction are exerting a powerful force for a changing American workplace. These changes—cost pressures, greater international and domestic competition, rapid technology change and the decline in the traditional dominance of the largest firms—have seriously weakened the bargaining power of unions. It has also led to 'downsizing' or 'rightsizing' of the workplace, costing many employees, including managers, their jobs.

In periods of relative economic growth, collective bargaining demands and results were historically favourable to labour. However, after the general prosperity of the late 1980s resumed in the mid-1990s, following the 1991–92 recession, unions remained weak and wage improvements were only moderate. This phenomenon of relatively strong economic growth in conjunction with declining real wages has come to be viewed as potentially a contradiction.

American politics is largely politics of the Centre. The two major parties, Republicans and Democrats, dominate national politics and have generally absorbed and moderated the ideas of more extreme groups. Distinctions between them are further blurred by the fact that, unlike the situation in other English-speaking countries, party discipline has historically been weak. However, a major swing to the Right occurred in the Republican Party in recent years, culminating in a historic election victory in 1994 in which that party gained the majority in both houses of Congress for the first time in decades.

The two political parties do differ with respect to the area of the Centre that they occupy. The Democrats, while not a labour party, are generally more sympathetic to employees than are the Republicans. In general, the Democrats have more 'liberal' political goals, and are more supportive of government action to achieve social and economic justice. The swing to the Right by the Republican Party may lead to increased efforts to dismantle existing laws designed to protect employee and union interests.

As it relates to employment relations, the political environment in the USA, with its representative democratic institutions, has provided a structure for the development of both free trade unions and free management. The political strength of capital and its representatives has always been sufficient to preserve broad areas of managerial discretion from government regulation. Yet the balance of political forces has historically permitted the development of reasonably strong trade unions and the imposition of some governmental constraints upon managerial freedom in the employment relations arena.

During the 1980s and early 1990s the political environment accentuated the trend towards ever-increasing management power in employment relations. Prior to 1992, relatively conservative national administrations, both Democratic and Republican, 'deregulated' the transport industry, increasing competition and placing downward pressure on wages. They lessened the influence of government upon employers generally by moderating the enforcement of laws protecting workers from health and safety hazards and from discrimination. President Reagan's appointees to the agency responsible for ensuring workers the right to organise, the National Labor Relations Board, instituted major policy changes unfavourable to unions. All of this combined with the heightened conservatism of the Republican-appointed federal judiciary to create a very hostile legal environment for unions. At the same time, as discussed below, protections for individual workers were increasing in some respects.

The national political landscape changed considerably with the election of a Democratic President, Bill Clinton, in 1992. He moved very quickly to sign into law the Family and Medical Leave Act, entitling employees to unpaid leave for family and medical reasons. Also, albeit after considerable delays in their appointments, the new Democrat-appointed members of the National Labor Relations Board and its General Counsel moved, largely through procedural changes, to make this agency once again an effective instrument for facilitating unionisation and collective bargaining. However, this has not yet had any perceptible effect on the level of unionisation. Although not always highly energetic in supporting organised labour's political agenda, President Clinton has been much more friendly towards it than have Republican Presidents.

The importance to unions of the legal outcomes of the political system was dramatically demonstrated in the 1992 strike by 13 000 United Auto Workers against Caterpillar Corporation. Because the law permits strikers to be replaced permanently, Caterpillar was able to use the threat of replacement to break the strike, with the union surrendering and ordering strikers back to work. Similar experiences in industries ranging from airlines to professional baseball have highlighted the importance of unions having at least a modicum of *political* power in order to be effective in pursuing their *economic* strike-based strategy.

In 1994, the Republicans, led by Newt Gingrich, came to power in Congress with the promise to turn back the clock, reducing the extent of the federal government and many of its social programs. Although not included in the 'Contract with America' that constituted the Republican platform, the weakening of employment protection seems to be rapidly gaining prominence on the Republican agenda. If the 1994 Republican success is a passing fancy of an increasingly fickle American electorate, it may not matter very much in the long run. If, however, the change in the political landscape continues, we can look for massive changes in the political environment relative to workplace issues. For example, health and safety standards, among others, will no doubt be made subject to cost-benefit analysis. Legislation to weaken the National Labor Relations Act and prohibitions against company unions will be adopted. A wide array of worker protections will probably be challenged. If all of this occurs, we will indeed be witnessing a sea change in the traditional American employment relations system.

The employment relations parties

In the USA, all of the participants in the employment relations system still have a significant role. However, it is the employers that have generally been the most powerful of the actors and that, as will be argued below, are becoming increasingly dominant.

Employers and their organisations

Thomas Kochan argues that 'management is the driving force in any advanced industrial relations system' (1980:179). This is especially true in the USA. In the USA and in other industrialised countries it derives, at least in part, from the crucial role of management in ensuring the efficiency and survival of the work organisation. It may further stem from the high general social status of managers and their relatively high position in the organisational hierarchy.

The non-union sector of the American workforce includes the vast majority of workers. Throughout most of this sector, redundant workers can be laid off in whatever order the employer desires, and terminated for any, or no, reason—with the exception of particular illegal grounds, such as race and sex, and some court-made exceptions such as discharges that violate public policy. Furthermore, the conditions under which employment takes place are essentially employer-determined, although limited by labour market forces.

Employer organisations are relatively unimportant in the USA (Adams 1980:4). In contrast to many other countries, there have never been national employers' confederations engaging in the full range of employment relations activities. There have, however, long been employer organisations with the mission of avoiding the unionisation of their members' employees. The National Association of Manufacturers was formed for this purpose in the nineteenth century. In addition, many regional Chambers of Commerce include union avoidance in their activities. These employer groups and others engage in anti-union litigation, lobbying and publicity campaigns. They, along with management consultants, engage in the lucrative business of educating employers in techniques of union avoidance.

There has been a considerable increase in employer anti-union activities since the mid-1970s. These actions have ranged from locating enterprises in non-union areas in the south and west (the so-called 'Sun Belt') and openly violating the labour laws, to the positive action of intentionally providing pay higher than the union range. The reasons for this increase in anti-union activities are not entirely clear. However, immediately prior to this period the union–non-union wage differential had grown to a margin so large as to tempt employers to go to considerable lengths to be non-union. Another cause of increased employer resistance may be managers seizing the opportunity to defeat their historic adversary when it is weak. The acceptance of unions by American managers has always been rather grudging, and based more upon necessity than choice.

The unions

The fundamental characteristics of the American labour movement are as follows:

1 Goals that are largely those of 'bread and butter' unionism.
2 A strategy that is mainly economic.
3 Collective bargaining as a central well-developed activity.
4 Relatively low total union density.
5 Strength *vis-à-vis* the employer on the shop floor (job control).
6 An organisational governance structure in which the national union holds the reins of power within the union.
7 Financial strength.
8 Leadership drawn largely from the rank and file.

Selig Perlman long ago argued that the American labour movement exhibited a 'Tom, Dick and Harry' idealism—an idealism derived from the ordinary worker (1970:274–5). Perlman believed that unions, because they reflected the aspirations of their members, adopted those goals that seemed most important to the workers. These goals, said Perlman, had nothing to do with the imagined utopia of the Marxist 'intellectuals', but rather reflected the 'pure and simple' goals espoused by such labour leaders as Samuel Gompers, the 'father' of the American labour movement. Perlman's argument still affords a basic understanding of the American labour movement. Although American unions have also pursued wider goals, and have become more interested in cooperation with management to increase worker feelings of self-worth, what has endured has been their emphasis upon practical improvements in wages, hours and conditions of work. Of course, unions in other countries have also sought 'bread and butter', but American unions have focused more closely upon this outcome than have most others.

The ideology of American unions is still much as it was expressed in 1911 by Samuel Gompers:

> The ground-work principle of America's labor movement has been to recognise that first things must come first. The primary essential in our mission has been the protection of the wage workers, now; to increase his wages; to cut hours off the long workday, which was killing him; to improve the safety and the sanitary conditions of the workshop; to free him from the tyrannies, petty or otherwise, which served to make his existence a slavery. (Gompers 1919:20)

American unions have relied upon collective bargaining, accompanied by the strike threat, as their main weapon. This strategy has influenced the other characteristics of the American labour movement. It has provided the basis for an effective role on the shop floor, as the day-to-day work of administering the agreement requires this. It has required unions to be solvent financially in order to have a credible strike threat. It has resulted in an organisational structure in which the power within the union is placed where it can best be used for collective bargaining—with the national union (Barbash 1967:69). Centralisation of power over strike funds in the national union has been a crucial source of union ability to develop common rules and to strike effectively. It has facilitated, and perhaps even required, an independence from political parties that might be tempted to subordinate the economic to the political. It is one reason why there is a relatively low total union density, as collective bargaining organisations need to have a concern about density only as it pertains to their individual economic territories. Bargaining outcomes are only indirectly affected by the overall strength of labour in the society, except where—as may be the case at the present—political strength gets so low as to impede bargaining. It has also contributed to one of the concomitants of low density, weak political power.

Although American unions have emphasised collective bargaining, they have also engaged in politics. Their political action has for the most part taken the form of rewarding friends and punishing enemies among politicians, and lobbying for legislation. They have avoided being involved in the formation of a labour party. The American Federation of Labor–Congress of Industrial Organizations' (AFL–CIO) Committee on Political Education (COPE) and similar union political agencies are major financial contributors to political campaigns. The goals of such political activity have often been closely related to unions' economic goals, being aimed at making collective bargaining more effective. However, the American labour movement has also been a major proponent of progressive political causes such as laws on civil rights, minimum wages, plant-closing notice, and other subjects of benefit to citizens generally.

Since the 1980s, the AFL–CIO has moved towards greater identification with a particular political party, the Democrats. A large amount of resources were devoted to the 1996 elections in an attempt to elect officials, mainly Democrats, more friendly to labour. This suggests a new awareness of the importance of politics. It is possible that 12 years under Presidents Ronald Reagan and George Bush helped move the AFL–CIO to this conclusion, and experience with the Republican right-wing majority in Congress, beginning in the mid-1990s, has tended to confirm this.

The structure of the American labour movement is rather loose compared with that of other Western union movements, as the national unions have never been willing to cede power over the function of collective bargaining to the AFL–CIO. The AFL–CIO is a federation of national unions that includes approximately 85 to 90 per cent of American union members. It was strengthened in the 1980s by the reaffiliation of several major unions, which has given the American labour movement the greatest degree of cohesiveness it has seen in 30 years. The AFL–CIO serves as the chief political and public relations voice for the American labour movement, settles jurisdictional disputes among its members, enforces codes of ethical practices and policies against racial and sex discrimination, and is American labour's main link to the international labour movement.

A major change in the AFL–CIO occurred in October 1995 with the unprecedented election challenge for the federation's presidency by John Sweeney. As President of the Service Employees International Union (SEIU), Sweeney successfully organised a coalition of union leaders within the federation's member unions and defeated the chosen successor of the previous president who had retired as a result of the Sweeney-led challenge. In an effort to address the decline in union density, Sweeney's administration has adopted a major emphasis on organising new membership.

The national unions have been described as occupying the 'kingpin' position in the American labour movement (Barbash 1967:69). They maintain ultimate power over the important function of collective bargaining, in large part through their control of strike funds. The national unions can establish and disestablish local unions, and can withdraw from the AFL–CIO if they wish. The national presidents of unions are generally considered to be the most powerful figures in the American labour movement.

Continuing a trend that began in the early 1980s, several mergers and proposals for mergers among national unions have occurred. Recent examples of mergers include the combination of the two largest textile unions as well as the proposed combination of the Steelworkers, Autoworkers and Machinists. In addition, many small independent unions have begun to choose to be absorbed into major national unions, further consolidating the structure of US unionism (McClendon, Kriesky & Eaton 1995).

The local unions perform the day-to-day work of the labour movement. They usually conduct bargaining over the terms of new agreements and conduct strikes, although in some industries national unions do this. They administer the agreement, performing the important function of enforcing the complex set of rights that the American collective bargaining agreement creates. Social activities among union members take place at the local level; what there is of a union culture in the US exists here (Barbash 1967:26–41).

As mentioned, union membership in 1996 constituted less than 15 per cent of wage and salary workers. This compares with a union membership density of about 20 per cent of wage and salary earners as recently as 1983 (see US BLS 1997). Union membership as a proportion of the labour force reached its peak in 1956 at approximately 35 per cent. However, between 1975 and 1996, government and service employee unions experienced substantial growth. One of the old construction unions, the International Union of Operating Engineers, has also grown impressively. The National Education Association is the largest union, with a membership of 2 million. It is mainly in the manufacturing sector that union membership has been lost (Gifford 1992). Many unions have abandoned their traditional jurisdictions and are in fact general unions that will organise virtually anyone.

The American labour movement is generally considered an exceptional case because of its apolitical 'business unionism' ideology, focusing rather narrowly on benefits to existing membership. The most convincing explanations for this are historical (Kassalow 1974). First, there is no feudal tradition in the USA, which has made the distinctions among classes less obvious than in much of Europe and the USA lacks any other special historical circumstances giving rise to class consciousness. Second, American capitalism developed in a form that allowed fairly widespread prosperity. Third, the great diversity of the population, divided particularly along racial and ethnic lines, has always hampered the organisation of a broad-based working-class movement. Fourth, the early establishment of voting rights and free universal public education eliminated those particular potential working-class issues in the nineteenth century. Fifth, social mobility from the working class to the entrepreneurial class blurred class lines, creating a basis for the widely held belief in the 'log cabin to White House' myth. In consequence, the American labour movement has seldom defined itself in class terms. Additionally, the historic experience of American trade unionists was that class-conscious unions (i.e. those that assumed the 'burden of socialism') tended to be repressed by the strong forces of American capitalism (see Sexton 1991). A related but somewhat different explanation (Sturmthal 1973) is that American labour formed an economic strike-based strategy in its early years because this was appropriate to the conditions of labour shortage under which it began, and has continued to pursue this course, even at times when it is inappropriate.

Why is the USA unique among the countries in this book in having no labour-style party? First, it would be difficult to operate as an independent national political force when representing only a small proportion of the workforce. Second, American workers have traditionally been highly independent politically, often voting in ways other than those desired by their union leaders. Third, the limited American experience with separate labour parties has not been favourable. Formed in 1828, the Working Men's Party was arguably the first labour party in the world. A reading of minutes of union conventions for many years afterwards shows that its collapse, and the severe problems that it engendered, caused unions to steer clear of repeating that experience. Some later attempts were made, but were not much more successful. These were probably hindered by the fact that it has historically been difficult to form any third party in the USA. Fourth, the idea of a labour party is one that has often been urged by left-wing unionists who were the losers in struggles for control of unions in the 1930s and 1940s, and who were purged during the 'Red scare' years of the 1950s. In our view, the failure to form a labour party may be accounted for in part by the narrow economic orientation of American unions, which makes the unions economic actors rather than political parties that pursue political outcomes. As others are puzzled by the American failure to have a labour party, American trade unionists are unable to see why they should do such an odd thing.

American unions, to a much greater extent than those in many other countries, have had longstanding problems with corruption, and a history in some unions of undemocratic practices (Hutchison 1972). The Landrum-Griffin Act was enacted in 1959 as an attempt to control these practices. While there have been successful reform efforts in recent years in such unions as the Teamsters, organised labour is still burdened by a reputation for corruption, of which their enemies take full advantage.

Government

The rapid increase in public sector unionisation in the 1960s and 1970s was probably the most important development in the American labour movement since the 1930s. Teachers initiated this, as they successfully protested about declines in their salaries and benefits relative to those of other workers. Unionisation spread rapidly through most areas of government employment. As a result of this wave of unionising, there has been an important change in the composition of the American labour movement, with public employee unions in 1991 representing 37 per cent of union members (Gifford 1992). Subsequent surveys suggest that this percentage continued to rise in the late 1990s (US BLS 1997).

Government has three main roles in employment relations in the USA. These roles include, firstly, the direct regulation of terms and conditions of employment; secondly, regulation of the manner in which organised labour and management relate to each other; and thirdly, that of employer.

Until quite recently, the direct regulation of terms and conditions of employment was limited to the areas of employment discrimination, worker safety, unemployment compensation, minimum wages and max-imum hours, and retirement (Ledvinka & Scarpello 1991). In 1964, the government acted to prohibit discrimination in employment on the grounds of race, colour, sex, religion or national origin. This law was strengthened in 1991. It has also proscribed discrimination on the basis of age, and against Vietnam War veterans. Effective in 1992, it acted to broadly prohibit discrimination against disabled workers.

The government has addressed problems of worker safety, mainly through the Federal Occupational Safety and Health Act of 1970 (OSHA), state health and safety laws, and state workers' compensation laws. OSHA mandates a safe workplace, both by imposing a general duty of safety upon employers and by providing a detailed set of regulations for each industry. Employers violating safety and health standards are subject to fines and remedial orders. These regulations are not subject to justification on a cost-benefit basis, but there is in progress a powerful effort by Congressional Republicans to impose such a requirement on this and other federal regulations.

Workers' compensation laws provide for medical care and income protection for workers injured on the job. Also, they encourage safety indirectly by increasing the costs of insurance for employers that experience a large number of on-the-job injuries.

Unemployment compensation is provided for on a State-by-State basis, but with some federal control and funding. It involves payments to persons who have become involuntarily unemployed and are seeking work. The duration of payments is less than in most of the other countries in this book. It is usually limited to a period of 26 weeks, although with federal support this may be extended to 39 weeks in a particular State when unemployment is high (Commerce Clearing House 1987:4409). Federal and State wage and hour laws provide for a minimum level of pay and a premium pay rate for overtime work, although many workers are excluded from the coverage of these laws. Following a strong legislative battle in the US Congress, the minimum pay level was raised to $4.75 per hour effective in the fall of 1996 and then raised to $5.15 in 1997, although there is a lower 'training' wage for young workers. Employers are also required to pay one-and-a-half the employee's regular rate of pay for hours worked in excess of 40 in a particular work week.

Retirement benefits are regulated in two main ways. First, through the Social Security system, employers and employees are required to pay a proportion of wages (7.65 per cent each in 1995) into a govern-ment fund. It is out of this fund that pensions are paid by the government to eligible retired employees (Social Security Act). The second way in which government controls pensions is by regulation of the private pension funds that are set up voluntarily by employers. The Employee Retirement Income Security Act of 1974 requires retirement plans to be financially secure, and insures these plans. It also mandates that employees become permanently vested in their retirement rights after a certain period.

Government regulation of the labour–management relationship consists largely of a set of ground rules through which these actors establish, and work out the terms of, their relationship. Through the National Labor Relations Act (NLRA) of 1935, as amended in 1947 and 1959, government provides a structure of rules that establishes certain employee rights with respect to collective action.

The process and ground rules established by law for union certification and bargaining in the private sector represent one of the more unusual features of US labour–management relations. The NLRA (1935) specifies a multi-step organising process ordinarily culminating in a secret ballot election by employees to determine whether they want union certification. The objective of the law regulating union representation elections is to ensure employees have a free choice. To achieve this objective, the National Labor Relations Board (NLRB) determines the appropriate voting unit, conducts the secret ballot election, certifies the union as the exclusive bargaining agent for the unit when the union achieves a majority of the votes cast, and rules on charges of unfair labour practices such as employer retribution against employees who support the union. When the union is victorious in the election, the NLRB issues a certification that requires the employer to bargain in good faith with the union. The union has the same obligation.

A good deal of controversy in recent years has focused on whether or not the election process is working in accordance with the original legislative intent. This has led to a continuing debate over the adequacy of laws protecting workers' rights to form and join unions. The Commission on the Future of Worker–Management Relations (Dunlop Commission), reporting in 1994, reached the conclusion that the labour laws did indeed need to be changed to facilitate union organising. To the dismay of the unions, it also recommended weakening the legal prohibition against company-dominated unions. The Republican Congress elected in 1994 has, we believe, used this as an excuse for proposing a very broad authorisation of company-dominated worker organisations in the so-called TEAM Act.

In the USA, government plays a very limited role in the collective bargaining process in the private sector. Although it requires 'good faith' bargaining efforts, government generally takes a 'hands-off' position—with notable exceptions such as the railroad industry—in influencing contract outcomes achieved between labour and the employer in private sector collective bargaining.

Since 1959, by the enactment of the Landrum-Griffin Act, the federal government has regulated the internal affairs of unions. This law creates a 'Bill of Rights' for union members, requiring that unions accord them rights of free speech and political action. It also punishes union officials who mishandle union funds and outlaws certain anti-democratic practices by unions. In 1991, an election held under government supervision resulted in a slate of 'reform' candidates taking power in the historically corrupt Teamsters union (International Brotherhood of Teamsters—IBT).

A great deal of federal employment legislation took place in 1988. In that year the Employee Polygraph Protection Act placed limitations on the use of lie detectors by employers. These machines, notorious for their unreliability and degrading uses, were being widely utilised by employers for both pre-employment testing and investigations of employee wrongdoing. This increased protection of employees was balanced, however, by the Drug-Free Workplace Act of 1988 which strongly encourages drug testing and punishment of employees for drug use by employers that do business with the federal government. Employer actions in this area have received further encouragement from regulations of the US Department of Transportation and Department of Defense requiring broad drug testing of employees in those industries. Drug testing of federal and railroad employees, at least under some circumstances, was approved by the US Supreme Court in two 1989 decisions.

An additional piece of legislation adopted in 1988 is the Worker Adjustment and Retraining Notification Act (WARN), or 'plant-closing' law. This federal statute requires employers, with some exceptions, to give 60 days advance notice of a plant closing or mass layoff.

The trend in government action has continued into the 1990s. Congress passed the Civil Rights Act in 1991. This statute re-established the requirement that the employer had the burden of justifying, on the basis of business necessity, an employment practice having discriminatory effects; this was an important action by Congress to reverse the weakening of anti-discrimination laws by conservative judges. However, consistent with recent conservative trends, there is currently an intense public debate about rescinding legislation such as current 'affirmative action' policies on discrimination. Also of great practical importance is the Americans With Disabilities Act, effective in 1992, which imposes on most employers the obligation to make reasonable accommodation to the needs of disabled employees. This may even include protection for employees with infectious diseases such as AIDS. A recent action, mentioned above, is the passage of the Family and Medical Leave Act, which provides for 12 weeks of unpaid leave for family or medical reasons.

Government is an employer of considerable consequence. In 1994 it employed 14 per cent of the workforce (OECD 1997). Government employment, including both national and State levels, increased by 32 per cent between 1970 and 1988 (Bureau of the Census 1989; Bauman 1989). In 1996, 38 per cent of government workers were unionised, a slightly higher proportion than in 1983 (Gifford 1992; US BLS 1997). This represents a public sector membership density that is considerably greater than the private sector's density rate of less than 11 per cent.

The main processes of employment relations

In the *non-union sector*, employers have devised a set of management practices to systematically determine pay and conditions of work. With respect to compensation, a combination of job evaluation and individual performance evaluation systems is common. The range of possible wage rates to be paid to workers in the job of, say, clerk are determined by an assessment of the worth of the job to the firm (i.e. job evaluation). A particular employee is assigned a wage rate within this range depending upon seniority, performance or other factors. In addition to pay, fringe benefits such as health insurance, pensions, vacations and holidays are determined by company policy. All of this is done with an eye to the external labour market, with total compensation having to be adequate to attract and keep needed workers (Gomez-Mejia, Balkin & Cardy 1995).

Collective bargaining, which chiefly determines the outcomes in the *unionised sector*, has reached an advanced stage of development in the USA. Since the 1940s, collective bargaining has produced a high standard of living for most unionised workers, protection for the worker interest in fair treatment and a complex and detailed set of rules governing the employment relationship, while generally preserving the managerial ability to ensure efficiency.

The collective bargaining structure is highly fragmented, and this fragmentation is increasing. As is the case in a number of countries, trends since the early 1980s suggest the locus of collective bargaining is shifting downwards towards the firm or workplace level (Katz 1993). Single-company or single-workplace agreements are the norm in manufacturing. Most collective bargaining takes place at such levels. Even where national agreements exist, as in the car industry, substantial scope is left for local variation.

Third-party intervention is widespread. Although the USA is noted for the very limited role government plays in determining collective bargaining agreements in the private sector, mediators employed by the national government through the Federal Mediation and Conciliation Service (FMCS) are active in the negotiation of new agreements, and their work is generally popular with the parties. In negotiations involving government employees, many State laws provide for binding arbitration of unresolved disputes over the terms of a new agreement. This is especially common where the government employees involved, such as firefighters or police officers, are considered to be 'essential'.

'Interest' arbitration of the terms of a new agreement is very rare in the private sector.

Although there is considerable variety in collective bargaining agreements (contracts), they share certain nearly universal aspects. Most are very detailed, although the craft union contracts are less so. Agreements generally cover wages, hours of work, holidays, pensions, health insurance, life insurance, union recognition, management rights, the role of seniority in determining promotions and layoffs, and the handling and arbitration of grievances. Most agreements have a limited duration, usually of one, two or three years (BNA 1995).

In both the private and public sectors, the vast majority of agreements provide a formal multi-step grievance procedure that culminates in 'rights' arbitration. The formal procedure specifies a series of steps through which the parties can resolve disagreements over the application and interpretation of an existing collective bargaining agreement. The procedures are almost always capped by the provision for an independent arbitrator to be selected jointly by the union and the employer. Compared with most industrialised countries, the emphasis on formal grievance arbitration represents one of the more unusual features of labour–management relations in the USA. A substantial body of private 'law' has grown up through arbitral decisions, providing employment relations with a set of norms that are used in the non-union sector as well as in the union sector. Decisions of arbitrators have historically been treated by the courts as final, binding and unappealable (Feuille & Wheeler 1981:270–81).

An important issue related to grievance handling and rights arbitration is the duty of fair representation. In return for the right to exclusive representation, the union has the obligation to represent all bargaining unit members impartially and in good faith. This issue of fair representation has grown in importance in recent years as workers have become increasingly willing to bring legal claims against unions for failure to represent them fairly. One result of the rise in litigation dealing with fair representation is an increasing reluctance of unions to drop grievances of questionable merit short of arbitration for fear of being sued.

At least for unionised workers, the relative lack of government welfare programs in the USA is somewhat compensated for by the extensive protections included in these agreements. However, declines in health insurance coverage and automatic wage adjustments in collective bargaining agreements, although balanced to an extent by gains in other areas, reflect the somewhat decreased strength of American unions in what has traditionally been their bailiwick. Furthermore, although union wages and benefits continue to be substantially higher than those of non-union workers, their *increases* have been slightly smaller than those of non-union workers in several recent years.

Given the challenges with which it has been faced in the 1980s and 1990s, collective bargaining in the USA has survived well. Although the American collective bargaining system is currently being widely criticised for its adversarial nature and obsolescence, a review of its recent accomplishments would seem to provide clear testimony to its strength and flexibility. However, it may bear some share of blame for the problems of American competitiveness, at least for its invention of the automatic wage adjustment based upon increases in the consumer price index (COLA clauses) that raised wages unexpectedly during the high inflation of the 1970s.

The rapid rise of health-care costs, most of which had been borne by employers, has prompted employers to shift some of this burden to employees, with unions and employers working together to contain these costs. Profit-sharing plans have been proposed and accepted at such firms as Weyerhauser, Chrysler and Uniroyal-Goodrich. Corporate mergers and acquisitions have given rise to union insistence on 'successorship clauses' in contracts with such diverse employers as Bloomingdale's and Firestone. In such a clause the company agrees to require a buyer of the business to retain the union relationship. Technological changes have sparked agreements on early retirement, preferential hiring, pay continuance guarantees and retraining (Kempski 1989).

Current issues of importance

Although there are many current issues concerning American employment relations, we will briefly review two categories of issues that pose especially significant challenges: workplace transformations, and the decline of unions and the rise of management power.

Workplace transformation

There is little doubt that the American workplace is experiencing a transformation, mainly through the adoption of new human resource techniques. Many American firms, in an effort to enhance performance and remain competitive, have initiated changes in the very nature of work. These include changes in work process design; employee ownership through employee stock ownership plans (ESOPs); and cost-reduction efforts through downsizing, out-sourcing, and contingent employment. Each of the changes is undoubtedly significant. However, there are many questions about this transformation with respect to its permanence, true essence, effectiveness, and its desirability from the perspectives of employees and society at large. This broad array of changes, while they are related, and are intended to achieve similar goals, can be divided into those programs designed to improve work processes and those initiated with the primary purpose of reducing costs.

As in many other countries, much attention is currently being devoted to work process approaches. The nature of the work system transformations, which are designed to improve organisation performance and product/service quality, vary considerably in terms of specific design and technique. Most commonly, however, these new approaches involve some form of employee involvement or managerial work system redesign that emphasises coordination and decision making. Specific examples of current workplace changes range from total quality management (TQM) programs to self-directed work teams within a socio-technical work system approach (Applebaum & Batt 1994).

Although there is considerable diversity among the emerging new work systems, two related models can be identified: the 'lean' production and the 'team' production systems. The lean model programs rely to a greater extent on managerial and technical expertise, and involve centralised coordination and decision making. In contrast, 'team-based' approaches use a more decentralised decision-making structure and focus on continuous improvement. The team-based model also places greater emphasis on structures for representation of employee interests at all organisation levels and is, therefore, more consistent with and adaptable to unionised settings than the lean production model. The team-based programs are also more likely to engender valued outcomes for employees such as increased job security, greater autonomy and a greater guaranteed share in performance gains.

There is, however, another category of changes in the American workforce that represents very different outcomes for employees in comparison with the workplace transformations utilising employee involvement. The same competitive pressures that have led to work systems change have also led employers to implement changes focused on cost cutting. These include downsizing, use of contingent workers and out-sourcing of work. For example, in 1994 many of the largest firms in the USA made permanent reductions in employment despite the fact it was a record year for corporate profits among these firms.

What is needed is real employee involvement. In addition to serving the interests of the employer, appropriate employee involvement— regardless of the specific technique used—should be consistent with worker goals such as improved quality of work life and enhanced job security and compensation (Voos 1994:16). Programs that fail to directly and positively affect worker interests are unlikely to have a long-term positive impact on performance; and evidence suggests that programs that serve employee interests and improve organisational performance are more likely to occur in unionised settings (Eaton & Kriesky 1994).

The decline of unions and the rise in management power

Although there are many reasons for membership decline, it appears most of the loss of union membership as a percentage of the workforce is rooted in two basic factors: an economic environment that encourages competition based on labour costs, and a legal framework that allows employers leeway in avoiding unionisation (Voos 1994).

Although union membership has declined sharply since the late 1970s, unions have achieved an improved victory rate in union certification elections in some recent years. In addition, under the new AFL–CIO leadership, organising new members has become a high priority for the labour movement. Given managements' market-driven incentives, and barring unlikely major revisions in public policy that would address some of the basic problems of organising, it appears likely organised labour will continue to face daunting challenges with respect to new membership organising.

Although membership decline is one of the more obvious measures of organised labour's difficulties, recent history suggests additional indicators of declining union strength. First, bargaining structures have become more decentralised in recent years as reflected by the declining prevalence of 'bargaining patterns', multi-employer bargaining, and the increased emphasis on agreements that are tailored to specific companies. Given that management has been the principal force behind this trend towards more decentralised bargaining, this, too, reflects the rising power of management relative to organised labour.

Another indication of the rise of management power is the frequent use of confrontational bargaining tactics. In an era of reduced union bargaining power, management has often used highly aggressive tactics at the bargaining table, which in some cases has served to eliminate union representation altogether. The most conspicuous and most controversial example involves employer use of permanent striker replacements.

The future of organised labour in the USA is difficult to predict, but without question the challenges are formidable. In the 1930s organised labour grew only after major transformations of the political environment, labour law reform, and changes in the strategies and structure of the labour movement. Perhaps today a confluence of changes both within organised labour and in the political environment will be necessary for improvement. The trend towards more conservative government, however, suggests major labour law reform in favour of organised labour is highly unlikely in the foreseeable future.

Conclusions

The pressures of increased market competition have, for American employment relations systems as for others, opened a Pandora's box of troubles. These troubles have produced a crisis for organised labour that brings into question the future viability of America's form of workplace democracy. We believe that it is in the interest of American society as well as workers that the American employment relations system survive and prosper. For this to occur, many argue that a fundamental transformation of employment relations must also occur.

It may be that the pressures discussed in this chapter have already fundamentally altered the American employment relations system. Alternatively, perhaps the recent trends are simply the expected response of established actors within the American employment relations system to great political and economic changes.

Certainly, the dramatic increase in competition has created the need to develop new ways to organise work and reduce costs. As discussed earlier, in recent years there has been a proliferation in new workplace systems and organisation restructuring. Some organisations—by providing for genuine employee involvement and enhanced job security in the context of a real employee voice—have created appropriate as well as effective cooperative work methods. Other organisations, however, have responded by undertaking drastic downsizing measures without regard to the long-term implications for the organisation or its employees. In general, although evidence suggests the changes currently underway represent a long-term trend, it remains unclear whether more cooperative work mechanisms can endure under American capitalism, where the 'fast buck' is held in reverence; the pressures of predatory take-over artists keep management constantly watching for profits; managers hold opposition to unions to be a holy cause; and hierarchical habits are deeply ingrained. The trust that is the foundation stone of labour–management cooperation is difficult to build in such an environment. For example, empirical evidence suggests that the use of permanent striker replacements at the International Paper Company in the late 1980s made it difficult to gain employee cooperation in employee participation schemes (at non-strike locations) (Eaton & Kriesky 1994).

It appears that the best chance for effective work system change lies in the team-based approaches that emphasise cooperation on the shop floor where workers have expertise, power, and the desire to exercise both. These approaches are more consistent with unionised settings and are more likely to provide for meaningful participation (Voos 1994). We remain, however, sceptical that management will undertake programs that relinquish real power to workers, especially power at the higher levels of corporate decision making. It is also unclear whether these programs are economically viable.

What is clear is that unions have shown a willingness to cooperate with workplace changes that attempt to increase productivity and product/service quality, given that the innovations also include attention to the union's goals. As such, consistent with the American 'business unionism', the collective bargaining process has shown flexibility in responding to the new competitive markets.

An enduring concern is the future strength of the American labour movement. However, as noted earlier, in labour's Pandora's box of troubles there is one remaining item: 'hope'. There is also a fundamental logic to collective action of workers that is not repealed by greater competition. In sum, the parties in the American employment relations system continue to muddle through. As the only certainty appears to be change, a history of muddling through reasonably well is rather reassuring.

A chronology of US employment relations

1794	Federal Society of Cordwainers founded in Philadelphia—first permanent US union.
1828	Working Men's Party founded.
1834	National Trades Union founded—first national labour organisation.
1866	National Labor Union formed—first national 'reformist' union.
1869	Knights of Labor founded: a 'reformist' organisation dedicated to changing society, which nevertheless was involved in strikes for higher wages and improved conditions.
1886	Formation of the American Federation of Labor (AFL), a loose confederation of unions with largely 'bread-and-butter' goals. Peak of membership of the Knights of Labor (700 000 members), which then began to decline.
1905	Formation of the Industrial Workers of the World (IWW), the 'Wobblies', an anarcho-syndicalist union.
1914–22	Repression of radical unions because of their opposition to war, and during the 'Red scare' after the Russian Revolution.
1915	Establishment of the first company-dominated union, Ludlow, Colorado.
1920s	Decline and retrenchment of the American labour movement.
1932	Election of Franklin D. Roosevelt as President of the USA—a 'New Deal' for unions.
1935	National Labor Relations (Wagner) Act gave employees a federally protected right to organise and

	bargain collectively. Also, the formation of the Congress of Industrial Organizations (CIO), a federation of industrial unions.
1935–39	Rapid growth of unions covering major mass production industries.
1941–45	Growth of unions and development of the collective bargaining system during the war.
1946	Massive post-war strike wave in major industries.
1947	Enactment of Taft-Hartley Act, which prohibited unions from certain organising and bargaining practices.
1955	Merger of AFL and CIO to form the AFL–CIO.
1959	Landrum-Griffin Act, which regulated the internal operations of unions.
1960	New York City teachers' strike—the beginning of mass organisation of public employees.
1962	Adoption of Executive Order 10988 by President John F. Kennedy, providing for limited collective bargaining by federal government employees. Also the beginning of the movement of the National Education Association towards collective bargaining by teachers.
1960–80	Growth of unionism of public employees. Decline of union density in manufacturing.
1977–78	Defeat of Labor Law Reform Bill in Congress, as the employer movement in opposition to unions gained strength.
1980	Election of President Ronald Reagan—new Federal policies generally adverse to organised labour.
1981	Economic recession.
1988–89	Federal legislation on drugs, lie detectors, plant closing, minimum wages. Court decisions on drug testing and termination of employment.
1991	Federal legislation prohibiting discrimination against disabled workers. Federal legislation strengthening employment discrimination laws.
1991–92	Extended economic recession.
1992	Election of President Bill Clinton—a more labour-friendly national administration comes to power.
1994	Republicans win Congressional elections—a very conservative Congress comes into being.
1995	Increases in the minimum wage.
1996	Re-election of President Clinton.

4 Employment relations in Canada

Mark Thompson

For many years students of comparative employment relations neglected Canada, treating it as part of a continental system or as a minor variant of the US approach. While the two nations have similar legal regulations, unions with formal organisational links and workplace-level collective bargaining, the Canadian employment relations system is distinct from that of the United States (USA) in many ways. It is very decentralised, characterised by relatively high levels of conflict, a labour movement that is growing slowly, and frequent amendments to labour legislation. Periodically, the employment relations system is perceived as a serious national or regional issue.

The environment of employment relations

The economic, social and political contexts of Canadian employment relations are different from those of most other developed nations. The nation enjoys a standard of living equal to that of the more prosperous nations in Western Europe, but depends heavily on the production and export of raw materials and semi-processed products—mineral ores, food grains and forest products. Although Canada enjoys a comparative advantage in the production of most of these commodities, their markets are unstable and primary industries do not generate substantial direct employment. A large manufacturing sector does exist in the provinces of Ontario and Quebec, but it accounts for only 19 per cent of the gross domestic product (GDP) (OECD 1996:183). Because Canada lacks a large domestic market, it signed the Free Trade Agreement (FTA) with the USA and the North American Free Trade Agreement (NAFTA) with Mexico and the USA, in 1988 and 1993 respectively (with NAFTA taking effect on 1 January 1994). The immediate impact of free trade was to accelerate the integration of the manufacturing sector into a larger North American economy. Levels of activity in traditional industries, such as textiles and furniture, fell substantially, while other sectors, such as automobiles and chemicals, expanded.

In 1995 Canada exported about 38 per cent of its gross national product, and imported almost as much, with the USA accounting for almost 80 per cent of exports. Trade with Mexico is relatively insignificant. Apart from proximity and a natural complementarity of the two economies, Canadian–American trade relations are encouraged by extensive US ownership in many primary and secondary industries, as well as by the free trade agreements.

Canada has a mixed economy, with active roles for both public and private sectors, often in the same industries. Older public enterprises typically came into being for pragmatic reasons—provision of a necessary service, development of natural resources or the preservation of jobs. Thus, many public utilities, transportation and communications companies are government-owned. In the 1960s and 1970s, government ownership served nationalistic goals of the reduction of foreign ownership or stimulation of technological development. Public sector companies and their employment relations generally are run with relatively little political interference. Privatisation gained favour in the mid-1980s, as the federal and provincial governments disposed of natural resources and transportation companies, in addition to smaller holdings. This trend continued at a modest level in the 1990s.

Canada's most pressing economic problems in the 1990s were high government deficits and unemployment, difficulties it shared with most other developed nations. After a period of inflation in the mid-1970s, unemployment, always substantial by international standards, rose sharply and remained high, as Table 4.1 demonstrates.

During the inflationary periods of the 1970s, governments intervened directly to reduce inflation. Between October 1975 and September 1978, the federal government and nine of ten provinces imposed anti-inflation programs. These included comprehensive wage and price controls, limits on growth in government spending and restrictive monetary and fiscal policies. The weight of controls fell most heavily on public-sector workers and, consequently, their unions. Although opinions differ about the impact of the program, the rate of inflation declined during its life, and the rate of wage increases fell even more sharply. However, both labour and management resented the restrictions in the program, so it was not extended.

Table 4.1   Earnings, prices and unemployment

Year	% change in wages: major collective agreements	Annual rate of change: consumer price index	Annual rate of unemployment
1974–1978	11.4	9.2	7.1
1979–1983	9.8	9.7	9.0
1984–1988	3.8	4.2	9.6
1989	5.3	5.0	7.5
1990	5.6	4.8	8.1
1991	3.6	5.6	10.3
1992	2.1	1.5	11.3
1993	0.6	1.8	11.2
1994	0.3	0.2	10.4
1995	0.9	2.1	9.5
1996	1.6	1.6	9.7

Sources: Statistics Canada, *Canadian Economic Observer*, various issues; *Historical Statistical Supplement*, 1989/90; Bank of Canada, *Review*, various issues.

Since the 1980s, the national bank has followed a modified monetarist economic policy. In the early 1980s it kept interest rates high, restrained the growth of the money supply and accepted the basic thrust of US economic policy by intervening to maintain a stable exchange rate with the US dollar. When the 1982 recession grew serious, federal and provincial governments reimposed public sector wage controls in order to reduce government spending. These policies provoked scattered labour disputes and held public sector compensation down, but did little to reduce deficits or stimulate the private sector. Since the recession of the 1980s, Canada has experienced slow economic growth. Rates of inflation are among the lowest of any industrialised nation, while unemployment has remained high.

Politically, Canada has a modified two-party system. For the past 60 years the Liberal Party has dominated federal politics, occasionally forming a minority government or yielding power to the Conservatives, who won large majorities in 1984 and 1988. The Liberals are a pragmatic, reformist party, with a traditional base of support in Quebec. The Conservatives are a right-of-centre party, normally drawing votes from the eastern and western regions. While it has a market orientation, the Conservative government did not embrace the more extreme social and economic policies of the Thatcher or Reagan administrations. In a stunning reversal of fortunes, the Conservatives were virtually eliminated from Parliament in the 1993 election. The New Democratic Party (NDP), with a social-democratic philosophy and strong union support, had traditionally held a small number of parliamentary seats and 15 to 20 per cent of the popular vote. It too was decimated in 1993, but recovered slightly in 1997, to 11 per cent of the popular vote. The NDP was not able to achieve a high profile nationally after 1993. Other parties appear from time to time. In the early 1990s, a pro-independence party from Quebec and a conservative party from the western provinces both had substantial representation in Parliament. None of the federal parties is strong in all the provinces, and purely provincial parties have normally governed in two large provinces, Quebec and British Columbia. A pro-independence party formed the government in Quebec in 1994, though provincial referendums in 1980 and 1995 favoured remaining in Canada.

Official efforts to deal with economic problems have been hindered by the nation's political structure. Like Australia, Canada is a confederation with a parliamentary government. The ten provinces hold substantial powers, including the primary authority to regulate industrial relations, leaving only a few industries, principally transportation and communications, to federal authority. The political structure reflects strongly held regional sentiments, accentuated by distance and language. The second most populous province, Quebec, is predominantly French-speaking and has strong separatist tendencies. The provinces, often led by Quebec, have not only resisted any efforts to expand federal powers, but also have gradually gained greater powers at the expense of the federal authorities.

A fundamental change in Canadian political life occurred in 1982. The Liberal government produced the nation's first written constitution, which included a 'Charter of Rights and Freedoms'. The charter contained a number of protections for individuals and groups from government action. Among these are freedom of association and speech and the right to live and work anywhere in the nation, all of which have a potential impact on employment relations law and practice.

As a 'new' country, Canada has received immigrants throughout its history. The largest source of immigrants has been Britain, followed by other European countries after the Second World War, and by citizens of developing Commonwealth nations in the 1960s and 1970s. Most of the immigrants came to improve their economic status, but many also brought a tradition of working-class politics. Simultaneously, the relatively conservative political tradition of the USA has been a powerful model to Canadians. These influences, combined with a parliamentary political system and its acceptance of third parties, have combined to produce a value system that includes both the individualism of an expanding capitalist economy and the collectivism of mature industrial nations in Western Europe. Thus, conservative governments occasionally have nationalised private companies and NDP regimes have encouraged small businesses. Even political parties that govern for long periods of time, such as the Liberals nationally, may alternate between conservative and liberal economic policies.

The employment relations parties

The unions

The Canadian labour movement has displayed steady, though unspectacular, growth since the 1930s, despite a longstanding tradition of disunity. Membership passed 4 million in 1994, which constituted 37.5 per cent of paid non-agricultural employees, an increase from 1.4 million and 32.2 per cent in 1960. This membership was divided among two national centres and a large number of unaffiliated unions.

The greatest penetration of unionism is in primary industries, construction, transportation, manufacturing and the public sector. In the late nineteenth and early twentieth centuries, Canadian unions were established first in construction and transportation, mostly on a craft basis. During the 1930s and 1940s, industrial unionism spread to manufacturing and primary industries, without including white-collar workers in the private sector. Since the late 1960s, the major source of growth in the labour movement has been the public sector. First public servants, then health and education workers, joined unions. Professionals, notably teachers and nurses, had long been members of their own associations, and these transformed themselves into unions as their members' interest in collective bargaining grew. By 1980, nearly all eligible workers in the public sector had joined unions. Table 4.2 shows the relative rate of unionisation by industry.

Unionisation of the public sector raised the proportion of female union members. By the mid-1990s, approximately 40 per cent of all union members were women. Union organisations, including the large congresses discussed below, made special efforts to include women in senior leadership roles. Many unions have close ties to women's organisations.

Approximately 275 unions operate in Canada, ranging in size from less than 100 to more than 400 000 members. Two-thirds are affiliated with one of the central confederations discussed below, with the remainder, principally in the public sector, independent of any national body. The ten largest unions contain 44 per cent of all members. A variety of union philosophies are represented: most of the old craft groups still espouse apolitical business unionism, but larger number of unions see themselves fulfilling a broader role and actively support the NDP and various social causes. A few groups, principally in Quebec, are highly politicised and occasionally criticise the prevailing economic system from a socialist perspective. But rhetoric aside, the major function of all unions is collective bargaining.

The role of US-based 'international' unions is a unique feature of the Canadian labour movement which has affected its behaviour in many ways. Most of the oldest labour organisations in Canada began

Table 4.2 Union members as a percentage of paid workers[a]

Industry group	% unionised
Public administration	79.2
Construction	65.2
Transportation, communication and other utilities	53.4
Fishing and trapping	53.5
Forestry	53.1
Service industries	35.7
Manufacturing	35.2
Mines, quarries and oil wells	29.4
Trade	11.9
Finance	4.7

Note: a   1992.
Source: Ministry of Supply and Services (1994).

as part of American unions—hence the term 'international'. The cultural and economic ties between the two countries encouraged the trade union connection, while the greater size and earlier development of US labour unions attracted Canadian workers to them. For many years, the overwhelming majority of Canadian union members belonged to such international unions, which often exerted close control over their Canadian locals. But the spread of unionism in the public sector during the 1960s and 1970s brought national unions to the fore, as internationals were seldom active among public employees. As a result, the proportion of international union membership declined from more than 70 per cent in 1966 to less than 30 per cent in 1996.

Persistent complaints about the quality of service in Canada, American labour's support for economic protectionism and increased Canadian nationalism created pressures for change within the labour movement. During the 1970s a few unions in Canada seceded from internationals, and the largest international in Canada (the United Automobile Workers, UAW) separated in 1985. But a more common (and successful) change was agreement to grant special autonomous status to Canadians in international unions. In the past, internationals encouraged a conservative form of business unionism in Canada, discouraged political involvement and exerted a powerful influence over the policies of national centres. While a role in these areas continues, the impact of policies originating in the USA is low and seems destined to decline further.

The most important central confederation in Canada is the Canadian Labour Congress (CLC), with about 80 affiliated unions who represent 60 per cent of all union members. Members of CLC affiliates are in all regions and most industries except construction. It is the principal political spokesperson for Canadian labour, but is weaker than many other national centrals. It has no role in bargaining, for instance, and does not have substantial powers over its affiliates, unlike centrals in Germany and Scandinavia. The CLC's political role is further limited by the constitutionally weak position of the federal government, its natural contact point, in many areas the labour movement regards as important, such as labour legislation, regulation of industry or human rights. In national politics, it officially supports the NDP. The poor electoral record of the NDP federally (discussed below) further weakens its political role. In addition, the CLC has chartered federations in each province to which locals of affiliated unions belong, and some of these federations wield considerable influence in their provinces.

The Confederation of National Trade Unions (CNTU) represents about 6 per cent of all union members, virtually all in Quebec. It began early in the twentieth century under the sponsorship of the Catholic church as a conservative French-language alternative to the predominantly English-language secular unions operating elsewhere in Canada and in Quebec. As the province industrialised during and after the Second World War, members of the Catholic unions grew impatient with their organisations' lack of militancy and unwillingness to confront a conservative provincial government. Following an illegal strike against a powerful employer supported by the provincial government in 1949, the Catholic unions abandoned their former conservatism and moved into the vanguard of rapid social change in Quebec. In 1960, the federation adopted its present name and severed its ties with the Catholic church. Since then, ideological competition has prevailed in the Quebec labour movement, and the CNTU has become the most radical and politicised labour body in North America. It has supported Quebec independence actively and has adopted left-wing political positions. Unlike the CLC, it has a centralised structure that gives officers considerable authority over member unions. Because of its history, current political posture and the large provincial public sector in Quebec, the CNTU membership is concentrated heavily among public employees.

Management

Although the majority of unionised firms accept the role of labour grudgingly, open attacks on incumbent unions are rare. However, non-union firms strive to retain that status, some by matching the wages and working conditions in the unionised sector, others by combinations of paternalism and coercion. A small number of firms have union substitution policies, which replicate many of the forms of a unionised work environment with grievance procedures, quality circles or mechanisms for consultation. But in industries with a long history of unionism, such as manufacturing or transportation, unionism is accepted as a normal part of the business environment.

Unionised firms in Canada normally have a full-time industrial relations staff, though seldom a large one. Collective bargaining rounds usually occur at intervals of between one and three years, so it is not feasible for most firms to maintain large staffs for that purpose, and many staff have non-industrial-relations duties. Major decisions, such as whether to undertake strikes or the level of first wage offers, are highly centralised and taken at the corporate level. Overall, the employment relations expertise of Canadian management is not high: few have formal training; the cadre of specialists is not large; and key decisions may be taken by senior executives with little sensitivity for the issues.

The high degree of foreign ownership in the Canadian economy affects the Canadian economy generally, but seldom employment relations. About 25 per cent of the assets of all industrial firms are foreign-owned, chiefly by US corporations. Foreign ownership clearly affects a number of strategic managerial decisions, such as product lines or major investments. But the impact of non-Canadians on employment relations decisions in unionised sectors is almost non-existent. Foreign owners prefer to remain in the mainstream of Canadian employment relations for their industries rather than imposing home-country corporate policies.

The organisation of employers varies among regions. No national group participates directly in employment relations, although a number of employer organisations do present management viewpoints to government or the public. Since most labour relations law falls under provincial jurisdiction, few industries have national bargaining structures. In two provinces, Quebec and British Columbia, local economic conditions and public policy have encouraged bargaining by employer associations formed specifically for that purpose. Elsewhere single-workplace bargaining with single unions predominates, except in a few industries with many small firms, such as construction, longshoring or trucking, where multi-employer bargaining is the norm.

Government

The government in Canada has a dual role in employment relations—it regulates the actors' conduct and employs large numbers of people both directly and indirectly.

Government regulation of employment relations is very extensive, although it rests on an assumption of voluntarism. Constitutionally, the provinces have primary jurisdiction over labour relations, except for transportation and communications industries, which fall under federal jurisdiction. Each province, and the federal government, has at least one Act covering labour relations and employment standards in the industries under its jurisdiction. Employment standards legislation generally sets minimal standards for such areas as wages, vacations or holidays. In a few areas, such as maternity leave, the law has led most employers. Although the details vary considerably, labour relations legislation combines many features of the US National Labor Relations Act (Wagner Act) and an older Canadian pattern of reliance on conciliation of labour disputes. Each statute establishes and protects the right of most employees to form trade unions, and and sets out a procedure by which a union may demonstrate majority support from a group of employees in order to obtain the right of exclusive representation for them. The employer is required to bargain with a certified trade union. A quasi-judicial labour relations board administers this process and enforces the statute, although the legislation often specifies the procedural requirements in detail.

Labour relations legislation imposes few requirements on the substance of a collective agreement, though the exceptions are significant and expanding. For many years, Canadian laws have effectively prohibited strikes during the term of a collective agreement, while also requiring that each agreement contain a grievance procedure and a mechanism for the final resolution of mid-contract disputes. Despite these restrictions, as many as 15 per cent of all stoppages occur while a collective agreement is in force. Most of these stoppages are brief and seldom attract legal action. More recently, statutes have added requirements that the parties bargain over technological change and that management grant union security clauses. The federal labour code and a few provinces also provide rights of consultation for non-union workers on occupational health and safety.

Separate legislation exists federally and in eight of ten provinces for employees in the public sector. These statutes normally apply to government employees and occasionally to quasi-government workers, such as teachers or hospital workers. They are patterned after private sector labour relations Acts except for two broad areas. The scope of bargaining is restricted by previous civil service personnel practices and broader public policy considerations. In a majority of provinces, there are restrictions on the right to strike of at least some public employees, with police and firefighters being the most common categories affected by such limits; however, there is no other common pattern of restrictions. Employee groups without the right to strike have access to a system of compulsory arbitration. While a statute requires arbitration, the parties normally can determine the procedures to be followed and choose the arbitrator.

The processes of employment relations

In unionised sectors, the major formal process of Canadian employment relations is collective bargaining, with union power based on its ability to strike. Joint consultation is sporadic. Health and safety legislation in all jurisdictions requires joint consultation on those subjects for all but the smallest employers. The parties have initiated consultation outside of any legislative framework in 20 to 25 per cent of firms covering such subjects as product quality, technological change or performance. Other formal systems of worker participation in management are rare. Arbitration of interest disputes is largely confined to the public sector.

Collective bargaining

Collective bargaining in Canada is highly decentralised. The most common negotiating unit is a single establishment–single union, followed by multi-establishment–single union. Taken together these categories account for almost 90 per cent of all units and more than 80 per cent of all employees. Company-wide bargaining is common in the federal jurisdiction, where it occurs in railways, airlines and telecommunications, and in industries concentrated in a single province, such as automobile manufacturing. In response to increased union militancy, employer associations expanded in the 1970s, especially in the construction industry.

Despite the decentralised structure of negotiations, regional pattern bargaining is common. One or two key industries in each province usually influence negotiations in other firms and industries. In larger provinces, such as Ontario and Quebec, heavy industry patterns from steel, paper or autos often predominate.

The results of bargaining are detailed, complex collective bargaining agreements. Few of the terms are the result of the law, and negotiated provisions typically include pay; union security; hours of work; vacations and holidays; layoff provisions; and miscellaneous fringe benefits. Grievance procedures are legal requirements and invariably conclude with binding arbitration. In addition, there are often supplementary agreements covering work rules for specific situations or work areas. Seniority provisions are prominent features in almost all collective agreements and cover layoffs, promotions and transfers, with varying weight given to length of service or ability.

Given the detail in collective agreements and the parties' preference for litigation, arbitration is frequent and legalistic. In turn, this emphasis on precise written contracts often permeates labour–management relationships.

Another outcome of collective bargaining is labour stoppages, the most controversial single feature of Canadian industrial relations (discussed further below). In the decade 1986–95, in the production and construction industries, Canada lost more working days due to industrial disputes than any other country in this book (see Appendix). There have been frequent allegations, never really proven, that labour unrest has seriously hindered the nation's economic growth. These concerns are especially notable because Canada generally has low levels of social conflict.

Mediation has long been a common feature of Canadian collective bargaining. Two models currently exist: a tripartite board may be appointed and given authority to report publicly on a dispute; alternatively, single mediators function without the power to issue a report. In most jurisdictions participation in mediation is a precondition for a legal strike. Although elements of compulsion have diminished, over half of all collective agreements are achieved with some type of third-party intervention.

Outside of the public sector, compulsory arbitration of interest disputes is rare. However, special legislation to end particular disputes is not uncommon in public sector or essential service disputes. Back-to-work laws are extremely unpopular with the labour movement and have contributed to the politicisation of labour relations in some areas. In the public sector, interest arbitration is common, with arbitrators usually chosen on an *ad hoc* basis from among judges, lawyers or academics. The process is legalistic, without the use of sophisticated economic data. When collective bargaining first appeared in the public sector, there were concerns that compulsory arbitration would cause bargaining to atrophy. Experience of the 1970s demonstrated that collective bargaining and compulsory arbitration can co-exist successfully, though the availability of arbitration does reduce the incidence of negotiated settlements.

Issues of current and future importance

The future of collective bargaining is being questioned in most industrialised countries. In large measure, this debate revolves around the ability of labour organisations to retain, or even expand, their traditional bases of strength in heavy industry and blue-collar occupations. Union density in these industries in Canada has not declined materially and is consistently twice as high as that of the USA, for instance. However, Canadian unions have had the same difficulty as their counterparts elsewhere in extending their membership base into the more rapidly growing areas of the service sector and technologically advanced industries. As employment shifts from the goods-producing sectors to services, the traditional base of collective bargaining gradually shrinks as a proportion of the labour force. Historically, the organised elements of the labour force have led the non-union employers in the expansion of employee rights and improvement in wages and conditions of employment. If collective bargaining becomes confined to declining sectors of the economy, this role also will diminish.

The traditional centres of collective bargaining are also under pressure from foreign competition and deregulation, factors common among developed nations. Despite a tradition of high tariffs for parts of manufacturing, Canada has long relied heavily on foreign trade, so foreign competition is not new. Tariff barriers eroded slowly in the 1960s and 1970s and more rapidly after the FTA took effect in 1989. The Canadian manufacturing sector, aided by a depreciating currency, responded well to these challenges. The decentralised structure of collective bargaining seems to have facilitated adaptation to economic change. Exports rose steadily, while manufacturing employment was stagnant. These developments were sources of stress to employment relations institutions, but changes were incremental.

Similar results occurred after deregulation. Governments deregulated most of the transportation and communications sectors in the 1980s and 1990s, and several public enterprises in these sectors were privatised. Employment in the unionised firms in these industries shrank, while new competitors were largely non-union. These developments occurred gradually and did not provoke upheaval in industrial relations.

The immediate future of collective bargaining will be a function of the actions of government and management in the face of trade union economic and political power. Both federal and provincial governments continue to respect the legitimacy of collective bargaining and an active labour movement. A review of labour relations in federally regulated industries completed in 1995 found strong support for the institution of collective bargaining among the parties, for instance. Legislation and other public policies reflect that commitment, even when most right-of-centre parties govern. Few major changes in labour legislation occurred in the 1980s. The most important exception to the generalisation was in British Columbia, where a Conservative government made sweeping changes in the basic labour relations statute, without eliminating the basic protections that had been part of the legislative framework since the Second World War. However, these changes provoked vigorous reaction from the labour movement, which is especially strong in the province. Ultimately, the government was replaced by the NDP, which returned most legislative provisions to their previous state and added a number of protections for the labour movement in 1992. At about the same time, the NDP government of Ontario, the largest and most industrialised province, passed a new labour law that assisted organised labour substantially. In the case of British Columbia, the re-election of the NDP ensured the continuation of existing labour legislation. The NDP was defeated in Ontario, after which the victorious Conservative government rescinded the previous changes and enacted other measures to weaken unions. On balance, it appears that the legislative support for collective bargaining will not change markedly across Canada. However, further gains by labour are unlikely in the immediate future. Rather, a more likely scenario is further modest reductions in labour's legal position.

Management and collective bargaining

Canadian employers faced many of the same market forces to reduce costs in the 1980s and 1990s as their private sector counterparts in other developed nations: foreign trade; increased domestic competition in services; and deregulation. Public sector employers were required to either limit or reduce wage expenditures. The FTA with the USA, as well as NAFTA, added to competitive pressures. Many responses by employers to these changes were traditional: layoffs dramatically reduced employment in many industries, and the use of part-time and casual workers rose substantially. But there was no general movement to escape unionism.

In industries where unionism was well established, a combination of cultural and legal forces caused Canadian employers to work within the collective bargaining system to meet competitive pressures. Militant anti-unionism is not a popular public position among Canadian employers, although many managers privately express hostility to labour organisations. Major employer organisations normally advocate cooperative relations with unions and have not called for 'deregulation' of labour markets. At the firm level, surveys of industrial relations and human resource managers show little interest in unseating incumbent unions, although resistance to the spread of unionism may have strengthened.

Legal restrictions on employer tactics make de-unionisation very difficult, and protections for union organisation are effective. Employer success in bargaining has diminished pressures for structural changes. The decentralisation of bargaining structures in the private sector, driven by employers, effectively put wages into competition. Negotiated changes in work rules have been frequent, and in the 1990s negotiated wage freezes and concession bargaining became more common. In a few industries, the parties have negotiated collective agreements with terms as long as six years, typically incorporating wage freezes followed by modest wage increases coupled with employment guarantees for most bargaining unit members. The proportion of collective agreements with provisions for contingent pay actually fell in the 1980s.

At the level of the workplace in unionised industries, radical reorganisation of work and the implementation of work systems based on high levels of employee commitment have been limited, in part because of union resistance. Labour generally is concerned that these initiatives have the effect, and perhaps the goal, of reducing workers' support for their unions. Where changes have been introduced, the failure rate is relatively high; an average of only 30 per cent last more than five years. However, many employers are seeking to move away from the traditional adversarial system of labour relations, especially in manufacturing. Increased consultation and communication between management and unions is a common development, for instance. Modest changes in work practices, often outside of formal collective bargaining, have occurred frequently.

It is unclear to what extent Canadian employers' acceptance of collective bargaining in the face of difficult economic conditions is due to legal protections for unions and collective bargaining or to a philosophical acceptance of the legitimacy of these institutions. If employers are merely obeying the law, then support for collective bargaining obviously is subject to changing political and legal circumstances. If the support for collective bargaining is cultural, then employment relations institutions will probably survive and evolve gradually.

Labour disputes

As noted earlier, historically, the most important issue in Canadian industrial relations has been time lost due to strikes. These have gone in cycles. There was a wave of unrest early in the twentieth century, another around the time of the First World War, a third beginning in the late 1930s and a fourth in the 1970s (see Table 4.3). The latest wave abated in 1983, as the economy suffered a severe recession and unemployment rose, and most measures of labour disputes have fallen since then. By international standards, the two salient characteristics of Canadian strikes are their length and the concentration of time lost in a few disputes. Involvement is medium to low (3 to 10 per cent of union members annually), and the size of strikes is not especially large (350–450 workers per strike, on average). The largest five or six strikes typically account for 35 per cent of all time lost. In recent years, the average duration of strikes has been 10 to 15 days. These characteristics have not been explained fully, but may be due to the existence of major companies, such as General Motors or International Nickel, and large international unions that can withstand long strikes at individual production units without the parent organisations suffering major economic loss.

Despite public concern about strikes, there have been few efforts to deal with their underlying causes or even to understand them better. Certainly, the fragmented structure of bargaining is one factor that contributes to the pattern of strikes. Yet the causes of fragmentation lie in the nation's governmental structure and politics. Provincial governments resist virtually any effort to limit their powers, and the paramount importance of Quebec separatism on the national political agenda has restrained moves from the federal government to extend its authority over economic issues.

Governments have attempted to deal with labour unrest in a variety of ways. One model is to encourage consultation. During the 1970s and 1980s, several governments took initiatives directed at establishing labour–management consultation as practised in Western Europe. In cases of large-scale layoffs, joint labour–management committees (in union and non-union workforces) were mandated. Later the federal government sponsored tripartite sectoral committees to deal with the effects of restructuring. These committees function well, and their number is expanding, but there still is no evidence that cooperation at this level of the employment relations system affects the parties' actions at other levels.

Every province requires joint health and safety committees in most workplaces. In unionised organisations, such committees are an avenue of influence outside of collective bargaining. These committees operate in large workplaces, and disputes over health and safety are rare. However, employers resist vigorously any initiatives to strengthen the statutory authority of health and safety committees. Mandating labour–management cooperation represents a sharp departure from the North American traditions of government limiting its role in the workplace to the promulgation of minimum standards, and from the maintenance of a sharp distinction between the unionised and non-union sectors in matters of collective representation.

A second model for dealing with labour unrest has been to impose

Table 4.3   Strikes and lockouts in Canada, selected years

Year	Number	Workers involved	Days lost ('000)	Average length[a]	% of working time[b]
1966–70	572	291 109	5709	19.6	0.35
1971–75	856	473 795	7309	15.4	0.38
1976–80	1105	618 743	7824	12.6	0.35
1981–85	755	291 863	5226	17.9	0.22
1986–90	634	397 664	4929	12.4	0.18
1991	463	253 486	2530	10.4	0.09
1992	404	149 475	2108	14.1	0.08
1993	382	101 827	1519	14.9	0.05
1994	375	80 861	1607	19.9	0.06
1995	328	149 159	1582	10.6	0.05
1996	327	283 631	3342	11.8	0.11

Notes: a   Average length measured in days.
         b   Percentage of working time lost due to strikes.
Sources: Labour Canada, *Strikes and Lockouts in Canada*, various issues; unpublished data, Human Resources Development Canada.

legislative controls on the exercise of union power. One province enacted a new labour relations Act along those lines, and two others considered the same policies. As in Britain, government in these jurisdictions is more anxious to legislate against labour than are most employers, so the long-run prospects for this model are not good.

In the mid-1980s, unions demonstrated that they could mount large strikes and win concessions on significant issues—invariably involving job security. By the mid-1990s, the incidence of labour disputes had fallen considerably, as Table 4.3 indicates. The decline in labour unrest diverted interest from this issue and labour relations in general. In a time of low inflation and high unemployment, the incentives to strike over other issues fell and the costs of confrontation rose.

Public sector employment relations

The area of Canadian employment relations most subject to change is the public sector. From the mid-1960s through the 1980s, systems of employment relations developed in all provinces and in the federal government. Beginning with the 1982–83 recession, governments in several jurisdictions addressed budgetary shortfalls by restricting public sector compensation. In general, governments chose to deal with their fiscal problems by legislation rather than bargaining. By 1987 legal restraints had been removed. Early in 1991, the federal government led another round of restrictions on public sector bargaining and compensation. By 1995, a majority of all provinces had imposed restrictions on public sector bargaining as part of their programs of fiscal restraint.

One of the most comprehensive restraint programs was the misnamed 'Social Contract' in Ontario. In 1993, an NDP government attempted to negotiate substantial reductions in compensation with more than 100 public sector bargaining agents. When negotiations failed, the government threatened to impose cuts legislatively if agreements were not reached. Under such pressure, nearly all employee organisations agreed to cuts that did not entail reductions in rates of pay. Compulsory unpaid holidays became a common feature in the Ontario public sector. These policies split the Ontario labour movement, which had supported the government actively. Public sector unions were unanimous in their condemnation of the Social Contract. Except for the Canadian Auto Workers, one of the most militant major unions, private sector labour organisations were lukewarm in their reproaches to the government and made no move to withdraw political support. The vigorous action by an NDP government marked a shift in the politics of restrictions on public sector collective bargaining. No longer were severe policies regarded as aberrations of right-wing governments, making it easier for more conservative regimes to impose similar or more severe controls.

Public sector unions protested all the restraint programs, but generally in vain. Governments found that restricting public sector wages and bargaining rights was politically popular. Reliance on legislation or other means to impose freezes or reductions have brought into question the commitment of Canadian governments to collective bargaining systems enshrined in many statutes. Under these circumstances, labour's responses to government initiatives are likely to be political. In the 1980s, public sector unions in Quebec, Ontario and British Columbia (the three most populous provinces) organised major demonstrations and work stoppages that brought pressure on governments to moderate their policies. A major national strike by a federal public sector union with a tradition of moderation showed that public sector workers could be mobilised when they faced restrictions they regarded as unfair. In the end, however, government employers prevailed. Led by the federal government, controlled by the Liberal Party since 1993, deficit reduction became a dominant theme in the nation's political orthodoxy. Employment in the federal government fell substantially, and several provincial governments also cut employment as well as compensation. In such conditions, the labour movement could do little to resist these losses. Wage cuts, often presented as mandatory unpaid days off, were imposed in several provinces.

The political role of the labour movement

Although many Canadian unions and union leaders are active in partisan politics, the labour movement has been unable to define a political role for itself. Officially, the CLC supports the NDP, but this alliance has presented problems. Federally, the NDP has been unsuccessful in raising its share of the popular vote (and legislative seats) beyond about 20 per cent, and was only the fourth-largest party in the Parliament elected in 1997. The labour movement has been unable to deliver large blocs of votes to the federal NDP, though financial contributions and the diversion of staff to the party are invaluable. In Quebec the NDP has minimal influence, as most labour leaders support pro-independence parties. Even when the NDP has enjoyed greater success, the CLC has been left to deal with governments whose election it had opposed. For example, labour opposed the US–Canada Free Trade Agreement, a central issue in the 1988 national election. When the pro–free trade Conservatives triumphed, the CLC was in a poor position to secure assistance for workers who lost their jobs as a result of new trade patterns. The tensions created by this situation have hampered consultation on economic policies.

Provincially, the situation is different. The NDP has governed in Ontario and three western provinces. Labour's political role is better defined when the NDP is a viable option provincially. However, the labour movement's partisan position provincially risks making labour issues more political and subject to sharp variation after changes of government. Quebec unions have supported independence for the province and have enjoyed great political influence when parties that endorse this position have governed the province.

The Social Contract in Ontario sharpened labour's dilemma. Public sector unions withheld all support for the New Democrats in the 1995 election, contributing to the government's defeat. This experience revealed that the labour movement had no alternative to the election of the NDP. Punishing the NDP improved the electoral chances of more anti-labour parties. Yet the Ontario NDP proved willing to override valid collective agreements, attacking one of the fundamental principles of the Canadian employment relations system.

The practical result of these problems is that the CLC has vacillated between wholehearted commitment to the NDP and a more independent posture as workers' lobbyists before governments of any party. To further complicate the situation, some public sector unions avoid political endorsements. The founders of the NDP had the British Labour Party as a model, but were unsuccessful in achieving their goal. The American tradition of labour acting as an independent political force has adherents in Canada, despite its limited relevance in a parliamentary political system. It thus appears that the labour movement will continue to search for an effective political role.

Conclusion

Employment relations seldom has been a major issue in Canadian life, but the system is caught up in the central concerns of the nation: the division of powers between provinces and the national government; the relative importance of the public and private sectors; relations with the USA and other trading partners; and the performance of the national economy. While employment relations actors will contribute to the debates on these issues, the future direction of the system is likely to be determined by broader trends in Canadian life. But decisions on economic policy, changes in industrial structure and a new constitution will ensure that the Canadian employment relations system remains in a state of flux in the future.

The employment relations system itself displays few of the overt signs of structural changes found in other developed nations. Unlike in the USA, unionism and collective bargaining have not been subjected to an attack by management. By contrast with the United Kingdom, no government has undertaken a sustained anti-union campaign. The labour movement has a high degree of legitimacy in Canadian life, having close ties with the women's movement and consumer groups, for instance. The labour movement is recognised as a spokesperson for workers in economic and social consultations.

This degree of stability is unusual among employment relations systems covered in this book, especially in the 'Anglo-Saxon' countries. Three factors account for Canada's unusual status: the lack of a crisis sufficiently important to provoke change; the decentralised structure of employment relations and political systems; and the entrenched nature of employment relations institutions.

Canada's record of slow but steady economic growth, combined with almost a decade of stagnant wages, provide scant support for politicians or employers who wish to blame collective bargaining or unionism for the economy's performance. The collective bargaining system has responded successfully to most of the changes in economic conditions. A decade of high unemployment has reduced the militancy of Canadian workers except when job security is the central issue in dispute. The elimination of trade barriers undermines the bargaining power of Canadian workers in the manufacturing and transportation sectors, two major sources of industrial strength. Continued reductions in government service employment affect another pillar of collective bargaining. The lack of any crisis in the system has stifled debate over the broader questions of worker representation outside the traditional strongholds of the labour movement.

The large number of actors in the Canadian employment relations system and the weak links among them contribute to stability. In the provinces, for instance, economic or political changes occur in different time periods and at different magnitudes. A sharp shift to the Right in Ontario in the 1990s was partially offset by a moderate program of social reform in Quebec, Saskatchewan and British Columbia. A Liberal federal government bent on reducing the public sector compensated somewhat by strengthening private sector collective bargaining in industries under its jurisdiction. Employers and unions respond to economic and political conditions on a regional basis. Overall modest changes in specific regions or industries, not necessarily in the same directions, result in a relatively stable pattern nationally.

The Canadian system of employment relations, including a leading role for collective bargaining in determining conditions of employment, is broadly accepted in the nation's society. While business leaders privately decry the role of collective bargaining and unionisation in Canadian society, they seldom express such views publicly. No political party advocates wholesale changes to the Canadian employment relations system. Most business organisations, especially those representing large firms, advocate relatively modest (anti-labour) changes in the status quo. Business resists any efforts to foster the growth of unionism, however. In the absence of a major change in Canada's economic performance or political system (such as the separation of Quebec) the recent pattern of incremental adaptation will continue.

A chronology of Canadian employment relations

1825	Strike by carpenters in Lachine, Quebec, for higher wages.
1825–60	Numerous isolated local unions developed.
1867	Confederation—Canada became an independent nation.
1872	Unions exempted from criminal and civil liabilities imposed by British law.
1873	Local trade assemblies formed Canadian Labour Union, the first national labour central.
1886	Trades and Labour Congress (TLC) formed by 'international' craft unions.
1902	'Berlin Declaration'—TLC shunned unions not affiliated to international unions.
1906	Canadian chapter of Industrial Workers of the World (IWW) founded.
1907	Canadian Industrial Dispute Investigation Act—first national labour legislation, emphasised conciliation.
1919	Winnipeg General Strike—most complete general strike in North American history.
1921	Canadian and Catholic Confederation of Labour formed, the Quebec federation of Catholic unions.
1925	British courts ruled that the Canadian constitution put most labour legislation within provincial jurisdiction.
1927	All-Canadian Congress of Labour founded.
1935	Following the National Labor Relations (Wagner) Act in the USA, there were demands for similar Canadian legislation.
1937	Auto workers strike at General Motors, Oshawa, Ontario, established industrial unionism in Canada.
1939	TLC expelled Canadian affiliates of US Congress of Industrial Organizations (CIO).
1940	CIO affiliates joined All-Canadian Congress of Labour to form the Canadian Congress of Labour (CCL).
1944	Order-in-Council P.C. 1003 guaranteed unions' right to organise (combining principles of US Wagner Act with compulsory conciliation).
1949	Miners in Asbestos, Quebec, struck in defence of law, initiating the 'quiet revolution' in Quebec.
1956	Merger of TLC and CCL to form the Canadian Labour Congress (CLC).

1960	Canadian and Catholic Confederation of Labour severed ties with the Catholic church to become the Confederation of National Trade Unions.
1967	Federal government gave its employees bargaining rights; other jurisdictions followed suit.
1975	Federal government imposed the first peace-time wage and price controls.
1982	Federal government enacted Charter of Rights. Construction unions withdrew from CLC to form the Canadian Federation of Labour.
1987	Charter of Rights and Freedoms (enacted in 1982) took effect.
1991	Legislated pay freeze imposed on federal government employees.
1992	Major revisions to labour legislation in Ontario and British Columbia, making use of striker replacements illegal.
1995	Ontario government rescinds previous changes to labour legislation.
1997	Liberal Party re-elected in federal elections—led by Prime Minister Jean Chretien.

5 Employment relations in Australia

Edward M. Davis and Russell D. Lansbury

Like Canada, Australia was colonised by the British, has a wealth of mineral and energy resources and is sparsely populated. Australia has a population of 18 million people and a gross domestic product (GDP) of \$392 billion. Australia has developed a services sector that is almost as predominant as in the United States (USA) and Canada. Thus, out of its total civilian employment of 8.2 million people, 72 per cent are employed in services, 23 per cent in industry and 5 per cent in agriculture (also see Appendix). However, Australia's economy remains highly dependent on raw materials and rural products.

Strong economic growth in the middle of the 1980s and a reduction in real wages enabled the labour market to expand and reduced the rate of unemployment. However, as shown in Table 5.1, deteriorating economic conditions in the late 1980s and early 1990s resulted in a rise in the unemployment rate to 11 per cent in the period 1991–93. With a tightening of government economic policy and a sharp downturn in 1990–91, inflation fell to 1 per cent in 1992–93, but after this began to rise again, before declining again in 1997. Unemployment in the mid-1990s persisted at levels of 8 to 11 per cent and averaged 8.3 per cent in 1996. The growth rate for part-time employment was three times higher than for full-time employment in the period 1992–96.

Unlike the other three English-speaking countries discussed in this book, Australia had a Labor government in office from 1983 to 1996. It was the longest-serving Labor government at the national level in Australia's history. The federal Parliament remains the formal and symbolic focus for Australian political democracy, but the Australian executive and legislature are also particularly important, as are the six State governments.

Table 5.1   Selected economic variables

Year	GDP (% change[a])	Inflation (% change in CPI)	Current account (% of GDP)	Unemployment (% of the workforce)
1986–87	2.2	9.3	–4.4	8.0
1987–88	5.3	7.4	–3.4	7.5
1988–89	4.3	7.3	–5.0	6.1
1989–90	3.5	8.0	–5.7	6.6
1990–91	–0.9	5.3	–4.0	9.3
1991–92	0.6	1.9	–2.9	11.0
1992–93	3.1	1.0	–3.5	11.0
1993–94	4.4	1.8	–3.8	9.9
1994–95	4.1	3.2	–5.9	8.3
1995–96	4.1	4.2	–4.1	8.3

Note: a   GDP figures show percentage change in the gross domestic product average based on 1989–90 prices.

Source: ABS (1997), *Australian Economic Indicators*, Cat. No. 1350.0, June.

The legal, political and economic environment

Australia was founded in 1901. When the former colonial governments agreed to establish the Commonwealth of Australia, they insisted that the new federal government should have only a limited jurisdiction over employment and industrial relations. Thus, under the constitution of the Commonwealth of Australia (1901), federal government was empowered to make industrial laws only with respect to 'conciliation and arbitration for the prevention and settlement of industrial disputes extending beyond the limits of any one State' (Section 51, para. 35).

Employers were initially hostile to the Commonwealth Court of Conciliation and Arbitration (the forerunner to the Australian Industrial Relations Commission), established under the Conciliation and Arbitration Act 1904, since it forced them to recognise unions registered under the Act and empowered these unions to make claims on behalf of all employees within an industry. Having earlier rejected the notion of compulsory arbitration, the unions changed their stance after some disastrous defeats during the strikes of the 1890s. Under the 1904 Act unions could force employers to court even if they were unwilling to negotiate, and once the court made an award (i.e. ruled on pay or other terms of employment), its provisions were legally enforceable. The new federal government was attracted to compulsory arbitration because strikes were becoming a problem as they spread across State borders. Industrial agreements were being broken and it was felt that legislative enforcement was needed in order to gain compliance. Furthermore, if the parties were unable to settle disputes between them, an independent third party should be available.

Despite their initial opposition to the system, employers soon found that they could use arbitration procedures to their advantage and generally supported the system (see Macintyre & Mitchell 1989). The establishment of systems of conciliation and arbitration at the federal and State levels marked an important departure from the British-style industrial relations that had characterised Australia before the 1890s. That British traditions played a large part in Australian industrial relations was unsurprising. British law and notions of unionism were major imports in the nineteenth century, when the foundations of Australia's contemporary employment and industrial relations system were established.

The system of arbitration includes both federal and State industrial tribunals. Until 1956, the Commonwealth Court of Conciliation and Arbitration carried out both arbitral and judicial functions. After this, the industrial division of the Federal Court administered the judicial provisions of the Act while the Commonwealth Conciliation and Arbitration Commission (hereafter referred to as the Commission) carried out non-judicial functions. Federal awards that cover approximately a third of the workforce tended to set the pattern for all other tribunals, so that a high degree of uniformity emerged despite the multiplicity of tribunals. Although the Commission is empowered to intervene only in disputes extending to more than one State, most important cases fulfil this requirement or can be made to do so. Either party to a dispute may refer a case to the Commission, or it may intervene of its own accord 'in the public interest'. Thus, the powers of the Commission have become more extensive than originally intended. Some States have expressed concern at the drift of control to the federal level; others have been in favour. Attempts by the federal government to persuade all of the States to cede their industrial relations powers to the Commonwealth have so far failed, although the State government of Victoria did so in 1996. Most national industries, however, are covered by federal awards.

In 1988 the Labor government replaced the Conciliation and Arbitration Act 1904 with the Industrial Relations Act 1988. The name of the Commonwealth Conciliation and Arbitration Commission was changed to the Australian Industrial Relations Commission, but its function remained largely the same. The new Act was similar in approach in many ways to its predecessor. Under it, all federal unions were required to register with the arbitration authorities (represented by the Industrial Registrar) in order to gain access to the tribunal and to enjoy full corporate status under the law. Registration requirements operated for large employers and employers' associations, but registration was more significant for unions since it established the conditions for union security. The Act continued the longstanding 'conveniently belong' rule which made it difficult either for a new union to be registered, or to extend the coverage of an existing union, where it could be established that there already existed a union to which the employees in question could 'conveniently belong'. While this helped to reduce inter-union disputes, it also inhibited the development of new unions and helped preserve some whose principal industry had declined. The 1988 Act required unions seeking registration to have a minimum of 1000 members and be industry-based. The intent was to deter the further proliferation of small, craft-based unions. Existing unions with under 1000 members had to make a case before the Registrar in a bid to maintain their registration.

The federal government moved to amend the Act in 1990, increasing the minimum size of federal unions to 10 000 members. There was substantial opposition to this bold proposal. Indeed, the then Confederation of Australian Industry (CAI) lodged a complaint with the International Labour Organisation (ILO) claiming that the proposal breached the principle of freedom of association, and in any case could not be justified on economic or other grounds. In the Labor government's Industrial Relations Reform Bill 1993, this point was acknowledged and the minimum number of members for union registration was amended to 100, as existed prior to the 1988 Act (this was further reduced to a minimum of 50 members under the coalition government's Workplace Relations and other Legislative Amendments Act 1996, see below).

The provisions of the Reform Bill came into operation in early 1994. The amended Act permitted workplace agreements to be negotiated and considered for certification in non-unionised workplaces. The Reform Act also included a limited right to strike and a number of new legal rights for employees based on minimum standards of employment derived from ILO Conventions (Pittard 1994). Provisions in the Industrial Relations Reform Act 1993 proved to be controversial among both unions and employers. In the federal election campaign of March 1996, won by the Liberal–National Party coalition, employment and industrial relations were strongly debated. The incoming government, led by John Howard, was committed to a new round of major changes in industrial relations law, which led to the Workplace Relations and other Legislative Amendments Act 1996 (discussed later).

Since Federation, conservative political parties have generally dominated federal government. During their intermittent periods in office at the federal level, Labor governments made some significant changes in the economic management of the nation and were more sympathetic to union interests than their conservative counterparts. However, once in government, most political parties tended to favour protectionist policies. This resulted in the creation of a manufacturing sector that produced goods for a small domestic market behind high tariff barriers. These barriers, however, did restrain the decline of manufacturing employment that resulted from a combination of structural and technological changes in the Australian economy.

The tariff policy was originally designed to insulate the Australian economy from cheap imported goods and provide employment for an expanding labour force. It also enabled wages to be determined by tribunals more on social and equity grounds than in accordance with productivity and market forces. Many protected industries, anticipating the chill winds of unrestricted competition, tenaciously lobbied governments to retain significant tariff levels. The move of the Whitlam Labor government (1972–75) to reduce tariffs by 25 per cent 'at a single stroke', was strongly criticised both by Australian unions and employers as having led to increased levels of unemployment, especially in industries vulnerable to overseas competition.

The federal Labor government, between 1983 and 1996, sought to 'phase in' tariff reductions and stimulate competition. However, the lengths to which government policy should go to encourage competition has remained a matter of debate. In addition, while some have advocated the rapid dismantling of protective barriers, others have argued for a more selective and cautious approach. This has been particularly the case in regard to key manufacturing industries such as automotive assembly and components (see Lansbury 1994).

Employment relations in Australia are influenced by the nature of its mixed economy. There is a heavy concentration of power in a relatively small number of large enterprises. As in comparable countries there is a very uneven distribution of employees across organisations. The second Australian Workplace Industrial Relations Survey (AWIRS 2) found, in 1995, that the largest workplaces, employing 500 or more persons, accounted for 26 per cent of the total labour force. At the other end of the scale, workplaces with less than 50 employees accounted for 17 per cent of the total labour force. Workplaces in the public sector accounted for 35 per cent of the labour force, compared with the private sector which employed 65 per cent (Moorehead et al. 1997:399).

The employment relations parties

Employers' associations

The early growth of trade unions in Australia encouraged the development of employers' associations and led them to place greater emphasis on industrial relations functions than did their counterparts in some other countries. Numerous employers' associations have a direct role or interest in industrial relations (Plowman 1989). However, there is great variation in the size and complexity of employers' associations from small, single-industry bodies to large organisations that attempt to cover all employers within a particular State. In 1977, the Confederation of Australian Industry (CAI) was established as a single national employers' body, almost 50 years after the formation of the Australian Council of Trade Unions (ACTU). In 1983, a group of large employers set up the Business Council of Australia (BCA), partly as a result of their dissatisfaction with the ability of the CAI to service the needs of its large and diverse membership. Membership of the BCA comprises the chief executive officers of each member company, which has given it a high profile and significant authority when it makes pronouncements on matters such as employment relations.

Since the mid-1980s there have been several important secessions from the CAI. These included large affiliates such as the Metal Trades Industry Association (MTIA) in 1987 and the Australian Chamber of Manufacturers (ACM) in 1989. One repercussion has been employers airing their different viewpoints at events such as National Wage Case hearings. In 1992 the CAI attempted to present a more united front and to attract back former affiliates by merging with the Australian Chamber of Commerce to form a new organisation, the Australian Chamber of Commerce and Industry (ACCI). However, employer bodies have generally appeared to be less united than are the unions under the umbrella of the ACTU, especially during the period of federal Labor governments.

Unions

The establishment of the arbitration system in the early years of this century encouraged the rapid growth of unions and employers' associations. By 1921, approximately 50 per cent of the Australian labour force was unionised. Union density has fluctuated; during the depression of the early 1930s it dropped to around 40 per cent. The 1940s witnessed a steady increase in density, and a peak of 65 per cent was achieved in 1953. Surveys of the labour force conducted by the Australian Bureau of Statistics suggest that union density has suffered a steep decline since the mid-1970s. In 1976, 51 per cent of all employees were in unions (56 per cent males; 43 per cent females). By 1996 this figure had dropped to 31 per cent (34 per cent males; 28 per cent females) (ABS 1996).

Factors contributing to the fall in union density have included the relative decline in employment in manufacturing—a bastion for unions—and strong growth in the more poorly unionised services sector (approximately 72 per cent of the workforce). Significant growth in part-time and casual employment, also poorly unionised, has been an additional factor. The sharp fall in coverage has sparked a vigorous debate on reform within the movement (see below). As in Britain, unionism originally developed on a craft basis, but with the growth of manufacturing, general and industrial unions became more common. The basic unit of organisation for the Australian union is the branch, which may cover an entire State or a large district within a State. Workplace-level organisation tends to be informal, but shop-floor committees and shop steward organisations have developed more rapidly in recent years, in both blue-collar and white-collar sectors (see Peetz 1990).

Nevertheless, unionism in Australia tends to be comparatively weak at the workplace level, reflecting the reliance of many unions on the arbitration system rather than enterprise-level bargaining to achieve their objectives (see Lansbury & Macdonald 1992). In the second Australian Workplace Industrial Relations Survey (AWIRS 2), union density in workplaces with 20 or more employees in 1995 stood at 51 per cent, compared with 64 per cent in the first AWIRS survey in 1990 (Moorehead et al. 1997:141). The proportion of workplaces in which unions were active in negotiations was only 12 per cent in 1995, compared with 15 per cent in 1990 (Moorehead et al. 1997:330).

The main confederation for both manual and non-manual unions is the ACTU. It was formed in 1927 and currently covers around 95 per cent of all trade unionists. The ACTU expanded considerably following its merger with two other confederations that formerly represented white-collar unions. The Australian Council of Salaried and Professional Associations (ACSPA) joined the ACTU in 1979 and the Council of Australian Government Employee Organisations (CAGEO) followed in 1981. The ACTU's considerable influence over its affiliates was reflected at ACTU Congresses and Conferences throughout the 1980s and early 1990s which saw ACTU Executive recommendations, almost without fail, endorsed by affiliates (Davis 1996). Officers of the ACTU also play key roles in the presentation of the unions' case before the Australian Industrial Relations Commission and in the conduct of important industrial disputes.

As in the United Kingdom (UK) and the United States (USA), there is now only one main central union confederation. This is in contrast to some Western European countries that have several confederations. Nevertheless, in each of the States, trades and labour councils also play a significant role in industrial relations. Although the State trades and labour councils are formally branches of the ACTU, they generally have a much longer history than the ACTU and display some independence in the way they conduct their affairs.

By the early 1990s Australian unions were in the midst of an extraordinary period of change. Encouraged by ACTU policy and spurred on by federal legislation, unions sought to implement far-reaching reform.

The goal has been the restructuring of unions into some 20 industry or occupational unions. The ACTU President reported in 1991 that 'dozens of amalgamations' were underway. The objective of amalgamations was the establishment of larger, better-resourced unions, which would be better able to serve their members and assist them in workplace bargaining.

At the 1995 ACTU Congress it was announced that 98 per cent of workers covered by federally registered unions were now in 17 large unions. While this was a remarkable success in achieving ACTU policy, not all welcomed the amalgamation process, particularly the leaders of some State-based trades and labor councils, whose power and influenced waned in the face of larger federal unions. Furthermore, there were reports of dissatisfaction on the part of some officials with the operation of the new conglomerate unions, in which the balance of power between various groups was threatened or altered as the result of mergers.

During the mid-1990s, the ACTU undertook an active recruitment campaign to boost union membership by 200 000. The strategy involved hiring 300 recruitment officers to work with individual unions, targeting poorly unionised industries such as finance, recreation and hospitality, and marketing a range of new services to members such as discounted housing loans, travel and insurance. The ACTU strategy also included measures to pool union resources in regional and rural centres where unions had little presence. Under this initiative, a single union was given responsibility in a particular rural zone for signing up members in different industries and occupations. These new recruits would then have their membership transferred to the union with legal coverage rights once it was able to service the region.

The Liberal–National Party coalition government, elected in March 1996, pledged that it would introduce major reforms to union structures and operation. The Workplace Relations Act 1996 subsequently increased the potential for non-union bargaining. This could be achieved not only through a new stream of non-union certified agreements, but also through newly created Australian workplace agreements to be signed by employees and not unions (although employees may elect to have a union or any other appropriate body as their bargaining agent). The government also introduced new freedom of association provisions into the Act to ensure that employees and independent contractors were free to join or not join unions. A controversial proposal to facilitate the establishment of new enterprise unions was not enacted in its original form. This was largely as a result of employers' concerns that this proposal could generate a proliferation of small and potentially militant unions. Under the new Act, any new enterprise unions will require 50 or more members and will have to demonstrate proof of support of their fellow employees. New unions can register only if existing union(s) are not effectively representing their members. The Act also contains provisions enabling the 'de-amalgamation' of 'super unions', many of which amalgamated as part of the ACTU's drive to rationalise the large number of small unions. The process, however, looks hazardous; there are few early signs of union dis-amalgamation. While some of the government's reforms will make aspects of the unions' work more difficult, they may also stimulate a stronger degree of union solidarity.

Government

The powers of the federal government over industrial relations, as noted previously, are limited under the Commonwealth constitution. The lack of legislative power, particularly over prices and incomes, has frustrated federal governments of all political persuasions. During the period of the Fraser Liberal–National Party government (1975–83) there were occasional strong exchanges between the federal government and the Commission. For instance, in 1977 the Fraser government argued strenuously that its economic policy would be prejudiced unless the Commission's decisions on wage adjustments were framed in accord-ance with government wishes. The Commission responded that it was 'not an arm of the government's economic policy [but] an independent body . . . required under the Act to act according to equity, good conscience and the substantial merits of the case' (Isaac 1977:22).

The 1972–75 Whitlam Labor government sought to establish pace-setting conditions for its employees and encouraged the extension of union coverage. The election of the Liberal–National Party coalition government led by Malcolm Fraser in 1975 brought considerable change. The conditions of public servants began to fall behind those prevailing in the private sector, and legislation was introduced that strengthened the ability of the government as an employer to lay off or dismiss workers at will. A further measure was the cancellation of the system whereby members' dues in the two largest public-sector unions had been deducted from wages. The post-1983 Labor govern-ment repealed those laws regarded as least palatable by the unions and restored the automatic payroll deduction of union dues. Public sector employees failed, however, to regain their place as pace-setters. Indeed, experience during the 1980s and 1990s suggested a growing disparity in remuneration for public sector and private sector employees.

A feature of industrial relations during the period 1983–96 was the strength of ties between senior ministers in the federal Labor govern-ment and senior union officials. Contributing factors were that Bob Hawke, Prime Minister from 1983–91, was a former President of the ACTU and two of the four Ministers for Industrial Relations during this period were former ACTU officials. Paul Keating launched a successful challenge for the leadership of the Labor Party and became Prime Minister in December 1991. Although Keating developed a strong personal relationship with Bill Kelty, Secretary of the ACTU, he was not as closely aligned with the union movement as his predecessor. As detailed later in this chapter, the Hawke Labor government and the ACTU jointly supported a move towards a more decentralised approach to wage determination, beginning with the end of full wage indexation after a severe economic crisis in the mid-1980s.

During the period of the Keating Labor government (1993–96), there was a further shift towards decentralised bargaining at the enterprise level and a greater focus on achieving increased labour productivity. The union movement was on the defensive, finding little comfort in general policy developments, but seeing little alternative to the Accord with the government (see later in this chapter). Furthermore, the emphasis of the Keating government's Industrial Relations Reform Act 1993 was on strengthening individual legal rights rather than on collective advances for the unionised workforce. To achieve its objectives, the 1993 Act drew on other constitutional powers, namely the corporations power and the external affairs power. This was a departure from traditional reliance on the conciliation and arbitration power (Section 51, para. 35). By the time of its defeat in March 1996, the Keating government had moved a long way from the policy position espoused by the Hawke government in 1983. The emphasis on state intervention and centralisation of the first Hawke Labor government had been replaced by greater reliance on market forces and decentralisation, as well as an expansion of the federal government's industrial relations powers.

The Howard coalition government sought to hasten reform towards a more deregulated employment relations system through its Workplace Relations and other Legislative Amendments Act 1996 (discussed in greater detail later in this chapter). The main policy changes in the Act included a reduction in the role and importance of awards, which would be limited to an enforceable safety net of minimum wages and conditions; new arrangements for enterprise bargaining, which included individual agreements without union intervention; and removal of restrictions on the use of particular types of labour and hours of work. Not surprisingly, the union movement strongly opposed the new government's reform proposals on the grounds that workers' rights and conditions would be eroded. The unions sought to galvanise support among community and welfare organisations, and among the minor political parties holding the balance of power in the Senate, to block or amend the legislation. Although the minor parties holding the balance of power in the Senate forced a number of amendments to the government's original Bill, the principal reforms were retained in the new Act.

Employment relations processes

Although federal awards have had precedence, the State systems of employment and industrial relations are still very important. Problems arising from overlapping jurisdiction of the State and federal tribunals have long been a source of concern to reformers, but changes have been difficult to achieve. In the late 1980s, however, agreements were reached between the State and federal governments on the dual appointment of Heads and other members of the State industrial tribunals to the federal Commission. This was an important step towards the possible development of an integrated national industrial relations system. However, reforms introduced by the Howard government may reverse this trend (see below).

Historically, the Australian system of conciliation and arbitration was based on the assumption that the processes of conciliation would be exhausted before arbitration was undertaken. The system of arbitration was compulsory in two senses. First, once engaged, it required the parties in dispute to submit to a mandatory procedure for presenting their arguments. Second, tribunal awards were binding on the parties in dispute. Awards specified minimum standards of pay and conditions that employers must meet or if they were not to face legal penalties. However, unions and employers were free to negotiate above these minimum standards. It is necessary to distinguish between the formal provisions of the arbitration system and the way it worked in practice. In reality, there has always been a considerable amount of direct negotiation between the parties. Agreements directly negotiated between employers and unions coexist with or take the place of arbitrated awards. If these agreements were ratified by the Commission, they were known as 'consent awards' and could deal comprehensively with the terms and conditions of work in particular workplaces or supplement existing agreements. In this way, awards were more flexible in practice than they appeared to be in a formal sense.

Following a survey of 60 major unions, Niland (1976) reported that three-quarters of the respondents claimed to be using direct negotiation or bargaining procedures in dispute resolution. Some 30 per cent negotiated solely within the conciliation and arbitration framework and 20 per cent operated completely outside the system, while 50 per cent used a mixed approach. These findings provided support for an earlier study by Yerbury and Isaac (1971) that reported a substantial increase in the relative importance of directly negotiated agreements at both the federal and State levels. Yerbury and Isaac noted the emergence of a 'peculiar hybrid of quasi-collective bargaining' which, they argued, could well become the dominant feature of industrial relations in Australia. During the late 1980s there were moves towards greater industry and enterprise bargaining within limits set by the Commission. Decisions made at the centre were designed to encourage a more decentralised focus or 'managed decentralism' (McDonald & Rimmer 1989). The term pointed to the continuing hybrid nature of the Australian industrial relations system (Lansbury & Niland 1995).

The trend towards greater decentralisation of employment relations processes increased during the 1990s in response to economic recession and growing political pressures. The Industrial Relations Reform Act 1993 extended the scope for enterprise bargaining by introducing enterprise flexibility agreements (EFAs). These allowed workplace agreements to be negotiated in non-unionised workplaces. The Commission retained a role in ensuring that the terms and conditions of EFAs did not disadvantage employees when compared with the relevant award. Although there was a significant growth in the number of enterprise agreements during the 1990s, these largely supplemented rather than replaced existing awards. However, the effects of these changes were to widen the opportunities for employers, employees and unions to opt out of the traditional award system (Ludeke 1993). This tendency was further enhanced by the election of the coalition government in March 1996 and the passing of the Workplace Relations Act, which came into effect in January 1997.

The settlement of disputes

One of the principal motivations behind the introduction of compulsory arbitration was to render strikes unnecessary. The 'rule of law' provided under arbitration was supposed to displace the 'barbarous expedient of strike action'. For many years the Commonwealth Conciliation and Arbitration Act contained a provision making strike activity illegal and subject to penalties. Although this provision was removed in 1930, Australian workers in the federal system were only granted a qualified and limited right to strike in 1993.

The Industrial Relations Reform Act 1993 provided unions and employers with a period of immunity from common law and secondary boycott actions associated with strikes and lockouts. Under this Act, either party could notify the other of its intention to use industrial action during the designated bargaining period. The Commission could intervene and make use of its traditional arbitral functions if it believed that the parties were not acting in good faith, if there was little likelihood of an agreement being reached, or on the grounds of public interest. In seeking to resolve the dispute, parties that engaged in unlawful strikes could be fined and in addition have their awards suspended or cancelled. The Howard government has maintained a limited right to strike during the designated bargaining period in its Workplace Relations Act, but it has sought to strengthen the Commission's powers to address illegal industrial action, prohibited the payment and acceptance of pay or wages for workers when involved in strike action and restored secondary boycott provisions to the Trade Practices Act, with substantial fines for breaches.

Another sanction, used sparingly by tribunals, has been to deregister a union that has acted in defiance of a tribunal order. Since deregistration has tended to be difficult and complex, tribunals have generally hoped that its threat would be sufficient. Threats, though, made little impact on the Builders Labourers' Federation, deregistered in 1986; its members were quickly absorbed by other unions, leaving only the shell of a once-powerful union.

One of the main effects of arbitration has been to shorten the duration of strikes and to increase their frequency. Although international comparisons of strike statistics are notoriously difficult (see Appendix), the Australian experience is illuminating. During the 1960s and 1970s it was among those countries with a relatively high number of strike days per 1000 people employed. For instance, in a study by Creigh and Makeham (1982) of 20 Organisation for Economic Co-operation and Development (OECD) countries, Australia came sixth with an annual average of 675 working days lost per 1000 employees between 1970 and 1979. The five countries with a higher strike propensity were Italy, Iceland, Canada, the Irish Republic and Spain. Close behind Australia were the UK and the USA. A relatively adversarial style of employment relations prevailed in Australia, in comparison with countries such as Japan, Germany and Sweden, which recorded many fewer strike days each year per 1000 employees.

From 1983, the federal Labor government presided over a more peaceful employment relations climate. During the 1980s, average working days lost through disputes per 1000 employees were halved. Since the end of 1982, no calendar year has seen working days lost exceed 300 per 1000 employees per year (ABS 1995). Beggs and Chapman (1987) have argued that while changing macro-economic conditions played a part in this absolute and relative decline in the impact of industrial stoppages, so too did the ALP–ACTU Accord (see later in this chapter). In 1994, the number of industrial disputes fell to its lowest levels in 55 years. Only 76 working days were lost per 1000 employees, and this was the lowest level since the Australian Bureau of Statistics began to collect statistics in this form in 1967.

The 1991 AWIRS findings questioned the popular impression that Australian workplaces are strike-prone. It revealed that nearly three-quarters of workplaces with more than four employees had not experienced any type of industrial action (Callus et al. 1991). When launching the publication of the survey, the then Minister for Industrial Relations, Senator Peter Cook, commented:

> In the year preceding the survey (1988–89), only 12 per cent of workplaces had been involved in some form of industrial action. In most cases, these

were stop-work meetings, involving information sessions and the like as well as stoppages per se. Moreover, whether one relies on the account of managers or union representatives, management–employee relations are generally perceived as reasonably harmonious. (Cook 1991:4)

The BCA has been less sanguine. In a survey of BCA member companies the National Institute of Labour Studies reported that, during the 12-month period prior to its survey in 1988, two-thirds of establishments were affected by stoppages of less than a day's duration, with 50 per cent affected by stoppages of a day or more. It should be noted, however, that BCA member companies generally have larger than average workplaces. However, even the BCA's own statistics (drawn from OECD data) show that between 1983–87, the amount of time lost by employees on strike in Australia was on par with the average for all OECD countries, namely 0.25 of a day per year. Furthermore, as noted by Dabscheck (1991), Australian strike data are more inclusive than those of comparable countries, which 'biases' the Australian data upwards.

There are other expressions of industrial conflict besides industrial stoppages. These include accidents; absenteeism; labour turnover; working to rules; and bans and limitations (see Hyman 1989). There are much less comparative data available on such forms of conflict. Yet there is some evidence to suggest an increase in the use of bans during the past decade. A ban is defined as 'an organised refusal by employees to undertake certain work, to use certain equipment or to work with certain people' (Sheehan & Worland 1986:21). One of the reasons put forward for this is that 'bans minimise loss of pay and make it more difficult for employers to apply legal sanctions against unions' (Frenkel 1990:14).

The term 'silent strike' has been used to describe such phenomena as labour turnover, absenteeism and even industrial sabotage. The 1991 AWIRS reported that voluntary labour turnover (thereby excluding dismissals, retirement and retrenchments) was 19 per cent per annum and that an average of 4.5 per cent of employees were absent each day. This compares with a rate of absence due to strikes of about 0.23 per cent. The Australian Automotive Industry Council estimated that turnover and absenteeism add about A$850 to the ex-factory cost of an automobile manufactured in Australia (Automotive Industry Council 1990:1). These statistics help to place strikes and their costs in a broader perspective of days lost due to a range of other reasons.

The determination of wages

The arbitration system has led to a relatively centralised wages system. This has been achieved by increasing the influence of the federal Commission over key wage issues despite constitutional limitations. Its predecessor, the Commonwealth Court of Conciliation and Arbitration, initially became involved in fixing a minimum wage in 1907 when it described the 'basic wage' as intended to meet 'the normal needs of an average employee, regarded as a human being living in a civilised community'. The basic wage was set at a level sufficient to cover the minimum needs of a single-income family unit of five, and became the accepted wage for unskilled work. The custom of wage differentials (margins) for skills was formalised in the 1920s, based largely on historical differentials in the metal and engineering trades.

The Commonwealth Court thus began to regulate wages and differentials through its decisions on the 'basic wage' and 'margins' at National Wage Case hearings. These are a much-publicised ritual and occur at regular intervals, with usually one National Wage Decision per year. The employers, unions (through the ACTU) and governments (at federal and State levels) each make submissions to the Commission, which later hands down a decision. The Commission's decisions have, in the past, determined changes to wages and conditions. Depending on the nature of the decision these have at times, through a 'pipeline' effect, applied generally to employees throughout Australia. In 1967, the Commission ended the system of a basic wage and margins in favour of a 'total' award. It also introduced the concept of national minimum wages, representing the lowest wages permissible for a standard work week by any employee.

During the early 1970s, the Commission sought to adjust the relative structure of award wages in different industries and to limit over-award increases. But by 1973–74, the contribution of increases determined at National Wage Cases to total wage increases had declined to approximately 20 per cent as unions bargained directly with employers for large over-award payments (Howard 1977). Collective bargaining had therefore become the dominant force in wage increases, its leading settlements being generally extended to the whole economy (Isaac 1977:14). Faced with both rapidly rising inflation and unemployment, the Labor government moved to restore the authority of the Commission (Lansbury 1978). In 1974, both the federal government and the ACTU asked the Commission to introduce automatic cost-of-living adjustments to wages, to offset the effect of increased prices (i.e. full wage indexation). Non-Labor State governments and private employers opposed this approach.

In 1975, the Commission issued guidelines on the principles and procedures of the new wage-fixing system. Under these guidelines, no wage increase could be granted without the permission of the Commission (Yerbury 1980). In December 1975, however, the newly elected coalition government, led by Malcolm Fraser, opposed full wage indexation mainly on the grounds of the depressed state of the economy. It also argued that the unions had failed to comply with the Commission's indexation guidelines. Between 1975 and 1981, partial rather than full indexation was the norm. In other words, the wage increases determined by the Commission were regularly below the increases in the consumer price index (CPI). The system of wage indexation was abandoned by the Commission in 1981 (Dabscheck 1989). A round of direct negotiations followed, similar in style to the collective bargaining round of 1974. Some very large pay increases were won and these began to flow on to other sectors. At the same time, there was a sharp fall in demand for goods and services, and unemployment rose. The Fraser government then initiated a 'wage pause' within the federal public service and successfully sought its general implementation by the Commission. Wage determination under the Labor governments from 1983 to 1996 and the trend towards a decentralised, enterprise-based bargaining system are covered later in this chapter.

The Accord

The election of the Hawke Labor government in 1983 returned the Commission to a powerful role in wage determination. The Accord agreed between the Labor Party and the ACTU included a return to centralised wage determination with wage adjustments for price movements and, at longer intervals, for movements in national productivity (ALP–ACTU 1983; Lansbury 1985). In late 1983 the Commission agreed to reintroduce wage indexation. Among the principles announced by the Commission, however, was the requirement that each union pledge to make no 'extra claims' in return for receiving wage indexation (that is, make no demand for additional wage increases except under exceptional circumstances).

To the surprise of some commentators, most unions accepted this condition and subsequently there was little movement in wages beyond the nationally determined pay rates. Those unions seeking to press for wage increases outside the Accord found themselves isolated and their campaigns usually proved unsuccessful. Prominent examples included the Plumbers and Gasfitters Employees' Union (PGEU) in 1986–87 and the spectacular case of the Australian Federation of Air Pilots (AFAP) in 1989. The PGEU found itself confronted with a legal armory used by employers to force the lifting of specified bans on building sites. This resulted in substantial damages being incurred by the union and its return to the centralised wages fold. The AFAP fared even worse. Opposed by government and airline employers, it failed to make any gains for its members and found its base decimated. These exceptional episodes point to the more general observation of national wage guidelines by unions. The guidelines are discussed in more detail later in this chapter.

Some have argued that the Accord played a major role in generating higher levels of employment than would have been the case under more conventional alternative approaches. Former Minister for Industrial Relations and later Treasurer in the Labor government, Ralph Willis, stated that during the Accord employment grew at an annual rate of 2.2 per cent between 1983 and 1996; three times the previous growth rate, and the highest among the OECD countries. He also noted that 90 per cent of this growth was in the service industries (Willis 1997:2). A major factor was significant restraint in real wages, particularly during the first seven years of the Accord.

The pursuit of policy that led to a fall in real wages sparked debate within the union movement. ACTU officials contended that the impact of the fall in real wages was more than offset by increased employment (thereby increasing household incomes), tax reform, improved super-annuation and a raft of more generous social welfare provisions. These, it was claimed, had led to higher standards of living. The ACTU also pointed to the greater influence exercised by union representatives over economic, industry and social policies. The Accord, for instance, set out 'agreed policy details' on the treatment of prices and non-wage incomes, on taxation, and on supportive policies covering industrial relations legislation, social security, occupational health and safety, education, health and Australian government employment. Although the Accord underwent a number of significant 'adjustments', known col-loquially as Mark I to Mark VIII, it consistently provided the frame-work for union influence on government policies on economic, industry and social matters. The various phases of the Accord (from Mark I to Mark VIII) are summarised in Table 5.2.

The original Accord (which later became known as Mark I) envis-aged federal government support for full wage indexation. As can be seen in Table 5.3, the National Wage Case Decisions in 1983, 1984 and 1985 provided for full wage indexation, although they simul-taneously delivered reductions in real wages through a mixture of delays in the adjustment of money wages and other factors. The severe economic crisis of 1985–86 however—seen in the rapid and largely unanticipated fall in the exchange value of the Australian dollar, the accompanying stimulus to inflation, soaring levels of foreign debt and increasing levels of interest rates—led the government to abandon its commitment to full wage indexation. Wage fixing became a more complicated business thereafter.

Landmark decisions by the Australian Industrial Relations Commission

The 1987, 1988 and 1989 National Wage Case Decisions broke the nexus between price and wage movements. Wage increases, for the

Table 5.2 The Accord: Mark I to Mark VIII—selected features

Mark I	1983-85	Commitment by federal government and the ACTU to the maintenance of real wages, controls on prices and non-wage incomes and supportive government policies.
Mark II	1985–86	ACTU reduced National Wage Case claim from 4.3% to 2.3% in return for compensating tax cuts; 3% phased increases in occupational superannuation
Mark III	1987–88	Two-tier wage system, which initiated moves towards productivity bargaining.
Mark IV	1988–89	Package of wage increases and tax cuts linked to restructuring and greater efficiency at industry and enterprise levels.
Mark V	1989–90	Package of wage increases, tax cuts and social wage improvements linked to structural efficiency and award restructuring.
Mark VI	1990–92	Package of wage increases, tax cuts, increased superannuation, improved social welfare benefits and access to enterprise bargaining linked to greater structural efficiency and continued award restructuring.
Mark VII	1993–95	Package of agreed reforms with enterprise bargaining the primary means of obtaining wage improvements: but award-based increases possible as an alternative if bargaining is unsuccessful; proclaimed central goal: to reduce levels of unemployment and to create 500 000 additional jobs in the next three years.
Mark VIII	1995–99	Package of agreed reforms. Enterprise bargaining retains central role in industrial relations; awards to act as a safety-net setting minimum rates. Joint commitment to low inflation and reduced unemployment. Other issues include superannuation, training, work and family. This final Accord was aborted due to the loss of government by the Australian Labor Party in March 1996.

greater part, were linked to measures that increased, or were seen as likely to increase, productivity and performance. The 1987 National Wage Case Decision became known as the two-tier decision because it introduced a split system of wage adjustments. (This is quite different from the US notion of two-tier collective bargaining.) A first tier provided for an initial A\$10 to be paid to all workers. This was followed by a further A\$6 'across the board' some 11 months later. A second tier permitted further wage increases of up to 4 per cent. This depended on unions and employers agreeing to improve efficiency in their industry or workplaces. The Commission requested that the parties consider reforms to restrictive work and management practices, multi-skilling and broadbanding of work classifications, reduction of demarcation barriers and changes to award classifications.

The 1988 National Wage Case Decision took a similar path. It allowed increases of 3 per cent (and A$10 six months later) on the condition that discussions occur between employers and unions on 'structural efficiency'. Unions and employers were required to agree to review their awards, looking at issues such as skill-related career paths, award relativities, flexibility, minimum rates and 'any cases where award provisions discriminate against sections of the workforce'. This resulted in a mixture of industry-by-industry and employer-by-employer negotiations. The decision reflected the central role of the Commission while it also supported moves towards the establishment of enterprise agreements between employers and unions.

The 1989 National Wage Case Decision followed on. The Commission granted a wage increase in two instalments as the lever to maintain pressure for reform. The first increase of A$10 to A$15 (or 3 per cent) was to be paid following scrutiny of proposals for award restructuring by the Commission while the second would depend on the progress made. The post-1987 decisions had therefore provided the opportunity for unions and employers to address issues which had long bedevilled economic performance, but had been widely regarded as immutable.

At the 1990 National Wage Case, federal and State governments, the ACTU and employer groups requested the Commission to encourage greater reliance on enterprise bargaining. In addition, the ACTU and the federal government asked the Commission to ratify the agreement struck by them in February 1990 (known as Accord Mark VI). This sought centrally determined increases to wages and superannuation and the opportunity for further wage increases negotiated at industry or enterprise levels. The Commission, however, in its April 1991 National Wage Case Decision, rebuffed the government and ACTU, in particular declaring that employers and unions had not achieved the maturity required for greater reliance on enterprise bargaining.

The ACTU condemned the Commission's 1991 Decision and encouraged its affiliates to win pay increases by negotiating directly with employers. There followed a period of extraordinary acrimony with bitter attacks made on the Commission by leading union officials and senior government ministers. However, bargaining against the backdrop of economic recession proved difficult and only a minority of workers gained the benefits sought by unions. Later in 1991 the Commission began a new National Wage Case which heard submissions on the future of wage fixation. Governments, unions and employers again argued for greater reliance on enterprise bargaining. In its second 1991 Decision the Commission refashioned the principles governing wage fixation, giving greater encouragement to enterprise bargaining. Nonetheless, unions and employers remained obliged to pursue

Table 5.3   Wage and price movements

Quarters	Change in CPI (%)	National wage increases	Date paid
1983 March/June	4.3	4.3%	Sept 1983
Sept/Dec	4.0	4.1%	April 1984
1984 March/June	−0.2		–
Sept/Dec	2.7	2.6%	April 1985
1985 March/June	3.8	3.8%	Nov 1985
Sept/Dec	4.3	2.3%	July 1986
1986 March/June	4.0	–	–
Sept/Dec	5.5	–	–
1987 March/June	3.5	A$10.00	March 1987
Sept/Dec	3.4	A$6.00[a]	Feb 1988
1988 March/June	3.5	–	–
Sept/Dec	4.0	3.0% + $A10.00	from Sept 1988[b]
1989 March/June	4.0	–	–
Sept/Dec	4.2	3.0% + 3.0%	from Aug 1989[c]
1990 March/June	3.3	–	–
Sept/Dec	3.4	–	–
1991 March/June	−0.1	2.5%	from April 1991
Sept	0.6	–	–

Notes: a   Taking the A$10.00 and A$6.00 together, this represents a 3.5% increase for full-time adult males.

b   The date for the initial 3% payment depended on the finalisation of an agreement between employers and unions on structural efficiency. The A$10.00 was to be paid as a second instalment at least six months later.

c   The Commission determined that again there should be a six-month interval between instalments.

Sources: ABS, *Consumer Price Index*, Cat. No. 6401.0; National Wage Case Decisions 1983–91.

'structural efficiency' and their agreements were to be subject to scrutiny by the Commission.

The spread and impact of enterprise bargaining in 1992 and 1993 was rather slow, particularly with the economy in recession. Accord Mark VII was finalised in February 1993, just prior to the federal election in March. Under Accord Mark VII, the unions agreed to work for 'wage outcomes consistent with Australia maintaining an inflation rate comparable with (its) major trading partners'. An A$8 'safety net' wage rise was supported by the government for workers who did not achieve any increase through enterprise bargaining. This was subsequently ratified by the Commission. The main commitment by government under Accord Mark VII was the creation of 500 000 new jobs.

A similar approach was evident in Accord Mark VIII, finalised in June 1995, under which the unions agreed to recognise the continuing importance of low inflation, while the government pledged to generate 600 000 new jobs over the next three years. Prime Minister Keating admitted that the pace of enterprise bargaining had not been as fast as anticipated, mainly due to lack of progress within most of the State systems, but noted that 60 per cent of employees in the federal systems were now under registered enterprise agreements.

One source of friction between the Keating Labor government and both the unions and the Commission concerned the future of the award system (see also the later section on employment and industrial relations reform). In April 1993, soon after his election victory, Prime Minister Keating claimed that enterprise-level agreements would eventually replace the award system. After a number of union leaders objected to this statement, the Prime Minister 'clarified' his position and emphasised that the existing award system would continue to provide a 'safety net' of minimum wages and conditions, especially for those employees in a weak bargaining position. However, the government was critical of the Commission for constraining enterprise bargaining. In the 1994 National Wage Case, the Keating Labor government argued unsuccessfully that awards should be stripped back to 'essential standards' in terms of wages and conditions. This was opposed by the ACTU on the grounds that they wished to maintain a mechanism whereby awards could be periodically upgraded to reflect the standards achieved through enterprise bargaining. Even under the government's proposals, however, the Commission would continue to play an important role in reviewing awards and facilitating the enterprise bargaining process.

Employee participation and consultation

In the early 1970s, under the influence of two reforming Labor governments (led by Prime Minister Whitlam at the federal level and Premier Don Dunstan in South Australia), industrial democracy attracted considerable attention. There was much discussion of the need to extend decision-making rights to workers, establish joint councils and committees in the workplace, and place worker representatives on management boards. In addition it was argued by proponents of industrial democracy that jobs should be redesigned to facilitate the more direct control of workers over their work life (see Lansbury 1980).

Many employers indicated their support for reform, cherishing the hope that change would reduce problems such as absenteeism and poor-quality work, and encourage improved productivity. For their part unions wished to see the rights of their members extended and gave their blessing, through the ACTU, to both representative and participative schemes that led to an increase in workers' decision-making power. They made it clear that they strongly opposed plans that failed to provide for the sharing of gains flowing from the implementation of industrial democracy (see Lansbury & Davis 1990).

Under the 1975–83 coalition federal government and mounting levels of unemployment, the pressure for industrial democracy ebbed away. Unions became increasingly concerned with the defence of members' jobs and wages, and employers found themselves under less pressure to display a commitment to industrial democracy (see Davis & Lansbury 1986).

The change of federal government in 1983 led to renewed interest. The Accord emphasised the need for government, employer and union involvement in macro-economic and social policy decision making. To this end the government established tripartite committees and councils at national and industry levels. Some, such as the Economic Planning Advisory Council, proved influential in the determination of government policy. The Accord also argued specifically for workers' involvement in decision making on technological change. More generally, it stressed that 'consultation is a key factor in bringing about change in industry . . . (at) industry, company and workplace level' (ALP–ACTU 1983:9).

The 1980s saw several important developments. Both federal and State governments took steps to legislate for improved occupational health and safety. Crucial roles were identified for joint union–management workplace committees with rights to relevant information, powers to inspect the workplace, and the right to be consulted on all changes that affect health and safety. Many union–employer agreements went further, granting employee representatives access to the facilities required to perform their duties and in some cases rights to stop the production process when deemed necessary. The extent of effective employee participation in occupational health and safety matters is usually related to the vigour of the unions covering members in the workplace and to the attitude of management. The outcome across workplaces is inevitably mixed.

Adhering to its commitment in the Accord, the Hawke government supported the ACTU in a lengthy case before the Commission on employee rights to information and to consultation over technological change. Under the terms of the Commission's Termination, Change and Redundancy Decision of 1984, employers were required to consult their employees and unions before introducing major changes to production methods or to organisational structure. In addition, where redundancies were contemplated, the length of notice was increased. Account was taken of length of service so that, for instance, four weeks notice was granted to any employee with five years' service or more. Unions welcomed this decision. Many employers were less enthusiastic, seeing the decision as increasing costs and impinging on managerial prerogative.

In 1986 the federal government published a policy discussion paper on *Industrial Democracy and Employee Participation*. The paper stated that 'employee participation is now a major government priority and the government sees it as essential to a successful response to the significant challenges of the present time' (Department of Employment and Industrial Relations 1986). It pointed to alternative paths the government might take in its pursuit of more employee participation. Three in particular were noted: the enactment of legislation; stimulating progress through financial incentives and assistance; and encouragement through government provision of resources, education, training and information.

The National Wage Case Decisions of the late 1980s reflected the declared enthusiasm of government, unions and employers for more consultation and employee participation. They also provided the most effective stimulus to greater employee participation in the workplace. The 1987 Decision advocated pursuit of improved efficiency and stressed that the approach adopted by unions and employers should rely on 'cooperation and consultation' (National Wage Case Decision 1987). The 1988 Decision argued that further restructuring should be done 'primarily by consultation and at minimal cost' (National Wage Case Decision 1988). And in its 1989 Decision the Commission was explicit in its support for 'appropriate consultative procedures to deal with the day-to-day matters of concern to employers and workers' (National Wage Case Decision 1989).

In the 1990s there has been less direct reference made to industrial democracy and more to workplace reform and consultation. As Australia entered the 1990s, leaders in government, business and unions appeared almost to compete in their declared commitment to consultation and participation in the workplace. However, actual performance often seemed to fall short of stated goals. For example, in its report, *The Global Challenge: Australian Manufacturing in the 1990s*, the Australian Manufacturing Council stated that Australian managers 'lagged in their appreciation of employee participation' and did not make the link to improved performance (AMC 1990:73).

The two Australian Workplace Industrial Relations Surveys conducted in 1990 and 1995 shed interesting light on the extent of formal consultation practised in Australia. In 1995, joint consultative committees were reported in 33 per cent of workplaces with 20 or more employees, compared with only 14 per cent in 1990. Furthermore, in 1995, 16 per cent of workplaces had employee representatives on their boards compared with only 7 per cent in 1990 (Moorehead et al. 1997: 188). Some of the increased interest in joint consultative committees may be attributed to the spread of enterprise bargaining in the 1990s. However, while more than 80 per cent of workplaces introduced changes in the two years prior to the 1995 survey, in only 29 per cent of the workplaces surveyed were employees consulted and in only 18 per cent did employees have significant impact on these decisions. Hence, the presence of formal mechanisms for consultation does not necessarily mean that employees will be involved in decision making by management (Moorehead et al. 1997:244).

Amendments to the federal Industrial Relations Act in 1993 were designed not only to facilitate more enterprise bargaining but also to formalise the importance of consultation. However, a survey of a large sample of enterprise agreements in 1994 found that only 49 per cent of all agreements contained provisions dealing with consultative arrangements (ACIRRT 1995). Nevertheless the potential for enterprise bargaining to promote consultation and participation is evident in some leading examples of recent agreements, such as the Enterprise Development Agreement between Westpac bank and the Finance Sector Union in 1994 (see Davis & Lansbury 1996).

The Karpin Report on Leadership and Management Skills in Australia, commissioned by the federal government, criticised the performance of Australian management. Karpin identified weaknesses among Australian managers that included a lack of open-mindedness and a rigidity towards learning; deficiencies in teamwork and empowerment; an inability to cope with differences; and poor 'people skills' (Karpin 1995). These factors may have contributed to the slowness of Australian managers to adopt consultative approaches, despite the advocacy by leading organisations and management theorists. While the past decade has witnessed changes that have facilitated higher levels of consultation and employee participation in workplace decision making, there remains scope for greater progress in this area.

Equal opportunity in employment

During the 1980s, issues related to women in the workplace attracted increasing attention. In large measure this was linked to the remarkable growth in female participation in the workforce. In 1961, women comprised approximately 25 per cent of the workforce; by 1981 this figure had increased to 37 per cent and by 1996 it had reached 42 per cent (Eccles 1982; Davis & Harris 1996). Features of this expansion were the increasing propensity of married women to enter the workforce and the rapid growth of part-time work. Indeed the proportion of the labour force working part-time more than doubled between 1970 and the mid-1990s, moving from 10 per cent to 25 per cent. Part-time work has remained a female preserve; only one-quarter of this group are male.

The growth of women in the workforce has not, however, been accompanied by their greater dispersal across industries and occupations. Women workers have continued to be concentrated in a small number of industries and occupations. Women are overrepresented in industries such as wholesale and retail trade; finance, property and business services; community services; recreation; and personnel. Similarly, in occupational terms, over 50 per cent of female employees are concentrated in two groups—clerical, and sales and personal services. Features of these industries and occupations are relatively low rates of pay and poor conditions. The result has been that women's earnings on average have remained below male earnings. In the mid-1990s women's full-time, average weekly earnings were 83 per cent of the comparable male rate (Davis & Harris 1996; also see Appendix).

These conditions have focused attention on measures to improve women's pay and conditions. The decisions of the Commission in 1969 and 1972 on Equal Pay have been criticised for their failure to achieve equal pay in practice. The 1980s saw pressure from the ACTU and various women's groups designed to encourage the Commission to reassess the value of work in female-dominated occupations. One response of the Commission was to point to the opportunities to revise pay rates following the National Wage Decisions of the late 1980s. The results so far are patchy. It would appear that while some predominantly female groups have improved their relative position, others have not.

The federal Affirmative Action (Equal Employment Opportunity for Women) Act 1986 covers all private sector employers with 100 or more employees. These employers are obliged to take eight specific steps designed to remove discrimination towards women and promote equality in employment. Two of the steps entail, respectively, consultation with unions and consultation with employees on the desired approach. The evidence so far, however, indicates indifferent compliance (Davis & Pratt 1990).

Childcare, maternity and paternity leave, equal employment opportunity (EEO) and affirmative action, and efforts to tackle sexual harassment attracted increasing attention during the 1980s and the first half of the 1990s. Such matters are now generally treated as industrial in nature rather than exclusively women's issues. Champions of greater workplace equity have often cloaked their cause with claims that fairer workplaces 'make good business sense'. Rates of turnover and absenteeism will be lower; profitability will be advanced. The extent of managerial commitment to EEO, however, remains uncertain.

Employment relations reform

A centralised period (1983–86)

After the election of the Hawke Labor government in 1983, Australian employment and industrial relations experienced considerable reform.

In broad terms, four phases can be identified (see Wailes & Lansbury 1997). The first phase, from 1983 to 1986, saw a return to centralised wage determination in line with the initial Accord agreement between the ACTU and the ALP. During this period, wage restraint was delivered by the unions, macro-economic indicators improved significantly and a number of social policy initiatives were taken by the government. A Committee of Review was appointed by the government soon after it assumed office, chaired by Professor Keith Hancock, which assessed the changes required to develop a more effective system of employment and industrial relations. After two years of deliberation, the Hancock Report (1985) recommended the retention and consolidation of a centralised system on the grounds that it facilitated the enforcement of incomes policies and thereby helped to contain levels of unemployment and inflation. Hancock proposed a restructuring of the federal tribunal into the Australian Industrial Relations Commission (AIRC), with powers similar to the existing Commission, and a new Labour Court to replace the industrial division of the Federal Court. It also proposed widening the new Commission's powers to deal with all disputes that arose between employers and employees.

Managed decentralism (1987–90)

During the second phase of industrial relations reform, between 1987 and 1990, the Hawke government responded to a series of economic and political crises by reducing the traditional emphasis on state intervention and macro-level strategies. Balance of payment problems caused by changes in the global economy and structural imbalances in the domestic economy led to alarming declines in the exchange rates of the newly floated Australian dollar and massive increases in foreign debt. On the political front, the government was criticised by the BCA and other employer groups which advocated, among other things, deregulation of the labour market. The BCA argued that the key to improved competitiveness was a shift to enterprise-based negotiations, which would emphasise the mutuality of employee–management interests and the virtues of individualism and flexibility (BCA 1989). The BCA had commissioned an extensive survey of its member companies and used these findings to support its proposals. While the BCA's research methodology was criticised as 'unscientific' with 'sparse and unconvincing results' (Frenkel & Peetz 1990), and the philosophy behind the BCA report was seen by some as a return to 'unitarism: management knows best' (Dabscheck 1990), the BCA's arguments were influential in causing the Hawke government to reconsider its industrial relations strategies. At the State level, the Liberal government of New South Wales published a Green Paper entitled *Transforming Industrial Relations in New South Wales* (Niland 1989), which argued in a similar vein to the BCA for a shift towards workplace bargaining. Many of the Green Paper's recommendations were subsequently implemented in legislation by the New South Wales government.

The unions put forward counter-arguments to deregulation and decentralisation in their report *Australia Reconstructed* (ACTU/TDC 1987), following a 'mission' by senior union officials to European countries. In this report, the ACTU echoed the Hancock Report's support for retention of centralised wage determination, but it also argued that wages policy should be interlinked to taxation and social welfare. The ACTU conceded that wages policy should take into account productivity, international competitiveness and investment, but argued that it should be linked to training and skill development as a means of achieving greater efficiency and wealth creation. While the government supported award restructuring, which linked wages more closely to skills, it was less convinced by other aspects of the ACTU's report that involved greater intervention in the economy. Indeed, the emphasis of government policy became 'micro-economic efficiency' (Gerritsen 1994), and it proceeded to further reduce tariff protection in order to foster greater competitiveness.

The AIRC succeeded in adapting to the changes in government policy. The National Wage Cases set the framework for wage bargaining; the Commission sought to combine the advantages of a centralised framework with scope for direct bargaining between the parties. This approach was termed 'managed decentralism' (McDonald & Rimmer 1989; Evans 1989). The federal government sought to provide a stronger legislative basis for these reforms in the Industrial Relations Act 1988, which introduced the concept of certified agreements, albeit constrained by a 'public interest' test and confined to unionised enterprises.

Coordinated flexibility (1991–96)

The third phase of industrial relations reform covered the period 1991 to early 1996 and involved a transition towards an even more decentralised approach, albeit still within a framework of labour market regulation. In October 1991 the AIRC endorsed a new system of enterprise bargaining as the main mechanism for wage increases and workplace reform, although it retained a capacity to scrutinise agreements that did not meet 'public interest' criteria. Under pressure from employers, however, who complained that it was too difficult to achieve enterprise agreements under this system, the government introduced amendments to the Industrial Relations Act in 1992, which reduced the authority of the AIRC to veto enterprise agreements and widened the opportunities for employers and unions to opt out of the traditional award system (Ludeke 1993). However, the Commission retained an important role in maintaining a national 'safety net' of minimum wages and conditions for lowest paid workers by updating awards and conducting National Wage Cases (Dabscheck 1995; MacDermott 1995).

Following its surprise victory in the federal election of March 1993, the Keating government introduced further reforms to extend enterprise bargaining. In his first major speech following his electoral victory, Prime Minister Keating told a meeting of the Institute of Directors that 'we need to find a way of extending the coverage of agreements . . . to being full substitutes for awards' (Keating 1993). To this end, the government introduced the Industrial Relations Reform Act 1993, which came into effect in March 1994. It embodied significant changes to the operation of the Australian industrial relations system which went beyond simply encouraging greater enterprise bargaining (McCallum & Ronfeldt 1994). The AIRC was given the power to enforce bargaining in good faith and the responsibility to facilitate agreements. A new federal Industrial Relations Court was established with jurisdiction over unfair dismissals. A new object was also inserted into the Act to 'ensure that labour standards meet Australia's international obligations using the external affairs power under the Commonwealth constitution'. The Industrial Relations Reform Act 1993 gave effect to a series of ILO and United Nations conventions and recommendations on minimum entitlements in wages, equal pay for work of equal value, rights to redundancy pay and protection against unfair dismissals.

The government's actions were controversial because, among other things, they invoked the external affairs power rather than relying on the more limited industrial power under the Australian constitution. The government's motives for introducing the new minimum entitlements were related to the unions' concerns that a safety net of provisions was needed for workers in a weak bargaining position who might be left behind under a more decentralised system. However, like earlier anti-discrimination and equal employment opportunity initiatives, these new legal rights could be enforced by individual employees without union involvement, in a range of courts and specialised tribunals. Furthermore, the new legislation also included provisions that facilitated bargaining and the certification of agreements that did not require unions to represent workers. An enterprise flexibility agreement, for example, need not have included an eligible union unless employees chose its involvement. This was seen by unions as providing encouragement for employers who wished to avoid unions and move towards enterprise regimes based on individual contracts of employment (Bennett 1994). Indeed such fears were subsequently realised in a major dispute that occurred during 1995 between a large mining company, Rio Tinto (formerly CRA), and unions at Weipa in the north of Australia (McKinnon 1996).

Fragmented flexibility (1996 onwards)

The fourth phase of industrial reform began with the election of the Liberal–National coalition government led by John Howard, in March 1996. The Workplace Relations and other Legislation Amendment Bill 1996 was one of the first pieces of legislation introduced into the House of Representatives by the new government. Due to opposition by Labor and other minority parties, which held the balance of power in the Senate, the Bill was delayed by reference to a Senate Committee of Review, and passed only after a series of amendments by the Democrats was accepted by the government. The Act, which came into force in January 1997, signalled a more radical deregulation of industrial relations although it still provided parties with a choice between remaining in the award system or opting for a workplace agreement. The Act did not go as far as New Zealand's Employment Contracts Act 1991, which abolished that country's arbitration system (on which Australia's was partially modelled). Nevertheless, the Howard government sought to move the system away from a collectivist approach, in which there was a strong role for unions and tribunals, to a more fragmented system of individual bargaining between employees and employers. The new system envisaged by the Howard government could be characterised as emphasising 'fragmented flexibility' rather than the 'coordinated flexibility' that was introduced by the Keating government (Wailes & Lansbury 1997).

Key elements in the Workplace Relations Act 1996 included significant changes in the role of the AIRC, which had hitherto been able to make determinations about 'industrial matters' pertaining to the relationship between employers and employees. This provided the tribunal with wide powers to regulate employment conditions. The new Act restricted the Commission's determinations to a list of 20 'allowable matters', although it could still arbitrate on 'exceptional matters'. Awards were also required to be simplified in order to conform with the 20 allowable matters, which established a safety net of minimum standards. New arrangements for enterprise bargaining included a new form of agreement known as Australian Workplace Agreements (AWAs), which existed alongside certified agreements. Under AWA provisions, employers were able to enter into either a non-union collective agreement or a non-union individual contract with their employees. An AWA had to be lodged with the office of the Employee Advocate to ensure that the AWA met the 'no disadvantage test'; that is, did not lead to a reduction in the terms and conditions of employees when compared with their award entitlements. Where doubt existed, the AWA could be referred to the Commission as a final arbiter. The AWAs were greeted with hostility by unions as an attempt to further undermine the collective basis of industrial relations. Indeed, for the first time in Australian industrial relations history, registration of individual employment agreements was permitted to prevail over awards and certified agreements. While it was generally anticipated that AWAs would play a fairly minor role in regulating wages and conditions, they were part of both a broader trend towards greater diversity in labour market arrangements and the growing emphasis on the individualisation of employment relations.

Assessing the success of enterprise bargaining

The growth of enterprise agreements during the 1990s has been cited as a key indicator by both the proponents and critics of the trend towards a more decentralised industrial relations system in Australia. While there has been a definite shift towards enterprise bargaining, it has not led to a complete abandonment of awards. By late 1994 at the federal level, 5 per cent of employees had their conditions entirely determined by registered agreements. By contrast, 35 per cent of employees were entirely dependent on awards and 30 per cent relied on a mixture of awards and agreements, while 30 per cent had their conditions determined mainly on an informal basis (ACIRRT 1995). The vast majority of federal agreements are certified agreements that entail formal union involvement. Furthermore, most agreements involved additions to awards rather than comprehensive stand-alone documents. Although enterprise flexibility agreements (EFAs) were limited to a number of mainly small enterprises, unions expressed concerns that they could spread and become associated with attempts by larger employers to avoid or undermine union representation. This is more likely to be the case with the new AWAs than with EFAs.

A number of reasons have been advanced for the slow and modest growth of enterprise agreements. According to Dabscheck (1995:115) the traditional channels provided by tribunals to regulate industrial relations have continued to be actively utilised. Furthermore, according to the results of the first AWIRS (Callus et al. 1991) managers reported little difficulty in initiating workplace change irrespective of the operation of the AIRC. Economic factors may also have influenced the parties to stay within the traditional system of wage determination as economic recessions tend to be associated with low wage rounds. Quinlan (1996) also notes that despite the assertions that enterprise bargaining would bring about a significant improvement in productivity, through greater flexibility and workplace focus, there is little in the way of supporting evidence. Furthermore, flawed notions of productivity are commonly employed by organisations and there is only tenuous evidence of a direct relationship between labour flexibility, employment relations and productivity. Yet assertions about the productivity-enhancing aspects of enterprise agreements underpinned key arguments advanced by the BCA (1989; 1991).

Recent cross-country analysis by researchers at the Reserve Bank of Australia have questioned the arguments, advanced by the BCA and others, that the centralised system of industrial relations afforded insufficient flexibility to achieve economic efficiency (Coelli et al. 1994). It remains to be seen to what extent the opportunities provided by the Howard government to engage in greater enterprise bargaining will be taken up. Indeed, as Dabscheck (1995:115) points out, the measures undertaken by governments in recent years to facilitate enterprise agreements have in fact involved a re-regulation of employment relations, as their operation has required long and complex pieces of legislation.

Conclusion

The 1980s and the 1990s have proved to be periods of significant change in Australian employment relations, including the nature and strategies of the major parties and the structure of rules and regulations governing industrial relations. There was considerable economic turbulence, with mixed progress made in the quest to reduce high levels of inflation and unemployment. The Australian Labor Party governed at the federal level from 1983 to early 1996, when it was replaced by a Liberal–National Party coalition government. During the 1980s, under the Hawke Labor government, there was a gradual shift from a centralised system of industrial relations, administered by the AIRC, to a managed form of decentralism. Increased pressures for enterprise-based bargaining in the early 1990s, however, led the Keating Labor government in the direction of coordinated flexibility. While the Howard coalition government continued this general policy direction, the emphasis was on individualistic rather than collectivist approaches, and a system of fragmented flexibility in industrial relations was promoted.

The parties in employment relations underwent significant change during the 1980s. The major employer peak council, the former CAI, was beset by the departure of many of its leading affiliates. The impression of employer diversity was further strengthened by the emergence of a newly formed and high-profile employer pressure group, the BCA. By contrast, for unions, the 1980s witnessed unparalleled moves towards strategic coordination under the umbrella of the ACTU. The various State and federal industrial tribunals also experienced great change. Reviews of the federal system and most State systems of industrial relations resulted in alterations to the structure of the tribunals. Moreover, the focus of the tribunals shifted following the

1987 National Wage Case Decision. The federal Commission's centralised approach to wage determination was jettisoned in favour of moves to link wage increases to measures designed to improve efficiency and a trend towards more decentralised bargaining at the enterprise level.

In the late 1990s, employers, unions and governments have common and divergent concerns about future directions. Employers are concerned with economic performance in the face of increasingly competitive markets. Many employers continue to give a high priority to human resource strategies and place a greater enterprise focus on employment relations. They are, however, closely monitoring the outcome of enterprise agreements to see whether promises of increased productivity are realised.

Unions are also concerned with industry and enterprise performance since poor performance and low competitiveness constrain economic growth and exacerbate unemployment. Unions are looking closely at enterprise bargaining, charting the repercussions for members' wages, conditions and rights at work. Of particular concern is the position of low-paid workers. In addition, the ACTU and affiliated unions are busy implementing measures to improve services to members and so impress upon employees the relevance of unionism. Unions fear that failure to prove their relevance will result in diminished membership and reduced influence, neither outcome being attractive.

Federal and State governments of all political persuasions remain preoccupied with both the broader economic problems facing Australia and the related need for micro-economic reform. The federal Liberal–National Party coalition seems likely to pursue a diminished role for industrial tribunals and further curtail union power. It remains to be seen, however, whether support for the trend towards a decentralised system of industrial relations will continue. Whatever the outcome, it seems certain that employment relations will retain its place at the heart of political and economic debate in Australia.

A chronology of Australian employment relations

1788	European settlers arrived in New South Wales, with separate British colonies established subsequently.
1856	Unions won recognition of the eight-hour day. The Melbourne Trades Hall Council (THC) was formed.
1871	Sydney unions created a Trades and Labor Council (TLC); Brisbane and Adelaide unions followed.
1879	First Inter-Colonial Trade Union Conference.
1890–94	The Great Strikes. Following defeat by combined

employer and colonial government power, unions founded Labor parties in each colony.

1901	Commonwealth of Australia founded.
1904	Commonwealth Conciliation and Arbitration Court established under the Commonwealth Conciliation and Arbitration Act, with powers of legal enforcement.
1907	The *Harvester* Case established the principle of the basic wage above which the court could award a margin for skill.
1916	Widespread union opposition to the Labor government's conscription policy.
1917	The All-Australian Trade Union Congress adopted a socialist objective.
1927	Founding of the Australian Council of Trade Unions (ACTU).
1929	The Conservative government defeated in a federal election called over the proposed weakening of the Conciliation and Arbitration Court.
1949	A major coal strike, begun around economic demands, saw the federal Labor government take strong action to defeat the Miners' Union.
1950	Penal provisions, known as bans clauses, written into awards, enabled employers to seek an injunction from the court restraining unions taking industrial action.
1955	The Australian Labor Party split, with a breakaway group becoming the Democratic Labor Party.
1956	Following the Boilermakers' Case, the Arbitration Court was disbanded. The Conciliation and Arbitration Commission was set up with arbitral functions, and the Industrial Court with judicial responsibility.
1967	Metal Trades Work Value Case—the determination of a basic wage and margins was discontinued and a 'total wage' was introduced in lieu.
1969	The jailing of a union official for failure to pay fines for contempt of court led to extensive strike action throughout Australia.
1972	A federal Labor government was elected after 23 years of Liberal coalition government.
1975	Wage indexation introduced. Labor government dismissed.
1977	The CAI established as a national employers' confederation.
1979	The Australian Council of Salaried and Professional Associations merged with the ACTU.
1981	The Council of Australian Government Employee

	Organisations merged with the ACTU. Wage indexation abandoned.
1983	Hawke Labor government elected. ALP–ACTU Prices and Incomes Accord became the lynchpin of government policy. Return to centralised wage fixation and full wage indexation. Formation of Business Council of Australia.
1985	Report of Committee of Review of Australian Industrial Relations Law and Systems.
1987	Landmark National Wage Case Decision.
1988	Elaboration of structural efficiency principle. New federal Industrial Relations Act.
1989	Award restructuring. Domestic airline pilots' dispute.
1990	Accord Mark VI agreed between the ACTU and federal government.
1991	Acrimony over the April National Wage Case Decision. October National Wage Case Decision condones a shift to more enterprise bargaining. Paul Keating replaces Bob Hawke as Prime Minister.
1992	Further movement towards decentralisation of bargaining, including amendments to the Industrial Relations Act 1988.
1993	Labor government re-elected for an unprecedented fifth consecutive term (with Paul Keating as Prime Minister).
1994	The Industrial Relations Reform Act 1993 came into operation and extended the scope of enterprise bargaining.
1995	Amendment of unfair dismissal provisions of the 1993 Reform Act to simplify procedures.
1996	Election of the Liberal–National Party coalition government led by John Howard.
1997	The Workplace Relations and Other Legislation Amendment Act 1996 was proclaimed.

6 Employment relations in Italy

Claudio Pellegrini

This chapter starts by putting Italian employment relations into an economic, historical and political context. It describes the various union confederations, employers' organisations and the role of the state. It then considers the different levels and content of collective bargaining and concludes by commenting on recent issues.

Italy has a population of 57 million with a civilian employment-participation rate of only 60 per cent (see Appendix). This is a lower participation rate than in any of the other countries discussed in this book. One reason for this is a low official participation rate for women of only 44 per cent (see Appendix). As a consequence the employment population ratio is only 51 per cent, compared with 63 per cent in Germany and 73 per cent in the United States (USA).

Like most other industrialised market economies (IMEs), according to official statistics Italy has experienced a substantial rise in its unemployment rate. Between 1970 and 1996 the unemployment rate more than doubled from 5.3 per cent to 12 per cent (see Appendix). More than half of the unemployed are young people looking for their first job. In the 15–24 year age group the unemployment rate is 31 per cent. This evidence of a difficult transition from school to work partly reflects attitudes and family strategies. Sons and daughters remain longer in their parents' homes and may work in the informal sector while waiting for more stable jobs (Reyneri 1994). Long-term unemployment constitutes a large share of the unemployed: around 58 per cent were unemployed for more than 12 months during the mid-1990s.

For men in the 24–54 year age group unemployment is much lower, only 5 per cent; however, for women in this age group the rate is 10 per cent. In terms of human capital the younger generation have higher levels of schooling (6.2 per cent in the 20–24 year age group had only primary school education in 1991), but past poor school attendances will have an impact for a while (in the 45–55 year age group 47 per cent would have attended primary school only, compared with 29 per cent in France and none of this age group in Germany and the United Kingdom).

Relatively more people are employed in Italy's agricultural sector (7.5 per cent) than in any other country in this book, apart from Korea. However, this figure has declined from 34 per cent in 1959. Italy has a comparatively large industrial sector, which employs 32 per cent; only Germany, Japan and Korea employ relatively more people in this sector (see Appendix). Services employ the remaining 60 per cent. Another Italian characteristic is a large clandestine or 'informal' economy, which is unrecorded and untaxed. It has been estimated at 30 per cent of gross domestic product (GDP). This characteristic disguises the real rates of GDP, employment participation and unemployment.

In the period 1971–78, the average annual GDP increase was 3.7 per cent; in the European union (EU) the average was 3.2 per cent. In the period 1979–94, the annual increase was 2.2 per cent, about the average in the EU. Due to an increase in exports, GDP growth reached 2.9 per cent in 1995; however, in 1996 it declined to 0.8 per cent. There is a major cleavage between the north and south of Italy for all economic indicators. The labour force participation rate is much lower in the south, while pay levels are higher in the north. In the mid-1990s the unemployment rate in the south was around 20 per cent, compared with 6.5 per cent in the north. An average of 10 per cent of families in Italy live below the poverty line, but in the south the rate increases to 22 per cent. Such regional differences have a major influence on collective bargaining.

Italy's average rate of inflation between 1975 and 1984 was 16 per cent, higher than in any of the other countries discussed. During the period 1984–93 the average increase was 5.9 per cent, the third-highest rate of the countries discussed. However, inflation has declined substantially, being less than 2 per cent in 1997. Union wage restraint was a major component of this economic success.

The high level of public debt has been an increasing source of concern, particularly because the EU has set standards that have to be met by 1998. Government gross public debt reached 120 per cent of GDP in 1994; the EU guideline is 60 per cent. The budget deficit has declined sharply since 1991, and after a series of rigorous budgetary plans which included tax increases and cuts to public spending, Italy should reach the 3 per cent Maastricht deficit criterion by the late 1990s (see ch. 12). A large proportion of the deficit was accumulated in the 1980s due to increases in the cost of health, generous pension payments, more-than-average increases in public sector salaries, and subsidies to public-owned enterprises. The quality of many services provided by the public sector is, however, very low. This is especially apparent in areas such as post, railways and health care. Particularly worrisome for business leaders, who require efficient public services to compete internationally, are the slow public administration procedures. These impose many requirements and a heavy tax burden. While government spending has been reduced in recent years, interest payments on outstanding debt are a major burden that fuels a vicious circle of high lending rates—a major complaint for employers. The large presence of small and medium-sized enterprises (SMEs) and independent employment facilitates tax evasion. Because of this the tax burden is high, but not well distributed.

Another important development in the Italian economy has been the large role played by SMEs. Between 1971 and 1981, the percentage of employees in the manufacturing sector in workplaces of between ten and 49 employees increased from 20 to 26 per cent, while the percentage decreased in larger workplaces. In the early 1990s, 45 per cent of dependent employees were in firms with less than ten people—in the manufacturing sector the rate was 24 per cent. A consequence of this employment structure has been the high percentage of the self-employed: over 25 per cent (the highest level in Europe, except for Greece). This decentralised economic structure has several causes. Employers tried to avoid the rigidities of larger manufacturing workplaces where unions were stronger and labour relations more turbulent. However, the growth of smaller manufacturing workplaces gave rise in several areas to integrated manufacturing networks known as industrial districts (Pyke et al. 1990). These districts specialise in certain products that are manufactured by a large number of SMEs carrying out various stages of production. This allows the district to obtain significant economies of scale, while avoiding the rigidities of large corporations. Industrial districts are well adapted to flexible production processes needed for changing market requirements. Other elements that have made the system successful include an artisan tradition, strong family and community ties, and local government assistance. The strong performance of this type of manufacturing process has made an important contribution to overall economic growth.

The political context

After 1945, the major political parties that emerged were the Christian Democratic Party (*Democrazia Cristiana*, DC), a Catholic-oriented inter-class moderate party; the Communist Party (*Partito Comunista Italiano*, PCI), which from its revolutionary origins became a reform-oriented party and played the role of the major political opposition; the Socialist Party (*Partito Socialista Italiano*, PSI); other small Centre-oriented political parties; and a right-wing party, Italian Social Movement (*Movimento Sociale Italiano*, MSI), which was the heir of the Fascist tradition. Between 1945 and 1947 the anti-Fascist parties, including the PCI, formed a coalition government of national unity. The electoral success of the DC in 1948—the beginning of the Cold War—led to the exclusion of the PSI and the PCI from government. The DC Party remained in power until 1993, with about 35 per cent of the vote. Between 1948 and 1964 the government was based on a coalition between the DC and small Centre parties; after 1964 the PSI joined the coalition (Ginsborg 1990).

What were the consequences of this political context for employment relations? In countries such as Britain, Germany, Sweden and France, the functioning of the democratic system is based on competition between conservative and labour social-democratic parties, which alternate in power. In Italy, however, the main political opposition, the PCI, has never been in power since the post-war Government of National Unity ended in 1948. The lack of change between the two major parties was because the PCI (in its roots if not in its policies) was seen as too far to the Left to gain more support, or to form a coalition. The PCI was not considered a legitimate competitor for the national government. Some observers called this situation 'blocked democracy' and believed it had negative consequences for the political system. The party always in power perceived little risk of being challenged and became less accountable and less efficient in administration.

Unlike in other IMEs, a union–government relationship based on accords or social contracts (as in Sweden or formerly in Australia) was difficult to achieve and to enforce in Italy. First, because a government based on the major pro-labour party was never in power; second, because the presence of competing unions with different political orientations made it difficult to reach a long-lasting union commitment; and third, because the weaknesses of Italian government coalitions prevented the enforcement of agreements and the delivery of government promises that were part of the accord (Regini 1987; Golden 1988).

Because the government has been based on coalitions, conflicts among parties or divisions within the major party have often precipitated political crises, the formation of new governments and early elections. While the instability of governments tended to disguise the stability of the coalition that was in power until 1993, weak coalitions made it difficult to carry out government policies, especially when unpopular decisions had to be made. Weak government also required union consensus and consultation. For this reason, since the 1970s almost all governments have allowed unions to play a relatively large role in economic policy. Compared with other countries the degree of union involvement has been considerable, but this role has not been based on formal tripartite institutions or explicit incomes policies (Ferner & Hyman 1992; Compston 1995).

In the early 1990s political corruption was investigated by the judiciary and this accelerated the collapse of the traditional system. In the late 1990s the transition to the 'second Republic' had yet to be completed, and the goal of governmental stability and competition between two leading coalitions, alternating in power, had yet to be achieved. In 1997 a special commission investigated the constitutional changes required to provide greater stability for government coalitions and a federal system that would give more autonomy to the different regions.

Meanwhile the former political parties have disappeared. A change in the electoral system that was meant to limit political fragmentation did not achieve its intended result. Instead the number of political parties increased. The main political parties on the Right are *Alleanza Nazionale* (National Alliance, former MSI) and *Forza Italia* (Go on Italy), built on the media empire of Berlusconi. On the Left the PCI divided into two groups. The main one, *Partito Democratico della Sinistra* (Democratic Party of the Left, PDS) has embraced a more moderate political line, while *Rifondazione Comunista* (Communist Refoundation) is on the far Left. *Lega Nord* (Northern League) demands more autonomy for the northern part of the country. The DC splintered into several political groups, with some staying in coalitions of the Right, and one group moving to the Left.

In the general election of 1994 *Forza Italia*, leading a coalition with *Alleanza Nazionale* and *Lega Nord*, won the election. The government lasted only until the end of the year, however, as *Lega Nord* left the coalition. During this period the unions, for the first time, were faced by a government that had no ties with unions. An attempt at pension reform led to strong union opposition and made it clear that union consent was necessary for change in this area. The subsequent government was formed by technocrats but was sustained by a Centre–Left coalition based around the PDS. This government was able to change pension legislation and pass budgetary plans to reduce the deficit.

Early elections were held in April 1996 with the result favouring the Centre–Left coalition. For the first time, the strongest party of the Left was in government. In the economic arena the most impressive achievements were the reductions in inflation and public debt. Another important item on the agenda was to change the composition of welfare expenses. In Italy welfare expenses on average are similar to other EU countries (25 per cent of gross national product, GNP), but their composition is biased in favour of a very generous pension system. This absorbs 62 per cent of welfare payments, compared with around 45 per cent for other European countries. In the present situation few resources are left for other areas such as active labour market policies and income support for the unemployed.

The employment relations parties

It is important to consider some historical background. First, the late capitalist development of Italy: in 1901, only 238 out of every 1000 employees were in the industrial sector compared with 632 in Britain (Barbadoro 1973:21). Second, the weak democratic tradition: men over 30 gained the right to vote only in 1912 and women voted for the first time in 1946 in the first free general election after Fascism (voters had to choose between the monarchy and a republic and had to elect the Constituent Assembly to draft the new constitution). These two elements help to explain the strength of the revolutionary and socialist tradition within the Italian labour movement. Third, the large role played by the organisations of agricultural workers explains the importance in the union structure of the local geographical organisations called Chambers of Labour (*Camere del Lavoro*). Fourth, the absence of unions based on crafts was a result of unionism taking shape in Italy at the end of the nineteenth century (much later than in Britain) with socialists playing a determinant role. At that time the Second International considered industrial unionism the most appropriate form of organisation because it was the most conducive to worker unity, and because it was more suited to the organisation of the large manufacturing enterprises that were then emerging.

The Fascist period between 1922 and 1944 marked the end of all established unions. The corporatist experience left its marks in the following period, particularly in terms of the centralisation of the decision-making process and the use of government intervention. It also reinforced the industrial basis of unionism. For all these reasons, after 1944, all the confederations were determined to organise along industrial lines.

Another element to be considered is the presence of the Catholic tradition before and after Fascism. Compared with other countries, according to Jemolo (1963:6), 'the Italian Catholics were the last to join in organising the worker forces, in studying social problems . . . There was too long a tradition of agreements between the wealthy classes and the Church'.

The situation changed at the end of the nineteenth century. The *Encyclica Rerum Novarum* in 1891 encouraged the formation of Catholic organisations in the industrial sector, and competition with the socialist-oriented Chambers of Labour favoured the emergence of Catholic unionism. In 1918 the *Confederazione Italiana dei Lavoratori* was formed. In the same period, Catholics became active in the political arena for the first time since 1870 when the Papal States were annexed by the emerging Italian state.

The unions

The three major union confederations are the *Confederazione Generale Italiana del Lavoro* (CGIL), with about 5.2 million members; the *Confederazione Italiana Sindacati Lavoratori* (CISL), with 3.8 million; and the *Unione Italiana del Lavoro* (UIL), with 1.7 million in 1996. Also included in the membership are retired employees who belong to a separate structure in each confederation. Without the retirees, membership in the late 1990s for the CGIL, CISL and UIL was 2.4 million, 2 million and 1.3 million respectively. Union membership increased dramatically after 1969. In that year the three confederations had 2.6 million, 1.6 million and 0.7 million members respectively. Union density increased from 29 per cent in 1969 to nearly 50 per cent in 1980, before declining to 35 per cent in 1996. The largest organisation, CGIL, is Left-oriented; the CISL has a large, but not exclusively, Catholic component; the UIL has ties with Left and Centre parties. Dramatic changes in the political arena have transformed the traditional links between unions and political parties.

The relationship between unions and political parties has a long, complex history and only the most important phases and their consequences are highlighted in this chapter. In 1944, the representatives of the major political parties opposed to the Fascist regime (Communist, Catholic and Socialist) signed an agreement which later led to the formation of the CGIL. The three political components that formed the confederation remained together until 1948, when there was a rupture in the coalition government that had included Socialists and Communists. As a consequence there was a split in the CGIL. The Catholic component left the CGIL in 1948 and formed the CISL. In 1950 the Republicans and Social Democrats also left the CGIL and formed the UIL. Socialists remained in the CGIL but also gained strength in the UIL (Beccalli 1972). During the 1950s, the links between political parties and unions were more direct and the unions had little room for autonomous decision making. During the 1960s, inter-union cooperation began to emerge, together with a new political climate (a Centre–Left coalition) and the development of national and enterprise bargaining. This led to the unions becoming more politically independent. In 1973, when the three union confederations formed the *Federazione* CGIL–CISL–UIL, it was decided that their leaders would not also hold office in political parties or be members of Parliament

(Weitz 1975). In 1984 the unitary structure collapsed over disagreement regarding the change in the wage indexation system. Since then each confederation has regained autonomy of action, though this does not prevent unity on major issues.

While the political climate influenced union attitudes and decisions, there were many allegiances between unions and political parties; some unions had allegiances with parties in government and others with parties in opposition. Therefore, compromise was usually necessary between and within each organisation if the unions wanted to act together. The only time the unions have had to face a government with no union links was after the election of 1994, when a Centre–Right coalition held power for about six months. In this period union opposition to government policies became much stronger. The situation in the late 1990s, with a Left coalition in power, is different because the three major union confederations have no political links with parties in opposition. This has caused a realignment in union strategies and the idea of reunification is again on the agenda. The main difficulties are not from explicit political differences but from internal organisational resistance.

Besides the three major confederations in Italy there are also other unions. In 1950 the *Confederazione Italiana Sindacati Nazionali Lavoratori* (CISNAL) was founded by the heirs of the Fascist tradition. This confederation, however, plays no significant role in employment relations. There are also independent union organisations (so-called '*sindacati autonomi*'), which are particularly strong in the public sector, education, hospitals and transportation. The main peak councils are *Confederazione Italiana Sindacati Autonomi Lavoratori* (CISAL), strong in the municipalities and railways; *Confederazione Sindacati Autonomi Lavoratori* (CONFSAL), strong in education and public employees; and *Confederazione Italiana Sindacati Addetti ai Servizi* (CISAS) in other services. In the late 1980s many other powerful independent unions were formed in the education system, in transportation and in health services (Bordogna 1989).

Managers (*dirigenti*) also have their own organisations. The main peak council is *Confederazione Italiana Dirigenti di Azienda* (CIDA), with about 100 000 members. Forty per cent of them are in the industrial sector where the unionisation rate was 40 per cent in 1988 (Pellegrini 1989).

In analysing union structure it is important to keep in mind the differences between the legal framework, collective bargaining provisions and the *de facto* situation. From 1948 until 1970 the unions were not present as such in the workplace. By agreement with the major employers' organisation *Confindustria*, there were internal commissions (*commissioni interne*) that were elected by all the employees, mainly to administer the national agreements. The main competing unions presented candidates for the commissions, but the latter were not formal union structures as in the case of the French *comité d'entreprise* or the German *Betriebsrat* (see chs 7 and 8).

During the 1960s, when the economic situation was improving, the unions enjoyed more power; and as a result they tried to establish union representatives (*Rappresentanza Sindacale Aziendale*, RSA), similar to the *vertrauensmann* in Germany. In 1970 the Workers' Charter was enacted. Consequently workers had the right to establish RSA in the workplace, and to have them recognised as such by the most representative unions or those that had signed national–local collective agreements that applied in the workplace. RSA representatives had the right to a certain amount of working time for union activity, based upon the size of the firm, and were protected from dismissal.

During the early 1970s, there was also a large increase in the number of industrial disputes. During these conflicts new forms of worker representation were emerging based on shop stewards (*delegati*) for each work unit. Together the shop stewards formed the factory council (*consiglio di fabbrica*). Union and non-union members were eligible to vote and to be elected (Sciarra 1977). When the three main confederations formed the unitary structure in 1972 they decided to recognise the factory council as the union structure in the workplace, and the *delegati* enjoyed the legal protection given to RSA by the Workers' Charter in 1970.

Thus, at the workplace, employees had only one form of representation, which was also the basis of union organisation and played a major role in collective bargaining at enterprise level (Regalia et al. 1978). The collapse of the unitary process and the lack of agreed rules for electing the council prevented regular elections in these bodies. After many attempts, an agreement was finally reached in 1993. This agreement had many relevant elements regarding bargaining structures and incomes policies that will be examined later. According to the 1993 agreement, elections for the new unitary union representation (*Rappresentanza Sindacale Unitarie*, RSU) can be held in workplaces with more than 15 employees. Two-thirds of the seats are based on the results of an election among competing lists and the remaining seats are reserved for the unions that have signed agreements that apply in the workplace, and are assigned according to electoral results. The number of representatives ranges from three, in workplaces with less than 200 employees, to 30, in workplaces with 3000 employees. In larger workplaces, three representatives are added for each 500 employees. After the 1993 agreement about two million employees participated in an election. The average size of the workplaces was 190 employees, with a 72 per cent participation rate. The distribution of votes among the main unions was as follows: CGIL 48 per cent; CISL 28 per cent; UIL 16 per cent; other unions 4 per cent; null and void 4 per cent.

This confirmed the dominant role of the three major confederations, and among the 44 767 elected representatives the breakdown was 51 per cent, 30 per cent and 16 per cent respectively. There are regional variations. As an example, the CGIL reached 72 per cent in certain areas, such as Emilia-Romagna, but only 28 per cent in Sicily. The same is true for other unions. There are also differences based upon sectors but these are less pronounced.

Legislation on union representation and access to the bargaining table is particularly relevant in the public sector where union bargaining structures and representation have become fragmented. This has had negative consequences in terms of conflicts. The importance of legislative intervention in this area has become more urgent because of the problems created by the national referendum on union matters, held in 1995.[1]

Employers' organisations

The most important employers' organisation is the *Confindustria*, which represents associations of the largest firms, as well as SMEs. It is especially strong in the manufacturing and construction sectors. Firms may join both the regional multi-sector association and the national sector association: the two together form the *Confindustria*. In the late 1990s there were 18 regional federations, 107 local associations and about 140 sectoral organisations representing 107 000 firms with 4.2 million employees. There were 52 collective agreements.

The *Confindustria* has two main objectives: one concerns employment relations and the other concerns the broader economic, technical and political needs of members. Until 1994 public sector manufacturing enterprises had their own associations for the purpose of collective bargaining. The two most important were the ASAP and *Intersind*, which represented two large public conglomerates, the Italian National Institute for Hydrocarbons (*Ente Nazionale Idrocarburi*, ENI) and the Italian Institute for Industrial Reconstruction (*Istituto per la Ricostruzione Industriale*, IRI).

Public sector employers have been innovative and are often the first to make agreements during bargaining rounds. For instance, in the IRI group there was an important 1984 agreement that established joint committees for consultation on a large variety of issues related to strategic decisions and employment relations policies. However, retrenchments in the public sector and privatisation plans have imposed severe constraints on their innovative role. In 1994, the ASAP was dissolved and *Intersind* joined the *Confindustria*.

There are also private employers' organisations in the commercial sector (*Confcommercio*) and in agriculture (*Confagricoltura*), the latter with 648 000 local members; the banking and credit sector also has its own two organisations. Small firms are represented by the *Confapi*, which has 57 000 members, which employ about one million people, and has ten national agreements signed with different unions. Craft shops (*Affigiani*), cooperatives and small businesses (*Artigiani*) also have their own organisations and sectoral agreements.

Within the *Confindustria* there has been a tense relationship between large industrial groups and other firms over specific issues (Lanzalaco 1990). This has hindered the maintenance of a unified strategy towards the unions and the government. There have also been differences in employers' policies between capital- and labour-intensive industries, with the latter being more concerned with labour costs.

The *Confindustria* plays an important role in coordinating national bargaining in the major industrial sectors, and has a direct role in bargaining with the union confederations on agreements that apply nationally. This role is particularly vital during periods when national-level bargaining plays an important role, such as in the mid-1970s or after 1993. In the past the *Confindustria* traditionally had strong ties with the DC (Martinelli & Treu 1984:287). While relations were sometimes strained, in general it was pro-government. In the 1990s—a period of political turbulence—the *Confindustria* was successful in maintaining its independence, and judged government goals and achievements on the basis of issues that were important for its members.

When the leader of the Centre–Right coalition, Berlusconi (an influential member of the *Confindustria*) held power, his political efforts were not unanimously supported and the organisation was able to maintain its independence. When the Centre–Left coalition gained power in 1996 it chose Prodi as its leader, who for several years was president of the IRI group.

The role of the state

As in Britain, before the 1960s there was relatively little legal intervention in Italian employment relations in terms of regulating the parties. The new constitution established in 1948 had some provisions regarding the recognition of unions and the right to strike, but legislation on this issue was not enacted. Traditionally, many matters relating to social security and labour market institutions have been regulated by law. The importance of collective bargaining in determining conditions of employment has always been recognised by the government, and in 1959 all the existing agreements were transformed into law (the *erga omnes* provisions). They constitute minimum standards, often ameliorated by further legislation and bargaining (Giugni 1972).

Legislation, however, has played an increasingly prominent role since the late 1960s, but labour law does not generally regulate the bargaining process, the size of the bargaining unit, or the right to strike.

Nevertheless, in 1988, a law was passed that limited the right to strike in essential public services. Besides the earlier mentioned Workers' Charter, other significant laws regulate social security, minimum pay during layoffs and retirement benefits. In many cases, these laws were the result of direct bargaining between unions and government and were subsequently approved by Parliament and codified by law. In other cases there is a trilateral agreement between government, employers' associations and unions.

Bargained legislation was particularly important during the 1970s when unions initiated many changes in the social, as well as the political, arena. This was partly related to the immobility of the political structure: the unions became vocal on emerging national issues and thus compensated for the shortcomings of the political system (Giugni 1973:37–46). Although the unions succeeded in winning reforms in social security arrangements, they also sought reforms in housing, health services, transport and fiscal policies. In these latter areas they were less successful. In the late 1990s, legislation based on agreements with unions has become important to reach the economic indicators established by the EU's Maastricht Treaty (see ch. 12).

Changes in the pension system and the provision of health care were key issues that were bargained with the unions and later legislated by the Parliament. In September 1996 the social partners and the government signed a 'Pact for Jobs'; however, related legislation was not approved until mid-1997. The main elements concerned training, apprenticeships, school-to-work transition and efforts to create a more flexible labour market. Compared with the EU average, Italy has a lower percentage of workers employed on a part-time (6.1 per cent in Italy and 16.7 in the EU) and temporary basis (7.2 per cent in Italy and 11.4 per cent in the EU).

The government intervenes as a mediator during collective bargaining, particularly on national- or industry-level agreements. This mediation role increased during the late 1970s, and many settlements were possible only because employers' costs were subsidised by the state. When large firms downsized their workforces in the 1990s, the Labour Ministry played a role by favouring early retirement plans and offering other opportunities for redundant employees. Such possibilities have been much reduced due to the necessity of reducing the fiscal deficit.

The government can also have a major impact on employment relations when bargaining with unions in the public sector, which in Italy is relatively large. Besides administration and education it includes many services, such as health, transport and mail. In the 1990s many publicly owned enterprises were privatised or joined private employers' associations. This has considerably reduced direct government influence. By the late 1990s conditions of employment in the public sector had improved to a greater extent than those in comparable employment in the private sector. This improvement reflected the lack of international competition, political influence and in some cases the fact that essential services were being provided. In recent years there have been several attempts to correct the disparity between the private and public sectors. The responsibility for bargaining has been given to the *Agenzia per la Rappresentanza Negoziale delle Pubbliche Amministrazioni* (Agency for Bargaining in the Public Administrations, ARAN), an agency that is at arm's length from political pressure. This agency has to follow government guidelines in terms of the cost of any agreement that is reached. Agreements signed by the ARAN cover 3 million workers, or around 20 per cent of dependent employees. The most important groups are in schools, the health sector and municipalities. Judges, the army, university professors and other specific categories are outside the system and their conditions of employment are established by law. In 1993, legislation was enacted that transformed the legal basis of employment relations in the public sector and made it closer to that of the private sector. Moreover, public sector wage increases have been linked to private sector central agreements.

Government intervention is crucial when enterprises face economic difficulties and ask for the prolonged use of Wage Integration Funds (*Cassa Integrazione Guadagni*, CIG) (although the other social partners also participate in the decision process). These funds guarantee up to 80 per cent of pay during layoffs. The CIG has two main forms: the ordinary fund is financed by employers' contributions and used during temporary crises for three-month periods; the special fund is used for more serious and prolonged crises, and is financed by the state. The CIG has become essential for facilitating technological and structural change. Since 1980, it has been used more and more frequently. In 1994 the CIG paid 358 million hours; however, in 1995, an improvement in the economic situation reduced this to 243 million hours.

Another important role of the state is the opportunity it provides for union representation in a series of governmental organisations at national and local levels, and in many administrative structures— particularly those associated with the labour market and welfare administration. Nevertheless, during the 1990s there was a tendency for unions to leave many of the positions they held in ministries and social security institutions because it was felt that union representatives lacked administrative skill and risked being entangled in the internal politics of these organisations.

The main processes

In Italy there are three major bargaining levels: national, industry, and enterprise or workplace. There is also a regional level for certain issues.

In some sectors, such as agriculture and construction, there is also collective bargaining at a provincial level. The three major collective bargaining levels have played different roles over the years and in general they deal with different issues (Baglioni 1991). In the past, however, there were disputes between employers and unions, with employers wanting to avoid bargaining on issues that had already been settled at a higher bargaining level.

In 1993, for the first time an agreement established the role to be played by each level of collective bargaining. This agreement helped to establish procedures in the employment relations arena. It is important to note that Italian contract deadlines are not as important in the bargaining process as they are in the USA. Agreements are often signed months after the expiration of the contract and are applied retrospectively when possible; alternatively, a lump sum of money is given to the employees to compensate for such losses.

During the bargaining process there are also strikes that usually last only a few hours or one day at the most. The number of working days lost through industrial disputes in Italy is high compared with most of the other countries in this book (see Appendix). Italy appears to be in an even worse position in relation to the number of workers involved in disputes (Franzosi 1995); however, since the mid-1980s there has been a significant decline in strike activity. Days lost per 100 000 employees for economic strikes during the period 1990–94 averaged 1742 per year. Ten years before, in the period 1980–84, it was 8683. Strikes are the most commonly used form of industrial action and are often accompanied by widely attended street demonstrations. As in France (see ch. 7) the Italian unions do not have strike funds. Usually there are no peace clauses in agreements and consequently strikes can be held at any stage. These can be in solidarity with other workers, in opposition to government decisions and for issues not strictly related to wages and working conditions. During the period 1990–94, 44 per cent of the total number of days lost occurred in so-called 'political strikes'.

National bargaining

Agreements at the national level between major employers' associations such as the *Confindustria* and the union confederations have played an important role in different periods for different reasons. They were very important during the 1950s, became less so between 1965 and 1975 when bargaining increased at the enterprise and industry levels, and again became important after 1975. In the mid-1980s attempts at stable centralised agreements collapsed. In 1993 national agreements became prominent again and several major issues were settled at this level.

In the 1950s the unions were too weak to engage in much bargaining at the enterprise level and lacked legislation that favoured their presence in enterprises. For this reason the national agreement was the most important, and sectoral agreements (for such sectors as textiles and construction) merely adapted their contents to the specific conditions that prevailed in each sector.

National agreements could deal with hours, holidays, use of the CIG (later transformed into law), seniority pay, compulsory or voluntary retirement, and training. The bargaining process at this level is strongly centralised and highly politicised. Although unions consult members before and after the agreements, there is little rank-and-file participation. Nonetheless, bargaining is given wide media coverage, as in Australia and Britain. This is unlike the USA where the bargaining structure is too decentralised to be generally given much national attention.

National bargaining became prominent again after 1975 for many reasons. First, during a period of economic recession there was little scope for bargaining at lower levels where employers' resistance was high; second, in centralised bargaining the unions could use their influence in the political arena; and third, the employers could benefit from a type of bargaining that inevitably involved governments eager to reach a settlement and which were, therefore, often willing to mediate and share the cost of settlements (Treu 1983). In the mid-1980s national bargaining was less successful. After some progress during 1983 in slowing the pace of inflation following changes in the indexation system, further efforts at stable incomes policies collapsed in 1984. In the 1990s centralised agreements again play a leading role and the agreement reached in 1993 became a cornerstone for incomes policies and the regulation of collective bargaining structures.

The most crucial issue that was bargained at national level was the *scala mobile* (the national indexation agreement), which guaranteed automatic wage increases based upon the price index of a selection of basic goods. Because it has played such an important role the main phases of this agreement will be highlighted.

After its introduction in 1950 it was modified frequently; in 1969, for instance, differential increases based on gender or geographical differences were eliminated. A major change was agreed in 1975 to eliminate gradually any differences based on occupation or skill levels: henceforth, after 1977, all employees were to receive the same increase. The 1975 agreement increased the percentage of wages covered by indexation from 64 per cent in 1974, to 90 per cent in 1977. After 1977 the *scala mobile* had many, and often unforeseen, consequences. The persistently high level of inflation and the high percentage of wages affected by indexation, flattened wage differentials (Regalia & Regini 1995) and left little room for wage bargaining. Moreover, the apparently higher levels of pay pushed employees into higher tax brackets. This made it more difficult for unions to influence the real levels of pay. The unions that defended the indexation system were blamed for the high inflation. The agreement was seen by many as a further step towards the centralisation of bargaining and towards the establishment of continuing trilateral bargaining between employers, unions and government.

In 1984 there was disagreement within the *Federazione* CGIL–CISL–UIL about the decision to concede a further reduction of indexation in exchange for concessions on fiscal and other issues. The CISL, UIL and the socialist component of CGIL agreed that there were conditions for a settlement, while the communists disagreed. The result was a serious split between the unions and the end of the *Federazione* CGIL–CISL–UIL. In 1984, the government decided to use a decree (based upon the accord with CISL, UIL and part of CGIL) to put a ceiling on the amount of indexation that could be paid. In this period the Prime Minister was a Socialist (Craxi) while the PCI was the main opposition; this helps in understanding the division within CGIL. The PCI asked for a national referendum on the issue, which was held in 1985 and supported the government decision by 54 per cent to 46 per cent.

In subsequent years national bargaining continued in several areas but was not part of a stable trilateral agreement. The main issues dealt with at this level were fiscal policy, national health services, special contracts for training and work, apprenticeships, and non-standard contracts of employment ('solidarity contracts' and part-time contracts). Work-training contracts have been particularly successful; they are reserved for people up to 32 years of age and can last two years. The employer has to provide a minimum amount of training and can benefit from reduced wages and financial benefits. These agreements were first reached in 1984 and have subsequently been improved, particularly in the area of training. They have been instrumental in developing social dialogue in the area of training, which was not usually an area that received much attention from unions. Very slowly and with some delay joint committees and agencies concerned with this issue have been established (Pellegrini 1994).

In the early 1990s centralised bargaining regained prominence in a different economic and political setting. In 1992 the indexation system was abolished, there was a major political crisis due to corruption scandals, and a severe monetary crisis pushed the Italian currency out of the European monetary system (EMS). The 1993 agreement was particularly important because it settled procedural issues as well as substantive ones. The structure and content of collective bargaining, union representation at the workplace and several other issues formed part of this historic agreement. The Italian government (which at that time included expert technocrats with Giugni as Labour Minister) decided that dialogue with the social partners was indispensable to confront the economic crisis and to meet the deadline established by the EU for monetary union. This led to a new system for wage adjustments, with new procedures for industry- and enterprise-level agreements (discussed below).

Bargaining at national level is influenced by the politics of the current government. When the Centre–Right coalition led by Berlusconi was in power it was impossible to reach an agreement on pension reform, and by the autumn of 1994 there was significant confrontation between the social partners. Agreement on these issues was reached the following year when Treu became Minister of Labour in a different government coalition.

Industry-level bargaining

Agreements are signed for various segments of the economy by national unions. In the industrial sector there are four major agreements: metals, textiles, chemicals and construction. As in Australia, the metals agreement often sets a pattern that others follow. Even though there has been a reduction in the number of agreements, one union may be involved in negotiating many agreements with several employers' associations representing, for instance, artisans, SMEs and cooperatives. There are about 20 national unions in each of the three confederations and in manufacturing alone there are more than 25 agreements with private sector employers' associations.

Industry agreements began to play a larger role in the mid-1950s, but in the 1970s they became very important. Major bargaining rounds were held about every three years between 1969 and 1993.

From 1969 to 1976 such industry-level bargaining extended the settlements won in union strongholds to the entire country. This was particularly important given the economic and social differences between the north and the south, and in view of the differences in union strength between large and small enterprises. In many cases the agreements specified minimum conditions. These could be improved depending on the bargaining strength of the unions at enterprise level. Industry agreements have been used increasingly by the courts as a standard in disputes, even for employers that had not signed the agreements either directly or through their associations. Industry agreements usually exclude topics that have been regulated by national bargaining and/or legislation. The latter has a larger scope and extends to issues such as retirement, insurance and unemployment compensation, and union and employee rights. More controversial is the overlapping of issues in industrial and enterprise bargaining. This has occurred in several areas but is always opposed by employers.

The 1993 national agreement accorded a key role to sector agreements and regulated the timing, content and process. The new system provided for a national agreement lasting four years, to be reopened after two years for a wage adjustment. Almost all the sectors renewed their agreements. In the absence of an indexation system the wage adjustments were based on the difference between the inflation forecast, when the agreements were signed, for the period 1993–94, and the inflation that actually occurred. In the majority of cases renewals have been reached in a reasonable time, with increases in line with the inflationary target. In the metals sector in 1996, however, the bargaining period lasted nine months and there was a lengthy dispute. The main area of disagreement was the employers' position that with low levels of inflation, two levels of bargaining (industrial and enterprise) were too many. This position challenged the bargaining structure agreed in 1993. To understand the employers' position it is important to appreciate that in large enterprises where enterprise agreements are prevalent, economic increases are still not clearly linked to economic indicators. Increases at enterprise level tend not to be reversible when economic conditions become less favourable. It was also possible that the employers increased their opposition to obtain economic incentives from a government that was very keen to settle the controversy. Incentives for buying new cars were given and this, more than any other mediation effort tried by the government, was the decisive element.

Industry agreements tend to focus on job classifications and descriptions, hours and overtime, compensation and incentive systems, holidays, discipline, union rights and the disclosure of information to unions. In the metals agreements, for instance, the entire workforce is classified into eight classes. Classes 2–5 are shared by white-collar and blue-collar workers; consequently the traditional rigid separation between these categories has been reduced. Particularly innovative has been the reorganisation of the classification system in the chemical sector, which is based on six levels and 14 organisational positions, with provisions for job enlargement and career development.

The unions have generally achieved their goal of narrowing the differentials in terms of pay and fringe benefits. However, in relation to pay, it is generally accepted that differences have been squeezed too much. Inflation and *scala mobile* flat-rate increases reduced the average differential between white-collar workers and blue-collar workers to 30 per cent. This has become a crucial issue for unions because it has prompted more employers to give increases to employees individually, undermining the unions' role in representing the workforce collectively. Since the mid-1980s there has been an attempt to increase wage differentials between levels in the seven categories. In the metals sector, where all blue-collar and white-collar employees are classified, the basic wage has a range index of 100 to 146. Real wages however have a larger differential because increases to individual employees may not be based upon agreements, and tend to be concentrated at the higher echelon of the classification system.

Technological and organisational changes will make it necessary in the future to reconsider the classification system, and related issues including assigning employees to various levels, content of the jobs included within each level, job rotation and career development.

In the 1980s there was a small reduction in the 40-hour standard week in some manufacturing industries. In the 1990s there was usually a limit of 150 hours overtime per year. Each employee has four weeks annual vacation.

In the area of union rights in the workplace, the most important provisions are those related to the functioning of the RSU, direct deductions of union dues from wages, and time allowed off for union activity. By law, each employee can take up to eight hours each year for union meetings during working time, within the workplace. The unions usually use part of the paid time in order to employ a shop steward for full-time union activity—these provisions are often improved by industry and enterprise agreements. The impact of a 1995 national referendum, which abolished legislation related to the system of direct deductions of union dues from wages, has not yet been widely felt because the issue is also regulated by collective agreement.

Collective bargaining at industry level has also been used to influence employers' strategies in terms of investments, subcontracting and technological change. Information disclosure provisions were negotiated in the late 1970s and were considered a first step towards increased industrial democracy. As in Britain, Australia and other countries, the results have been disappointing partly because of employer resistance and partly because of lack of union expertise. In the early 1980s, this level of bargaining was frustrated because of the difficulties and delays in reaching agreements at the national level (particularly on *scala mobile*). In the following bargaining rounds there have been more items related to information disclosure and almost all the agreements provide for the creation of joint committees to collect and present data; however, the full implementation of these provisions has generally not occurred.

Most bargaining rounds have one or more key issues, such as information rights, working time, classification systems or wage increases. In the years when the indexation system was able to provide for wage increases, bargaining focused on other elements.

In recent years, some innovative issues that have been dealt with at this level include vocational training and the creation of joint agencies to administer it. Another relatively new issue introduced in collective bargaining is affirmative action in favour of people with disabilities and other disadvantaged groups. Following an EU directive, the issues of safety measures and related training are also growing in importance.

The agreements have also opened up the possibility of the creation of pension and health provisions—new territory in industrial agreements. In traditional services such as the railways, banks and postal services, the trend is towards a reduction in employment. Employment in the services sector has often grown in areas outside the realm of collective bargaining. The reorganisation of Italy's financial sector, considered to have higher costs and lower productivity than that of other comparable countries, is particularly painful. In this area, the agreement attempts to reduce the role played by seniority in wage determination.

In the public sector, bargaining activity was carried out by the ARAN and the renewed agreement provided increases in accord with government decisions. The most important issue remains the reduction of fringe benefits that are still found in the public sector in terms of pensions, security of employment and conditions of employment.

Enterprise bargaining

Enterprise-level collective bargaining has been important since 1969 as more stewards have been recognised in the workplace. Legislation in 1970 gave legal protection to union representatives in the workplace. In the early 1970s unions extended the scope of bargaining in enterprise agreements and later extended the scope in industry and national agreements.

Between 1975 and 1980 the role of enterprise bargaining was more limited, because the indexation system did not leave enough scope for wage bargaining. After the failure of national agreements in 1984, adjustments at the enterprise level were important for the success of the restructuring process, and 'micro-concertation' developed (Regini & Regalia 1997). In 1992, to reduce inflation, enterprise bargaining was blocked for more than one year.

During enterprise bargaining, stewards play a major role in formulating the claim, while the bargaining is usually conducted together with full-time union officials. In the 1993 national agreement, the rights to bargain were given to the RSU. This agreement also established that the duration of enterprise agreements would be four years and that the content of the bargaining would be established at industry level.

The contents of the agreements differ depending on the size of the enterprise, the type of product and the method of production. In general, at the enterprise level, an important issue has been supplementary pay increases. Actual wages in large establishments are much higher than the standards set at national level. The 1993 national agreement establishes that increases at enterprise level have to be linked to productivity increases. A major problem is selecting an appropriate indicator. Unions have demanded more participation to have a better understanding of the financial condition of the enterprise, while employers would like wage increases to be temporary. According to a 1997 Bank of Italy survey, in enterprises with more than 50 employees 20–25 per cent of firms made distinctions among the three main employee groups (blue-collar, white-collar and managers), 57 per cent of firms gave increases to all categories, while only 4 per cent had provisions related to individual employees.

The same survey indicated that in one-third of the firms the increases were not linked to performance. Around half of the agreements provided for increases that were flexible only with regard to improved economic circumstances, and made no allowance for deteriorating economic conditions.

Other elements included in enterprise agreements are the distribution of working hours, overtime, assignment of jobs to the national classifications, stewards' facilities, health hazards, canteen costs and food quality. Information rights have, to a certain extent, increased the unions' consideration of the economic constraints faced by firms, but bargaining continues to be confrontational. Such bargaining is the main process used by employees to influence managerial decisions; it often involves workers invoking sanctions.

There have been an increasing number of *ad hoc* joint committees formed by stewards and managers for handling issues on a more cooperative basis. In the economic recession the main controversies were related to layoffs, reductions in working hours, mobility and the consequences of technological change (Garonna & Pisani 1986).

A national survey of 793 establishments with more than 20 employees showed that in 1993 only 15 per cent had signed enterprise agreements (Pellegrini 1995). In the metals sector in the years 1991, 1992 and 1993 the percentage was 23, 27 and 17, while in retail the percentage was 3.5, 11 and 10. The level of enterprise bargaining was particularly low in 1993 because of an unfavourable economic situation and the larger role being played by centralised agreements. In 1994 the proportion of firms that signed an enterprise agreement declined to 10 per cent.

The proportion of workplaces that undertake collective bargaining increases with size. In 1993, in firms with less than 100 employees it was 9 per cent, but in those with more than 500 it reached 27 per cent. The only other variables that were statistically significant in explaining the presence of agreements were unionisation levels and serious economic crises.

The issues most frequently dealt with vary in different years and according to sectors. In the mid-1990s the issues most often dealt with were wages (63 per cent), hours (40 per cent), employee rights (13 per cent), health and safety (18 per cent), and training (5 per cent). Among the enterprises surveyed, 31 per cent had used integration funds to assist in laying off employees. During the period from 1991 to 1994, 48 per cent of firms had signed at least one agreement.

Conclusion

The 1990s have witnessed major changes in the political landscape. These developments were partly linked to international events. The collapse of the communist systems facilitated the final transformation of the PCI into a democratic Left-oriented party. Much corruption, caused by unchallenged long-held political power, was brought out into the open, while the resulting prosecutions led to the end of traditional parties and the formation of new coalitions. A stable government has yet to emerge and the necessary transformation of the constitution is still ongoing. The economic agenda, particularly in financial issues, has been largely established at the EU level. Painful steps have been made towards reducing the budget deficit, and moving towards the parameters set by the Maastricht Treaty—a position many had believed impossible. Particularly impressive were reductions in inflation and the fiscal deficit. Demographic changes—the population is ageing and Italy has the lowest birth rate in Europe—will necessitate tough readjustments in the social security system, especially in retirement and health services.

Partly aided by currency devaluation, economic activity recovered after the downturn of 1993 and small enterprises regained their competitiveness. This strategy will not be available in the future, however, as the Italian currency has rejoined the European monetary system, putting more pressure on firms to improve their competitiveness. Many weaknesses remain: the south is far behind; the recovery did not improve unemployment significantly; and public services are still less efficient than those of Italy's major competitors. In the public service area, changes in terms of privatisation, better administration and employment relations are still slow.

The employment relations system has performed surprisingly well. Major national agreements were concluded and made a large contribution towards lowering inflation. When the currency came under downward pressure, unions were helpful in restoring international confidence by making major concessions. At lower levels, industry agreements were reached in accordance with established procedures and wage increases were at levels compatible with the goal of lowering inflation. The picture of bargaining at the enterprise level is less clear, with wage increases linked to increases in productivity. This requires a set of agreed standards and a better developed information system.

Some problems have emerged with the 1993 bargaining structure. Employers would like to have only one level of bargaining because they believe the reduction in inflation does not allow for two levels. The unions oppose such a scenario and argue that both levels are necessary: an enterprise level, and an industry level for SMEs that do not have enterprise bargaining. In large workplaces, however, agreements are not yet linked to productivity. Hence further innovations are likely.

The agreed rules for the election of union representatives have confirmed the importance of the three major confederations at the expense of independent unions. In the service sector, however, there has been a fragmentation of union representation and legislation will be required to regulate the issue.

Looking at the role played by different bargaining levels, different periods exhibit cycles that alternate between centralisation and decentralisation. Devising a model that will explain these shifting trends for several countries is a major challenge for comparative research. In the case of Italy in the 1990s the trend has been towards centralisation. The need to achieve the standards required for EU monetary union, and the need for union consent for budgetary cuts implemented by governments based on weak coalitions, are key elements in explaining this shift. The future will probably see the pendulum shift again as enterprises adjust to specific conditions.

While changes in the political situation have led to less conflict among unions, it will be difficult to create a unitary structure of unions. The main challenge is still to reduce unemployment. Several changes have made the labour market more flexible. It remains to be seen if they will have a beneficial impact.

A chronology of Italian employment relations

1848	First printing workers' associations.
1872	National Printing Union formed.
1891	*Rerum Novarum* papal encyclical.
1893	The Italian Federation of Chambers of Labour (*Federazione Italiana delle Camere del Lavoro*) was formed by the union organisations of 12 northern cities.
1906	The General Confederation of Labour (*Confederazione Generale del Lavoro*, CGL) was founded, including the Chambers of Labour and national unions.
1907	The Catholic Economic and Social Union was founded (*Unione Economico-Sociale dei Cattolici d'Italia*).
1918	The above union became the Italian Confederation of Labour (*Confederazione Italiana dei Lavoratori*, CIL).
1922	After the March on Rome, Mussolini became Prime Minister.
1922	CGIL held its last congress.
1926	Only Fascist unions allowed, which together with the Employers' Confederation formed the National

	Council of Corporations (*Consiglio Nazionale delle Corporazioni*) as part of the corporate state.
1943	Fall of Fascism in the south. It remained in power in the north until 1945.
1944	Rome trade union pact among Communists, Christian Democrats and Socialists provided for the creation of the CGIL.
1945–48	Coalition government of anti-Fascist political parties, including Socialists and Communists.
1948	The Christian Democrats (DC) won a parliamentary majority and excluded left-wing parties from government. Catholics left the CGIL and later formed the CISL.
1949	Social Democrats and Republicans also left the CGIL and later formed UIL. Socialists continued in the CGIL, which remained the largest peak council.
1962	After a period of economic expansion, union weakness and bitter competition, union unity developed in some manufacturing sectors.
1963	The Socialists joined the coalition government.
1969	Following intense industrial conflict, new unitary forms of workers' representation developed and unions ended formal political links.
1970	The so-called Workers' Charter favoured and protected unions.
1973	Three major peak councils united to form the *Federazione* CGIL–CISL–UIL.
1974	The *Federazione* and the employers changed the *scala mobile* indexation system—lower paid workers were particularly favoured.
1977–79	The Communist Party supported the government, but with no direct participation in it.
1983	Tax structure and *scala mobile* changed after two years of controversy. Changes in other areas were also put into effect or promised with the leading role of government as mediator. A new law was passed that formalised collective bargaining in the public sector.
1984	Negotiations for another national agreement dealing with the indexation system broke off. Only the CISL and UIL agreed with the government offer. The *Federazione* CGIL–CISL–UIL ended. The government enforced the accord reached with the CISL and UIL by decree.
1985	The referendum narrowly supported cuts in wage indexation (54.3 per cent versus 45.7 per cent). New

bargaining rounds were held related to the indexation system and hours of work. New legislation introduced the category of cadres (before this there were only three groups of employees: top managers, white-collar and blue-collar workers).

1986   A new indexation system agreed in the private sector, by which the coverage was reduced.

1988–89   Autonomous unions challenged the leading role of the established confederation in the public sector.

1990   A new law was passed that gave some protection from unfair dismissal in small enterprises (less than 15 employees).

1991   New legislation regulated the labour market, introducing greater flexibility in hiring practices.

1992   A new central agreement between the social partners and government abolished the *scala mobile*. The judges began an investigation into political corruption: these inquiries eventually discovered widespread corruption in the political parties that held power.

1993   A new central agreement was reached regarding incomes policy, collective bargaining structure and union representation structure in enterprises.

1994   A Centre–Right coalition won the majority on the basis of a new electoral system; the government led by Berlusconi was in power from March to December.

1995   A new government headed by technocrats was formed with support from the Centre–Left. The pension system was changed. Attempts to again change the political system failed and new elections were held in April 1996.

1996   The election gave a parliamentary majority to the Centre–Left coalition. Severe budgetary plans were passed in order to reduce the public deficit and reach the standards established by the Maastricht Treaty for European monetary union.

1997   The government and unions signed pacts on job creation in the private and public sectors.

7 Employment relations in France[1]

Janine Goetschy and Annette Jobert

France has a population of 58 million and a gross domestic product (GDP) of \$1538 billion. Between 1985 and 1995 its average annual growth rate was 2 per cent. Its inflation rate in 1996 was 2 per cent (see Appendix). The budget deficit, which has increased markedly since 1992, represented 3.5 per cent of GDP in 1995—public debt has multiplied 7.5 times in 15 years. Public deficit reduction has become one of the major objectives of French economic policy, which reflects its membership of the European monetary union (EMU) and its wish to meet the Maastricht criteria (see ch. 12).

France was the Organisation for Economic Co-operation and Development (OECD) member country that experienced the longest and largest uninterrupted rise in unemployment after the first oil-price shock in 1973, with unemployment reaching 12.3 per cent in 1996. Moreover, the nation also suffers from severe problems associated with unemployed youth, unemployed women and the long-term unemployed. The unemployment rate among young people, those less than 25 years old, declined slightly between 1985 and 1991, from 25.8 per cent to 19.8 per cent, but increased to 29.5 per cent in 1994. Unemployment is highest among less-qualified youth. In addition, many jobs that young people manage to obtain are essentially 'precarious' and poorly paid. Job prospects generally deteriorated from 1973 onwards for those with low educational levels. In 1995, male unemployment reached 10.7 per cent compared with 14.8 per cent for women, while the difference between male and female unemployment has scarcely diminished in France since 1985. The share of the long-term unemployed—those unemployed for more than one year—in total unemployment rose from 21.6 per cent in 1973 to 37.3 per cent in 1994. However, the share of long-term unemployment in France has remained lower than the European Union (EU) average since the mid-1980s.

In line with the international trends, since the 1970s the forms of employment in France have been changing substantially. By the mid-1990s, those in temporary employment represented about 11 per cent of the labour force, while about 16 per cent were in part-time employment. Female employment has continued to grow. The employment participation rate of women increased from 46 per cent in 1963 to 60 per cent in 1995.

Before the advent of the Fifth Republic in 1958, politics in France were more volatile than in most of the other European countries discussed in this book. There are four main political parties in France. The *Rassemblement pour la République*—mainly Gaullists—and the *Union pour la Démocratie Française* (UDF)—a combination of Independent Republicans and Christian Democrats parties—are broadly towards the Right of the political spectrum, while the Communist Party and the Socialist Party are to the Left of Centre.

Between 1958 and 1981, France was governed by Right-of-Centre governments. The Socialists made a decisive gain in 1981, when a Socialist President, François Mitterrand, was elected. Initially his government was a Socialist–Communist coalition, but the Communists left the coalition in 1984. Although Mitterrand's first term as President did not finish until 1988, the Socialists lost the 1986 general election and were replaced by a right-wing government, under Prime Minister Jacques Chirac. In 1988, Mitterrand was re-elected for a second presidential mandate by a large majority vote and stayed in office until 1995, when Jacques Chirac of the Gaullist Party replaced him. Between 1988 and 1993, Socialist governments led by three successive Prime Ministers (Rocard, Cresson and Beregovoy) were in power. However, the general elections of March 1993 resulted in a crushing defeat for the Left and a victory for the Gaullists and the Centre–Right UDF. This resulted in the election of a government of the Right led by Edouard Balladur. After the 1995 presidential elections, Jacques Chirac chose Alain Juppé as Prime Minister in a Cabinet that also included members of the centrist UDF. The battle against unemployment, which involved a radical 'five-year employment' law, as well as the reform of the social protection system (social security and pensions), constituted two cornerstones of the governments of the Right from 1983 to 1997.

In June 1997, Jacques Chirac called an early general election. This resulted in a defeat for the Right and a win for the Socialist Party and its allies. Led by Prime Minister Lionel Jospin, the new government included three Communists and one 'Green'.

The employment relations parties

Industrialisation and urbanisation developed in France during the mid-nineteenth century, rather later than in Britain. Strikes were not permitted until 1864, but even then unions were still illegal. However, many informal unions were organised during this period on a local level. There were some parallels with the origins of unions in English-speaking countries. Craftsworkers were the first to organise, but craft unions were soon displaced by industrial unionism. The early unions were often involved in violent clashes with state agencies and employers, who tried to suppress them. Unions were eventually legalised in 1884.

The present features of French unions derive partly from their early history and their ideological complexion. The importance of anarchists and revolutionary socialists within the labour movement and the specific characteristics of French employers, who tended to be either paternalistic or reactionary in their attitudes, heavily influenced French employment relations. This helps explain the traditional lack of mutual recognition between the employment relations parties (the social partners) and the important interventionist role of the French state in industrial and social matters. This tends to make it difficult for unions and employer organisations to recruit and retain members.

The unions

The French union movement has been characterised by pluralism, rivalry and fragmentation on the one hand, and paucity of financial and organisational resources on the other. Since the 1970s, these structural weaknesses have been particularly apparent. Union density has traditionally been low in France. It was around 23 per cent in the mid-1970s, fell to about 16 per cent by 1985 (Mouriaux 1986), then declined to around 11 per cent by the mid-1990s (see Appendix).

There are five national union confederations in France (see Table 7.1). These are the *Confédération générale du travail* (CGT); the *Confédération française démocratique du travail* (CFDT); the *Force ouvrière* (FO); the *Confédération française de l'encadrement-Confédération générale des cadres* (CFE–CGC); and the *Confédération française des travailleurs chrétiens* (CFTC). The official figures reported by the unions themselves also show a steady decline in membership during the 1990s.

The CGT, the oldest French confederation, was established in 1895. With the 1906 Charter of Amiens the CGT adopted an anarcho-revolutionary program, with members being wary of political parties and political action. Interestingly, in the same year, the British unions turned in the opposite direction, by forming the Labour Party. The coexistence of Marxists with anarchist and social-reformist elements led to a major split in the CGT in 1921, with an expulsion of the Marxists, following the split in the Socialist Party after the Russian Revolution. The two wings reunited during the 1936 Popular Front; however, another split occurred in 1939 after the *Germano–Soviet* pact. A further reunification took place during the 'resistance' but the two wings split again in 1948 when the minority group rejected Marxism, as well as the strong ties between the CGT and the Communist Party, and established the current FO (see below). Since the 1940s, most of the CGT's leaders have been Communist Party members, both at the top and intermediate levels. The CGT remained faithful to the ideology of class struggle and to a large extent obedient to the French Communist Party.

The CGT's membership has gone through four phases since the 1940s. After having reached a peak in 1947, it declined until 1958; it then grew between 1959 and 1975; and declined again after the mid-1970s. Between 1976 and 1990, the CGT lost two-thirds of its members, with total membership being only 630 000 in the mid-1990s. The loss of membership is all the more dramatic as the CGT has always had a high turnover of members, who often remain in the union for only a short period. The membership is said to turn over approximately every five years. As with the other confederations, the CGT is organised into industry federations, and in geographically based local unions. It draws its main strength from skilled manual workers. The confederation's core membership is in the metal, building and chemical industries, and in municipal and health services. In addition, more specific organisations of the CGT represent certain broad categories of members. Among the most important is the *Union confédérale des retraités* (UCR) for pensioners created in 1969, with 240 000 members. The *Union générale des ingénieurs, cadres et techniciens* (UGICT) was also established in 1969 and has 57 000 members. They are mainly technical, managerial and professional staff.

The CGT was a member of the World Federation of Trade Unions (WFTU) and held the post of WFTU Secretary General continuously from 1947 until 1978. Krasucki, former Head of the CGT, also held the post of Vice-President of the WFTU. Since 1977, the CGT has tried to join the European Trade Union Confederation (ETUC). The ETUC refused to admit the CGT in view of its lack of independence from the Communist Party and its membership of the WFTU. In the elections related to the ratification of the Maastricht Treaty, the CGT gave its support to the 'no' vote. During its 45th Congress in December 1995, the CGT decided to leave the WFTU to improve its chances of joining the ETUC.

The FO was established in 1948 as a reaction to Communist Party interference in the CGT. It claims to be the true heir of the CGT's traditional policy of political independence and is staunchly anti-communist. By the mid-1980s, the FO claimed to have become the second-largest confederation, with nearly one million members; however, its membership has been decreasing and is estimated to be close to 400 000 members. It sees collective bargaining as the main element of union action, and aims to defend workers' job interests, independently of any political party. It emphasises the importance of the union's role in representing the interests of employees and distrusts direct forms of employee representation and participation. It is strongest among white-collar workers, particularly technical and professional groups in the public sector. The FO has also a small *cadre* (managerial) section, the *Union des cadres et ingénieurs* (UCI). The heterogeneous membership of the FO has impeded the development of an efficient organisational structure and hampered recruitment.

At the international level, the FO has been a member of the anti-communist International Confederation of Free Trade Unions (ICFTU) since its creation in 1949, and an affiliate of the ETUC since it began in 1973. Since the 1950s, the policy of the FO has been favourable towards European integration. However, in recent years the FO has been rather critical of the EU on the grounds that it is mainly an instrument for economic integration and the free circulation of capital. During the vote on ratification of the Maastricht Treaty in 1992, the FO did not provide any voting guidelines to its members.

Confessional unionism began in 1919 with the formation of the CFTC. Its main objective was to promote peaceful collaboration between capital and labour, according to the social doctrine of the Catholic church. The CFTC split in 1964, when the minority group retained the religious orientation and kept the name CFTC. Its centres of strength are among miners, Christian school teachers and health workers; and it has a total membership of around 100 000. The CFTC has a tiny *cadre* section, the *Union générale des ingénieurs et cadres* (UGICA), with some 20 000 members, and a specific union for retired members with 55 000 affiliates. As a member of the World Confederation of Labour (WCL) from its inception, and of the ETUC since 1990, the CFTC favours the development of a Social Europe and was in favour of the ratification of the Maastricht Treaty in 1992.

Following the CFTC's 1964 split, the majority group formally abandoned the Catholic connection and formed the CFDT. Between 1948 (as the old CFTC) and 1976, membership of the CFDT nearly doubled to more than 800 000 members, but it declined from 1977 onwards to about 600 000 in the early 1990s. In 1970, it adopted elements of a socialist–Marxist ideology with elements of Gramscism, and favoured workers' control. The radicalisation of its ideology put it in closer competition with the CGT. But after 1979, the CFDT played down its former ideological emphasis. It began to emphasise union adaptation to economic change and aimed at a process of 'resyndicalisation', which meant establishing closer links between union issues and the rank and file. From the mid-1980s onwards, this back-to-the-Centre strategy (*recentrage*) entailed keeping a greater distance from the Left and developing closer links with the reformist unions. It is strongest in the metals, chemical and oil industries and the health, banking and insurance sectors. The CFDT has a small *cadre* section, the *Union confédérale des ingénieurs et cadres* (UCC) with about 42 000 members. However, UCC membership is restricted to 'senior' *cadres*, which partly explains why it is smaller than some other unions' *cadres* sections.

At the international level, the CFDT is a member of the ETUC and has played an active role in the EU in the arguments in favour of a Social Europe. Some of its previous leaders have held key posts in several European institutions. In 1988, the CFDT left the WCL, of which it was a major constituent, and joined the ICFTU.

The *Confédération générale des cadres* (CGC) was formed in 1944. In 1981 this confederation changed its name to CFE–CGC (*Confédération française de l'encadrement–Confédération générale des cadres*), given that about half of its members were not really management staff, but were supervisors, technicians and commercial agents such as travelling salespeople. In the late 1970s its membership was around 394 000, and included engineers, executives, salespeople, supervisors and technicians, but its membership declined by nearly half during the 1980s, and it had only 110 000 members by the mid-1990s. It is strongest in the metals and chemical industries and among salespeople. Its goals focus on issues such as winning more participation in managerial decision making for *cadres;* maximising their pay differentials; and protecting their interests in relation to tax and social security. It claims not to be associated with any political parties.

All these confederations are known as 'representative unions' at national level. This is a legal attribute granted on the basis of five criteria, the most important of which is proving that the union is totally independent from the employer. This confers on the union some exclusive rights, such as the nomination of candidates in the system of employee representation within the firm during collective bargaining (see below), and in terms of representation on numerous governmental and other consultative bodies.

Except for the CGC, unions from all these five confederations recruit across all industries and trades and across all categories of employees. Thus, they compete with one another. However, they each have their traditional strengths in their own specific sectors, occupational groups and regions.

The *Fédération de l'éducation nationale* (FEN) is another important specialist union which is also 'representative', but only on a sectoral level, in the education sector. The FEN decided to remain independent

Table 7.1   **Membership figures of the main union confederations[e] (in thousands)**

	1976	1983	1987	1995[a]
CGT	2074	1622	1031	630
CFDT	829	681	600[a,c]	600[d]
FO	926	1150	1108	400
CFE–CGC	325	307	241[b]	110
CFTC	223	260	250	100
FEN	526	493	394[c]	140
FSU	—	—	—	140

Notes: a   Estimate.
         b   1986.
         c   1988.
         d   Early 1990s.
         e   The full name of each confederation is included in the text—see also list of abbreviations.

Sources: Adapted from Bibes and Mouriaux (1990); Labbé (1996).

at the time of the CGT split. It recruits staff in most types of state educational institutions, and had approximately 140 000 members in 1996. Its main component comprises primary school teachers of a socialist orientation. The FEN has been subject to severe internal tensions which led, in 1992, to the eviction of two left-wing federations. In 1993, these evicted left-wing federations founded the *Fédération syndicale unitaire de l'enseignement, de la recherche et de la culture* (FSU), which also has around 140 000 members. The FSU rejects the collaborative attitude of the FEN and condemned the 1995 Juppé proposed reforms of the social security system. In December 1995 it joined the CGT and FO in large-scale protests and strikes against the Juppé reforms.

Beside these confederations, a looser gathering of unions called 'the group of ten' was formed in 1981. Its objectives were to have the capability to carry out united actions, to function more democratically and to defend previously excluded groups such as the unemployed and the poor. It was, therefore, not created to cater exclusively for the interests of employed workers. The 'group of ten' played an important role in the 1995 December strikes. It includes 18 unions and 70 000 members, while its two major union affiliates are the tax collectors, *Syndicat national unitaire des impots* (SNUI) and post and telecommunication workers, *Solidaire unitaire démocratique–Poste, Télégraphe, Téléphone* (SUD–PTT) unions. The SUD grouping (post, railway, banks, education) has gathered ex-members of the CFDT (who left the CFDT in 1989 and 1996). Some of the unions among 'the group of ten' are considered 'representative' in their respective sectors.

There are also several other 'autonomous' unions, which organise specific sectors—such as the automobile industry—or certain groups of employees—such as air traffic controllers, train drivers, truck drivers and journalists. They are called 'autonomous' unions because they do not belong to any of the larger groups that benefit from being legally defined as 'representative'.

The employers

Although small and medium-sized enterprises (SMEs) had traditionally been important in the French economy, since the late 1950s large companies have had a more important role. By 1987, firms with 500 or more employees accounted for 36 per cent of the employed work-force, a figure comparable to that of Germany, Britain and the Nether-lands. Nevertheless, 36 per cent are still employed in firms of less than 50 employees. Such small firms are usually family businesses and often have a strong Catholic tradition of paternalism.

By contrast with the plurality of unionism within the various union confederations, at a national level the employers are more united in their main confederation, the *Conseil national du patronat français* (CNPF). The CNPF includes more than three-quarters of all French enterprises. However, CNPF members differ in terms of their size and sectoral interests, diversity of capital ownership and range of manage-ment origins. They have, then, a heterogeneous range of interests. There has been tension between the CNPF being merely a liaison body for its sectoral affiliates, as was the case in the 1950s and 1960s, and becoming a real decision-making centre, which was the case after the organisational reforms of 1969. Unlike its counterparts in Britain and Germany, the CNPF has engaged in negotiation on certain broad issues since the late 1960s, though not on wages or working hours, with rates of pay being determined at the industry level. The CNPF was estab-lished in 1946, though employers were already organised in a range of industry-level federations from the early nineteenth century, and at national level from 1919 onwards in a forerunner to the CNPF.

The post-1973 economic crisis stimulated important changes in the employers' strategy. After this they sought to convince the government, the unions and public opinion more generally that there was a crisis and that business was vulnerable. The employers' objective at the micro level was to increase the flexibility of the workforce, a choice that they preferred to drastic employment reductions. At that stage the employers did not see flexibility being achieved through training. Flexibility was reached partly through quantitative *external* flexibility, that is, by introducing shorter term contracts of employment and more temporary work. Employers were especially enthusiastic about such employment practices, as they disliked the constraints imposed by the 1976 law on economic redundancies introduced by the Chirac government. This law, requiring prior administrative permission before implementing redundancies, was abolished in 1986, also under a Chirac government.

Another method used from the end of the 1970s was quantitative *internal* flexibility of working time. The average length of the working week could vary and could be calculated on a yearly basis. This led to developments such as weekend work, shift work and flexi-time. In the mid-1980s, the CNPF launched a campaign in favour of more *wage* flexibility.

With regard to *functional* flexibility, such as new job content and work autonomy for specific groups of workers, there have been many experiments. As they depend on long-term training it is not yet practicable to evaluate fully their scope and diffusion.

Since 1977, the CNPF has exhorted managers to pursue an active social policy at plant level and take more initiatives, in order to facilitate the implementation of this whole range of flexibility practices. Managers have been encouraged to abandon their old autocratic behaviour, to bypass traditional union channels and to enter into direct dialogue with employees. Some employers enhanced the status of supervisory staff by letting them deal directly with grievances at a lower level in the managerial hierarchy than was hitherto the case. Having to face a Socialist government for much of the time from 1981, the CNPF adopted a policy of 'conflictual cooperation' with the government, rather than one of ideological confrontation. The election of Gandois as President of the CNPF in 1994 led to expectations of a better climate of cooperation with the unions.

The Confederation of small and medium-sized enterprises (*Confédération générale des petites et moyennes entreprises*, CGPME) is a rival employers' organisation, which nevertheless has common roots with the CNPF and often cooperates with it. This occurred in the industrial tribunal elections of 1992, when the CNPF presented a joint 'enterprise plus' list that obtained 91 per cent of the votes on the employers' side. Founded in 1944, its history has been marked by some of its members strongly opposing taxation, technocracy, Marxism and the nationalised sector. During the 1970s and 1980s, public authorities took greater care of SMEs' interests.

The state

State intervention is very important in French employment relations. This reflects the traditional reluctance of unions and employers to use voluntary collective agreements. In periods when the Left has been in the ascendancy, unions have pressed for new laws: in 1936 with the Popular Front; in 1945 after Liberation; in 1968 following the events of May; and in 1981 with the advent of the Socialist government.

Since the late 1960s, there have been closer links between the law and collective bargaining. Certain laws are based on the results of previously negotiated agreements or on earlier discussions between the employment relations parties and the state. The state, then, generally does not play an authoritarian role in labour relations. Moreover, the state has tended to enhance the social partners' autonomy by transforming the legal framework for collective bargaining in 1971 and 1982.

The state is also a major employer, with about a quarter of civilian employees working in the public sector. The French public sector embraces a wider range of nationalised industries than is usual in most Western countries. As an employer, the state also exerts great influence on pay settlements in the private sector too. It influences wages through legislated increases and index-linked adjustments of the national minimum wage, *Salaire Minimum Interprofessionnel de Croissance* (SMIC). The SMIC is adjusted according to the price index of consumer goods when the latter has risen by 2 per cent. Moreover, the government can also raise the SMIC independently whenever it wishes; in 1997 the SMIC was raised by 4 per cent, double the rate of inflation. From a legal point of view, the SMIC should not constitute a basis for remuneration packages as a whole, but inevitably it exerts a general ratchet effect on all wages. However, since 1981 successive governments, both Left and Right, have tended to avoid using the SMIC to raise average wage levels. According to a 1994 Ministry of Labour survey, 8.2 per cent of workers in France received only the SMIC.

Throughout the 1980s, Socialist government policies aimed to reduce unemployment through special programs, especially to help the young and long-term unemployed find work and to encourage employers to recruit by reducing their social security contributions (direct costs), rather than through macro-economic measures. When the Right was in power (1986–88) its main preoccupation was to introduce more flexible labour relations rules for employers by amending the laws on redundancy, working hours, fixed-term and part-time hiring. From 1988 onwards, the Socialist Rocard government launched three successive 'employment plans' with an array of policy measures. By the late 1980s it was clear, however, that the government had abandoned its expectation that unemployment would disappear with economic recovery and then believed that a continuing significant level of unemployment was unavoidable.

The 1986 legislation that had abolished official controls on redundancies was also reformed by the Socialist government in 1989 to enhance works committees' rights to information and consultation with regard to redundancy matters. Whatever their size, all companies had to prepare a 'social plan' before implementing redundancies. While the government did not reinstate official controls over redundancies, the High Court has since recognised the duty of lower courts to check not only the legality, but also the substantive contents, of the 'social plans'. This is largely equivalent to the former control, and is tantamount to a regulation of dismissals. The courts also gave employers a 'duty to retain' redundant employees before they could lawfully consider dismissing them.

The conservative Balladur government, which gained power in March 1993, introduced a 'five-year employment law' in December 1993 which aimed to remove rigidities that the government perceived as barriers to job creation. Among its many provisions the legislation included items such as reductions in employers' social security contributions; encouraging work sharing through hours and pay cuts; simplifying company employee representation procedures and reducing their costs; vocational training for adults; vocational integration of young people, especially at regional level; guidance and monitoring devices for the labour market; limiting the situations where work could be combined with receipt of a pension; and prohibiting clandestine employment. The most controversial measure was the introduction of a new 'vocational integration contract' for young people, which led to strong opposition from unions and youngsters who regarded it as a form of 'youth SMIC'. This led the government to withdraw its proposed new 'vocational integration contract' proposal (*contrat d'insertion professionnelle* or CIP).

The 1993 law was followed by a long implementation phase lasting for more than two-and-a-half years. The process entailed the publication of decrees and a reliance on collective bargaining developments at various levels. One of the most important and successful implementation measures was the 'de Robien law' of June 1996. Concerned with working-time reduction, working-time flexibility and job creation, it provides financial incentives for employers to reduce their employees' collectively agreed working time. Despite fierce opposition from the CNPF, which believes it to be too costly both for the state and employers, the de Robien law has been successful at an enterprise level. Its success has surprised even the government itself. By December 1996 some 160 agreements covering 100 000 employees had already been signed.

Employee representation within the enterprise

At enterprise level, there is a range of representative bodies set up by particular political institutions or in response to particular social events. Employee delegates (*délégués du personnel*) were instituted by the Popular Front in 1936; works committees (*comités d'entreprise*) in 1945 following Liberation; and workplace union branches (*sections syndicales*) in 1968. As a generalisation, employee delegates deal with individual employee grievances; works committees deal with workplace consultation; and union branches and stewards represent their union and participate in collective bargaining at the workplace. There is a legal framework for all these institutions.

Unlike shop stewards or workplace delegates in the English-speaking countries, who are union representatives, French employee delegates are not union representatives. However, in practice, a majority of them are elected from a union slate. Delegates must be elected every second year by the total workforce in all enterprises that employ ten people or more. The 1982 Act stipulates that delegates could also be elected in those workplaces with less than ten employees, where several firms operate on a common site, such as a building site or commercial centre, and if there is a total of at least 50 employees. Most of the private sector is covered by this Act.

Employee delegates deal with individual claims for wages, working conditions, the implementation of labour law and collective agreements. They may also call the Labour Inspector in cases where there is disagreement. The number of delegates elected varies according to the size of the firm. The employer must meet them collectively at least once a month. To fulfil their duties, they are allocated 15 hours paid working time per month.

Delegates are elected by proportional representation. Manual workers and lower clerical staff vote separately from technicians and *cadres*. The election procedures must be agreed between the employer and the unions. There is no exclusion of foreign 'guest workers' from voting or from eligibility as candidates.

Unlike other countries, under these election procedures there is a two-round secret ballot. In the first round, candidates can be nominated only by one of the main union confederations, or by any other affiliated union that is recognised as 'representative' within the firm. If less than half of the electorate votes in the first round, then any employee may stand as a candidate for the second round. In practice, however, a second round is rarely required.

Works committees are required in all firms employing at least 50 employees. They use election procedures similar to those summarised above. However, these committees have little real decision-making power, except in relation to welfare issues. They do have the right, however, to be informed and consulted at specific periods on the general management of the business, particularly in relation to the number and organisation of employees, their hours of work and employment conditions.

Each quarter, the employer is required to inform the works committee about the general progress of orders, output and finances. Employers should also provide employment data including details of any short-term contracts and subcontract work. The employer must justify the use of such measures. Once a year, the employer has to submit a general report in writing to the works committee, covering the business's activities; turnover; losses or profits; the production achievements; substantial capital transfers; subcontracting; the allocation of profits; subsidies from the state or other public authorities and their use; investments; and salaries. To help it to examine the annual accounts, the works committee may choose an expert accountant. Further, on an *ad hoc* basis, the committee must be informed and consulted on all changes in the economic or legal organisation of the business, in cases such as sales or mergers, for instance. Moreover, under the 1982 Act, the committee has to be informed and consulted prior to the implementation of any large project involving the introduction of new technologies, whenever there may be consequences related to employment, qualifications, pay, training and working conditions. In firms with at least 300 employees, an expert can be co-opted to advise (Rojot 1983).

The works committee does not only have to give its opinion; its agreement is also required on such issues as profit-sharing arrangements and changes in working hours. If the employer requests it, the representatives have to maintain confidentiality about the employer's information on production processes and finances. The works committee is composed of the employee representatives and the employer, or deputy, and the employer chairs the meeting, which takes place at least monthly. Each representative union can appoint a union observer to the committee. To fulfil their duties each employee representative can use 20 paid working hours per month. The works committee can create subcommittees to examine specific problems. *Health, safety and improvement of working conditions committees* are compulsory in firms with at least 50 employees, and firms with at least 300 employees have to set up an *employment-training committee*. Many employers initially resisted works committees, but most have gradually come to accept them as having a legitimate role.

Since 1968, there have also been workplace union delegates in parallel with the representative bodies. Before 1968, unions had no legal right to establish such union delegates. In firms of a certain size, they can have an office and other facilities. According to the law, workplace union delegates are appointed by the local union branch, but the designated union delegate must be an employee working in the firm. Each union appoints its own union delegates, with their number varying according to the size of the firm. Union delegates can collect dues during working hours, use notice boards, distribute leaflets, and organise monthly meetings (outside working time). The Mitterrand government improved union rights by increasing the number of paid hours allocated to employee representatives for union duties and allowing them to circulate freely within the workplace. All employee representatives are legally protected against dismissal. Hindering a representative or the various representation institutions is unlawful.

The representative institutions are not a coherent system, but have grown in an *ad hoc* way. Moreover, owing to the complex and occasionally imprecise legal framework, there is some confusion of functions, not least because individual representatives may fulfil several functions. Often there is a lack of candidates to fill the various elected positions. In the larger firms, these representatives often coordinate the activities of the works committees as well as being employee delegates. Although this may be accepted by managers in big firms, in smaller firms managers may resent what they see as union interference.

A major innovation of the 1982 Act was to set up a *group committee* within large multi-plant companies whose registered office is in France. The function of such committees is to receive, at least once a year, information about the financial and employment situation within the group. As these French group committees developed, several multinationals of French origin later concluded agreements that also provided information and consultation structures at a European level (Jobert 1990).

A government-commissioned report (*rapport Bélier*) found that the provisions for representation work poorly in SMEs. Some 64 per cent of firms with 11 to 49 employees and 60 per cent of firms with 50 to 100 employees have no union delegates. In the latter category around 30 per cent also have no company works committees.

The 1993 'five-year employment' law sought to simplify the legislation on employee representation, especially for SMEs. The mandate of the employee delegate, elected in enterprises with ten or more employees, was extended from one year to two. This brought delegates into line with employee representatives on works committees elected for two years and was compulsory in firms with 50 employees and more. Elections held simultaneously were intended to reduce the administrative burden on the employer. In small enterprises, the monthly minimum paid time for employee delegates to accomplish their duty was reduced from 15 to 10 hours. With regard to works committees, enterprises with less than 300 employees were entitled to provide information in a single document once a year rather than in four written reports. In firms with less than 150 employees, works committee meetings could be held every two months and not every month as before. Further, firms with 50–199 employees could opt for a single representative structure instead of two, with employee delegates taking over the works committee representatives' role. The government claimed that firms which could benefit from such measures represent around 60 per cent of all those with works committees, and 25 per cent of all those with 50 and more employees. Altogether, it resulted in a reduction of 40 per cent of employers' costs for the operation of representative structures.

Employee participation and collective bargaining

The Employee Participation Act of February 1982 (part of the Auroux laws) gave employees the right to withdraw from dangerous working conditions if they considered the job to be dangerous, but not the right to stop the machinery. The Act was further extended in August 1982 to give employees the right to have a say on the content and organisation of their work and, more generally, their working conditions. The Act prescribed that employees' views should be expressed 'directly' and 'collectively' on these matters. The law was innovative in two ways. First, it was intended to decentralise collective bargaining in all enterprises with at least 200 employees. However, while it was compulsory for employers to *initiate* negotiations with employees over arrangements for direct employee participation, they were not compelled to *conclude* the negotiations. Second, the Act was to be experimental. After a two-year trial period, the government evaluated the impact of the Act. An amended Act was introduced in 1986. This enlarged the range of issues subject to participation to include most activities associated with a firm's output. It also allowed managerial staff to be represented directly in *employee participation committees* (*groupes d'expression directe*).

A Ministry of Labour report in 1985 concluded that 45 per cent of firms covered by the Act had reached agreements with unions on employee participation. In addition there were several hundred agreements reached in smaller firms where collective bargaining remained optional. Most unions had signed such agreements when they were represented in a firm. The incidence of agreements signed by unions, as a percentage of the firms in which they were present, were CGT, 76 per cent; CFDT, 78 per cent; FO, 62 per cent; CFTC, 84 per cent; and CGC, 87 per cent.

The report noted discrepancies between the views expressed by union officials at the national level and those of shop stewards at the level of the enterprise or workplace. Furthermore, while CFDT officials supported employee participation, the FO was against any schemes that might enable the employer to manipulate employees and reduce the union role as the representative of employees. The CGC, representing executive *cadres*, feared that employee participation might jeopardise the power of the managerial and supervisory staff within the enterprise.

Most employee participation groups were based on workgroups with 15 to 20 members, and met for one or two hours on two to four occasions per year. Most agreements contained feedback procedures which required the employer to respond to requests from groups within a specified time period. The major achievements of the participation groups were in improving working conditions and work organisation; however, employers were criticised for not dealing with employee requests satisfactorily. Hence, many groups faded away. Nevertheless, by 1990, the Ministry of Labour estimated that between 10 000 and 12 000 enterprises had signed participation agreements, which covered some 3.5 million employees (Goetschy 1991).

The statutes on collective bargaining (1919, 1936, 1946, 1950, 1971 and 1982) illustrate typical French labour law prescriptions. These attempt to compensate for the unions' organisational weakness and the lack of effective collective bargaining. For example, all employees, whether or not they are unionised, may benefit from a collective agreement. Furthermore, French labour law reinforces union pluralism and in some ways even favours the minority organisations (such as the CFTC, CGC and formerly the FO). Thus, a collective agreement is valid even if only one representative union has signed it. To what extent has this provision divided the union confederations? Traditionally, before the mid-1970s, the most radical unions (CGT and CFDT) tended to adopt an uncompromising approach during the negotiation process, while the reformist ones (FO, CFTC, CGC) were usually more willing to compromise and sign agreements. In many instances, however, such an arrangement seems to have suited both categories of unions. The CGT and CFDT members could thus benefit from an agreement, even though their leaders had not compromised themselves by signing it.

Collective bargaining has traditionally taken place at industry level. Employer and union organisations preferred such bargaining for ideological as well as tactical reasons. This practice also reflected the lack of mutual recognition between unions and employers at plant or company level. Industry agreements covered the maximum number of employees, which was an advantage to the unions when their membership was low. The employers have favoured industry agreements that establish only minimal standards for a given industrial sector. Furthermore, for a long time this spared employers from having to recognise unions at plant level.

After 1968 there was a significant development in multi-industry bargaining and plant-level bargaining. Both practices were reinforced by the 1971 amendments to the 1950 Collective Bargaining Act. Innovative multi-industry bargaining dealt with such issues as job security, vocational training, the introduction of salaried status for manual workers, unemployment benefits following redundancies and working conditions. Such national agreements provided a framework that aimed to encourage collective bargaining at lower levels, such as in a specific industry or firm.

The increasing number of workplace-level agreements resulted, firstly, from the demands from employees after the extensive social protests of May 1968; secondly, from new strategies used by employers to reduce labour turnover by granting employees specific company benefits; and thirdly, from the 1968 Statute, which legalised union delegates at plant level and gave them a legitimate function within collective bargaining. The workplace-level agreements were generally not innovative, but rather improved on or adapted higher level agreements to local conditions. In practice, such domestic bargaining was generally confined to larger firms.

Following the 1973 energy crisis, there was a decline in the number of workplace-level agreements. Multi-industry enabling agreements were less often followed by agreements at lower levels. There were significant difficulties, for instance, in implementing the 1975 multi-industry agreement on working conditions. However, during this period the parties could still conclude multi-industry agreements that were not 'enabling', but which settled precise conditions, especially about employment issues such as redundancy.

In the 1980s, the election of the Socialist government induced a different political and legal context for collective bargaining. A major objective of the Mitterrand government was the reform of workplace relations. It was outlined in the *Report on the Rights of Workers* by the Minister of Labour, Jean Auroux. This Auroux Report aimed to provide employees with real 'citizenship within the firm' and to create new opportunities so that 'employees may become actors of change within the enterprise'. The report was not completely new; it adopted a gradual rather than a radical approach and partly reflected the 1975 Sudreau Report. Though the report paid heed to the unions' platforms (especially those of the CGT and CFDT), it followed the government's own employment relations policy and thus received varying responses from the different union and employer organisations (Goetschy 1983).

The Auroux Report enumerated the following deficiencies of the French system of collective bargaining. First, many wage earners were not covered by any collective agreements, whether at industry or workplace level. As such, 11 per cent of wage earners in firms of at least ten employees were not covered by any collective agreement, while only a quarter of wage earners were covered by a workplace agreement. Such 'excluded workers' were particularly concentrated among temporary employees, such as in the distributive trades and in hotels and restaurants. Second, many agreements lacked job-classification structures. Third, there was a large gap between basic minimum wages and actual pay, with the average difference being 30 per cent. Fourth, collective agreements were highly fragmented (40 of the 1023 national- or regional-level collective agreements covered more than half of the total number of wage earners). Lastly, the low density of unionism and the divisions between unions undermined the 'legitimacy' of agreements.

The 1982 Collective Bargaining Act followed the Auroux Report. The 1982 Act included many prescriptions, most of which aimed to improve the existing system—although some of them were innovative. For instance, in firms that had union branches, employers were obliged to open negotiations every year on pay and working hours. However, there was no obligation to reach an agreement and the employer had the final say. Unlike in the USA, there was no requirement to bargain 'in good faith'.

Such provisions aimed to foster collective bargaining within the firm. The intention was to induce more 'integrative' attitudes, whereby employers would become more aware of their social responsibilities and unions more attentive to economic constraints.

As another innovation, non-signatory unions could veto a workplace-level agreement; for example, if an agreement included an 'opt-out' clause in relation to shorter working hours. Before using a veto, the non-signatory opponents had to win more than half of the votes in the works committees or employee delegates' elections. Granting such veto rights to the largest opposition unions was expected to lead to more legitimate agreements.

Further, in national industry agreements, the obligation to meet once a year to negotiate wages and every fifth year to discuss possible job classification revision should bring the agreed basic minimum pay rates and other conditions closer to actual practice. At the firm or industry level, the frequency of meetings (for a compulsory 'social dialogue') was expected to strengthen the negotiators' sense of responsibility in collective bargaining and to make them more responsive to their constituents.

After the 1982 Collective Bargaining Act, employers raised fierce criticisms of the novel obligation requiring them to negotiate at company level. However, their criticisms seemed to fade as the Act was implemented.

There were also several prescriptions that aimed to enlarge unions' rights to information and to provide expert help in the bargaining process. The Act further improved the existing procedures whereby the Minister of Labour could extend certain collective agreements to non-signatory firms. These extension procedures were important, given that the employer might initially refuse to sign an agreement.

Both the Act and some other 1982 ordinances gave priority to collective bargaining rather than to the law. The search for a new balance between state intervention and collective bargaining was the hallmark of Mitterrand's post-1981 strategy of social reform. However, this strategy was based on the 1969–71 employment relations policy of the then right-wing government, when Delors was the adviser to Prime Minister Chaban-Delmas.

The attempts by the early Mitterrand government to promote collective bargaining became entangled with its 'austerity plans' of 1982 and 1983. Nevertheless, workplace-level bargaining was subject to a new boost, not only by the Auroux laws, but also because it suited employers' interests. Since 1987, on average, 6000 agreements have been made each year.

In 1994, of the total number of company agreements signed, 45 per cent were concerned with work-time issues while 47 per cent dealt with pay. About a third of wage agreements at enterprise level contained individualised pay-increase clauses, most often linked to a general pay increase. About 7500 company agreements were signed in 1994 covering 2.9 million employees (20 per cent of the workforce). Collective bargaining remains essentially an industry-level activity. Most wage earners are covered by an industry agreement that was one of the objectives of the Auroux laws. Around 75 per cent of industry agreements concern pay issues.

Another trend of French collective bargaining has been the development of financial participation. The number of French employees covered by voluntary profit-sharing schemes *(accords d'intéressement)* has increased significantly. Similarly there have been a growing number of agreements on employee participation involving company results or growth, known as capital sharing *(accords de participation)*.

An assessment of the effects of the Auroux laws during the ten years after they were first introduced revealed that collective bargaining had been developing well (Coffineau 1993). Many of its conclusions have been confirmed by the subsequent collective bargaining experiences.

After a decline in multi-industry bargaining in the late 1970s and early 1980s, it increased in importance in the 1990s. The development of multi-industry bargaining was supported by the government and the CNPF which favoured a 'consensus approach' for achieving the modernisation of French enterprises. Among the unions, the CFDT has been most prominent in supporting such an approach. In 1988, a national orientation agreement on *technological change* was signed, with the aim of encouraging negotiations on this issue. The consensus approach also inspired the 1989 national framework agreement on the *flexible organisation of work time.*

There have been similar agreements on such issues as equal employment, working environment and occupational training. In 1994, multi-industry bargaining related mainly to training, employment, supplementary pensions and welfare. Sectoral and multi-industry bargaining activity were given a new impetus by the 'five-year employment' law of the Balladur government. In 1995, three major multi-industry agreements were reached on vocational integration for young people.

Whereas the CGT has opposed such 'enabling' arrangements, the CFDT and CGC have supported these arrangements being agreed with the CNPF. By contrast, the FO and the CFTC have been critical and have refused to sign some of the agreements.

Training has been one of the main issues of multi-industry bargaining. It was initiated by the law of 1971, which was influenced by Jacques Delors, then social adviser to the government. Originally the law made it a collective bargaining issue and required employers to pay 0.9 per cent of their wages bill towards vocational training (later increased to 1.5 per cent in 1994). In practice, French companies spend around 3.2 per cent on employee training. In order to be more legitimate, laws on training are often preceded by multi-industry agreements. Vocational training has given rise to many public and private organisations providing courses. Most of the multi-industry agreements provide frameworks that imply further industry-level bargaining. They are generally signed by all union confederations.

More fundamentally, the procedural agreement on 'the articulation of bargaining levels and the possibility of negotiations in companies without union representatives' (October 1995), which was not signed by the CGT and FO, entails two key changes for the French system of collective bargaining. Its first aim is to tackle the three traditional bargaining levels (multi-industry, industry and enterprise) as complementary rather than hierarchical. The second objective of the agreement makes it possible, in situations where union delegates are absent, for company agreements to be signed either by employees specifically mandated by unions, or by elected employee representatives (e.g. works committee members or employee delegates). Nevertheless, defining the choice and modalities of the two options would be left to industry bargaining, and such company agreements could also be denounced after signature by a majority of the sector's trade unions.

However, the agreement remains on trial for a three-year period and is intended to involve the traditional representative unions in an experimental process, by combining in a new way industry- and enterprise-level negotiations. Its aim is to circumvent two specific features of French employment relations. First, to develop collective bargaining in SMEs where there is often no union presence, and second, to counter increasing legislative intervention from the 'five-year employment law'. Moreover, the agreement is an attempt to answer the numerous pressures linked to economic globalisation. A draft Bill of May 1996 provides the necessary legislative backing allowing company agreements to be signed where there are no union representatives.

Representative elections

Besides their formal membership, then, unions' support can also be assessed on the basis of the results from 'social' elections such as the representatives on works committees, social welfare boards (*Sécurité Sociale*) and industrial tribunals (*Prud'hommes*).

The works committee election results for 1995 showed that, in total, the five representative unions obtained nearly 65 per cent of the votes (see Table 7.2). Thus the unions have a much higher degree of support than might be inferred from their low membership. However, between

Table 7.2 **Results of works committee elections (as a percentage of the votes cast)**

	1981	1982	1985	1987	1989	1991	1993	1995
CGT	32.0	28.5	25.9	24.6	23.0	20.4	19.6	19.7
CFDT	22.3	21.9	20.8	20.5	20.3	20.5	20.8	20.5
CFTC	2.9	4.0	4.7	4.6	4.4	4.4	4.9	5.1
FO	9.9	11.1	13.0	11.7	11.6	11.7	11.5	12.3
CFE–CGC	6.1	6.5	6.7	6.5	6.9	6.5	6.5	6.4
Other unions	4.1	4.7	5.1	5.2	5.6	5.6	6.3	6.2
Non-unions	22.2	22.8	23.8	27.0	29.1	30.9	30.3	29.9

Source: MTEFP–DARES (1995).

1981 and 1995 there was a significant increase for non-union representatives as shown by the voting results.

The participation rate for the works committee elections remains fairly high, being 66 per cent in 1995, though it has been declining. As Table 7.2 shows, the support obtained by the CGT, in percentage of votes received, declined from 32 per cent in 1981 to 19.7 per cent in 1995. By 1987 the CGT's percentage of the vote had fallen to second position behind the non-union representatives, and in 1995 it was in third position after the CFDT. Support for the CFDT seems to have remained relatively stable over the 1981–95 period, while the CFTC has gradually increased its share of the vote during the same period. Support for the FO grew until 1985 before falling slightly and then stabilising in the 1987–95 period. The FO's works committee votes have increased less than its membership. The CFE–CGC's percentage of the vote has remained fairly stable.

Turning to industrial tribunals (see Table 7.3), it appears that although the CGT has remained the leading confederation, its support has greatly declined since 1979. The support for the CFDT remained stable, whereas the FO's support increased. Despite their low membership, the support unions obtain through 'social' elections is relatively important. However, in general the various election results indicate that there has been declining support for the unions.

When comparing these results it must be kept in mind that the voting constituencies are widely different for the three types of elections. Those for social welfare boards and industrial tribunals cover a much larger electorate than those of the works committees.

Why is union density low and declining?

Following the Left's 1981 electoral success, an increase in the CGT and CFDT membership might have been expected, as was the case in

Table 7.3   Elections for industrial tribunals (as a percentage of the votes cast)

Year	CGT	CFDT	FO	CFTC	CGC	Others
1979	42.3	23.2	17.3	7.2	5.2	4.8
1982	37.0	23.5	17.7	8.5	9.6	3.7
1987	36.5	23.0	20.4	8.3	7.4	4.5
1992	33.3	23.8	20.4	8.5	6.9	6.8

Source: Liaisons Sociales (1993).

1936 and 1945, but throughout the 1980s these unions continued to lose members. Why has French unionism declined since the 1970s, even though the political environment has apparently been beneficial to unions, with the Left in power for much of the period (apart from 1986 to 1988 and 1993 to 1997)?

First, major restructuring has taken place in the French economy. There has been a movement away from traditionally well organised industrial sectors (such as coal, steel, metals and shipbuilding) to new industrial sectors, and a shift of jobs from industry to the services sector. The increasing number of small firms has also contributed to the decline of union membership.

Second, major changes in the labour market were detrimental to unionisation, with rising unemployment. Furthermore there were changes in employment contracts and employment practices that caused the number of people working on a part-time basis to increase, while the number working on a temporary basis also increased significantly. Both these categories are difficult to unionise. By the late 1990s over 70 per cent of all new recruits were working under fixed contracts or with agencies. This corresponded to a rise in the use of temporary workers from about 2.5 per cent of all employment in 1977 to around 6 per cent in 1994.

Third, young people's changing attitudes to unions, caused by an increasing scepticism about the efficiency of union action, versus their own individual capacity to negotiate, has contributed to the decline (Linhart & Mallan 1988). The decline in unionisation also appears to have been higher among women than among men.

Fourth, employers' social policies have been changing a great deal since 1977 (Morville 1985). The CNPF sought to establish a direct dialogue with employees and pursued a more active social policy by mobilising middle managers. Employers, then, were increasingly aiming to communicate with the workforce outside the formal employee representation system. Therefore unions were often bypassed and this tended to diminish their role even further. Employers developed a more participative style of management and introduced innovations. This led, for instance, to the number of quality circles increasing to a greater extent than in many other European countries. In practice, although the CNPF had expressed some initial ideological fears, employers welcomed the Auroux law granting employees the right to direct participation (Goetschy 1991). Moreover, employers initiated a whole range of flexibility practices in regard to working time and recruitment such as flexible hours, short-time and part-time work. Such practices often met employees' wishes, but led to the individualisation of employment relations within the firm. In 1987, the CNPF issued guidelines promoting the individualisation of pay, including the de-indexation of wages and the development of merit pay, which impinged on the unions' wage bargaining function.

Fifth, there was increasing self-criticism by unions due to their ineffective strategies in the face of new challenges. On the one hand, the gap between the union leadership and the rank and file appears to have been increasing. This is due to the unions' workload—including the numerous duties resulting from the Auroux laws (see below) and their increasing participation in welfare state institutions (social security, unemployment insurance, training, employment and administrative committees in the public sector)—and to the developing trend of multi-industry bargaining. Such an 'institutionalisation' of unionism seems to have isolated unions from those they were supposed to represent (Adam 1983; Rosanvallon 1986).

On the other hand, union fragmentation was exacerbated during the 1980s due to conflict and increasing animosity between unions. Rivalry between the CGT and CFDT led to the breaking up of their Union of the Left in 1977. After the Left's 1978 electoral failure, the CGT and CFDT both initiated a process of self-criticism. The CFDT admitted that it had been too dogmatic and that it had been insufficiently attentive to workers' daily preoccupations. The CGT was less self-critical and did not question its fundamental strategies or links with the declining Communist Party, which had exacerbated its own decline. Inter-union rivalry became even more acute when confronted with the Socialist government's austerity, modernisation and flexibility policies. The CGT was isolated whereas the CFDT continued to follow its reformist *recentrage* strategy that had begun in 1979, and launched the idea of the merger of non-communist unions.

In 1990, leaders of the CFDT and the FEN called for a 'labour axis' plan, which appealed for a united front between non-communist confederations, excluding the CGT. This call did not generate much enthusiasm among the other unions. Part of the aim of such an axis would be to counterbalance the influence of large national groups such as the DGB (see ch. 8) or TUC (see ch. 2) in the EU. This represented a move away from the 'unity of action' practices of the 1970s, when the CGT and CFDT managed to agree on a range of issues. There was considerable turmoil between confederations in December 1984 with the failure of the national multi-industry negotiations on flexibility of employment. Whereas the chief negotiators of the FO and CFDT were ready to accept the package deal, they faced tough opposition from elements within their own organisations. Between 1986 and 1988 official union practices were challenged, with strikes in the public sector and the setting up of informal 'coordination' groups outside the formal unions.

In short, the decline of unionism is explicable in terms of several factors, including the unions' work overload, their fragmentation, the disappointing results of the CFDT's *recentrage* strategy and the Left unions' policy disarray when confronted with a Left government in power.

Even before the problems of declining support in the 1980s, the weakness of the French union movement was a major issue. The *traditional* explanations of low union density can be summarised as follows. First, closed shop practices were prohibited to safeguard individual freedom to choose whether to join a union, although there are some *de facto* closed shops in sectors such as the docks and printing. Second, as a legacy of their anarcho-syndicalist roots, French unions have traditionally put more emphasis on having an active core of 'militant' organisers, rather than recruiting a stable mass membership. This also explains why they have rarely built up bureaucratic organisations on the scale of those in Germany, for instance. Following this early ideological choice, militants tended to see their role as fostering strikes and political action, rather than engaging in collective bargaining with employers, which made it difficult to demonstrate clear bargaining results to their members. Third, all wage earners benefit from any improvement won by the unions; after it is signed, a collective agreement applies to all employees whether unionised or not. Fourth, in general, no specific welfare benefits accrue to a union member, as may be the case in other countries. Fifth, employers have often opposed any extension of union influence, and have long used paternalistic practices, particularly in the numerous small firms. Sixth, the fragmentation of unions on ideological and political grounds hampered the recruitment and retention of members.

The low union membership created other problems such as poor financial resources and small organisational infrastructures in comparison with many other European unions. Their financial resources are strained, given that dues are paid irregularly. On average, a union member pays only half the required dues per year (Mouriaux 1983), and union dues are relatively low, being on average less than 1 per cent of wages.

Nevertheless, unions do have more political and industrial influence than their low density implies. They play an important role in collective bargaining and in representative elections. They also play a role in public tripartite or bipartite institutions transforming unions into a 'public service agency' (Rosanvallon 1986).

Industrial disputes

The right to strike is guaranteed by the French constitution, but as with any other right, it is qualified. In the public sector since 1963, the unions have had to give five days notice before a strike; however, there is little legal regulation of strikes in the private sector. The distinction between legal and illegal strikes is drawn by the courts. In the private sector, a strike is legally defined as a stoppage of work, hence other actions such as industrial sabotage, working to rule or slowing down are unlawful. A lawful strike has to concern 'industrial relations issues'. Despite legal constraints on sit-ins, such actions are permitted when their primary aim is to seek negotiations, rather than merely to disrupt output. Nevertheless, excessive disruption of output through strikes is illegal, and lockouts are generally illegal.

Although there is little legislation on strikes, there are elaborate procedures for the settlement of disputes, including conciliation, mediation and arbitration; but these procedures are rarely used in practice. Industrial disputes tend to be unpredictable in France, but, as in Australia, they are usually short-lived. Strikes tend to be short because, as a legacy of the anarcho-syndicalist tradition, French unions have few financial reserves and generally do not grant strike pay. Moreover, France loses relatively few days due to stoppages compared with Italy and the English-speaking countries (see Appendix).

When comparing strikes over a longer period the following trends can be noticed. First, compared with the 1970s, there was a significant decline in the number of days lost during the 1980s. This tendency has been accentuated in the 1990s. On average, there were 3.6 million days lost per year in the 1970s, 1.2 million days lost per year in the 1980s and less than 600 000 days lost per year between 1990 and 1995 (the trends concern market sector strikes—private- and public-owned companies—but the general picture does not change much when civil servants are included). Second, the proportion of 'generalised conflicts' (multi-employer strikes) decreased significantly in the 1980s and 1990s to only about 10–15 per cent of the level of such strikes that occurred in the 1970s. Third, the public non-market sector was more strike-prone than the private sector: 'throughout the period since 1982, public-sector workers were on average between half (1980s) and one-third (1990–1995) more likely to experience strikes than their fellow market sector workers' (Jefferys 1996). From 1982 to 1987, enterprises subject to competition, including public-owned companies, represented an average of 70 per cent of days lost, whereas between 1988 and 1994 their share had declined to 60 per cent.

The most salient factor is the relatively high proportion of strikes in the public sector. They accounted for around 45 per cent of strikes in the late 1980s and 1990s. Some of the public sector strikes were characterised by the establishment of rank-and-file 'coordination groups' to organise strikes alongside or in opposition to official union channels, such as among administration workers and nurses. These coordinated activities were a clear reflection of some of the deficiencies of French unions. In the public sector, claims were a combination of classic pay claims and demands to improve working conditions, career opportunities and human resource policies. Another feature of strikes is the growing importance of wider employment issues as the motive for strike action. In 1992, strikes about pay issues accounted for 35 per cent of the total, whereas strikes on employment topics accounted for 39 per cent.

Are some unions more strike-prone than others? Around 80 per cent of strikes result from union action, whereas 20 per cent are triggered by employees' initiatives. On average, 40 per cent of strikes are initiated by the CGT, 30 per cent by more than one union and 10 per cent by the CFDT. Strikes on employment issues are more likely to be the result of the initiatives of several unions, compared with strikes over pay issues.

In December 1995 an important strike took place against the reform plan of Prime Minister Alain Juppé. The aims of this reform were firstly to reduce the deficit arising from the social security system through fiscal measures, and secondly to align the pension system of civil servants with those in the private sector and to end certain more favourable pension systems enjoyed by some public sector categories, such as railway workers. The 1995 strikes were launched by the unions in the public sector (public transport, post, electricity and education), these being mainly the CGT and FO. Apart from their long duration, the disputes had three major characteristics. First, they were mainly restricted to the public sector and generally did not spread to the private sector. Second, the strikes took place throughout France, and mobilisation was high in certain large towns in the provinces. Third, they obtained much public support despite the great inconvenience. While their immediate cause was the Juppé plan, the strikes reflected fears of increasing unemployment and precarious employment. Further, the strikes were a reaction against the threat to 'public services'. More generally, these strikes illustrated the weaknesses of the French employment relations system and its difficulty in concluding collective agreements unless subject to acute pressures. Finally, it reflected a crisis of confidence between the state and its experts, on the one hand, and between the state and the French population, on the other.

With the Juppé social security reform plan and the 1995 December strikes, union divisions at national level became accentuated. While the FO came closer to its former enemy the CGT during the strikes, tensions increased with the more reformist CFDT. Further, the 1995 December strikes have led to internal tensions both within the FO and within the CFDT. The former has been accused by some of its affiliates of becoming too influenced by internal Trotskyist and/or external communist interests. The leader of the CFDT, Nicole Notat, has been attacked from the Left opposition within the CFDT for supporting part of Juppé's plan and for trying to attain a privileged position with the government and employers.

Conclusions

Although France had a Socialist President from 1981 to 1995, and despite labour legislation tending to reinforce their position, French union confederations have continued to decline. This decline seems unlikely to be reversed in the near future. This is largely due to changes in the labour market, high unemployment, employers' policies and unsatisfactory union strategies. Since the strikes of 1995, rivalries between and inside unions have increased, which has further weakened them. The French model of employment relations remains characterised by a structural gap between large companies—where unions are active participants in company-level bargaining and where representative institutions exercise their rights—and SMEs—where unions and representative institutions are rarely present, making company-level bargaining impossible. The reforms undertaken by the government or implemented through collective agreements have not yet succeeded in changing the situation. This is largely because of the opposition by some unions and the large number of employers who still consider the presence of unions in their enterprises as having a negative effect. One survey indicated that a third of employers share this opinion.

The main key players have to face new issues involved in the decentralisation of employment relations to the regions and the Europeanisation of employment relations. One aspect of decentralisation is the increasing importance of enterprise bargaining. Another aspect results from the 1982 law that helped initiate the decentralisation process by transferring some state powers to the regions. Since 1982, other laws have widened regional powers, such as the 1993 Vocational Training Act. If regional policies are to be properly defined, political authorities, local representatives of the state, unions and employers' associations have to cooperate. However, there have been great difficulties in assuming this new role because of the weaknesses of regional structures. This can be explained by the centralised tradition in France and the preference given to national/industry-level structures. The adaptation of these structures is a challenge for unions and employers' associations if they want to be involved in the increasing regional decentralisation.

Turning to improvements of employment rights in Europe: what is the role of European Works Councils (EWCs)? Among the nearly 120 French companies affected by the 1994 Directive, 34 have implemented EWCs. This raises three questions. First, how should the parties integrate the group committees, set up by the 1982 Act, with the EWCs? French works and group committees have more rights than the EWC, as they have to be consulted before certain decisions are taken by employers. This is not the case with the EWC. Therefore, French unions will probably not use the French Act of Transposition of the Directive to merge their institutions with EWCs. There are, however, guarantees that all the rights of the French institutions can be transferred to the EWC.

Second, how will the unions handle the selection process for representatives in the EWCs, when the number of representatives will be less than the number of unions? Will the unions cooperate and designate representatives who will speak for all employees and not just for some of them? The chances of union cooperation are not high. There are intense rivalries between the unions and the CGT is not a member of the ETUC (mainly because of the opposition of the CFDT).

Third, the integration of national industry-level bargaining with the European bargaining model will be important in the future because of the globalisation of markets and the role of large companies in that process. The advent of EWCs will help to diminish the extent of national industry-level regulation.

During their successful 1997 election campaign, the Socialists promised to create 350 000 jobs in the public sector (to be reserved for young people); introduce new laws allowing for the reduction of working time to 35 hours per week; and increase the national minimum wage (SMIC).

These issues are priorities for the union movement, which was invited to participate (along with the employers' confederations) at the national conference on employment, wages and working time in October 1997. This conference was organised by the government to define the priorities and content of employment strategies.

At the end of this conference, in line with his party's election commitment, the socialist French prime minister announced a bill to introduce a 35-hour working week for all employees by the year 2000. He recommended that the social partners negotiate the implementation at a decentralised enterprise level. To achieve a 35-hour week, with no reduction in salary, employers would need to improve productivity, while unions would need to accept more flexible working arrangements;

employers may also need to hire more workers. While the unions approved this basic framework, the employers' associations refused to accept the bill and tried to delay its implementation. This led to the resignation of the president of the CNPF, Gandois, who tended to support collective bargaining and social dialogue. He advised that the next CNPF president should be more combative. If the employers refuse to accept state financial incentives to introduce shorter working hours and do not negotiate with the unions, it could precipitate more industrial action and social unrest.

A chronology of French employment relations

1791	Le Chapelier law forbad strikes and unions, but not employers' associations.
1821	Building industry employers' association established.
1830s–1840s	Many illegal combinations of workers and some collective agreements.
1864	Abolition of Le Chapelier law.
1871	Paris Commune.
1884	Unions were entitled to organise on a craft or industry basis, but not at the enterprise or plant level.
1895	Anarcho-syndicalist Amiens Charter asserted the CGT's independence of political parties.
1919	The CFTC established following the Pope's 1891 encyclical (see Chronology, ch. 6, on Italy). First national industrial employers' confederation founded.
1920	Peak of union density—approximately 25–30 per cent.
1921	CGT split, following Russian Revolution.
1934	General strike called by the CGT.
1936	Election of the Popular Front coalition of Socialists, Communists and radicals. Many strikes and sit-ins. Agreements between the employers' association and the reunited CGT heralded major social reforms including the introduction of employee delegates.
1944	The CGC established.
1945	The Liberation government initiated works committees within enterprises.
1946	The CNPF established as the main employers' association.
1948	Creation of the FO after a split within the CGT.
1950	Law on collective bargaining and the establishment of a minimum wage system.
1958	Multi-industry unemployment insurance agreement introduced the principle of national agreements.

1964	CFDT established as a secular breakaway from CFTC.
1965	Multi-industry four-week holiday agreement.
1966	Works committees' role extended in relation to training and profit sharing.
1968	Events of May precipitated a general strike. Workplace union branches permitted.
1970	Multi-industry job security agreement; a multi-industry *mensualisation* agreement granted 'single status' for blue-collar workers.
1971	Amendment to 1950 Act to permit plant-level bargaining.
1975	A multi-industry redundancy agreement, including a continuation of 90 per cent of previous job's pay levels.
1981	Mitterrand's Socialist–Communist coalition formed the government. The 39-hour working week ordinance.
1982	Auroux laws enacted. Prices and incomes policy initiated. Retirement age reduced from 65 to 60.
1983	Major strikes in the car factories.
1984	Abortive multi-industry negotiations to introduce more flexibility in employment protection laws (initiated by the CNPF). The Communists left the 1981 coalition.
1986	Socialist government replaced by a Right-of-Centre government.
1987	New Redundancy Act repealed the earlier requirement for administrative approval before redundancies. New flexible work-time law.
1988	Socialist government returns to power and announces its first social program.
1988	Bill on minimum integration income (*Revenu minimum d'insertion*).
1989	Socialist government announces its second social program.
1990	Important multi-industry agreements are reached.
1991	Restructuring of the national employment office.
1992	The government launched significant job-creation programs to counter long-term unemployment.
1993	Socialist government overwhelmingly lost the legislative elections. A right-wing coalition government took office under Prime Minister Balladur, but President Mitterrand continued in his post.
1994	Implementation of the 'five-year employment plan' of the Balladur government.
1995	Jacques Chirac elected President. Major public sector strikes against the policies of the Juppé government.

1997 General election called prematurely by President Jacques Chirac; advent of a left-wing government headed by Prime Minister Lionel Jospin.

8 Employment relations in Germany

Friedrich Fürstenberg

Modern German industrial relations history can be divided into at least four periods: first, the pre-Hitler period, before 1933; second, the Hitler period between 1933 and 1945; third, the post-Hitler period of 1945–90, when there was a political division between West and East Germany; and fourth, the post-1990 period of reunification. This chapter starts by putting German employment relations into context. It discusses the unions' and employers' roles before considering two main processes of employment relations—collective bargaining and co-determination.

West Germany (the Federal Republic) was founded in 1949 within the western territories of the former German Reich. Almost a quarter of the population originally entered the country as refugees. Following reunification, Germany had a total population of 82 million people, with the new eastern federal States having a population of 15.5 million; 44 per cent of the population were in civilian employment. In the western federal States the male participation rate was 80 per cent and the female participation rate was 61 per cent. Relatively more people were employed in industry (38 per cent) than in any other Organisation for Economic Co-operation and Development (OECD) country. The services sector employed 59 per cent, while 3.3 per cent were in the agricultural sector (see Appendix). The most substantial shift has been from the agricultural sector, which employed 25 per cent in 1950 (*Statistisches Jahrbuch* 1967:138). These shifts also had a profound impact on the structure of the labour force, as shown in Table 8.1. Germany has a low birth rate, about 11 per 1000, but is densely populated with 225 people per square kilometre.

The reconstruction of industry after the Second World War has been

Table 8.1   Status categories of the German labour force (as a percentage)

	1950[a]	1961[a]	1970[b]	1983[b]	1988[a]	1994[a]
Blue-collar	51	49	47	40	38	36
White-collar (incl. civil service)	21	29	36	47	51	54
Independently employed	14	12	10	9	9	9.1
Assisting family member	14	10	7	4	2	1.4
Total	100	100	100	100	100	100

Sources: a   Statistisches Jahrbuch (various years).
           b   Wirtschaft und Statistik (various years).

termed an 'economic miracle'; however, this country has experienced some of the greatest increases in unemployment since 1970 of any of the countries in this book. Unemployment rose from 0.6 per cent in 1970 to 9.7 per cent in March 1997 (OECD 1997). This dramatic rise in unemployment is due to economic restructuring and a general recession, but there are indications that economic growth will resume again, especially once reunification has been fully implemented. Germany is the most powerful economy in Europe. While the unification process is difficult and causing some setbacks, a reunited Germany should create an even more powerful economy in due course.

Between 1991 and 1997 there was a 34 per cent increase in the cost of living for an average, middle-income four-person household. The average annual income of workers increased between 1972 and 1992 by 193 per cent. Since 1992 *real* wages have shown a slightly diminishing tendency. However, international comparisons show Germany has high labour costs, partly due to steady increases in the cost of benefits that are a consequence of social regulations. Also, due to high social-insurance contributions, the average take-home pay of a production worker in manufacturing (single-earner household with two children) is only 77 per cent of gross earnings (Hart 1996).

West German politics have been dominated by three political parties since the Second World War:

1   the Christian Democratic Union (CDU) and its sister party in Bavaria, the Christian Social Union (CSU);
2   the Social Democratic Party of Germany (*Sozialdemokratische Partei Deutschlands*, SPD);
3   the Free Democratic Party (FDP).

At regional and local levels, the Green Movement has had an increasing impact. In view of the system of 'personalised proportional

representation', it is extremely difficult for one party to win an absolute majority in elections. Only in 1957 did the CDU–CSU succeed in
so doing. Otherwise, at the federal level in West Germany there has
always been a coalition government, with the FDP playing an important
role in spite of its small share of votes. This might change, however,
as the FDP faces a severe structural crisis. Before 1966 and since 1982,
the CDU–CSU have had the majority in Cabinet, but from 1966
until 1969 there was a 'Great Coalition' between CDU–CSU and SPD.
From 1969 until 1982 the SPD had the majority. Since 1990, the
CDU–CSU has continued to form the government, while radical parties
have dwindled. In the East, however, former communists formed the
Party of Democratic Socialism (PDS), which gained more than a fifth
of the votes in the 1994 federal elections, and has subsequently been
present in the federal Parliament. The rate of participation in elections
has been declining slightly and 'floating voters' have become increasingly important.

As they are 'integrative' parties opposing radicalism, CDU–CSU
and SPD have strong factions representing workers' interests. From
1987 till 1990, within the federal Parliament, 2 per cent of CDU–CSU
deputies and 8.9 per cent of SPD deputies were *employees* of unions
or other workers' organisations, while 35 per cent of CDU–CSU
deputies and 99 per cent of SPD deputies were union members. Following the principle of 'bargaining autonomy', the federal government
abstains from direct interference in employment relations; governments
generally do not adopt definite pro- or anti-union policies, despite
frequent controversies regarding social and labour legislation. Thus, for
example, co-determination was introduced in 1951 under a government
dominated by the CDU–CSU and led by Adenauer.

The employment relations parties

Industrialisation in Germany began later than in Britain, but earlier than
in Sweden. German industrialisation took off relatively quickly in the
closing decades of the nineteenth century. Unlike that of Britain, the
German factory system developed within a society that retained a legacy
of paternalism. Notions of a 'vertically-bonded works community' grew
in this context (cf. Fox 1985).

Unions

The German labour movement grew out of the 1848 Revolution (see
the Chronology at the end of this chapter). German unions were mainly
occupationally based with strong ideological affiliations. They were
strongly opposed by the state and employers at the beginning of

Germany's Imperial era, but later won significant social and political roles, especially in the post-1918 Weimar Republic. However, the unions were abolished by Hitler under national socialism in 1933. Following this traumatic experience, after the Second World War the surviving union leaders aimed to establish a more unified union movement as an important way of fostering democracy.

There are four major union confederations:

1   the German Trade Union Federation (*Deutscher Gewerkschaftsbund*, DGB) with 16 affiliated unions and 9.4 million members, which is the most influential confederation.
2   the Confederation of German Civil Service Officials (*Deutscher Beamtenbund*, DBB) with 1.1 million members;
3   the German Salaried Employees' Union (*Deutsche Angestelltengewerkschaft*, DAG) with 507 000 members;
4   the Confederation of Christian Trade Unions of Germany (*Christlicher Gewerkschaftsbund Deutschlands*, CGB), which has no role in collective bargaining and operates in some regions, with 304 000 members.

The relative density of organisation is shown in Table 8.2. There is also a much smaller confederation: the Union of Senior Managers (*Union der Leitenden Angestellten*, ULA). It does not generally identify itself with the labour movement and aims to represent senior executives.

Table 8.2   Union density[a]

		Employees				
		Civil service	White-collar	Blue-collar	Total	Women
Employees	Total (millions)	2.5	16.8	13.0	32.2	13.8
	% of all employees	7.6	52.1	40.3	100	42.9
% of unions' share among organised employees	DGB	47.8	73.9	97.7	83.2	81.1
	DBB	49.7	7.8	0.3	9.6	9.0
	DAG	—	14.1	—	4.5	7.8
	CGB	2.5	4.2	2.0	2.7	2.2
	Total %	100	100	100	100	100
Union density (% of union members)	Total %	64.0	21.4	45.1	34.9	25.5
	DGB	30.6	15.8	44.1	29.0	20.7
	DBB	31.8	1.7	0.1	3.3	2.3
	DAG	—	3.0	—	1.6	2.0
	CGB	1.6	0.9	0.9	0.9	0.6

Note: a   1995 data.
Source: Institut der Deutschen Wirtschaft, Köln 1996 (figures rounded).

However, it has only about 43 000 members and only two of its affiliates are recognised for collective bargaining.

Under its federal structure, the real power within the DGB lies with the industrial unions. The three largest among them are the Union of Metal Industry Workers (*IG Metall*) with 3.1 million members; the Union of Public Service, Transport and Communications Workers (*Gewerkschaft Öffentliche Dienste, Transport und Verkehr*) with 2 million members; and the Union of Chemical, Paper and Ceramics Industry Workers (*IG Chemie-Papier-Keramik*) with 778 000 members. These three unions dominate the triennial congress of the DGB. The DGB mainly performs coordinating and representative functions for the union movement. It also maintains a major research institute (*Wirtschafts und Sozialwissenschaftliches Institut des DGB*). It regularly publishes survey results and monographs about the issues of working life. Like many German enterprises, it has been 'downsized'.

With the exception of the CGB, German unions are based upon an ideological pluralism, which leaves scope for internal competition among factions. The social-democratic group is the most influential. Radical factions have attained influence only at local levels. The internal structure of the unions is characterised by representative democracy. But there is still an important element of direct member participation. With the exception of the Union of Printing Workers, a union may call a strike only after having won a 75 per cent majority in favour, in a secret ballot. On the whole, however, union policy is highly centralised for three reasons. Firstly, collective bargaining is conducted mainly at industry and regional levels; secondly, unions pursue policies that embrace wider social issues; and thirdly, employment relations are highly bureaucratic and legalistic, which has induced the involvement of experts.

It is important to note the broad scope of the DGB's policies. These aim to safeguard and improve workers' rights, not only at the workplace and enterprise levels, but also at the level of industry and wider society. Union activity thus transcends the realm of working conditions to embrace, for instance, concern about work organisation and technological change. The unions also participate in adult education activities through their well-equipped training centres.

Union policy is 'cooperative', in so far as unions receive information and are consulted about all major areas of social and economic policy. This extends to practically all public policy relating to the quality of life of the working population and their dependants. Technically, the unions are neutral in party politics; nevertheless, their political presence is obvious. The German unions are not only powerful partners in collective bargaining, but they also exert great influence on political and social life. Their structural power, gained from institutionalised participation (see below), was augmented in the 1970s by an increase in unionisation, due to favourable labour market conditions and the politicisation of younger, especially female, employees. Density of the DGB unions increased between 1970 and 1985 from 30 to 35 per cent. The economic recession and the restructuring of German industry caused a decline in union membership as well as a financial weakening of the DGB. Union density in the DGB was reduced between 1992 and 1994 by 3 per cent to 36 per cent, and this decline has continued (see Appendix for union density data). This is the main reason behind attempts at reform discussed at the end of the chapter.

Employers

There is considerable industrial concentration. In 1989, more than 39 per cent of those in employment worked in establishments with more than 1000 employees (compared with less than 1 per cent who worked in establishments with less than 20 employees). Nevertheless, small and medium-sized enterprises shape the employment structure in several important sectors.

Unlike those from English-speaking countries, for instance, German corporations have a two-tier board structure. It is the lower, management board (*Vorstand*) that runs the firm and implements most decisions. However, the strategic decisions are formally endorsed by the upper, supervisory board (*Aufsichtsrat*) that reviews managerial performance. The supervisory board appoints the top managers, but generally meets only four times per year, and so cannot interfere directly in management (as discussed later).

Employers' associations began for defensive purposes as a response to the growth of unions in the second half of the nineteenth century (Bunn 1984). Neither unions nor employers' associations were allowed under the Third Reich period. After 1945, the employers' associations re-emerged, following the return of unions. Employers' interests were organised centrally in parallel with those of the unions. The Confederation of German Employers' Associations (*Bundesvereinigung Deutscher Arbeitgeberverbände*, BDA) represents 48 national branch federations and 15 regional federations, comprising about 80 per cent of all enterprises. The confederation has a range of committees and working groups, which provide expert opinions and prepare political platforms. For this purpose, the employers' federations also jointly operate two research institutes (*Institut der Deutschen Wirtschaft* and *Institut für Angewandte Arbeitswissenschaft*).

Neither the BDA nor DGB participate directly in collective bargaining, but they coordinate and provide information. The member organisations, however, are the real centres of employers' power. They have substantial 'strike protection funds' and are the partners of unions in collective bargaining, except where there is company bargaining (e.g. at VW, which is an unusual case). Unlike their equivalent associations in the English-speaking countries, the German employers organise lockouts of workers in response to industry-wide strikes, especially in major metalworkers' disputes (Owen Smith 1981:199). In common with most other countries, the employers' organisations are ideologically conservative and act as the employers' voice to the state.

In spite of the large variety of enterprises, differing in size, production and market situation, the employers try to maintain solidarity during industry-wide negotiations. However, there is increasing flexibility provided by the system of enterprise, or plant-centred negotiations between works councils and management. These negotiations implement and augment collective agreements at industry level (see below).

There are different organisations in the public sector. At municipal level, the Federation of Local Government Employers' Associations (*Vereinigung der Kommunalen Arbeitgeberverbände*, VKA), and at State government level, the German State Government Employers' Association (*Tarifgemeinschaft der Deutschen Länder*, TDL), have operated since 1949. At national level, since 1960 the Federal Minister of the Interior has been 'the employer' in negotiations.

The role of government

Germany has an extensive framework of labour law. The Federal constitution (1949) grants the freedom of association and right to organise. Employment relations are generally regulated by statutory law. There is a division of labour between local courts, regional appeal courts and a Federal Labour Court.

There is extensive legislation, for example, on labour standards; hours of work; sick pay; protection against summary dismissals; and establishing employment rights for young workers, women and disabled people, as well as expectant or nursing mothers. In addition there are health and safety laws, which are implemented by Industrial Injuries Insurance Institutes. These are self-governing public corporations under state supervision. Labour and management are equally represented on the decision-making bodies of these institutions. In many other areas of public concern there are also administrative networks for institutionalised cooperation between government, employer and labour representatives.

A comprehensive social security system has developed since the first introduction of social insurance in the 1880s. It is administered by self-governing agencies with either bipartite or tripartite boards. There is a Federal Institute for Labour at Nuremberg, which administers the Federal Employment Service and the Unemployment Insurance Fund as well as Unemployment Assistance and Family Allowances. It also operates a large research institute on all matters of labour market policy.

There is much vocational training in Germany; in this regard it is often seen by other countries as a role model. In 1991, about 55 per cent of all people over 15 years of age had completed a three-year period of such training, and/or vocational school attendance, after having finished full-time education. Further, 8.8 per cent had completed technical college training, had graduated from professional schools, or were university graduates (*Wirtschaft und Statistik*). Moreover there is a continuing trend towards higher qualifications in the upper grades of the labour force.

The attempt to create a form of 'concerted action', aimed at a kind of national incomes policy, failed due to disagreement about the goals (cf. Clark et al. 1980). On the other hand, the main strategies of employers and unions cannot succeed without taking government action into consideration (e.g. in the case of policy options for or against state-financed additional employment). Government policy on employment relations, however, is not to interfere, thus respecting the principle of collective bargaining autonomy (*Tarifautonomie*). State influence is generally limited to setting a normative framework and publishing basic pay data, especially on socio-economic targets and on trends in planning the federal budget.

The main processes

Governmental interference in collective bargaining is rare. There is no governmental mediation, as the parties provide their own voluntary conciliation system. Nevertheless, in major disputes the government usually gets involved, informally.

Collective bargaining

German employment relations has a dual structure. At workplace and plant levels there is no direct bargaining between unions and employers. Instead, works councils and employers negotiate on a statutory basis. It is at industry-wide and regional levels (and less often at enterprise levels) that unions and the employers' federations enter into negotiations, which usually result in collective agreements. There were 45 000 registered collective agreements in 1996. The Collective Bargaining Law 1952 grants legal enforcement of agreements only to union members. However, most agreements apply to all employees in the particular sector of the economy. Distinctions between unionised and non-unionised workers are not allowed in collective agreements, following a Federal Labour Court decision in 1967.

There is a distinction between master agreements, which have a relatively long duration, and ordinary agreements, which usually last for a year and regulate major conditions of work such as pay, working time and leave of absence. Enterprise agreements cover a relatively small percentage of the workforce, mostly those employed in firms that do not belong to an employers' association. As can be seen from Table 8.3, a wide range of special provisions may become the subject of collective agreements. There is a growing tendency to cover pay issues for white-collar and blue-collar employees jointly.

Procedures in collective bargaining are highly formalised and even ritualised, as illustrated in the following example of a typical set of *IG Metall* negotiations:

1 The claim is discussed at plant level by the members and officers and then screened by negotiation committees, which make recommendations about the form and extent of the claim to the collective bargaining committee. Four weeks before termination of the collective agreement, the union informs the employers about the claim.
2 A negotiating committee is established. Bargaining starts two weeks before the expiry date of the current collective agreement.
3 There is a peace obligation which continues to apply for four weeks after the expiry date. After this period, the workers may initiate demonstrations and other sanctions.
4 A new collective agreement is negotiated or, in case of a failure to agree, one or both parties may declare a breakdown of the negotiations; then the union negotiating committee may propose a strike ballot.

Under stage 4, after a failure to agree, the parties may jointly appeal to a conciliation board within two working days; after another working

Table 8.3   Some contents of collective agreements

Contents	1974 (%)	1978 (%)	1988 (%)
Fringe benefits:			
holiday pay	79	93	94
annual bonus	60	76	92
profit/capital sharing	77	92	95
Social security:			
job security	32	52	—
wage guarantees	40	62	—
protection in case of rationalisation	45	48	55
extra unemployment compensation	21	—	—
sick pay	30	42	—

Source: Boedler & Kaiser (1979:26); Clasen (1989:17).

day this may be done by either party, unilaterally; the other would then have to join after two more working days. Then an independent chair of the conciliation board, usually a well-known retired politician or public servant, has to be nominated without delay. The board must convene within three working days and present a proposal within five working days. After six more working days, the parties in dispute have to decide whether or not to accept this proposal.

Unlike the position in Britain or Australia, such procedures are usually followed strictly. Moreover, there are relatively few stoppages in spite of the lack of legislation concerning strikes or lockouts (see Appendix). However, there are many legal constraints on industrial action, partly deriving from court decisions. Legal strikes are strictly limited to employment relations topics. It is generally illegal to call a strike about a wider political issue.

However, there have been some major disputes. There were stoppages in 1984, both in the printing and the metal industries. In the latter, the union wanted a reduction in the basic working week from 40 to 35 hours, with no loss of pay. This was part of the union's strategy to counter high levels of unemployment. But the employers insisted that such a reduction in hours would render German goods less competitive in international markets. Following a nine-week stoppage, as an alternative to reducing hours the employers proposed to introduce more flexible working hours. The government did not support the union's campaign, though it proposed to introduce early retirement provisions from the age of 58.

The outcome of this dispute was a compromise. The average basic week would become 38.5 hours in 1985, but by the late 1990s it had shrunk to 35 hours. Such variations could be negotiated at plant level. This represents a decentralisation of collective bargaining and increases the role of works councillors. The 1984 dispute revealed a new set of union tactics, called 'the new flexibility'. These tactics included local strikes, for example, in component-making firms, which in effect would stop production in much of the car-manufacturing industry, without the unions calling a general industry-wide stoppage.

There was another tough industrial dispute in 1992, when the public service union assumed leadership in the annual sequence of collective bargaining, and demanded a general wage increase in spite of the government's increasing difficulties in financing German reunification. The public service union members returned to work after an 11-day strike that brought chaos to the nation's transport system and left garbage lying uncollected in the streets. A general wage increase of 5.4 per cent was agreed with the government, but did not win the support of the rank and file. As a consequence, the position of the union's top leaders was severely weakened and there were moves to decentralise the union's power structure. Another potentially disruptive strike in the metal industry was narrowly averted two weeks later when employers agreed to an increase of 5.8 per cent (compared with the union's original demand for an increase of 9.5 per cent).

Although for Germany these were uncharacteristically controversial disputes, there is still a widespread consensus that stoppages should be a last resort and only about fundamental issues.

Co-determination

There is a long tradition of attempts to introduce industrial democracy in Germany. Works councils were first established by law in 1916, in industries that were important for the economy in the First World War. They became obligatory under the Works Councils Act of 1920.

Since the Second World War, various laws on co-determination have enlarged union influence at the enterprise level. These laws include:

1   the Works Constitution Act 1952–72, which enlarged the legal rights of works councils in private enterprises;
2   the Co-Determination Act 1951, which established full parity co-determination within the supervisory boards of the coal and steel industries, and a labour director as full member of the management board;
3   the Co-Determination Act 1976, which established countervailing parity in supervisory boards of limited liability companies with more than 2000 employees;
4   the Personnel Representation Act 1974, which provided for the election of staff councils in public services and enterprises.

The main instrument for implementing co-determination is the works council, elected by all employees of a firm regardless of their union affiliation, and operating on a defined legal basis (see Table 8.4). However, works councillors usually cooperate closely with union officers or hold union office themselves. Works councils cannot call a strike, but they have the right to sue management in a case of alleged breach of contractual rights. In such rare cases, the issue is referred to an arbitration tribunal.

Works councils have many rights to information, consultation and co-determination. The 1972 Works Constitution Act, for example, requires works council consent on works discipline; daily working hours and breaks; temporary short-time or overtime work; the fixing of piece rates; pay systems; suggestion schemes; holiday schedules; any monitoring of employee performance; safety regulations; welfare services in the establishment; and the administration of works housing for employees.

Works councils can also co-determine any changes to the pace of work or the working environment. In such cases, works councils may

Table 8.4   Results of works council elections (as a percentage)

	1981	1984	1987	1990	1994
Participation rate (total)	80	84	83	NA	NA
Participation rate blue-collar	80	83	83	79	79
Participation rate white-collar	79	83	84	76	77
Re-election works councillors	66	70	68	68	67
Re-election works council chairpersons	75	73	72	72	71
1st election works councillors	34	30	32	32	33
1st election works council chairpersons	25	27	29	28	29
Organisation density:					
DGB works councillors	63	64	65	69	67
DGB works council chairpersons	80	75	75	78	75
DAG works councillors	8.5	8.9	5.6	4.0	4.3
DAG works council chairpersons	5.2	6.8	3.6	3.8	4.5
CGB works councillors	3.7	0.8	1.0	1.0	1.6
CGB works council chairpersons	0.5	0.1	0.3	0.5	0.2
ULA works councillors	0.4	0.3	0.1	0.06	0.0
ULA works council chairpersons	0.5	0.04	0.01	0.1	0.1
Other works councillors	0.9	0.7	0.4	0.5	0.9
Other works council chairpersons	3.4	0.9	1.2	0.7	0.7
Non-organised works councillors	23	25	28	25	27
Non-organised works council chairpersons	11	17	20	16	20

Note: NA Not available.
Sources: Institut der Deutschen Wirtschaft (1988); Niedenhoff (1995).

demand ergonomic data, with the expense borne by the employer. They can also co-determine the process of personnel selection and occupational training. In the event of any major operational changes in the enterprise, the employer and the works council have to negotiate over the change and, in the case of any economic disadvantages for employees, agree on adequate layoff and compensation arrangements.

A representative system of co-determination always poses the problem of adequately representing all the different interests in a constituency. Works councils do reflect the relative strength of blue-collar and white-collar interests. Some groups, such as younger workers, the unskilled, women and foreign workers, tend to be proportionately under-represented, even though there is a trend towards increasing the proportion of women and foreign workers.

Relations between works councils and unions are usually close. In most enterprises, union officers participate in works council meetings from time to time. They regularly address works assemblies. Communication and cooperation between works councils and unions vary according to the degree of unionisation of the employees.

Labour directors were first established in the coal and steel (*Montan*) industries in 1951. They are appointed in the same way as other members of the management board, but they cannot be appointed against the wishes of the employees' representatives on the supervisory board, who usually initiate such an appointment. Usually these directors are well-qualified and experienced union members (but not officials). Labour directors have a special concern with personnel and social policy, but also participate fully in the shaping of general company policy, which has to be jointly agreed by the members of the managing board. Thus a dual allegiance is established: the labour director is responsible both for effective management and for effective representation of the workers' points of view.

In other industries, labour directors are not institutionally linked with unions and have clearly defined managerial functions. Therefore, there is no question of a dual or conflicting loyalty. In dealing with co-determination in supervisory boards, two types of legal provisions have to be considered. In the case of a minority representation, members elected by the workforce cannot determine decisions against the will of shareholders' representatives. Outside the coal and steel industries, such situations are typical. For companies with less than 2000 but more than 500 employees, only one-third of each company's supervisory board members must be employee representatives, nominated by the works councils.

Parity of workers' representation has been achieved only in the coal and steel industries. In these industries, since 1951, representatives of capital have been nominated by the shareholders' meeting, while the labour representatives have been nominated by works councils and unions. The parties choose a chair by co-opting a 'neutral' person. In 1976, this system was extended to all German companies with more than 2000 employees. There are, however, two major differences between the 1951 and 1976 laws. With the exception of the coal and steel industries, in each company at least one employee representative is nominated by the *Leitende Angestellte* (senior executives). Furthermore, in impasse situations, the chair (nominated by the shareholders) has a casting vote.

From the employers' point of view there are five problems with the 1976 Co-Determination Act: the contradiction between parity and the property principle; the endangered autonomy of collective bargaining; the representation of middle-managerial employees below the senior executive level; the election procedures for nominating workers' representatives for the supervisory board; and the position of the labour director.

By contrast, the unions see other problems, especially the evasion tactics of some firms. By reorganising, altering the capital composition and changing the legal form of the enterprise, in 1978 alone about 30 companies tried to avoid extended co-determination in supervisory boards. Some other companies tried to change their statutes.

Subsequently, however, the situation stabilised. Between 1985 and 1992 the number of co-determined companies increased from 477 to 709 (in 1992 an extra 102 co-determined companies came from the new eastern federal States). Unions were also concerned about companies' secrecy, the lack of information disclosure, and about procedures that gave advantages to shareholders' representatives, such as the double vote for the chair in committees with a non-parity composition. In spite of such problems for unions, co-determination at supervisory board levels has generally led to a gradual modification of entrepreneurial goals, towards more socio-economic goals. This has included introducing social planning and implementing more retraining strategies in the face of technological change.

Current and future issues

Co-determination fosters a strategy of 'co-operative unionism', for several reasons. The unions were re-established after the Second World War as integrative associations, jointly representing the interests of workers with different political and ideological affiliations. The resulting concentration on social and economic issues and the independence from political parties marks a decisive difference when compared with employment relations in France or Italy, for example. Traditionally, German unions did not consider themselves merely as labour market institutions or 'business unions', unlike those in North America. The German unions generally aimed at settling larger issues in the wider society. There are still minorities of radicals and reformers who have different orientations, but most of them hold that the design and realisation of reforms are possible only by getting involved in decision-making processes. In the course of implementing the different co-determination laws, thousands of new functions and positions for union officials have been created, thus establishing a network of influence that cannot easily be abandoned. The knowledge they have gained has enabled unions to investigate new types of problems. Gradually the unions have developed an infrastructure matching their claim for co-determination, enabling them to deal with the employers on many more issues than traditionally defined by the scope of collective bargaining.

The relative success of co-determination was possible only because the employers and the managers became convinced that such a system provided an efficient way of managing employment relationships. The relatively low number of stoppages in Germany reflects its alternative means for preventing and settling disputes. Works councils provide an efficient grievance machinery at the enterprise level. Co-determination in supervisory boards is a form of conflict management; it provides for discussion of major issues and possible problems for the workforce before final decisions are taken. Consultation and negotiation start before the two sides become entrenched. The unions have an involvement at the early stages of social, technological and economic change. Strikes as an ultimate means for pressing workers' claims become necessary only in rare cases of fundamental dissent. As a consequence, however, bureaucratic procedures and oligarchic structures develop. These may exclude the shop floor from direct participation. In practice then, co-determination institutions at a higher level may lose touch with the rank and file.

Those who argue for more militancy and direct democracy in employment relations usually deplore strong union involvement in managerial affairs. But, putting ideological considerations aside, the growth of a segmented internal labour market in large companies calls for new union strategies. Co-determination is a pragmatic approach towards influencing working conditions. The effects of investment policy, for instance, on the organisation of work, qualifications and skills, cannot be influenced by traditional bargaining techniques. Instead, the whole process of making investment decisions and implementing them by technological, economic and possibly social planning needs to be accompanied by continuous communication and consultation in order to avoid outcomes detrimental to workers' interests. It is this communication and consultation structure, combined with the opportunities for greater influence, that co-determination provides. Its greater efficiency, however, is offset by complaints about the lack of direct participation. Thus, demands for more workplace-level democracy are an inherent dynamic factor in German industrial relations. Therefore, new managerial strategies like human resource management (HRM), which aim at increased employee commitments, challenge the often bureaucratic structures of plant co-management in personnel matters. Unlike in the English-speaking countries, the introduction of HRM has generally not been used to restrict the role of workers' representatives. Rather, HRM has added extra communication channels at workplace level.

Technological change and flexibility

Since the 1980s, the German economy has faced structural changes. Their impact upon employment relations can be illustrated by the changes in technology, often aimed at the reduction of labour costs. Union strategies focus upon protection against increases in work load and stress; prevention of de-skilling; and the reduction of working time as a protection against job losses. As there has not yet been a general policy of job creation by reducing working time, a possible consequence—an equivalent reduction of workers' income—is still controversial, despite the 1984 metal industry dispute (discussed further below).

Table 8.5   Government regulations on humane work design

Regulation	Year	Contents
Safety of Machines Act	1963	Obliges all users of machines and equipment to ensure that all safety rules are observed.
Works Constitution Act	1972	Regulates cooperation between works councils (i.e. shop committee) and management; contains special information rights and participation of workers in job design (workplaces, processes, technologies and the environment.
Occupational Safety Act	1973	Regulates the employment of security staff (medical and engineering) and the application of research findings on work humanisation.
Workplace Decree	1975	Contains minimum requirements for the work environment (noise, lighting, climate etc.).
Decree of Toxic Substances	1986	Sets maximum workplace concentrations of toxic substances to be observed.

Source: Projektträger Humanisierung des Arbeitslebens (1981).

Demands for government action usually focus on job creation and the maintenance of skills and qualifications. Unions are demanding a better linkage between the government's labour market and educational policies on the one hand, and its measures to improve the economic structure on the other. They advocate improving the policies on technological change. The research program for the 'humanisation of work life', administered by the Federal Ministry for Research and Technology, is supported in principle by all unions. However, as a prerequisite for this support the unions want to be involved in the design of research projects, through their representatives on advisory boards, and in their implementation, through works council participation at enterprise level. There have been many such action-research projects, though they have mainly been pilot studies. There is still a need to foster more implementation of the results.

Employers and their associations also assume some social responsibility for technological change. The challenge for them is to develop and utilise new technologies to foster productivity and competitiveness, while also providing more humane forms of job design and employment security. It is not easy for employers to find workable compromises between social, economic and technological considerations, which may be to some extent conflicting. Nevertheless, there is considerable scope for them to discuss such matters with unions and works councils. There

Figure 8.1   Regulation of issues associated with technological change under the Works Constitution Act[a]

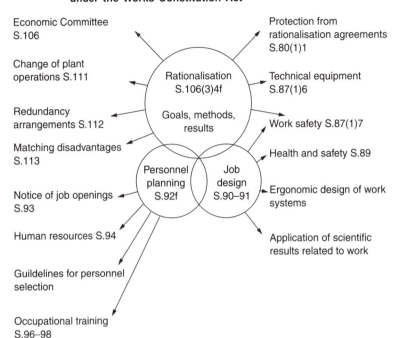

Economic Committee S.106		Protection from rationalisation agreements S.80(1)1
Change of plant operations S.111	Rationalisation S.106(3)4f	Technical equipment S.87(1)6
Redundancy arrangements S.112	Goals, methods, results	Work safety S.87(1)7
Matching disadvantages S.113		Health and safety S.89
	Personnel planning S.92f / Job design S.90–91	
Notice of job openings S.93		Ergonomic design of work systems
Human resources S.94		Application of scientific results related to work
Guildelines for personnel selection		
Occupational training S.96–98		

Notes: a   Adapted from Wiesner (1979:46).
          b   S refers to paragraphs of the Works Constitution Act.

are numerous cases of management, union and works council participation in the humanisation of work programs.

Government strategies to improve employment relations in view of technological change primarily focus upon adjusting the legal framework (see Table 8.5). As a result, the socio-economic environment for introducing technological change has been profoundly restructured. In particular, the Works Constitution Act provides considerable information, consultation and co-determination on plant-level employment relations issues, including those associated with technological change (see Figure 8.1).

Such regulations help the parties to cope successfully with the problems of introducing innovative applications of technology while maintaining consensus between the employment relations parties. Nevertheless, there are also other relevant factors. Perhaps the most important is job security. Between 1980 and 1989 the potential labour force increased by 2.1 million people, while the number of people employed remained stable. Most Germans, then, still seemed to accept that new technology was not generally destroying jobs; rather, its impact on employment depended on how it was introduced and on market conditions. Nevertheless, the rise in long-term unemployment rates in the late 1990s has become a more acute political problem. The reduction of employment opportunities for less-qualified groups of the labour force, however, is primarily seen as reflecting economic pressures, changes in demand, high levels of labour costs, and a relatively inflexible economy.

Reduction and flexibility of working time

The DGB hopes that the gradual introduction of a 35-hour week will have a lasting, positive effect on employment. By contrast, the employers advocate the notion of a 'new policy on working hours', which promotes more flexibility of working time, to be attained by a more economically efficient deployment of labour. The employers argue that this will result in the creation of new jobs. This trend towards a reduction in working time has led to a difficult situation in which employers, employees and their representatives are faced with a complex challenge.

Appropriate working-time arrangements must take account of specific work situations. It is necessary to distinguish between sectors of industry, levels (workplace, enterprise, industry), categories of workers (shift workers, etc.) and the scope of regulations (weekly working time, holidays, retirement). To what extent are collective and individual working-time arrangements effective in attaining general employment policy objectives? Linked to this important question is the unions' basic problem of trying to ensure that individual flexible working-time arrangements do not lead to unduly flexible and fragmented working conditions.

A major union strategy is to neutralise the adverse effects of productivity increases on employment by the reduction of weekly working hours. However, this approach, when combined with claims for a full wage adjustment, is precipitating conflict with employers. The employers' strategies have usually been to retain a cost-benefit advantage. Such strategies could overcome the unions' initial successes in wining reduced working hours.

It is difficult to coordinate working-time objectives with a general employment policy. As the organisation of working time affects the whole way of life of workers, as well as that of their families, it cannot be reduced to a single dimension—employment policy considerations. Accordingly unions are concerned about possible increases in work intensity as a result of reductions in working hours.

One possible way to resolve these difficulties would be to try to analyse the competing interests in a general framework. The outcome of labour disputes in the metal and printing industries led initially to a fairly general introduction of the 38.5-hour week (but in the metal industry a 35-hour week was subsequently introduced). This has shown that a realistic reorganisation of working time must allow for a general reduction in working time and flexible implementation, depending upon the particular contexts. However, the only system likely to be acceptable to all would have to be economically viable and feasible from the employers' standpoint. From the workers' perspective, such a system would have to guarantee that their right of co-determination and their influence in collective bargaining would not be reduced.

This problem has to be tackled at several levels. At the level of the national economy, changes need to be made to the system of working hours; at sectoral or regional levels, new regulations must be incorporated into collective agreements; and new works agreements must be signed at the level of enterprises and workplaces. Flexibility in working hours may be attained in particular enterprises provided that it is not at the expense of workers' interests, and that it remains within the regulatory framework.

Consequences of German reunification

The reunification of East and West Germany has had a profound impact on employment relations. Within the former German Democratic Republic, free and independent unions did not exist. The 'Free German Trade Union Federation' (*Freier Deutscher Gewerkschaftsbund*, FDGB), with 9.6 million compulsory members, and therefore a density of 98 per cent, recognised the leadership of the Communist Party (*Sozialistische Einheitspartei Deutschlands*, SED) in its constitution. Its main functions were cooperation in implementing centralised economic planning, and the administration of fringe benefits and welfare agencies. It had no experience with collective bargaining and freely elected works councils. As a consequence, the FDGB had no role in the opposition to and overthrow of the old regime. In September 1990 the FDGB dissolved and since October 1990 the DGB has claimed coverage of the whole of reunited Germany. West German legislation, including the Collective Agreements Act and the Works Constitution Act, has been introduced. Works council elections have taken place and collective agreements have been concluded. Unionisation was organised reasonably successfully with the support of West German union staff. As a result, union members in the new eastern federal States were integrated into the German union structure. There have been similar developments on the employers' side.

But this organisational restructuring is overshadowed by the employment crisis in what was East Germany. Major parts of its industry had to close, usually as a consequence of outdated plant and equipment and the loss of markets in Eastern Europe. More than a third of workers in the former GDR lost their jobs following reunification. Furthermore, nearly all of the former GDR's 8.5 million workers required new qualifications or refresher courses to raise their skill levels to the standards of the West (McCathie 1992:16). The policy of equalising wage levels between the eastern and western federal States, such as occurred in the metal industry, exacerbates the problem of a substantial productivity gap. Special agreements at enterprise and workplace levels appeared to be necessary in many cases. In economically weak enterprises facing the threat of unemployment and shutdown, many works councils in the new eastern federal States formed a *Notgemeinschaft*, an emergency association with their employer, resulting in a kind of co-management as a defence against external pressures. Thus emerging employment relations structures in the new eastern federal States may exhibit such innovations.

Conclusion

The German employment relations system is facing major challenges due to internal and external structural changes. There are increasing moves to reorganise unions and employers' federations, as they are considered to be inflexible and no longer adequate for changing economic and employment structures. Some smaller unions are experiencing dwindling memberships due to the transfer of production into low-wage countries or, as in the mining industry, site closures. One remedy is union mergers, such as that between the Chemical and Mining Workers, or at least close cooperation, as between the DAG and the Commercial Workers.

In the face of continuing de-industrialisation, particularly in the former East Germany, unions have to turn their attention to new sectors and forms of employment where traditional attitudes towards union membership do not prevail. The dwindling share of young people in unions is concentrating the minds of union leaders. It is encouraging them to develop new services for members.

Employers' associations have also experienced pressures from their members. Firms suffering from the recession and structural change plead for lower margins in settling work conditions, especially pay rates, and sometimes prefer to quit the employer associations and escape from their collective agreements.

This also indicates a fundamental change in the negotiation levels. The prevailing industry-wide, or regional, collective bargaining is increasingly criticised, especially by employers within the metal manufacturing industries. Bargaining at enterprise and plant levels is increasing in importance to cope with a growing diversity of business circumstances and the need to increase productivity. This may result in a growing role for works councils; however, legal regulations limit their bargaining scope.

Externally, since 1993 the single European market and the planned EMU have been challenging the maintenance of the post-1949 West German traditions of co-operation within a national *Soziale Marktwirtschaft* (socially-negotiated market economy). Increased transnational pressures towards deregulating labour markets are precipitating organisational innovations. Nation-based structures and strategies are further weakened by the trends towards globalisation of finance, marketing and production operations in key industries. These economic constraints narrow the scope for implementing socially acceptable policies.

The situation is aggravated by enormous transfer payments from the former West Germany to the new eastern federal States, which will continue well into the twenty-first century. Pressures on the labour market are also likely to be compounded by the influx of migrant workers from Eastern European countries, such as in the building and construction industries. The future development of employment relations in Germany, therefore, will reflect not only German issues, but will also increasingly reflect the challenges at the levels of the European Union and beyond.

Generally, there are good prospects for Germany to maintain and further develop its post-1949 innovations in employment relations, if the key players pay attention to the need to increase flexibility and participation, especially at the enterprise and workplace level.

A chronology of German employment relations

1832	Secret association of German craftsworkers in France, Switzerland and Britain.
1844	Silesian weavers' revolt.
1846	*Gesellenverein* (journeymen's association) founded.
1848	Year of revolutions.
1848–54	General German Workers' Fraternity, comprising 31 workers' associations and three workers' committees.
1848–53	Association of cigar-producing workers.
1849–53	Printers' association formed.
1863	Foundation of the General German Workers' Association.
1865–67	First national associations of cigar workers, printers and tailors.

1869	Foundation of Social Democratic Workers' Party.
1869	Prussian Trades Law grants freedom of coalition.
1873	First collective agreement (in the printing trade).
1878–90	Anti-socialist legislation.
1891	First industrial union—German Metal Workers' Association.
1892	First trades union congress.
1894	Foundation of first large Christian trade union (coal miners).
1899	Congress of Free Trade Unions recommends collective agreements.
1904	Main employers' association founded.
1905	First long strike by the German miners' union.
1913	Association of German Employers' Federations established, with 3 million union members; 10 885 collective agreements cover 1.4 million employees.
1914–18	First World War.
1916	Law to enforce works committees in all production establishments with more than 50 workers.
1918	Law on collective agreements.
1918–24	Central Working Commission of employers and workers in manufacturing industries and trades.
1919	Foundation of General German Trades Union Federation (ADGB).
1920	General Strike against rightist riot (*Kapp-Putsch*).
1920	Works Councils Act.
1921	Foundation of *Akademie der Arbeit* (Academy for Labour Studies).
1927	Law on labour courts.
1928	Law on collective agreements.
1928	Thirteenth ADGB Congress discusses co-determination.
1933	Unions abolished by National Socialist government.
1939–45	Second World War.
1945	Decision to found the DGB
1949	Founding Congress of DGB.
1951	Co-determination Act for coal and steel industries.
1952	Works Constitution Act.
1955	Personnel Representation Act (for employees in the public sector).
1963	Foundation of Christian Trade Union Movement.
1963	Lockout of metal workers.
1967	'Concerted action' begins.
1972	New Works Constitution Act.
1974	New Personnel Representation Act.

1976	Co-determination Act for firms with more than 2000 employees.
1978–79	Steel strike: dispute about shorter working week.
1984	Metal workers' dispute about a shorter working week.
1989	Amendment of the Works Constitution Act, including minority protection, definition of managerial employees, and consultation in technological change.
1990	Reunification of West and East Germany. Dissolution of FDGB.
1992	Public services strike.
1995	Failure of attempts to establish a joint platform between the government, employers and unions to confront increasing unemployment.
1996	Attempts to cut the costs of social security by restricting sick pay precipitated some industrial disputes. Various settlements resulted in the maintenance of sick pay but cuts in the level of Christmas bonuses.

9 Employment relations in Sweden

Olle Hammarström and Tommy Nilsson

Sweden became an industrial society later than most of the other countries covered in this book. At the turn of the century, Sweden was a poor agrarian society with high emigration. Sweden today is to a large extent a welfare-oriented, service society. Sweden has 26 per cent of its civilian workforce employed in industry; 3 per cent are still in agriculture; while 71 per cent are in services, partly as a result of the very strong growth of local and regional government since the 1960s (see Appendix).

Swedish employment relations have long fascinated foreign observers. With a total population of 8.8 million and with 4.3 million in the labour force, Sweden is the smallest of the countries discussed in this book. However, 75 per cent of its women are in the labour force, which is still the highest female participation rate of any Organisation for Economic Co-operation and Development (OECD) country (although the female participation rate has fallen in recent years.).

After the 1994 election, there were seven political parties represented in the Parliament. (The percentage of the popular vote that they each received is given here in brackets.) Four of them are liberal conservative *(bourgeois)* parties: the Conservative Party (22 per cent); the Centre Party (7 per cent); the Liberal Party (7 per cent); and the Christian Democratic Party (4 per cent). The Social Democratic Party *(Socialdemokratiska Arbetarpartiet*, SAP) was returned in 1994 and formed a minority government. A new 'green' party called the Environment Party received 5 per cent of the popular vote. The small Left Party (6 per cent) has never been part of any Swedish government, but it has often been an ally to the much more important Social Democratic Party (42 per cent), which formed the government for 53 years of the

59 year period from 1932 to 1991, including a continuous period of 44 years between 1932 and 1976 (Hammarström & Mahon 1994).

During the long period of Social Democratic government, Sweden became known as a country of high taxes and as a highly developed welfare state. In the 1980s, the average *take home* pay in Swedish manufacturing industry was only 66 per cent of *gross earnings* (after tax and social security contributions, but excluding family benefits), which was a lower percentage than in any of the other countries. In the period 1984–93, there was an average annual increase in the consumer price index (CPA) in Sweden of about 6.2 per cent, higher than for any of the other countries in this book (see Appendix).

After a marked shift in economic policy in the early 1990s, the inflation rate fell below the European Union (EU) average. At the same time the previously low level of unemployment (1.8 per cent in 1990) increased and reached 10 per cent in 1996. Nevertheless, for most of the post-war period, Swedish unemployment has consistently been less than in most of the other countries discussed in this book. Some years it has been even lower than in Japan (see Appendix).

Historical context

Following its relatively late industrialisation, Sweden also became unionised somewhat later than other countries. The trade union movement started to develop during the 1880s. At first, the Social Democratic Party, which was established in 1889, functioned as a union confederation, but then the Swedish Trade Union Confederation (*Landsorganisationen i Sverige*, LO) was formed in 1898. The employer organisations developed as a response to the growth of the unions. The Swedish Employers' Confederation (*Svenska Arbetsgivareföreningen*, SAF) was established in 1902 (Korpi 1978).

The Swedish union movement began with craft unions but by 1910 the concept of industry unions was dominant. Several factors explain this shift. Social democratic union organisers worked hard to have industrial unionism accepted by the union movement, but it must be noted that craft training was also poorly developed at the time when the first unions were formed. Furthermore, industrialisation occurred to a large extent in the form of '*bruk*', or one-company towns or villages, where it was natural to form one union against the one employer (Fulcher 1988).

The right to organise and bargain collectively had no legal basis at first and was strongly contested by the employers. The first industrial disputes were combined struggles for the right to organise and for higher pay in the 1870s. These struggles intensified around the turn of the century; for example, in a lockout in the engineering industry in

1905. These conflicts led to the recognition of union rights in the so-called 'December compromise' of 1906. In an agreement with LO, SAF acknowledged the unions' right to organise and bargain collectively. For its part, LO accepted that all collective agreements were to include a clause giving the employer 'the full right to hire and fire and to organise production'. The agreement was seen as a major step forward by the union side. The right to organise had been achieved, even though the precedence of employers' rights was then commonly seen as the natural state of affairs. This was the first example of a major agreement reached by the central organisations on behalf of their affiliated unions and employer associations.

However, the 'December compromise' was not fully recognised by all employers, and some of them therefore continued to implement anti-union policies. The first nation-wide dispute was in 1909. The legendary 'Great Strike' started as a lockout by employers in an attempt to weaken the unions. The dispute ended with the workers returning to work without an agreement. It was a heavy defeat for the unions, whose membership declined from 162 000 members in 1908 to 85 000 members in 1910 (Tilton 1990).

Industrial relations legislation developed slowly. It was reactive rather than promoting reform. In 1906 an Act on voluntary mediation was passed and a small mediation office was established. During the period 1910–20, employers and conservative politicians tried on several occasions to introduce legislation that would restrict unions' rights to strike. These attempts were blocked by socialist and liberal interests. As strikes continued to be seen as a major social problem, Acts on Collective Bargaining and the Labour Court were passed in 1928, despite union opposition. These Acts were the first legal recognition of union rights (Johnson 1962; Hanami & Blanpain 1987).

In 1932, after the election of the first Social Democratic government with a workable parliamentary majority, the situation changed. The unions adopted a new strategy as they no longer saw the government as a natural ally of the employers. The new relationship between capital and labour led to the Basic Agreement of 1938 (also known as the Saltsjöbaden Agreement, named after the place where the negotiations took place), which laid the foundation for labour–management cooperation and consultation. This spirit of cooperation became known as 'the Swedish model' during the 1950s and 1960s.

There are no official definitions of the 'Swedish model'. Various writers have given it different meanings (e.g. Rehn & Viklund 1990). Common to all definitions, however, is the philosophy that unions and employers should take full responsibility for wage formation and industrial peace, whereas the government should take responsibility for upholding full employment and economic stability. The factors that brought unions and employers together to form the Swedish model were the common interest to stimulate economic rationalisation and productivity growth and the desire to avoid government interference in collective bargaining (see Olsson 1989; Brulin & Nilsson 1991; Brulin 1995).

The cooperative spirit of the Swedish model was codified into the Basic or Industrial Peace Agreement of 1938. After that followed other agreements that together formed the collective bargaining base for the Swedish model. They were the Industrial Welfare Agreement of 1942; the Works Council Agreement of 1946; the Vocational Training Apprentices Agreement of 1947; and the Time and Motion Studies Agreement of 1948.

Before the Second World War the Social Democratic government largely followed a Keynesian economic policy, which used budget deficits to fight unemployment. After the war, a significantly modified version of Keynesian policy was developed. In 1951, the LO Congress adopted a policy based on the so-called 'Rehn–Meidner' model, named after two prominent LO economists who proposed a new approach to economic policy. LO advanced the view that trade unions should take into account the government's economic policy when formulating their wage demands. In exchange for union support, the government agreed to pursue a policy of full employment. Economic growth was secured by union commitment to rationalisation and technical development. This government also gave support to an 'active labour market policy' that encouraged both geographical and skill mobility for displaced workers. The Labour Market Board (*Arbetsmarknadsstyrelsen*, AMS) was established in 1948 and has subsequently assumed a strong role in developing labour market policies (Meidner 1983). This national and largely centralised 'active labour market policy', however, has recently been regarded as decreasing in effectiveness. Hence, a change is under way to decentralise labour market policy, involving local politicians as well as representatives of unions and employers.

In adopting the program based on the Rehn–Meidner model, the unions assumed partial responsibility for national economic performance, thereby changing their policy from that of the early 1930s. Thus, industrial conflict was partly transferred to the political arena with the state taking an active part in income redistribution through taxation and social security legislation. The period from 1950 to the end of the 1960s was one of stability in the labour market. Steady economic growth, particularly through the 1960s, meant that wage disputes were settled without great difficulties. Unions accepted management's right to 'hire and fire' and to rationalise production within the expanding sectors of the economy. This transition process was facilitated by the government's active labour market policy. The main emphasis of union demands during this period was on improved social security.

Major reforms in the old-age pension system, known as the *Allmän tilläggspension* (ATP), were introduced in 1960 along with other social benefits. The ATP scheme is an earnings-related indexed pension system, funded by employer contributions. It allows employees to retire at 65 years of age, with a pension of 65 per cent of their income during their ten best working years. The political controversy over the pension system (compulsory system or voluntary system) dominated political debate for almost ten years and contributed to a continuation of the political domination by the Social Democrat Party.

During this period, LO implemented its policy of a 'solidaristic' wage policy, which was an essential element of the Rehn–Meidner model. The policy had two ingredients. One was 'equal pay for equal work' regardless of industry or company. That meant that company profit levels were not the main basis for negotiations. Subsequently, poor economic performers were forced out of business, while the profits in the most successful companies were not challenged by the unions. The other dimension of the 'solidaristic' wage policy was the narrowing of the gap between the lower paid and the higher paid workers. The gap was attacked by both a progressive taxation system and pay contracts that gave extra wage increases to low-income earners (Delsen & Van Veen 1992).

The harmonious pattern of industrial relations that emerged in Sweden during the 1950s and 1960s was facilitated by steady economic growth. The industrial development of Sweden was originally based on natural resources: iron, timber and hydro-electric power. In addition, some important innovations allowed a number of Swedish firms to become major players in world markets, for example AGA (light-houses), ASEA (power generation, electrical and diesel motors), SKF (ball bearings), Nobel (explosives), Ericsson (telephones), Electrolux (refrigerators), Atlas Copco (rockdrilling) and Alfa-Laval (separators). Sweden became the home base for multinationals, rather than merely a host country. This is still true although foreign investment in Sweden primarily occurs through foreign acquisitions. The number of people employed by Swedish multinationals outside of Sweden is larger than the number of Swedes working in foreign-owned multinationals. Industrial relations in Sweden has thus developed on a national basis without strong influence from other countries.

Sweden is more dependent on international trade than any of the other countries discussed in this book. Around 28 per cent of Sweden's gross domestic product (GDP) is exported. This includes approximately half of the production of the engineering industry, which is dominant in the Swedish economy. The figures are even higher for other sectors such as the iron, steel and wood industries. The strong dependence on international competition has also been a factor that has inclined Swedish unions in the private sector to accept productivity improvements. Both technical and administrative rationalisation have been accepted and often welcomed by Swedish unions.

The employment relations parties

Unions

The establishment of a union in Sweden does not require any registration or acceptance by government authorities or courts. Any group of employees is free to form its own union and will be automatically covered by labour legislation. The more advanced union rights are, however, reserved for unions holding contracts. The most significant of these rights is access to company information and the right to initiate bargaining on any major changes before they take place. There are very few newly organised unions in Sweden, mainly because the existing unions appear to serve their members effectively and they protect their area of interest from competing unions.

There are three main union confederations. LO (the Swedish Trade Union Confederation) and TCO (*Tjänstemännens Centralorganisation*, the Swedish Confederation of Salaried Employees) dominate the blue-collar and white-collar sectors respectively. A third confederation, SACO (*Sveriges Akademikers Centralorganisation*, the Swedish Confederation of Professional Associations), consists of professional unions organising employees who generally possess an academic degree.

LO's 20 affiliated unions have a total membership of 2.2 million people including retired members. This means that LO covers more than 90 per cent of blue-collar employees. Most affiliated unions are organised on an industrial basis with one union in each company or site. The largest unions are the Swedish Municipal Workers' Union (661 000 members) and the Swedish Metal Workers' Union (443 000 members). LO represents its affiliated unions in the areas of social and economic policy. Traditionally, it also bargained collectively on behalf of all members in the private sector. In the public sector, however, the two major unions bargain directly, without the direct involvement of LO.

TCO was formed in 1944 by the merger of two organisations, one covering private sector employees and the other covering public sector employees. The 19 unions affiliated to TCO have 1.3 million members. It does not take part in collective bargaining, but is active in training and represents its unions in consultations with the government on general economic and social policies. The largest member unions are SIF (*Svenska Industritjänstemannaförbundet*, the Swedish Union of Clerical and Technical Employees in Industry) (300 000 members), *Lärarförbundet,* the Teachers' Union (200 000 members) and SKTF

(Svenska Kommunaltjänstemannaförbundet, the Swedish Union of Local Government Officers) (185 000 members). The largest member unions are 'vertical' industry unions, which means they organise all white-collar employees at all levels in an enterprise. They make up three-quarters of total TCO membership. The other member unions are organised on an occupational basis. For the purpose of collective bargaining, the TCO-affiliated unions were organised into two bargaining cartels: PTK (*Privattjänstemannakartellen*, Federation of Salaried Employees in Industry and Services) for the private sector and TCO–OF (TCOs *förhandlingsråd för offentliganställda*, Confederation of Professional Employees, Public Sector Negotiations Council) for the public sector. However, PTK also includes unions outside TCO that are affiliated to SACO.

SACO is the smallest of the three confederations. The 25-member unions of SACO have around 385 000 members. The unions are organised primarily on the basis of common academic background. The largest unions are those that organise teachers in secondary education and graduate engineers. SACO has bargaining cartels for the state and local government sectors. In the private sector most SACO unions are affiliated to PTK.

Union organisation has developed rapidly during the 1990s. A number of mergers and coalitions have taken place and more are under way. One example is in the private sector manufacturing industry where the unions Metal, SIF and CF, affiliated to the three different central confederations, have formed a joint bargaining body.

The links between LO and the Social Democratic Party (SAP) are traditionally very strong. LO's financial support to the party is of prime importance, particularly in election campaigns. A significant part of the local electoral work is also carried out by union activists. The strong links between the LO and SAP were also demonstrated through the system of collective membership, though this was recently abolished. The relationship continues, but both organisations have found reasons to operate with more independence during the 1990s.

Most employees in Sweden are members of unions (see Appendix): about 90 per cent of blue-collar employees and 80 per cent of white-collar employees. This exceptionally high union density by international standards is explained by several factors. One is that the unemployment benefits system is administered by the unions. Most workers regard it as natural to belong to a union for protection against possible unemployment. Other benefits offered by the unions also help them in recruiting members. However, perhaps the most important reason is the degree of union influence achieved during the long period of Social Democratic government. The close relationship between successive Social Democratic governments and LO helped the unions to establish themselves as a significant and well-established force in society. Thus, most Swedes see joining a union as normal when entering the labour market. In contrast to LO's affiliation with the Social Democratic Party, TCO and SACO have no formal political affiliation. Union membership, as a total, has increased in recent years, but membership as a proportion of the labour force fell marginally in the 1985–95 period (see Appendix).

Employers' organisations

Employers in Sweden are also well organised. There are four employer confederations: one for the private sector and three for the public sector. The Swedish Employers' Confederation (SAF) organises employers in the private sector. SAF acts for more than 41 000 affiliated companies organised in 38 sectoral associations. The SAF-affiliated companies employ some 1.3 million people. In 1991 SAF decided to withdraw from engaging in central wage negotiations on behalf of the members.

For the national government authorities there is the Swedish Agency for Government Employers (*Statens Arbetsgivarverk*, SAV) and for the local government sector there are two organisations. The municipalities collaborate through the Swedish Association of Local Authorities (*Kommunförbundet*) and the county councils through the Federation of County Councils (*Landstingsförbundet*). These organisations act on behalf of 278 municipalities and 23 county councils. The public sector has more than 1.5 million employees, of whom more than half a million are national government employees.

Characteristics of the social partners

Swedish unions and employers' organisations (the 'social partners') are large and well funded by international standards, in view of their high density of membership and their relatively high level of subscriptions. Union subscriptions are normally in the range of 1 to 2 per cent of gross earnings. The unions accumulate funds to meet the costs of industrial disputes. The size of funds varies, but is large by international standards. Most unions can compensate their members during industrial disputes for two to four weeks on full pay. The employers' associations also accumulate such funds.

Another feature of Swedish unions is the high degree of centralisation in decision making. Decisions about strikes and accepting collective agreements are normally taken by central bodies such as the executive committees. Even in cases where centralisation in decision making is not formally regulated in the statutes, members usually follow the recommendations of their leaders. Although Swedish unions are centralised, this does not mean that they are weak or inactive at the local level. On the contrary, in comparison with unions in other countries, the level of local activity is high. Wherever there are ten or more members, it is usual that a local branch of the union will be formed. Approximately 10 per cent of union members hold an elected position in their union organisation and 15–20 per cent of the membership receive some form of union training each year. Participation in union meetings, however, is usually low. It is common to find only 5–10 per cent attendance at regular meetings. Attendance of 50 per cent or more is common only for annual meetings or when decisions are to be taken on collective agreements or strike action.

The role of the government

The Swedish state is a large employer. Pay negotiations are handled by the Swedish Agency for Government Employers (SAV), an association of the government agencies. There is no political control over SAV.

The private sector has been the traditional pace-setter in Swedish pay negotiations. It is also widely accepted that the production costs and productivity of the export sector are of prime importance in pay determination. However, there are cases where the public sector takes the lead and reaches agreements ahead of the private sector. In non-pay issues it has been common for SAV to break new ground, ahead of the private sector. One example is the area of industrial democracy, which is examined later in this chapter.

The government exerts its main influence on industrial relations through its political role. Traditionally, employment relations have been left to the employers and unions. However, during the 1970s a number of new laws were introduced, constituting a new framework of employment relations. These laws deal with issues such as industrial democracy, the work environment, security of employment, and union rights. They generally limit the rights of employers and strengthen those of employees and their unions. After the union 'harvest years' of the 1970s came a period of strong employers' offensives in the 1980s and a dramatic increase in unemployment in the early 1990s. These have contributed to a major setback in the status and influence of unions, as discussed later.

The main processes of employment relations

Every union has its own statutes, including rules about how to enter into collective agreements. It is common practice that the right to conclude agreements is entrusted to a union's executive committee. A union may give its mandate to a central union council or a bargaining cartel to bargain on its behalf. Central agreements were the general practice between 1956 and 1982. A central agreement is normally a recommendation that has to be endorsed by each participating union before it is binding.

Such central agreements include a peace obligation, whereby the employers agree to increase economic rewards in exchange for a guaranteed period of labour peace. Once an agreement is ratified, the detailed applications are worked out through industry-wide and local agreements. Any disputes must be referred to the central level rather than being settled by industrial action.

Central agreements usually include several pay components. It is common to have a general pay increase (either in percentage or absolute terms) as well as specific increases directed towards special groups such as low-income earners, women, shift workers, or tradespeople. Agreements may also include guarantee clauses that permit an adjustment of pay according to changes in the CPI or wage increases in other sectors. This means that central agreements are supplemented by industry-, plant- or company-level agreements before the individual wage increases are finally determined. Central agreements generally cover a period of one to three years. During this period, there may also be local bargaining. Increases in pay outside of the central agreement are called 'wage drift'. Wage drift has traditionally been in the range of 25–50 per cent of the centrally agreed wage increase. During the 1980s, wage drift increased and in some instances equalled the increase provided for by the central contract. This was caused partly by market forces and partly by the employers' wish to widen wage differentials (Ahlén 1989).

In addition to the pay agreement, there are other central agreements. They cover such subjects as working hours, the working environment, joint consultation and equal opportunities for women. Central agreements may also be supplemented by local agreements that specify how the rules are to be applied in particular situations. Collective agreements sometimes replace or supplement the law in regard to non-pay issues (Elvander 1992).

Local bargaining

Although the structure of local bargaining differs markedly from one workplace to another, we will describe the process in a typical medium-sized private sector company with 300–400 employees. The employees would be organised in three or four local union clubs. All manual workers would belong to a LO-affiliated union. The first-line supervisors would belong to Ledarna (the supervisors' union) and most of the rest of the white-collar employees would belong to SIF (the main white-collar union in private industry).

Ledarna and SIF would cooperate in the bargaining cartel PTK. The local unions would be represented on the company board with one LO and one PTK representative, and their deputies would also attend. There would be a work environment committee with a majority of union representatives. The economic performance of the company would be regularly discussed in the economic committee, where the LO and PTK representatives would meet with management. There would be regular meetings every month in which management would report about production and investment plans, among other things. The unions would indicate if they wished to take an issue further, in which case separate negotiations about that issue would be organised. The unions would initiate negotiations about grievances, as requested by their members. Most of the contacts between management and unions would be informal. Formal labour–management contacts would be limited to four or five board meetings, three or four meetings of the work environment committee and four to six cases of collective bargaining, besides the pay negotiations.

Public sector

Union–management relations in the public sector are similar to those in the private sector. However, some differences should be mentioned. There are usually more unions among salaried employees, as professional unions are more strongly represented in the public sector where there tend to be larger concentrations of employees. Another difference is the greater degree of formalisation in union–management contacts. The employer fulfils the 'primary duty of negotiation before deciding on a change of the operation' by sending a written proposition in the form of 'draft minutes' that describe the proposition. The union representatives confirm that they accept by signing the minutes. A formal document confirming the agreement is completed, but no meeting is ever held. This greater formality in the public sector can, in part, be seen as a reflection of the more bureaucratic traditions in the public sector, but can also be explained by the large size of most public sector organisations.

Dispute settlement

The Swedish government plays only a limited role in settling disputes. The Swedes differentiate between 'interest' disputes and 'rights' disputes (see ch. 1). In the case of interest disputes, parties have the right to engage in industrial action after giving proper notice (usually one week). A small state agency provides mediation. However, the mediator has only an advisory role and there is no formal obligation for the parties to accept the mediator's proposal or to withdraw industrial action if requested by the mediator. In most years there are 30 to 40 cases of mediation. Parliament can in theory legislate to seek an end to an industrial dispute, but such action is very unusual (Olsson 1990).

In the case of rights disputes, there should be no industrial action. Disputes about the interpretation of laws or agreements must be referred to the National Labour Court or, in some cases, to regional lower civil courts or magistrates. Verdicts of the lower courts may be appealed to the Labour Court, which is the final arbiter for all labour disputes. The Labour Court hears around 250 cases per year, including individual grievances. Unlike the position in most other countries, individual workers are virtually precluded from making claims other than through a union.

The right to engage in industrial action includes lockouts as well as strikes. In addition, there are milder forms of industrial action such as bans on overtime and new recruitment, as well as 'black bans' on certain jobs. However, industrial action is only allowed when contracts have either expired or been properly terminated. Industrial action undertaken during a contract period is prohibited by law. Actions in support of other unions (secondary conflicts) are, however, always allowed. If a union engages in an illegal strike, either at the local or central level, the employer may sue the union for damages. To avoid responsibility for an illegal strike, union officials must actively discourage their members from taking part. Only in this way can they avoid being fined or sued for damages. Individual union members who take part in unlawful industrial action can also be fined by the Labour Court. These fines have traditionally been limited to a maximum of SEK200, but this was increased to SEK5000 in 1992.

Issues of current and future importance

During the 1960s, when Sweden experienced a period of high economic growth and continuous industrial peace, the concept of the 'Swedish model' became well known internationally. The model can briefly be described as having relatively few, but well organised and strong, employers' associations and unions. The unions have positive attitudes to rationalisation and rely upon the government to pursue an active labour market policy in order to absorb technological and structural unemployment. As noted previously, the Swedish model is normally traced from 1938 when LO and SAF reached the first so-called Basic Agreement, which regulates procedures of collective bargaining and matters of cooperation. Under the Basic Agreement, decisions about what to produce and how to organise production were managerial prerogatives. Pay and conditions have always been subject to bargaining, with the right to take industrial action when the contracts are to be renewed.

The first Basic Agreement was reached after a long period of sustained conflict. Throughout the 1920s and 1930s Sweden had one of the highest levels of industrial disputation in Europe. There were strong demands for legislation that would restrict the right to strike, to hold lockouts, and to engage in free collective bargaining.

The Swedish model worked well until the early 1970s, and then came under increased strain. The unions' radical demands for economic and industrial democracy met with strong employer resistance. The political and economic scene changed when 44 years of Social Democratic government came to an end in 1976. In common with other OECD countries at that time, Sweden was confronting considerable economic turbulence in the wake of the oil crisis. The employers felt that it was both politically and economically necessary to fight back. The unions' demands for 'economic democracy', in the form of wage-earner funds, were strongly opposed by the three liberal conservative political parties and by SAF, which has played an increasingly visible role in politics since the late 1970s.

In 1980 there occurred the largest-ever industrial dispute in Sweden. A strike was met by an employer lockout of 80 per cent of the workforce. The dispute was settled after two weeks on the basis of a mediated proposal. Some commentators claimed that this conflict symbolised the end of the Swedish model and its spirit of cooperation. The dispute indeed symbolised the end of an era of relatively peaceful central collective bargaining; however, the Swedish model had never precluded the possibility of industrial disputes.

The 1980 dispute can be attributed partly to the role of the government in the pay-determination process. Throughout the 1970s, government had sought to influence this process in various ways. Public statements on what was acceptable were issued and adjustments of the taxation system were frequently used. Furthermore, the government's intervention in the 1980 pay round was ill-timed. The pay settlements in 1981 and 1983, however, were achieved without disputes. During 1983 and 1984 agreements were reached, in the main, without the assistance of mediators.

An important new element in Swedish industrial relations is the move towards decentralised bargaining. Following the failure of their 1980 lockout, the private employers realised that such tactics would no longer be effective in opposing union power. The employers gradually adopted the view that wage solidarity had gone too far and that employers were losing ground within the existing central model. They decided to break with the centralised bargaining arrangement. The first step was taken in 1983 when the influential Engineering Employers' Association and its counterpart unions reached agreements outside of the central round of negotiations. Since then the Engineering Employers' Confederation and the Metal Workers' Union have continued to negotiate without the involvement of SAF and LO. Increasingly, the other employers' associations and unions followed suit. By 1991 SAF had decided that it would no longer take part in any central wage bargaining with LO.

Another new element in the 1980s was the introduction of profit-sharing systems and employee stock-ownership systems. Such systems were strongly advocated by management but were met with scepticism or outright opposition from certain unions. By 1989 one-quarter of private sector employees were covered by profit-sharing systems and almost one-third by employee stock-ownership systems.

Industrial democracy

Industrial democracy is a broad term that refers to the influence of employees on their own working lives or, more precisely, on 'what and how they produce'. The debate in Sweden has concentrated on two areas: first, work organisation and the individual's influence over his or her job; and second, union influence over top management decisions via collective bargaining and through representation on company boards (Schmidt 1976; Brulin 1995).

As in many other countries, industrial democracy has been part of the debate on the radical Left in Sweden for many years. Towards the end of the 1960s, demands for increased employee influence were raised within the unions. The debate was influenced by the effects of technological change in the workplace, the growing awareness of work environment issues, health hazards and the wave of radical political ideas that swept through Europe. Some union demands were heeded in the political arena and a number of reforms were introduced (Olson 1992).

In a simplified form, the union strategy on industrial democracy can be described as follows. Mobilisation of interested members and union activists was achieved by focusing on problems of health and safety at work. This created a political climate in which laws and regulations in support of industrial democracy could be introduced, which culminated in a revision of the employment relations legislation with the passing of an Act on Co-determination at Work: *Medbestämmandelagen* (MBL) 1976. These laws were supplemented by financial support for training and research, which to a large extent was channelled through the unions.

MBL has provided the legal framework for employment relations in general and industrial democracy in particular in Sweden. Since 1977, MBL has prescribed that management should be a joint effort by capital and labour, that is, managers and union representatives. Both parties should have equal rights to information, which means that unions should be able to obtain all the relevant information available from the company. Further, MBL stipulates that management has to consult the unions before any decision is taken on major changes in the company (such changes range from reorganisation to the introduction of new technology). Although management is not obliged to reach agreement, it has to allow time for unions to investigate the matters being decided, and consult at either local or central level before it implements decisions. MBL also gives the unions priority rights in interpreting agreements in some cases. They also have rights of veto over the hiring of subcontractors if they suspect that their use might violate laws or agreements. By law, the local union has the right to appoint two directors (and two deputies) to the board of most private companies that employ at least 25 people (in some cases they can appoint three directors). This right is commonly used in large and medium-sized companies but is less commonly used in small companies.

The introduction of MBL and other laws that constitute the legal base for reform of working life was very controversial in the 1970s. The employers strongly opposed most of the laws and predicted that reforms would lead to inefficiency, and would increase costs and inhibit the decision-making process. Employers also argued that this legislation would be preferable if it promoted individual employee involvement, rather than union activity. In spite of this resistance, in 1982 SAF reached a new basic agreement on efficiency and participation with LO and the Federation of Salaried Employees (PTK). This agreement was an attempt to implement MBL in the private sector by setting up a joint Development Council that would promote efficiency and participation in individual firms. Significantly, this agreement provided for considerable adaptation depending on local circumstances; for instance, in relation to technological change (Hammarström 1978a; Brulin & Nilsson 1991).

The legal reforms had limited impact. From the unions' perspective, there was a general feeling of disappointment about the reforms. No significant change in the power situation at the workplace occurred. While the reforms were seen as a definite step forward, the step was too short and too slow for most union activists. However, MBL has led to an improved provision of information by management to the local unions. Consultation by management with the unions before deciding on changes has become standard procedure. It is also reported that the operation of the board has improved in some companies as the result of participation by union representatives at this level.

Technological change

During much of the 1970s, industrial democracy was a focal point of debate. During the 1980s, however, the call for industrial democracy has gradually receded and been replaced by a debate on new technology—including the widespread introduction of microprocessors into process technology. In common with their counterparts in other advanced industrial societies, Swedish employers support the introduction of new technology on the grounds of economic necessity. To remain competitive, they argue, there is no choice but to introduce technological change. Although such changes may have negative effects on the level of employment, failure to keep abreast of technological developments in the short run will mean failure in the long run (Sandberg 1992).

Swedish unions have traditionally sympathised with economic rationalisation and technological development. The success of several large Swedish multinational enterprises in the engineering industry, such as Volvo, Saab, Scania and Ericsson, has had considerable influence on the thinking of the unions. One debate within the union movement has been whether computer technology represents 'traditional' technological change or should be regarded as a new and different phenomenon that requires a different strategy. By and large, Swedish unions have favoured the former approach. Computer technology may have far-reaching consequences for the nature and level of employment; however, Swedish unions feel that their traditional policies and practices can be applied to most forms of new technology.

An example of an innovative approach to technology is TCO's work with visual display units (VDUs). TCO was concerned about electrical and magnetic radiation and other health aspects of VDUs. The Worker Health and Safety Authority in Sweden refused to regulate VDU standards as they found no scientific evidence of harmful effects. TCO, therefore, developed a do-it-yourself test instrument to enable members to test their own VDUs and demand better equipment. TCO's work led to a situation where the major producers saw TCO as a consumer group and accepted TCO's recommendations as a consumer demand. Since 1992, TCO has had a licensing procedure whereby it offers producers who meet the TCO standard a label of approval. The producers pay a fee to TCO for the licence and can then put the TCO sticker of approval on their products. By the end of 1995, 200 licences had been sold and many producers claim that the TCO label is a must for their product.

LO has also taken the initiative with a licensing procedure concerning information technology (IT) and its application in the production process.

Economic democracy (wage-earner funds)

Economic democracy has been a dominant issue in the Swedish political debate since the 1971 decision of the LO Congress to investigate the matter. The concept has included two ideas: profit sharing and collective ownership. The arguments in favour of these developments have been both economic and power related. Employees should get a share of the profits, but part of the wealth that is generated should be reinvested in Swedish industry through a system of collective ownership. LO saw economic democracy as a necessary complement to the 'solidaristic' wages policy, whereby wages are related not to the profits in an individual company but to the economy as a whole. The argument in favour of expanding workers' power through wage-earner funds was advanced as a result of the limitations of industrial democracy. Employees would exert more genuine influence, it was argued, if they were part-owners of their firms through the funds (Olson 1992; Pontusson 1992).

The first radical proposal for wage-earner funds, the Meidner Plan, was adopted by LO in 1976. It aimed, in the long run, to make the unions the majority shareholders in all major industries in Sweden. The proposal was for the compulsory issuing of new shares based on company profits. These shares would then be transferred to funds controlled by the unions.

The plan met unprecedented opposition from the employers. SAP was largely positive in its support, but had some reservations. The Liberal Party and the Centre Party acknowledged the need for such reforms but favoured individual rather than collective profit-sharing arrangements.

The wage-earner funds proposal was discussed at length by LO and SAP but they had difficulty finding a proposition that was radical enough to satisfy LO, yet practical enough to be politically feasible. The whole issue became a political burden to SAP and it lost the elections in 1976 and 1979 partly on this issue. However, it managed to be re-elected in 1982, despite continuing controversy surrounding the wage-earner fund issue. Following the long and intensive counter-campaign by the employers, the three non-socialist parties did not promote their own separate propositions. Instead, they all focused their campaign on criticising the LO/SAP proposals. The employers and the supporters of the wage-earner funds were totally opposed to each other. Unions made several different proposals, but the coalition of employers and the non-socialist parties used the same argument against all of them.

Although the issue had become a political problem, SAP was committed to implementing a form of wage-earners' funds. In October 1983, the opponents of these funds mounted a massive protest demonstration in Stockholm, when more than 100 000 members of the business community marched on Parliament. Nevertheless, in November 1983, the new government introduced a diluted version of the original proposal. This included the establishment of five regional funds, which started to operate in 1984. Each of the regional funds was administered by a separate board appointed by the government after consultation with the unions.

The five wage-earner funds operated in the same manner as insurance companies and pension funds. There were few signs of their precipitating a 'fundamental change of the economic system in the direction of state socialism' as had been predicted by earlier opponents of the funds. The funds were used for research and for incentives for savings. A proportion of the funds was invested in a new venture capital fund. Following the defeat of the Social Democratic government in 1991, the incoming Conservative–Liberal coalition government abolished the wage-earner funds (Pontusson & Kuruvilla 1992).

Associate agreements

The traditional Swedish model has come under pressure in the face of increasing globalisation. As noted previously, the employers in the large export companies have argued in favour of decentralised negotiations on an enterprise level. Parallel with this development, many Swedish employers have introduced the idea of 'associates'. This strategy was first announced at the SAF Conference in 1987. The employers argued that following the introduction of integrated and flexible production systems, there was no room for a division between blue-collar and white-collar workers. Rather, there should be a single category of employees. Consequently, associate agreements were promoted by SAF. The stated objective of associate agreements is to provide equal terms of employment for all the employees in a company whereby everybody shares the same wages system, even though they may be members of different trade union organisations.

New forms of work organisation tend to dissolve the old demarcation line between blue-collar and white-collar workers. The new principles of work, by contrast with the old Tayloristic ones, are meant to increase the adaptability of employees to customers' needs, as well as boosting productivity. A major trend in Swedish industry is for more or less self-regulating teams to be established on the shop floor. This means that traditional supervisors disappear and are replaced by 'production leaders'; they are not supposed to control the teams, but are intended to support them. This also means that many traditional white-collar roles and duties, such as planning, production–engineering improvements and administration, are being integrated into the teams. At the same time, white-collar staff are moved closer to the shop floor. A new phenomenon is the so-called customer-orientated *complete team*. This team consists of generalists and has the capacity to handle the manufacturing process, the planning, the purchasing and the design of standard products. In order to take full advantage of the potential of the new work principles, management argues that the traditional contractual boundaries between workers and officials must be eliminated.

According to SAF, associate agreements must be negotiated at the local level. This argument is related to the employers' objective, which is to gain greater control over the wage structure. Many employers want to reduce the power of the local union clubs in regard to the setting of wage rates. They believe that if the central authorities, LO and the unions, were weakened, local union clubs would become more business-oriented which, in turn, would increase the power of employers. It is important to SAF that managers at the enterprise level gain more influence over the wage structure. The goal is that each company will achieve its own collective agreement with the employees. Management in large export-oriented companies such as Volvo, ABB and Ericsson have all actively supported the idea of associate agreements. However, by 1996, only a few local agreements had been signed (Nilsson 1996).

The unions' perspective on associate agreements

The Swedish unions have long favoured measures that support increases in productivity and competitiveness. Consequently they generally have a constructive attitude to the introduction of a single category of employees and associate agreements. However, trade union organisations also strive to maintain their influence on the wage structure and to gain greater influence over the organisation of work. With this in mind, unions have been willing to discuss associate agreements with employers. Accordingly, unions wish to achieve a central associate agreement which, in turn, will form the basis for concluding local agreements. The central agreement, under these arrangements, will consist of an overall arrangement on issues such as working hours, holidays, notice to quit and subsistence allowances. In regard to the wage structure, unions seek general principles to control the local setting of wage rates, although they would accept a distribution of wages decided locally and based on work demands, performance and ability.

During recent years it has been clear that trade unions are willing to accept more locally oriented wage structures. The agreement concluded in the engineering sector during 1993 is an example of the decentralisation process and the productivity orientation that are influencing Swedish working life. For the first time in the history of metal industry agreements, the Metal Workers' Union has argued that the setting of wage rates should be 'individual and differentiated'. Furthermore, wages should increase with higher levels of responsibility and degrees of difficulty, as well as with levels of competence and performance demonstrated by the workers. Under the previously centralised model, the exact amount of wages was decided for each worker within the central agreement.

Unemployment

During the 1990s, unemployment problems have dominated labour market debates in Sweden. As mentioned, unemployment began to rise in 1991, reaching 10 per cent by 1996. In addition, approximately 5 per cent of the workforce were engaged in labour market training or relief programs. Traditionally, unemployment has been tackled by Social Democratic governments using active labour market policies. This means priority has been given to active measures for the unemployed, rather than cash benefits. The approach taken by the Conservative–Liberal Party coalition government to labour market programs between 1991 and 1994 differed from that taken by the Social Democratic government since 1994. The emphasis in the Social Democrats' policy has been on training and active measures.

The unemployment problem has had a profound impact on employment relations. The employers have strengthened their position and the union movement has become weaker. The unions have had to allocate increasing resources to assisting their unemployed members and to supporting labour market policy. Hence, fewer resources have been available for offensive measures to improve wages and conditions.

One dimension of the unemployment problem is the relationship between unemployment and the wage-formation process. Since the employers' withdrawal from the central bargaining system there has been a general dissatisfaction with the wage-setting system on all sides: unions, employers and government. All agree that increased wages have added to inflation pressures and that there is a need for a non-inflationary wage-setting system. However, there is no agreement on how to achieve this. Unions claim that it can only be achieved under centralised coordinated processes, whereas the employers claim that local bargaining is the solution to the problem. While the issue has been extensively debated, so far no agreement has been reached (Johannesson & Wadensjö 1995).

Conclusions

Employment relations in Sweden have passed through three broad stages during the past 100 years. The first stage was from the beginning of the union movement in the 1890s to the mid-1930s. During this period the unions were established. The relationship between capital and labour was antagonistic and there was a high level of industrial disputes. The government was either passive or supported the owners of capital.

The second stage lasted for most of the 44 years of Social Democratic government from the mid-1930s to the early 1970s. The Swedish model was established during this period, with a low level of industrial conflict, a 'solidaristic' wage policy, an active human resources policy and labour–management cooperation. An economic policy reliant on economic growth subsumed many of the pay-related problems for the unions and paved the way for a pattern of labour–management relations with few industrial disputes.

A third stage emerged in the 1970s. More radical union ambitions, the election of a non-socialist government in 1976, severe economic problems and a strategy based on free enterprise and a market economy, on the employer side, represented significant changes. The 1980 dispute symbolised these new developments. Wage-earner funds were introduced after a bitter and drawn-out conflict, but were not seen as a complete victory by the unions. The wage-earner fund system became a political burden for SAP and did not result in a basic change in Sweden's economic system. The employers tried to reverse the trends as much as they could. Their prime objective was to deregulate Sweden and facilitate more market influences. Fragmentation of the bargaining structures, more flexible working-time arrangements, profit sharing, and payment-by-results systems became examples of initiatives advanced by their associations.

During the 1980s a new collective bargaining structure emerged. The centralised bargaining structure that had been dominant during the 1960s and 1970s was replaced by a more fragmented and decentralised bargaining structure. This development was led by the Engineering Employers' Association against the ambitions of most unions and some of the employers' organisations. SAF's 1991 decision to withdraw from the central bargaining process marked the end of the bargaining pattern that had begun in 1956. The 1991–93 agreement was reached only after pressure from a special government commission. Since then, wage negotiations have taken place on an industry level.

By the end of the 1980s a new phenomenon had appeared in the form of associate agreements. With new forms of work organisation and more diffuse demarcation lines between blue-collar and white-collar workers, it was more efficient to have a single status for all employees, who then enjoyed similar employment conditions. A debate has persisted between the employers and the unions concerning the level at which these associate agreements are to be settled. Employers in the large companies want to have separate agreements at the enterprise level, while the unions seek a central associate agreement that would provide the basis of all local agreements. In this way, the unions seek to preserve their solidaristic wages policy principle.

During the 1980s SAF withdrew from most of the cooperative institutions that had been established during earlier decades. Yet there were still some cooperative approaches that focused on work organisation, technical development and skill formation. However, arrangements in the non-wage areas were hampered by disagreements between employers and unions about the locus of wage negotiations.

After SAP was voted back into office in 1982, the direction of economic policy changed. A number of devaluations led towards an expansionist export-led recovery. This proved successful for a few years, but it delayed tougher structural decisions that the government was forced to make after 1989. Sweden subsequently reduced its budget deficit and restored balance to its foreign trade. The unemployment rate, which was already low by international standards (3.7 per cent in 1983), was brought down to a historically very low level (1.2 per cent in mid-1989). The government gave high priority to measures to restructure industry and stimulate flexibility within the labour force. By 1990, however, fighting inflation had become the government's main priority and unemployment increased dramatically during the early 1990s.

The incidence of industrial conflicts during the 1980s was slightly higher than in previous decades. A new element was that white-collar workers accounted for the majority of the working days lost in industrial stoppages. White-collar unions were more often involved in industrial disputes, particularly public sector employees. Groups that have participated in major conflicts include nurses, fire fighters and physicians. The involvement of public sector employees in industrial conflict resulted in the government playing a new role in industrial relations. However, the Social Democratic government did not attempt to change or interfere with the basic employment relations rules. It was still unions and employers who took primary responsibility for negotiating agreements and resolving conflicts.

Does the Swedish model still exist? This question has been debated on numerous occasions since the industrial conflict in 1980. Several commentators announced the death of the model after this dispute. The model is no longer the same, and the employers are continuing to distance themselves from it. However, basic common values between employees and employers still exist. They both have a joint interest in efficiency and rationalisation of production and a commitment to take responsibility for industrial peace. The Swedish government, in turn, still accepts responsibility for an active labour market policy and gives high priority to maintaining relatively full employment. However, due to the huge state deficit, the Social Democratic government had difficulty solving problems arising from high levels of unemployment.

One new feature is the role of the employers. Through the 1980s, they were more interested in changing wage relativities and increasing wage differentials than in limiting total employment costs. This put pressure on governments to fight inflation without the support of employers. Other new elements in the employment relations scene are the increasing prominence of white-collar unions and the growth of the service sector. It is no longer possible for blue-collar unions to dominate the unions' agenda. The existence of more than one powerful union confederation has also complicated the employment relations system. However, Sweden has not managed to resolve the conflict between inflationary wages and full employment. The pay-determination machinery has demonstrated its inability to control wage drift. This is a serious threat to the Swedish model.

In 1994 Sweden joined the European Union (EU) and the debate on harmonisation of employment relations began. It is now likely that labour–management relations in Sweden will move in a 'continental European' direction, which could lead to more fragmented bargaining structures, greater government intervention, and a consequent weakening of the unions. On the other hand, if a Social Democratic government continues to dominate the political scene, there may be a return to a modified version of the Swedish model (Higgins 1996).

A chronology of Swedish employment relations

1898	LO founded.
1902	SAF founded.
1906	December Compromise Agreement—employers accepted the right for workers to organise.
1909	General strike of 1909 followed by a severe decline in union membership.
1928	Establishment of Labour Court and a Collective Bargaining Act.
1936	Law regulated unfair dismissal for union activity, and the social partners' rights to negotiate.
1938	SAF–LO Basic Agreement at Saltsjöbaden, which set a cooperative 'spirit' for labour relations.
1944	TCO founded.
1946	SAF–LO–TCO Works Councils Agreement, which was revised in 1966 and ended in 1977 by MBL.
1956	Beginning of LO–SAF central bargaining.
1971	LO and TCO adopted policies for industrial democracy.
1972	LO–SAF Rationalisation Agreement on productivity, job satisfaction and job security.
1973	Initial law on board representation for local unions.
1974	Law made it difficult for employers to dismiss employees, and for companies to hire workers on

	probation without union approval. Law gave local union representatives time off for union work with pay.
1975	The wage-earner funds debate began. Law gave employees educational leave.
1976	Non-socialist coalition government replaced the Social Democratic Party (SAP).
1977	Co-determination at Work Act (MBL) implemented.
1980	Lockout/strike throughout most of the private sector—largest labour market conflict.
1981	LO and SAP congresses approved principles for wage-earner funds.
1982	SAP re-elected. SAF–LO–PTK Agreement on Efficiency and Participation.
1983	Wage-earner funds implemented. Industry-wide bargaining replaced the 1956–83 centralised pattern.
1984	Government initiative to introduce new three-party model for central wage fixation based on a 'social contract'.
1985	Widespread introduction of a profit-sharing system and employee stock-ownership system in the private sector.
1986	Major public sector conflict led to the break-up of a traditional, rigid wage structure in the public sector.
1989	New leadership in SAF sought a final breakaway from centralised wage-formation models.
1990	SAF decided that it would no longer take part in wage bargaining. A new form of wage commission *(Rehnberg-gruppen)* managed to establish a two-year wage agreement covering almost the entire labour market.
1991	SAF decided that it would no longer nominate representatives to decision-making state authorities such as the Labour Market Board (AMS). Change of government to a four-party Conservative–Liberal coalition.
1992	The new government changed the composition of boards and statutory organisations; representatives from union and employer groups were replaced by members of Parliament and independent experts. Changes in the industrial relations laws to meet employer demands.
1993	Unemployment reached a record high level for the post-1945 period.
1994	Election of a Social Democratic government. Re-establishment of industrial relations rules that

	applied before 1992. Entry by Sweden into the European Union.
1995	Major reforms of the social welfare system; reduced levels of compensation in several benefits from the traditional 90 per cent of earnings, to between 75 per cent and 85 per cent of earnings.
1996	Major reductions in employment in the public sector. Strict budget restrictions in the public sector.
1996–97	Government industry and labour-market policies orientated towards small and medium sized firms; policies aimed to increase economic growth and reduce unemployment.

10 Employment relations in Japan

Yasuo Kuwahara

This chapter starts by putting Japanese industrial relations into context, sketches some historical background, then discusses the roles of unions and employers, and the Japanese approach to collective bargaining and labour–management consultation. The issues discussed include job security, labour shortages, foreign workers, technological change, and small and medium-sized enterprises.

In terms of its population of 125 million people and its gross domestic product (GDP) of $4578 billion (see Appendix), Japan is the second-largest economy of the ten countries discussed in this book; the United States (USA) being the largest. In the last ten years for which data are available, Japan's economy had the second-highest growth rate (along with Australia) of all the countries, after South Korea. In terms of GDP per capita, on a nominal basis, Japan ranks first out of the ten countries; however, on the basis of 'purchasing power parities', Japan ranks second after the USA (see Appendix).

Japan has a labour force of 67 million; the labour force participation rate is 77 per cent. Some 82 per cent of the labour force are *employees*. About 6 per cent of the labour force work in primary industries, including agriculture and fisheries. Manufacturing, mining and construction industries employ 34 per cent, while 61 per cent of the labour force work in the tertiary industries, including services, wholesale and retail, finance, utilities and government.

In many respects Japan appears to be different from most other countries. On average, the Japanese enjoy the longest life span (82 years for women and 76 years for men). It is estimated that the

Japanese ageing ratio (the total of people 65 years old and over, divided by the total population) will be the highest among the major developed countries by the year 2025, according to the Ministry of Health and Welfare (Koseisho 1989). The structure of Japan's population will change substantially from the pyramid shape of the 1950s to a top-heavy shape by 2025. Japanese workers generally work more hours, and lose relatively fewer working days in industrial disputes,[1] than those in other industrialised market economies (IMEs). The population density of 326 people per square kilometre is higher than in any of the other countries discussed in this book. The unemployment rate, at about 3 per cent, is the second-lowest of the ten countries—Korea has the lowest rate—although the rate is one of the highest in post-war Japanese history. In May 1996 the unemployment rate peaked at 3.5 per cent, the highest since the current statistical method was introduced.[2]

The post-1945 period has seen Japanese politics dominated by the conservative Liberal Democratic Party (LDP). Opposition parties have exerted influence from time to time; however, apart from a brief period after the war, none obtained enough power to hold office in national politics. In this context, a remarkable change occurred in the election of the House of Councillors (*Sangiin*) in 1989 when the Japan Socialist Party (JSP) and other opposition parties won more seats than the LDP. However in the more important House of Representatives (*Shugiin*), the LDP maintained its majority. Both the LDP and JSP substantially increased their numbers at the elections of 1990, at the expense of the other parties. In the election of July 1993 the JSP had a historic victory, when the leftist and rightest factions integrated. The LDP, the JSP and the *Sakigake* (Harbinger) Party formed a coalition Cabinet. While a leader of the JSP initially became Prime Minister, this position was assumed by Hashimoto Ryutaro from the LDP in January 1996—and in the same month the JSP changed its name to the Social Democratic Party of Japan (SDP).

Depending on their dominant ideology, unions are associated with various parties including the SDP (formally the JSP), Democratic Socialist Party (DSP) and the Japan Communist Party (JCP). Successful candidates from these parties may be either recommended or supported by a union, or may have been associated with a union in the past. Despite these relationships between parties and unions, rank-and-file members of unions tend to vote for candidates of their choice. A recent notable change has been the increase in voters who do not adhere to particular parties.

The fragmentation of voters was illustrated especially clearly by the election of the House of Representatives in October 1996. The LDP won 239 seats, which exceeded the previous number of 211, while the SDP and the *Sakigake* (Harbinger) Party had a decisive defeat. Many

Figure 10.1   Changes in the population pyramid

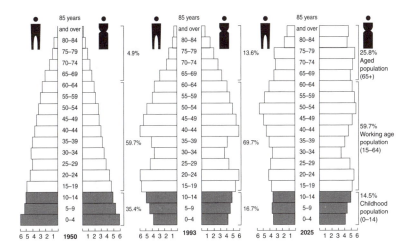

Sources: Management and Coordination Agency (1993) *Population Estimates as of 1 October 1993*; Ministry of Health and Welfare (1992) Estimates of Future

of the former supporters of the SDP and the *Sakigake* (Harbinger) Party switched votes to the newly established Democratic Party, the LDP and the Japan Communist Party. Many members of the SDP and the *Sakigake (*Harbinger) Party moved to the Democratic Party. The voter turnout rate of 59 per cent was the lowest in the post-war period and the widespread political apathy among voters has left a serious problem for political leaders. Interestingly, the voter turnout from among women was higher than that of men. The relationship between unions and political parties was also further eroded.

The 'Japanese' model of employment relations

Since the mid-1970s, Japan has attracted much attention for its favourable economic performance and for its 'cooperative' employment relations, which has allegedly supported this economic performance. The growing international interest in Japanese management and employment relations has been perplexing to Japanese people, since throughout the twentieth century Japan has tried to follow models derived from the West (for example, Britain, the USA and Germany). Before the 1973 oil crisis, the Japanese tended to see such countries as much more advanced, so that various management techniques and technologies were imported from them.

However, many of the Western countries that once led Japan in economic prosperity have had sluggish economies for some time. By contrast, the economy of Japan developed steadily, although it too has problems. Some of these other countries have lost their legitimacy as models. Moreover, the former models are now looking for a new model themselves, and, ironically, Japan often has been the source of inspiration. Many commentators in other countries, both developed and developing, have advocated 'importing' the 'Japanese' model—but to what extent is it transferable to other countries?

To begin to answer such a question some historical background is required. Japan's feudal era ended with the Meiji Restoration of 1868. Hitherto, Japan had little contact with Western countries. Industrialisation began in the following decade, a century later than in Britain. Japan's early factories in major industries were begun by the state, but in 1880 it sold most of them to a few selected families. These were the origin of what later became the powerful *zaibatsu* groups of holding companies, which were based on these groups' commercial banks.

Although some unions, such as those covering printers and ironworkers, began during this period, the familial basis of industrialisation continued well into the twentieth century. Many factories had their own dormitories, especially in the textiles industry. In many industries, they had master workers (*oyakata*) who were subcontractors, like the early British foremen. Following the First World War, there was an acute shortage of skilled workers. Firms wanted to recruit workers directly, hence many large firms intervened in the *oyakata*'s prerogative to recruit. With the rapid development of industries, the system of skill formation through apprenticeship was absorbed into internal training within firms.

As the paternalistic tradition developed in the 1920s and 1930s, the unions did not exert much sustained influence. With the increasing pressure of a militaristic regime, unions were dissolved between 1938 and 1943 and the employers' associations were absorbed into the mobilisation for war production.

After Japan's unconditional surrender in 1945, the Allied powers' General Headquarters (GHQ) sought to reshape the organisation of work and employment relations as part of the post-war reconstruction. The main elements of the present model, then, were established after the war under American influence.

Unions

The Japanese labour movement developed rapidly under GHQ's democratisation program. Although much of Japan's industrial base was destroyed during the war, only four months after its end union membership had reached pre-war levels and by 1949 there were 6.6 million

Table 10.1 Number of unions and their membership density

Year	Labour unions[a]	Union membership[b] (persons)	Estimated union density (%)
1935[c]	993	408 662	6.9
1940[c]	49	9 455	0.1
1945[c]	509	380 677	3.2
1949	34 688	6 655 483	55.8
1950	29 144	5 773 908	46.2
1955	32 012	6 285 878	35.6
1960	41 561	7 661 568	32.2
1965	52 879	10 146 872	34.8
1970	60 954	11 604 770	35.4
1975	69 333	12 590 400	34.4
1980	72 693	12 369 262	30.8
1982	74 091	12 525 619	30.5
1983	74 486	12 519 530	29.7
1984	74 579	12 463 755	29.1
1985	74 499	12 417 527	28.9
1986	74 183	12 342 853	28.2
1987	73 138	12 271 909	27.6
1988	72 792	12 227 223	26.8
1989	72 605	12 227 073	25.9
1990	72 202	12 264 509	25.2
1991	71 685	12 396 592	24.5
1992	71 881	12 540 691	24.4
1993	71 501	12 663 484	24.2
1994	71 674	12 699 000	24.1
1995	70 839	12 613 582	23.8
1996	70 699	12 451 000	23.2

Notes: a Based on *tan-i rodo kumiai* (unit labour unions). This is the basic organisational unit for unions in Japan and is comprised of workers in the factory, office site, etc. or in an enterprise.

  b Based on *tan-itsu rodo kumiai* (enterprise labour unions) which, in most cases, are comprised of the unions of a single enterprise.

  c The numbers are as at 30 June, except for 1935, 1940 and 1945 which are for the end of the year.

Sources: Ministry of Labor, *Basic Survey on Trade Unions; Year Book of Labor Statistics & Research, 1948, 1950, 1992 and 1996*.

union members, a peak density level of 56 per cent. There were, nonetheless, some setbacks for the unions. For instance, their plans to hold a general strike in 1947 were countermanded by GHQ. However, the unions continued to grow and in 1970 recorded a density of 35 per cent.

After 1970, membership and density of unionisation stagnated. By the mid-1990s membership density had declined to around 23 per cent. What was responsible for this decline? One of the main causes has been the change in industrial structure, especially the shift towards the service sector.

During the decade after the 1973 oil crisis, there was substantial rationalisation in the manufacturing sector, which was highly unionised. Since most larger establishments adopt union shop clauses, union membership varies with the rise and fall of the unionised firms or industries. When the firm is expanding, union membership generally increases, and vice versa. Although there has been an increase in the number of employees in the service sector, the average size of firms in terms of employment tends to be relatively small, and it is generally more difficult and costly for unions to organise in small firms than in large ones. Another cause of union decline has been the general improvement in living standards, which has tended to make employees less enthusiastic about union activities.

Unemployment was about 1.1 per cent at the end of the 1960s, when the economy enjoyed high growth. Although the level of unemployment in Japan has remained less than in most Western countries, it has more than doubled since 1970 (see Appendix). In the recessionary period after the 1973 oil crisis, many companies adopted a tougher stance towards unions, claiming public support for such policies. Employees have become more concerned about the competitive position of the companies for which they work and most seem to have a high degree of commitment to the firm.

This reflects their expectation of 'lifetime employment' and seniority-based wages; such practices were consolidated after the Second World War. Permanent manual and non-manual staff are employed not for specific jobs or occupations, but as company employees. Companies prefer to employ new school leavers or university graduates rather than experienced workers who have been trained in other firms. Their induction program is designed to encourage them to conform to the company's norms.

Young recruits start at a comparatively low level of pay, which is based on their educational qualifications. Their pay increases in proportion to their length of service in the firm. Promotion is largely based on length of service, which is assumed to correlate with the employee's level of skill developed within the enterprise. Therefore, it is disadvantageous for workers to change employers and for employers to lay off employees who have accumulated specific skills required in that particular enterprise. Typically, in the so-called primary labour market, comprised of permanent or regular employees working for large enterprises, there is a tacit understanding about the long-term commitment between employer and employee. However, this is not confirmed in a written contract. Although the length of service among female workers is steadily increasing, 'lifetime employment' generally describes patterns for male rather than female workers.

Most unions in Japan are organised not by occupation or by job, but by enterprise or establishment. An enterprise union consists solely of regular employees of a single firm, regardless of their occupational status. Since enterprise unions usually include both blue-collar and white-collar workers as members, the union density among white-collar workers is relatively high. These employees are expected to stay in the same company until their mandatory retirement age, unless they are made redundant or leave voluntarily (both acts are less usual than in most Western countries).

An increasing number of companies are raising the retirement age from 55 to 60 years old, in accordance with the lengthening average life span of the Japanese. By 1995, about 86 per cent of the firms surveyed had adopted a retirement age of 60 years or more. Many workers remain in work even after reaching their mandatory retirement age. They find other jobs in subsidiaries or similar enterprises by recommendation of the parent companies, or they start small businesses by investing their retirement allowances and other financial resources.

Only about a third of all employees are part of the core of genuinely regular employees. This is an estimate of the percentage of employees working in the public sector and for big enterprises listed at the major stock exchanges. Many of the remaining two-thirds of the labour force work for smaller businesses, or on a temporary or part-time basis, and are often excluded from unions. Therefore, union density among female employees, who constitute the majority of part-time workers, is lower than among male employees. The density is generally low in small and medium-sized enterprises (SMEs). However, in SMEs that are stable or expanding, there are many regular employees who stay in the same company for most of their working lives. In practice, therefore, it is difficult to draw a clear line between the primary and secondary labour markets in Japan. The dominance of SMEs is a notable factor in maintaining flexibility in the Japanese labour market.

A worker leaving the company automatically loses union membership. The same is true for employees who are promoted to managerial positions. In spite of its name, an enterprise union does not only function for the benefit of the enterprise; it has legal protection against employer interference into its affairs and other unfair labour practices.

Many enterprise unions grew sporadically in the period of turmoil after 1945. Some of them evolved from the factory- and company-based war-time production committees. Since most Japanese unions are organised for individual enterprises or plants, there are many unions: more than 70 839 according to one estimate (Rodosho 1996). Union density is greatest among regular employees in large firms. About 97 per cent of enterprise union members work in firms that employ more than 100 employees. Although there are other types of union organisations, such as industrial, craft and general unions, these are exceptions. *Kaiin*, the Seamen's Union, is a rare example of an industrial union.

Most enterprise unions within the same industry join an industrial federation of unions. There are more than 100 such federations. The major functions of the industrial federations include coordinating the activities of the member enterprise unions with the aim of increasing wages and improving working conditions; dealing with problems common to a whole industry; guiding and assisting member unions in specific disputes; and political lobbying in the interest of workers. These industrial federations themselves belong to national centres, of which *Rengo* (Japan Trade Union Confederation, JTUC) is the largest.

After the two oil crises of the 1970s, unions at industrial and national levels led what they called a 'policy-oriented struggle' with the aim of ensuring stable employment and maintaining their members' standards of living. In the course of such labour activities, another movement 'to unite the labour front under the initiative of private sector unions' emerged in December 1982—*Zenminrokyo*, the Japanese Private Sector Union Council. It was formed by the labour federations in the private sector and reflected their enthusiasm for further unification to increase their strength. This organisation developed into a larger union centre, *Rengo*, which integrated the public sector unions. The new *Rengo* was established in 1989, when it had 78 industrial federations with nearly 8 million members. Public sector unions used to have more power compared with those in the private sector. However, in general, union membership has decreased since 1978 and the leading edge of unionism has shifted towards unions in the private sector.

Rengo has pursued cooperative labour management relations. In the political dimension, it supported the establishment of a coalition Cabinet in 1994 and sought to form an expanded liberal–democratic league. However, it has had to endure the fragmentation of the political parties. Unions have been regarded as a source of gaining voters for the new political parties. The defeat of the Social Democratic Party (the former JSP) has aggravated the situation. *Rengo*, which is an association of enterprise unions and their umbrella organisations, has found it difficult to represent the interests of union members at the grass-roots level. As a result, *Rengo* has focused on political campaigns, but these have further widened the gap between union leaders and members. The structure of *Rengo* has been seriously challenged by the unfavourable economic climate, high unemployment, the shortage of jobs for university graduates, and the restructuring of industries and enterprises.

Although the national confederations play important roles, the enterprise unions have more resources and are more powerful. The latter are autonomous in running their organisations and in promoting their members' interests. Furthermore, they are financially independent and self-supporting. Most union activities occur at the enterprise level, rather than at federation level. As the company's success greatly influences members' working conditions and employment opportunities, enterprise unions usually have a cooperative attitude towards management. Employees generally identify with their employer in making decisions that would enhance the employer's competitiveness. Thus, a key aspect of the work environment in the Japanese company is this interdependence and the belief that the company is a 'community of shared fate', where 'everyone is in the same big family'. In addition, the relatively modest wage differentials between managers, white-collar workers and blue-collar workers tend to reinforce the workers' sense of identification with the firm. This contrasts with some Western countries where there is a more rigid class differentiation and much larger differentials.

Are enterprise unions really independent from the control of the employer? If a company is unionised, the enterprise union is usually the only organisation that is recognised as representing the employees at the enterprise. Employers usually offer various facilities to the union, including an office; however, such facilities are offered on a voluntary basis after negotiations between the parties. To a certain extent, the availability of these facilities helps to establish a basis for cooperative labour–management relations in enterprises.

It is generally believed that an advantage of enterprise unionism lies in its policies being adapted to each enterprise, rather than reflecting any broader craft or political issues. Labour–management relations based on enterprise unionism will usually be more flexible than those based on, for example, craft unionism. On the other hand, there are disadvantages from a union's point of view. Newly employed workers automatically acquire union membership and their union dues are 'checked off' from their pay automatically; thus their 'union consciousness' is generally less than their 'enterprise consciousness'. Union membership usually ceases on retirement, which also reduces the commitment by workers to the union.

Furthermore, a serious barrier for unionisation is that membership of an enterprise union is usually limited to those who are regular employees, or core workers. Non-regular employees such as part-time workers, seasonal workers and immigrant workers are usually not effectively organised by unions. Although some part-time workers are unionised (mainly in the retail sector), the percentage is low.[3] While some new types of organisations, such as unions for female workers and managers' unions, are emerging, they are rather exceptional.

Employers

During the period immediately after 1945, there were many violent labour disputes in Japan. These tended to reflect the economic disorder and the shortage of food and other necessities. Neither employers nor workers then had much industrial relations experience. To cope with this labour offensive and to establish industrial peace and order, employers organised regional and industrial associations. However, partly because of the so-called 'democratisation' policy of GHQ, employers were often obliged to yield to union pressures, thus facing an erosion of their managerial prerogatives.

Although most bargaining takes place at the enterprise level, some industries engage in collective bargaining at industry level; for example, in private railways, bus services and textiles. Apart from these few examples, none of the other national or regional employers' organisations engage in collective bargaining.

Nikkeiren, the Japan Federation of Employers' Associations, was founded in 1948. It is the most important employers' organisation from an employment relations point of view, and it has many functions. It coordinates and publicises employers' opinions on labour problems; selects employer representatives to the various government commissions, councils and International Labour Organisation (ILO) delegations; and provides its member organisations with advice and services on labour conditions and employment practices. *Nikkeiren's* members include employers' associations organised at both prefectural and industry level.[4] Every year at the time of *Shunto*, the Spring Labour Offensive, *Nikkeiren* releases guidelines for employers to follow when dealing with demands from the various unions during collective bargaining. Thus, although many of them do not have a direct role in bargaining, the employers' associations seem to have an important role behind the scenes (Levine 1984:318ff.). The main determinant of the outcome of collective bargaining is the individual company's business performance.

Employee-managed firms?

The basic structure of Japanese companies, particularly the large ones, is quite different from the structures found in most North American and European companies. The corporate structure of large Japanese companies may be closer to a model of 'employee-managed firms', unlike large companies in Western, particularly Anglo-American, countries which are often characterised as 'shareholders' prerogative' firms. The structural characteristics of Japanese companies should not be seen as barriers to international competition; the Japanese corporate system is legitimate, even though it is different.

The economic literature on employee-managed firms usually distinguishes them from other firms by assuming that they have a distinct functional objective. It is assumed that employee-managed, or *Illyria* firms, seek to maximise the dividend or net income per worker, while stereotypically capitalist firms seek to maximise total profit (Ward 1958).

Figure 10.2   A model of a typical large Japanese company

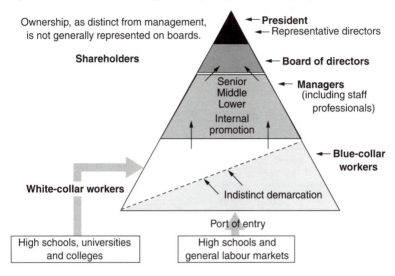

Source: Kuwahara (1989).

In addition, an employee-managed firm implies a type of partici-patory management. Although various definitions could be formulated, a generally acceptable one would be that an employee-managed firm is a productive enterprise where ultimate decision-making rights are held by member-workers on an equal basis regardless of job, skill-grade, or capital contribution. Using this definition, the typical Japanese firm might be called 'quasi employee-managed', even if, strictly speak-ing, it is not managed by all the workers. Although boards of directors are not officially elected or nominated by employees through a system of voting, most directors are ex-employees. They are recommended as candidates for a directorship to the shareholders' meeting by the pres-ident, who usually has been promoted from within. Thus, most de-cisions are executed by board directors who have been promoted from within the same corporation. Nevertheless, independent directors rep-resenting large shareholders such as banks, insurance companies and parent companies are sometimes also included as members of the board, when the company is a subsidiary or is financially supported by the parent company or banks or insurance companies.

Directors are usually promoted from among the senior managers who have worked for the company for a long time, often 25 to 30 years, after graduating from university, college or high school. Some of these people had been leaders of enterprise unions when they were rank-and-file employees. Indeed, many employees who have been promoted to supervisory and/or managerial positions were previously union members. When promoted from senior managerial positions to become board directors, individuals are asked to adopt a different role as members of the senior executive. However, this change takes place on a continuum from being an employee to being a top manager. Directors who have been promoted internally after a long career might be expected to place the interests of the enterprise community, consisting of executive members and employees, above the interests of stockholders. Even if there are few independent directors, however, the interests of large shareholders are rarely neglected, and senior executives, such as the CEO, generally consult them before making important decisions. Larger shareholders are generally more interested in capital gain rather than increasing dividends.

Since internal promotion is the usual path for advancement, most employees have a strong commitment to the firm. In Japanese companies, the word *shain* is often used. (It means literally 'member of the company'.) This word contains nuances that do not have an equivalent in Western terminology. It means more than a mere hired worker; rather, it implies belonging to a community formed by people with the same interests. There is a sense that a Japanese corporation is a social entity of its own.

Employees participate in the various stages of the decision-making process. Small-group activities such as quality control circles (QCC) or total quality control (TQC) are widespread. With a reduction in the degree of explicit industrial conflict and the increasing development of 'internal labour markets', the difference between collective bargaining and joint consultation is becoming less distinct.

Most blue-collar workers are paid on a monthly salary basis, as are white-collar workers. The performance-related remuneration system is important. In addition to wages or salaries, most Japanese workers receive two large seasonal payments worth about 3.9 months' salary a year (the industry average in 1996). Prosperous industries, such as petroleum, pay bonuses worth about 5.1 months' salary a year, while declining industries such as garments pay about 2.1 months' salary a year. This practice originated from the employers' consideration of the extra expenditure required for the Buddhist *bon festival*, a kind of ancestor worship ritual observed in summer, and for the end-of-year and New Year celebrations. The amount of the payment fluctuates according to the performance of the company or industry and according to the merit of employees. However, it does not fluctuate a great deal, and workers assume that the payments are an integral part of their annual income. Despite the relative stability of the amount, employees do relate any small changes to variations in the company's profit. This increases employees' interest in the operation and performance of the company for which they work. The bonus system has attracted the interest of some Western economists as an effective measure to combat stagflation (Weitzman 1984).

Collective bargaining

Pay agreements may be concluded separately from agreements on other matters. Most unions conduct pay negotiations during *Shunto* in April and May each year, while negotiations on more comprehensive labour agreements may be conducted at other times. However, an increasing number of unions also make other claims during the *Shunto*; for example, for increases in overtime rates, revisions of allowances, shorter working hours, raising the retirement age and expanding private pensions. A decline in union density and a sluggish economic climate have helped to change the characteristics of the *Shunto*. Its relative importance in national wage bargaining has declined, with the locus of wage bargaining shifting towards the enterprise level. Increasing differences in the profitability of firms, brought on by increased competition, have been a major cause of this change.

The structure of enterprise unions usually corresponds to the organisation of the enterprise, and its establishment, department or divisional groupings. Grievances are often settled informally, with formal procedures rarely used. Managers often attempt to subdue tensions and conflict and to reinforce a feeling of community. This does not mean that industrial disputes are unheard of; there were many large-scale and long disputes in mining and major manufacturing industries in the 1940s and 1950s. Some strikes were led by radical, leftist leaders. Many of these disputes left deep wounds in employment relationships which were not easily healed.

Such disputes taught the unions and employers some important lessons. Although there were many stoppages in 1974, there was a substantial reduction subsequently. Disputes are usually settled directly between the parties concerned, but sometimes a third party conciliates. Conciliation machinery for the private and public sectors is provided by the central and local labour relations commissions. Special commissions act for public sector employees and for seamen. Nearly all the disputes brought before these commissions are settled either by conciliation or mediation; few disputes go as far as arbitration. Most disputes presented to the labour relations commissions are those that go beyond the limits of labour–management relations at the enterprise level. The relative importance of the commissions has declined as there has been an increase in the extent of cooperation between labour and management at the enterprise level.

Contemporary Japanese industrial relations is relatively stable, and relations between the parties can generally be characterised as cooperative. Some see this in a positive light. Others have a more negative view, arguing that enterprise unions are too dependent on employers, and that the relationship is one of collaboration and incorporation. However, enterprise unions may be more appropriate than traditional occupationally based unions in firms that are 'quasi employee-managed', in terms of decision making and in fostering workplace democracy and employee morale. Nonetheless, it is open to question to what extent Japanese firms fulfil this description; the pursuit of company profits tends to come before consideration of the individual employee.

Unions represent sectional interests, and enterprise unions are no exception. Since many employees expect to work for many years for the same enterprise, they tend to place considerable emphasis on the improvement of their own working conditions, but do not pay as much attention to the interests of the temporary workers at the same establishment. This may be an unfortunate characteristic of quasi employee-managed firms, where regular employees want to maintain their positions even if this is at the expense of non-regular employees, such as part-time workers and temporary workers who are disproportionately likely to be women.[5]

Why has the relationship between unions and employers changed so fundamentally since the 1950s? There has been increased competition among firms, improved standards of living and a shift towards a service-oriented economy, and public opinion is more conservative than it was in the 1950s. The 1970s oil crises further accelerated the trend in this direction. But is cooperative employment relations desirable under all circumstances? Relations may come under severe stress when labour and management have to face a crisis or a serious economic recession, which may precipitate redundancies, but these are a last resort.

Contemporary issues

The social and economic environment in Japan is still changing rapidly. There is an ageing population, an increasing proportion of highly educated workers, growing participation by women in the labour market, increased immigration of foreign workers, and moves towards an 'information society'. One impact of globalisation is a growing view that in several sectors Japanese economic prowess is being challenged by competition from other countries. A major issue is the high appreciation and volatility of the yen, which has induced radical changes in product and labour markets. In 1980 the rate was 217 yen to the US dollar, but by 1995 this had decreased to 84 yen per US dollar. To cope with the difficulties caused by the appreciation of the yen, many Japanese firms shifted some production to other countries, including

China. Another consequence has been the rise in migrant workers, attracted to Japan by high wages. Although the value of the yen fell in relation to the US dollar after 1995 (see Appendix), there has been little change in the trend of foreign direct investment and immigration. This volatility in the value of the yen has made it difficult for managers and other players to make appropriate decisions.

Also, the globalisation of markets is having a radical impact on many industries. This has been particularly apparent in the finance, communication and service sectors. An example is the remarkable development of the information and communication industries, which has seen the number of firms in communications and broadcasting rise dramatically, from 85 in 1985 to 4305 in 1997 (Keizai Kikakucho 1997). The development of information and communication technologies is transforming traditional patterns of employment by generating new working styles, such as working from home, tele-work and satellite offices.

Job security and employment practices

In the post-1973 recession, many countries experienced increases in unemployment. Unemployment in Japan was 1.2 per cent in 1965 and remained less than 1.5 per cent until 1974. It then increased to 2 per cent in 1980 and 2.8 per cent in 1986–87; at that time the highest rate since these statistics were first collected in the early 1950s. Unemployment had particularly increased among those less than 24 years old and those over 40 years old. The level of unemployment subsequently declined, but rose again after 1992.

Total employment has continued to increase, despite the increase in unemployment. In the 1985–95 period, employment rose by 9.4 million, from 42.9 million to 52.3 million employees. The industries that recorded the greatest increase in jobs were retailing and wholesaling, business services, construction and medical services. The new high-technology industries also expanded. Heavy manufacturing industries contracted, however, including textiles, shipbuilding, steel and non-ferrous metals, lumber and industrial machinery. In declining industries affected by the oil crises, many unions, especially the federations at the industrial level, participated (sometimes for the first time) in the reorganisation of industry by asking the government to establish industrial policies that took the unions' viewpoint into account.

The stagnation following the oil crises taught employers some important lessons about the difficulties of laying off redundant workers. Companies generally do not dismiss permanent employees, since there is no institutionalised layoff system. Moreover, if firms did lay off people, this could destroy the 'high trust relations' that usually prevail between managers and employees. Hence, one strategy adopted in Japan was to increase flexibility by minimising the number of permanent (regular) employees, and by employing temporary and part-time workers instead. On the other hand, raising the mandatory retirement age from 55 to 60 or even to 65 may increase the commitment of employees to particular enterprises. Since retirement allowances and private pensions are generally related to length of service, employees usually want to stay with enterprises for as long as possible.

Many companies are modifying their traditional employment and pay system to achieve more flexible human resources management (HRM) practices. The innovations include 'plateauing' the age–wage profile after a certain age, so that an automatic seniority pay increase is not expected after, say, 45 years of age, and introducing selective career paths that induce early retirement. Some firms have reduced their total number of employees by 'natural wastage' or attrition.

Labour shortages

Since the late 1980s, there has been a significant shift in the supply–demand relationship in the labour market. The increase in the value of the yen in the 1980s led to a threat of a recession, particularly among export industries. Japanese industry responded positively to this situation by reorienting itself towards developing domestic demand, and the economy began to grow again. With firms showing a greater propensity to recruit more workers, the number of employees increased.

From 1987, the job-offers ratio (the number of job offers divided by job seekers) increased as the Japanese economy overcame the yen's appreciation and grew again (see Figure 10.3). Furthermore, unemployment declined again, after having temporarily risen to 3 per cent in 1987. In 1986–87 Japan was plagued by fears of unemployment induced by the soaring yen.

In June 1988 the job-offers ratio exceeded 1.0 for the first time in 14 years. The October 1989 ratio was 1.03. It increased to 1.4 in October 1990. Thus, the employment situation improved from the macro viewpoint, but the extent of labour shortages varied in different sectors of the labour market.

The labour shortages in the early 1990s gradually spread to many industries, and were especially serious in construction, retailing and other elements of the service sector as well as in the machinery and metals segments of the manufacturing sector. Many of these industries offered working conditions that were not attractive to young workers and many firms encountered difficulties caused by an acute shortage of new young employees.

However, the economy cannot escape from business cycles. After March 1991, the job-offers ratio declined again. It recorded the lowest level of 0.6 in September 1995. Although the ratio has recovered since

Figure 10.3   Trends in the rate of unemployment and job-offers ratio

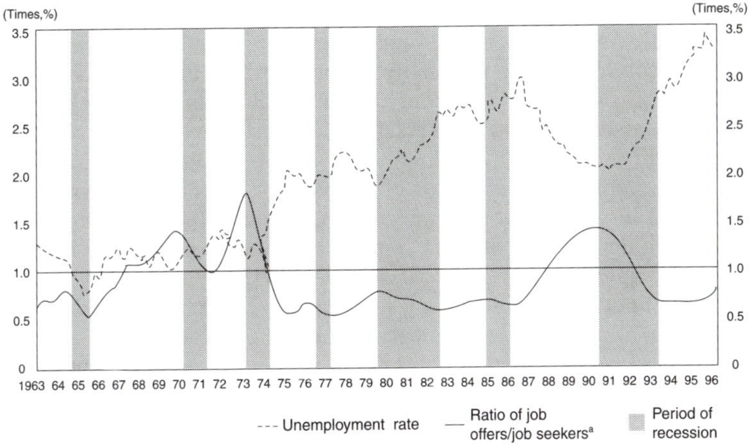

Note: a   Number of registered job openings/number of registered job applicants.

Source: Ministry of Labour (1997).

then, it was still below 1.0 during 1996. Many firms reduced the number of employees in various ways. However, in view of their poor working conditions, some small firms had difficulties in hiring adequate numbers of Japanese workers, allowing immigrant workers to find openings in these relatively low-skilled jobs. A mismatch of workers in terms of skill and industry developed. How did industries respond to this mismatch? Strategies used by employers included technological innovation, flexible use of workers, shifting production bases to Asian countries, and the employment of more foreign workers.

The foreign labour issue

When faced with a serious shortage of labour in the mid-1980s, many employers hired foreign workers, who were often 'illegal labourers' from developing countries. Until the mid-1980s, there was little discussion about the employment of foreign workers. However, given the subsequent appreciation of the yen and the tight labour market, the wage differentials between Japan and developing countries have increased.

Partly due to the government's slow response to the foreign labour issue, an increasing number of foreigners entered Japan with tourist or student visas, but then unlawfully entered the labour market. This includes those who are engaged in activities not allowed by law, or who have stayed in Japan longer than permitted by their visa. It is estimated that by 1995, at least 285 000 foreign workers were employed unofficially in construction, some aspects of manufacturing and the service sector. They are especially engaged in jobs that are considered demanding, dirty and dangerous. When legal immigrant workers are included, about 600 000 workers from various countries are currently working in the labour market.

In the construction sector, for instance, foreign labourers are employed through personal connections with a subsidiary firm's boss or through employment agencies, including brokers or syndicates. They are also employed on a daily basis in the day-labourer market. Regrettably, an undercover network of syndicates or brokers has been established which provides bridges between Japan and the foreign workers' countries of origin. Many immigrants who look for employment opportunities in Japan depend on such a network. The 'trade' in foreign workers often involves the use of professional smugglers who extract exorbitant fees for transport and for providing false documents, such as visas and Japanese passports. Workers who find employment opportunities through these channels are often exploited and forced to work in substandard conditions for low wages. A substantial number of cases involving illegal foreign workers are reported each year.

Under these circumstances, the Japanese government introduced an amendment to the Immigration Control and Refugee Recognition Act, which was implemented in June 1990. The amendment expanded the categories of authorised legal residence and employment, while introducing penalties against employers and brokers who employ illegal workers or who facilitate such employment. The government's policy is to prohibit unskilled workers, or those looking for simple jobs, from seeking employment in Japan. The amendment has not changed this. This policy is rationalised by arguing that if there is an abundant supply of cheap labour, it will obstruct the progress of rationalisation and industrial restructuring in desirable directions such as high-value-added industries or high-technology industries. Unless there is strong support for the maintenance of fair working conditions for foreign workers, it may be necessary to continue to prohibit the inflow of unskilled workers.

The pressure from Asian developing countries to supply the required labour is very strong. Recent evidence of this includes the sudden increase in illegal landings by Chinese stowaways since 1996. This has attracted much attention from the Japanese Maritime Safety Agency and the National Police Agency, because of a perceived link between such 'illegals' and increases in serious crime. In this environment, Japan must develop long-term policies to accommodate the increasing number of immigrants who are attempting to adapt to Japanese society, while also preparing measures that will stem the inflow of illegals. Such policies should cover not only working conditions but also broader issues such as housing, education, social security, regional issues, police and political rights. This should allow foreign workers to be satisfactorily absorbed into Japanese society for the mutual benefit of all concerned.

Technological innovation

There was great concern in the 1950s and in the 1970s that technological change and innovation would so improve productivity and save labour that it would lead to decreased employment opportunities and worse unemployment. However, subsequent developments have diminished such concerns. The movement towards a service-based economy and the introduction of new technologies have not been seen as reducing job opportunities in Japan.

Japan is leading the world in the diffusion of labour-saving technologies. A variety of technologies (factory automation and office automation) have been introduced. According to a survey by the Association of Industrial Robot Producers, by 1987 Japan was ahead of the other major industrialised market economies (IMEs) in terms of its having more than a 60 per cent share of all the industrial robots in the Organisation for Economic Co-operation and Development (OECD) countries.

New technologies, particularly micro-electronics, were used to create many new products including videotape recorders, word processors and personal computers, which in turn expanded employment opportunities to a great extent. Many labour-saving technologies have also been introduced to cope with the shortage of labour. However, this has raised other problems. With the proportion of school leavers declining, along with the ageing of the labour force, restructuring through technological innovation may prove difficult for some groups in the years ahead. Middle-aged and older people, for example, are not well prepared to respond to new technologies, although it is less of a problem for younger members of the workforce. It has long been advocated that older people should be assisted in terms of retraining and redeployment, but this has not been easily accomplished.

Flexibility

Another way to cope with the mismatch of labour and job opportunities is to introduce greater labour market flexibility. Since the late 1970s, there has been a considerable expansion in the employment of part-time workers and those available from temporary agencies. The job-offers ratio for part-time workers was 4.0 in 1990. Most part-time workers are female, particularly middle-aged married women. The percentage of part-time female workers who work less than a 35-hour week had risen to more than 32 per cent by 1995. In addition, the average length of service for part-time workers with one employer has gradually become longer. In 1988 they worked an average of 4.1 years. The rate of turnover among part-time workers has remained stable in recent years.

By contrast, the rate of turnover of young workers has tended to rise. Furthermore, it remains high against the backdrop of the tight labour market. Approximately 20 per cent of young workers with high school diplomas left their initial place of work within a year and 40 per cent left within three years. An increase in the number of young workers (known as *freeters*) who do not want to stay with a single firm, is contributing to such changes. Simultaneously, the average length of service among 'core-workers' (regular employees) is getting longer. It is around 12.4 years for men and 7.1 years for women (Rodosho 1987). Hence, changes are taking place in Japan's so-called 'lifetime' employment practices.

Many firms are trying to introduce HRM pay and promotion policies based on performance rather than the length of service or age of employees. They also classify the types of employees according to their characteristics, such as core-workers, specialists and temporary (flexible) workers.

Small and medium-sized enterprises (SMEs)

The stereotypical Japanese employment practices mentioned above (e.g. long-term commitment and enterprise unions) are usual for most *large* employing organisations, but are also found, albeit to a lesser extent, in SMEs. In 1991, some 70 per cent of all Japanese employees worked in SMEs (defined as establishments with less than 100 employees).

There are wide differences in wages and working conditions, depending upon a firm's size, capital/labour ratios, and other factors, which result in higher value-added productivity in large firms. SMEs are not an inefficient and declining sector. SMEs account for a wide range of economic activity, and increasing support for them is emerging from many diverse quarters, because they can be innovative and more flexible.

It is difficult to generalise about the characteristics of employment relations in SMEs because of their wide variety. Subcontractors are one type of SME which play an important role in manufacturing industries; however, the percentage of subcontractors in other industries is low. Although it is hard to obtain an exact picture, about 66 per cent of manufacturing firms are subcontractors of one type or another. Industries that have many subcontractors include motor vehicle, textiles, clothing, general machinery, electrical machinery and metal industries.

Table 10.2   Private establishments and number of people employed by size of establishment and by sector

Year	Total industry (%)			Manufacturing industry (%)			Non-manufacturing industry (%)		
	Small firm[a]	Medium firm[b]	Large firm[c]	Small firm	Medium firm	Large firm	Small firm	Medium firm	Large firm
1975	69.1	12.2	18.7	57.6	13.4	29.0	77.9	11.3	10.8
1985	71.5	10.9	17.7	60.9	11.7	27.4	78.3	10.3	11.4
1990	69.3	11.4	19.3	57.6	12.2	30.2	75.7	10.9	13.4
1994	69.4	11.6	19.0	57.7	12.1	30.2	75.3	11.3	13.4

Notes: a   Small firms denote those capitalised at less than 100 million yen.
         b   Medium firms denote those capitalised at between 100 million and 1 billion yen.
         c   Large firms denote those capitalised at 1 billion yen or more.
Source: Keizai Kikakucho (1996).

The percentage of subcontractors increased in each of these industries in the 1970s. However, as a firm increases in size, it tends to be less dependent on other firms (Chusho Kigyo Cho 1983).

Independent firms constitute another type of SME; they compete with one another in the market. In this category, there are a growing number of SMEs based on high technologies. This category of firm typically combines advanced technology with high levels of business acumen and technical ability. There are still relatively few of these firms compared with the traditional type of SMEs; however, they are expected to have a great impact on their product and labour markets.

Since union density is low in SMEs, the terms and conditions of employment are generally determined by market factors. In the case of subcontractors in very competitive areas, profit margins are low. Wage levels in the primary labour market do not correspond directly with those in SMEs, although there is a spillover effect.

As mentioned earlier, there has been an increase in the number of part-time workers. About 31 per cent of women workers were part-timers in 1995. Such workers are more likely to enter and leave the labour force. The motivation of such employees is changing. Increasing numbers of them are entering the labour market not only for economic reasons but also for socio-cultural reasons—such as to escape from the tedium of being a 'housewife'. Employers are also increasingly seeking to employ more part-time workers to gain greater flexibility in their labour force.

When considering the dynamic role of SMEs, and the characteristics of Japan's part-time or temporary workforce, the simple stereotype of a dual labour market should not be automatically applied to the Japanese situation. Japanese labour markets are complex and segmented.

Even the so-called primary labour market in the manufacturing sector has stagnated since the oil crises, especially in basic industries such as steel, nonferrous metals and chemicals. On the other hand, many SMEs have emerged as being more dynamic and profitable, though they are often characterised as using secondary labour markets.

SMEs are playing a larger role in the Japanese economy. The growth of the service sector has led to an increasing diversity in workers' conditions; these reflect their employer's specific business conditions. By the late 1990s, over 60 per cent of civilian employees were in the service sector. The future of unionism in Japan greatly depends on whether unions can recruit such employees.

Conclusion

Japanese employment relations are changing. One of the most important characteristics of Japanese society, reflected in HRM and industrial relations, has been its adaptability. There are various characteristics of Japanese HRM and industrial relations that help maintain flexibility, and facilitate adaptation to change. Some examples include relatively vague and wide job descriptions; flexibility of workforce allocation in organisations; lack of rigid work rules compared with those found in other IMEs; widespread use of bonus pay systems; and long-term merit ratings for managers and employees. These are not exclusive to Japan, but are generally found more frequently in combination, compared with other countries.

Before the 1970s, some union leaders and academic critics of the Japanese system saw certain characteristics of the Japanese model, such as lifetime employment, seniority-based wages and enterprise unions, as feudalistic practices which should be abandoned. During the mid-1970s however, such characteristics came to be seen as important explanations of the post-war Japanese economic miracle.

By comparison with most other OECD countries, Japan enjoyed high rates of economic growth. This may have been an unexpected result of the Second World War, which destroyed most of the special interest organisations that, as Olson (1982) argued, may hinder the growth of an economy. Various bottlenecks in the supply of oil and other raw materials have impeded Japan's growth, particularly since 1973. By the mid-1980s, Japan had entered a stage of slower growth, though it continued to grow more rapidly than most other IMEs.

Nevertheless, lower rates of economic growth and the ageing of the population have induced some rigidities into Japanese society. The narrowing of promotion opportunities for managers is becoming a serious issue for those in the prime age group of 35–45 years of age.

The position of white-collar workers is also of major concern. Their status in enterprises and society is undergoing substantial change. Since production workers have attained high levels of labour productivity, white-collar workers are emerging as targets for rationalisation. However, unlike some countries in Europe, Japan is not likely to see the emergence of radical white-collar unionists.

The future of the Japanese model of industrialisation depends upon its ability to continue to adjust to change by eliminating barriers to economic growth, with the help of various innovations. The model is changing, as there is continuing structural change in the face of strong international competition. New technologies are being used widely; these also may thwart rigidities in the labour market and in the wider society. Hitherto, the process of 'creative destruction' has generally had a positive impact on the Japanese labour market and has had favourable consequences for employers and most workers.

Despite its overwhelming success, particularly after the first oil crisis, the Japanese still see their economy as 'fragile' or 'precarious'. It has overcome the many difficulties of the post-war period including oil crises and the appreciation of the yen. Japanese economic and corporate policy makers have demonstrated their flexible but tough characteristics.

Japanese management is regarded in other IMEs and newly industrialising economies (NIEs) as a model that is suitable in the face of global competition. Japanese styles of management are being transferred through direct foreign investment by Japanese firms to developing as well as developed countries. Such direct foreign investment increased greatly in the late 1980s and early 1990s. The value of the yen strongly influences the competitiveness of Japanese enterprises. Not only large firms but also SMEs have shifted their production bases to developing countries in Asia and some IMEs. This shift has evoked considerable controversy about the future of Japan (i.e. is deindustrialisation inevitable or not?).

As Japanese firms move operations overseas, local employees may have promotion opportunities in such international enterprises. About 10 per cent of employees of Japanese companies outside Japan are managerial and white-collar staff. It makes sense for the Japanese to train and promote non-Japanese employees for senior managerial positions overseas. But for this to happen successfully, both sides have to accept considerable changes in their expectations.

Establishing an overseas subsidiary presents challenges of cross-cultural adaptation. Rather than merely creating new management strategies in a foreign country, a learning process is involved. It is not a one-way transplant of technology; the host country's interests should also be considered. The continued viability of Japanese management strategies will be tested as Japanese enterprises try to create new international hybrid best-practice approaches to management.

A chronology of Japanese employment relations

1868	*Meiji* Restoration ended the feudal era.
1880	Early government factories sold to family groups, the genesis of *zaibatsu*, or holding companies.
1887	Unionisation movement among printers, ironworkers and other craftsworkers (which soon disappeared).
1892	Formation of National Federation of Chambers of Commerce.
1894–95	Sino-Japanese War.
1897	Founding of *Rodokumiai-kiseikai*, the first successful union in Japan. Ironworkers' Union (*Tekko Kumiai*) and Japan Railway Union (*Nittetsu Kyoseikai*) organised.
1900	Enactment of *Chian-iji-ho* (Maintenance of the Public Order Act) with provisions to prohibit workers' right to organise.
1901	Government-owned Yawata Ironworks opened.
1903	Ministry of Agriculture and Commerce issued 'Status of Factory Workers'.
1904–05	The Russo–Japanese War.
1906	Japan Socialist Party organised.
1907	Violent strikes at Ashio and Besshi copper mines.
1911	Factory Law promulgated.
1912	Founding of *Yuaikai* (Friendly Society).
1914–18	First World War.
1920	Great Depression. Large-scale labour disputes at Yawata Ironworks. First May Day.
1921	Founding of *Nippon Rodo Sodomei* (Japan Labour Foundation).
1922	Japan Communist Party organised.
1925	General Election Law promulgated. Public Peace Maintenance Law promulgated.
1927	A large-scale strike at *Noda Shoyu*.
1929	Lifting of the gold embargo. *Showa* panic.
1931	Pre-war record for the number of labour disputes. The Manchurian Incident started.
1937	Sino-Japanese War started. Founding of *Sangyo-hokokukai* (Association for Services to the State through Industry)—a labour–management cooperative association.
1940	Organisations of workers and farmers dismissed. *Dainihon Sangyo Hokokukai* (The Great Japan Federation of Patriotic Industries) inaugurated. *Taisei Yokusankai* (The

	Imperial Rule Assistance Association) organised; merged with *Dainihon Sangyo Hokokukai* in 1942.
1941–45	Second World War.
1945	Hiroshima and Nagasaki reduced to ashes by atomic bomb explosion. The Potsdam Declaration accepted. Japan's unconditional surrender. The Trade Union Law promulgated.
1946	Workers' control of Tsurumi Works, *Nippon Kokan K.K.* Six labour unions, including the labour union of Tsurumi Workers, *Nippon Kokan* and the labour union of Toshiba Corporation, started production control. Labour disputes at the *Yomiuri Shimbun.* Japanese Confederation of Labour (*Sodomei*) organised. Labour Relations Adjustment Law promulgated. The constitution of Japan promulgated (effective on 3 May 1947). *Nichirokaigi* (Congress of Labour Unions of Japan) organised.
1947	The General Headquarters ordered the suspension of 1 February general strike. The constitution of Japan came into effect. *Densan* (Japan Electric Industry Workers' Union) and *Tanro* (Japan Coal Miners' Union) organised. Ministry of Labour established.
1948	The Japan Federation of Employers' Associations (*Nikkeiren*) organised. Revised National Public Service Law and Public Corporation and National Enterprise Labour Relations Law promulgated. Trade Union Law and Labour Relations Adjustment Law revised. Dodge Line introduced. The Korean War broke out. Conference for organising General Council of Trade Unions of Japan (*Sohyo*). Communist purge occurs. The Peace Treaty with Japan signed; the Japan–US Security Treaty signed.
1952	The Third May Day; bloodshed at the Palace Plaza. Third labour law revised.
1954	Human rights disputes at Omi Kenshi Co. Ltd. All Japan Federation of Labour Unions (*Zenro*) organised. *Sohyo* consolidated five industry-level offensives into a united wage increase in spring.
1956	Japan joins the United Nations.
1958	Labour disputes at Oji Paper Co., Ltd.
1959	Minimum Wages Law passed by the Diet. United movement to stop the revision of the Japan–US Security Treaty. Labour disputes at Miike Coal Mines.
1964	Japan joins the OECD. Federation of IMF–JC.
1965	Japan ratified ILO's Convention 87.

1973	First oil crisis.
1974	The biggest strike in the history of the Spring Labour Offensive—about 6 million participants.
1980	UAW (International Union, United Automobile, Aerospace and Agricultural Workers of America) asked for the Japanese automobile manufacturers direct investment in the USA.
1982	Japanese Private Sector Trade Union Council (*Zenminrokyo*) formed.
1987	Japanese Private Sector Trade Union Confederation (*Rengo*) formed.
1988	Revision of Labour Standard Act (promotion of shorter working hours).
1989	Start of new *Rengo* (Japan Trade Union Confederation) which merged the public sector unions.
1990	Revision of the Immigration Control and Refugee Recognition Act.
1991	Japan International Training Cooperation Organisation (JITCO) was established.
1992	Child Care Leave Law introduced.
1993	Skill Training System for Foreign Workers established.
1994	Yen recorded its highest rate against US dollar. The LDP, JSP and *Sakigake* (Harbinger) Party formed a coalition Cabinet. Law for Improving Working Conditions of Part-time Workers.
1996	The LDP formed a new Cabinet.
1997	Agreement between universities and employers on new graduates. Introduction of harsh penalties against brokers who assisted in illegal landings. Introduction of penalties under the Equal Employment Opportunity Act. Instability in financial markets in Asia-Pacific countries, including Japan, induced uncertainties in the labour market.

11 | Employment relations in the Republic of Korea

Park Young-bum[1] and Chris Leggett

The Republic of [South] Korea (hereafter Korea) has a population of 45 million; by the late 1990s almost 80 per cent was urban, an increase from only around 30 per cent in 1962. This compares with urbanisation rates of virtually 100 per cent in Hong Kong and Singapore and 58 per cent in Taiwan, the other Asian newly industrialised economies (NIEs) that are often discussed in relation to Korea. Ethnically homogeneous, about half of South Korea's population are Buddhist, although there is a substantial and significant Christian presence; all have inherited Confucian values. In the late 1990s, the labour force was 20 million with a participation rate of 62 per cent (76 per cent for males and 49 per cent for females), and unemployment was not much above 2 per cent; yet weekly working hours remained the longest for any country reported by the International Labour Organisation (ILO). The tight labour market has led to an increase in the employment of foreign workers, as it has in the other Asian NIEs.

Rapid industrialisation through export-oriented manufacturing has resulted in Korea's per capita gross national product (GNP) increasing from $87 in 1962 to more than $10 000 in 1997, an annual average growth rate of 8 per cent, but within a range of between −3.7 per cent in 1980 and 12.3 per cent in 1987. These fluctuations in growth rates reflect political crises and Korea's sensitivity to changes in the world economy. Korea is the world's twelfth largest economy and it became a member of the Organisation for Economic Co-operation and Development (OECD) in 1996. However, in 1997, Korea, along with several other Asian countries, experienced a major economic crisis that required International Monetary Fund (IMF) intervention.

Since the Second World War, Korea has been governed by an American military occupation (until 1948) and six republics. The first extended from 1948 to 1960 under Syngman Rhee; during part of this

275

time the Korean peninsula was devastated by a civil war, which ended with the 1953 armistice and the division of the peninsula between the People's Republic of Korea in the north and the Republic of Korea in the south. The second lasted from 1960 to 1961 under Chang Myeon; the third from 1961 to 1972 under Park Chung-hee; the fourth from 1972 to 1980 under Park Chung-hee and, in an interim, Choi Kyu-ha; the fifth from 1980 to 1987 under Chun Doo-hwan; the sixth since 1987 under Roh Tae-woo and Kim Young-sam. Rhee was ousted by student demonstrations and Park was assassinated, and in 1996 Roh and Chun were tried and sentenced for crimes committed during their presidencies. Although Rhee started the process, Presidents Park and Chun were the political driving forces of Korea's rapid industrialisation. Apart from a brief spell during the Second Republic, Korea began to function democratically only in 1987, but an opposition candidate was not elected to the presidency until after the 1997 election.

The development of Korean employment relations

At the time it was opened to the outside world by the Kangwha Treaty of 1876, and until it was colonised by Japan in 1910, Korea was the 500-year-old feudal kingdom of Chosun, ruled by the Yi Dynasty according to the Confucian code of personal, social and civic behaviour. Its society was rigidly stratified into *Yangban* (ruling class), *Jungin* or *Seoin* (middle class), *Sangmin* (peasant farmers and craftsworkers), and *Cheonmin* (underprivileged class). Although workers' handicrafts were made in *Sangmin* and *Cheonmin* family workshops, wage labour was rare. Organised labour can trace its origins to the late eighteenth century, but its extent was minimal until Japanese imperialism in the late nineteenth century resulted in workforce expansion in mining, stevedoring, transport, municipal services and trade-related occupations.

During the Japanese colonial administration from 1910 to 1945, Korean industrial relations were restrained by the Japanese authorities. Nevertheless, the labour movement drew support from nationalist and socialist leaders, but their incompatibilities led to communist-backed unions being driven underground, while other unions tended to accommodate the colonial regime.

In spite of a brief renaissance after liberation in 1945, unionism was restructured according to the division of the Korean peninsula. As a result, the leftist *Chun Pyung* (the General Council of Korean Trade Unions) was banned in 1947 by the American Military Government (AMG) and soon replaced by its rival, the *Daehan Nochong* (General Federation of Korean Trade Unions, or GFKTU). Another attempt at independent trade unionism was made with the formation of the *Cheonkuk Nodongjohab Hyeobuiehyo* (National Council of Trade

Unions, or NCTU) in 1959 and, in 1960, the GFKTU and the NCTU merged. In 1961, unions were obliged to affiliate to industry federations under a government-sponsored national centre known as *Hankuk Nochong* (Federation of Korean Trade Unions, or FKTU). Meanwhile, the family business beneficiaries of state largesse under the First Republic, the *chaebol*, had been incorporated by the governments of Park Chung-hee and Chun Doo-hwan as capitalist partners in development, thus completing the basic institutional character of Korean employment relations until the re-emergence of an independent trade union movement in the mid-1980s. Because the success of Korea's industrialisation was dependent on the supply of cheap labour to ensure the competitiveness of *chaebol* products in world markets, for Korean governments and the *chaebol* the control of industrial relations was of central importance.

Protests in the 1980s led by students and union activists against the Chun Doo-hwan government came to a head in June 1987 when the presidential candidate and Chun protégé, Roh Tae-woo, presaged political liberalisation, including direct elections. This was a turning point in Korean employment relations, with government subsequently withdrawing from its authoritarian approach to become more of a conciliator within its legal framework, while still committed to the maintenance of economic growth (Woo 1996:165).

There immediately followed a revival of the labour movement, manifested in dramatic increases in the number of unions, in union membership and in disputes; but only minor amendments were made to labour laws, which continue to recognise only one union peak body, the FKTU, and to lock out 'third parties' (i.e. union officials not employed by the enterprise concerned) from collective bargaining (Paisley 1994:54). However, in April 1996, a presidential address from Kim Young-sam announced a New Conception of Industrial Relations (NCIR) with the purpose of reforming Korean industrial relations through the deliberations of a multi-representative Industrial Relations Reform Commission (IRRC).

The employment relations parties

According to the systems model (see ch. 1) the main participants in a country's employment relations are tripartite: workers and their organisations, employers and their associations, and government and private agencies (Dunlop 1958). The IRRC (mentioned above) advising Korea's President on the reform of the country's industrial relations is comprised of representatives from unions, employers, academics, lawyers, religious leaders and the press (Woo 1996:166). It is therefore important to note the influence on industrial relations of other organisations, for example, the influence of such professional bodies as the Korea Labour Institute (KLI) and academics from the economics and law faculties of Korea's prestigious universities. Neither should it be overlooked that before 1987 the Korean CIA played a covert but significant role in the repression of labour activism. Finally, some of the young activists in the radical union and student movements in the 1990s appear to be inspired by values deriving from their Christian, mainly Presbyterian and Catholic, beliefs.

Unions

Korean unions are represented on three levels. There are local unions based on a plant, an enterprise, a region or an occupation, most commonly at the plant or enterprise. Thus all union members at a particular plant or enterprise, regardless of their occupation, join the one local union. Local union leaders are directly elected by the members and bargain collectively with their employer. The consequence of the local enterprise union structure is that collective bargaining issues tend to be firm-specific. Although the local unions make up occupational federations and regional councils, and these in turn form a national centre, the right to negotiate is vested in the local unions with regional councils and industrial federations having only the right to consult and discuss. However, there are a few unions, such as the Korean Federation of Communication Trade Unions and the Federation of Korean Taxi Transport Workers' Unions, which are structured on an occupational basis and collectively bargain at regional and national levels.

Since 1987, there have been many attempts by labour activists to organise a national centre as a rival to the FKTU. For example, in 1991 *Cheonnohyeob* (Korea Trade Union Congress, or KTUC) was formed and soon had more than 300 000 members. In 1995, it joined with other officially non-recognised centres to form the *Minju Nochong* (Korea Confederation of Trade Unions, KCTU). In spite of the official non-recognition of their centre, some KCTU leaders were invited to join the IRRC (mentioned above) as representatives of a single union.

Korean unionism has changed dramatically since 1987 (Kim 1993:133; Park 1993:159; Kwon & Leggett 1994:20; Moon 1994:142; Wilkinson 1994:5). Most important has been the emergence of the dual union movement of the officially recognised FKTU affiliates, and the affiliates of the KCTU.

The KCTU claims a membership of 400 000, organised in 907 affiliated unions, including those of the *chaebol* of Hyundai, Daewoo and Kia. The unions of other car companies are also affiliated to the KCTU as are unions from other key sectors of the Korean economy. Consequently, the KCTU, although not officially recognised until 1997,

Table 11.1   Korean trade union numbers, membership and density

	Membership ('000)	Eligible ('000)	Density (%)	Number of unions
1970	473	3746	12.6	3500
1975	750	4751	15.8	4091
1980	948	6454	14.7	2635
1985	1004	8104	12.4	2551
1986	1036	8433	12.3	2675
1987	1267	9191	13.8	4103
1988	1707	9610	17.8	6164
1989	1932	10 389	18.6	7883
1990	1887	10 950	17.2	7698
1991	1803	11 349	15.9	7656
1992	1735	11 568	15.0	7527
1993	1667	11 751	14.2	7147
1994	1659	12 297	13.5	7025
1995	1615	12 736	12.7	6606

Source: Korea Labor Institute.

could not be ignored (Park 1996). Its unions, in tune with contemporary developments, tend to be more assertive and independent than the FKTU's.

Amendments to the labour laws, such as that to the Labour Dispute Adjustment Law in 1987, which made it easier for unions to use the official conciliation machinery (Park 1993:165), were followed by a jump in the number of unions, but not by a proportionate increase in membership.

Kim (1993) makes a number of points concerning union membership in Korea. First, with the growth of heavy industry, men have displaced women in union activity. Second, white-collar workers have become increasingly unionised as their numbers in the workforce have grown. Third, he points to the development of structures within unions that promote 'solidarity' and 'cleavage', for example, the formation of joint councils based on region, occupation and industry, as well as enterprises. Enterprise councils to promote solidarity have been a response to divisive tactics of the *chaebol* which have been difficult to counter. Hyundai, in particular, has taken a strong confrontational approach to the new unionism. The labour militancy of the late 1980s and early 1990s appeared to have subsided, until late in 1996 when amended legislation provoked its revival (see below). It is possible to speculate that the human resource management (HRM) policies of some *chaebol*, like Samsung, and other exemplars, such as the government-owned Pohang Iron and Steel Corporation (POSCO), may have had an influence on those who might otherwise have followed Hyundai's strategy.

The slight decline in union membership in the 1990s may be partly attributed to industrial restructuring. First, employment in mining and manufacturing, where unionisation is usually strong, has been declining—by about 150 000 between 1990 and 1995—and many small firms in these sectors have collapsed. Consequently, between 1989 and 1995 the number of unions fell by 1287—from 7883 to 6606 (Table 11.1). Nevertheless, the union presence is strong in large companies and the average membership of a union remained at about 250.

Employers

Korean employers are organised in several employers' associations. The oldest, founded in 1884, is the Korean Chamber of Commerce and Industry (KCCI), which represents all business sectors; membership is mandatory. Membership of the Korean Foreign Trade Association (KFTA), established in 1947, is compulsory for all businesses engaged in import and export. The Federation of Korean Industries (FKI), which was founded in 1961, represents its (voluntary) member organisations on business and labour matters, and the Korean Employers' Federation (KEF) deals exclusively with labour matters, being the official counterpart of the FKTU (Park 1993:142–3). However, it is by focusing on the companies themselves, especially the *chaebol*, that the employer role in Korean employment relations is best understood, since collective bargaining generally occurs at the workplace or enterprise level.

As the government's chosen agency for the country's economic development, symbolically and industrially, the *chaebol* distinguish Korea from the other NIEs. It is in the *chaebol* that economic activities are highly concentrated—the top 30 *chaebol*, each a concentration of large firms, contribute about 95 per cent of the nation's GNP and the top five, that is Hyundai, Samsung, Lucky Goldstar, Daewoo and Sunkyong, contribute about 60 per cent (Bank of Korea 1990). It follows that they are a major influence on the character of Korean employment relations. Hence, the *chaebol* are a major employer of Korean workers and, as indicated by the post-1987 enterprise union activism, employ a substantial proportion of Korean trade unionists (Chun 1989:318–21)—around 60 per cent of strikes occur in large corporations (Korean Chamber of Commerce and Industry 1988:56–9).

The government's growth strategy—large-scale economies for low-cost competition through the agency of the *chaebol*—expanded employment, especially of blue-collar workers, and promoted the development of internal labour markets (Chun 1985:247). Further, some *chaebol* businesses, such as those of Hyundai, were under unified control through the concentration of related industries or factories in one region, called a 'one set approach' (Kong 1992:138–42). Thus, similar workers doing similar work in similar working conditions were concentrated by *chaebol* in one place or region. Further, in the government-induced process of industrial development, a number of industrial parks have been developed, where several plants are concentrated. This has facilitated the growth of collective consciousness and enhanced the power of workers and their unions. Structurally, the unions, often large, developed along regional or *chaebol*-based lines; for example, the Mansan-Changwon Union Coalition in the Mansan-Changwon region and the Hyundai Group Union Association (HGUA) respectively. With the support of the government, Hyundai established its related heavy manufacturing factories, such as car assembly and its shipyards, in the city of Woolsan (Chun 1985:319–22). It was in this city, site of the first industrial park in Korea, that in 1987 Hyundai workers first unionised at the workplace level, and then went on to organise at the Hyundai group level.

In line with its diversification and expansion and the requirements of mass production, the founders of the *chaebol* formalised their employment frameworks for workers into paternalistic, hierarchical and authoritarian structures. Typically, family members of the *chaebol* founders are located in key management positions (Kuk 1987:144–58).

Reinforced by the threat of North Korean communism and the legacy of immediate post-1945 militant unionism, the government built a legislative framework for Korean industrial relations (discussed below). However, the *chaebol* aimed to control the unions directly. On the one hand, they attempted to incorporate unions into the framework of their management structure as compliant and subordinated labour agents for settling industrial conflicts. But, on the other hand, with the support of the state, they prescriptively expelled militant unionists and workers from the workplace, being unwilling to accept what they saw as intermediary–political agents in their organisations. For the *chaebol*, the activities of unions should align with the hierarchical structure of the organisation rather than constrain the authority of management, a view especially reflected in the labour–management relations of Samsung and Hyundai (Ogle 1990). Therefore, although the *chaebol* suppressed the activities of unions, they also sought their compliance as 'company unions'.

After 1987, as we have seen, Korean employment relations began to undergo fundamental changes. The broader social influences enabled workers and unions to regain their rights from the *chaebol*. The approach of the *chaebol* to collective bargaining is decentralised, with the intention of protecting managerial prerogatives at the highest level.

The effect of the new vitality of the Korean unions on the *chaebol* has varied. Many *chaebol* have met union demands to end or avoid strike action and have lost some of the direct control they exercised over production workers. Many of the larger companies employed only permanent workers whose job security was well protected—retrenchment from restructuring has been limited in Korea. Since 1987, union-ised workers have become even more protected, often at the insistence of the union, without being subject to either individual or team performance evaluation. In some cases, bonus payments are made without reference to performance (Park & Lee 1996). Unlike the Daewoo shipping company in the early 1990s, small and medium-sized employers—who are not cushioned within a *chaebol* and who cannot expect to receive government help if they get into difficulties—have generally not had to make the same concessions as have *chaebol* companies, partly because of the relative weakness of the unions outside the *chaebol* (Park & Lee 1995:50–1).

The role of the state

Due to its dominant role in economic development through industrialisation, the prevalent theme of most analyses of Korean employment relations has been the central role of the state. The assumption is that the state is a central authority in shaping employment relations and, in particular, the character of the country's union movement. Tangential to the main theme is the corporatist nature of the state and its changes (Choi 1989; Park 1992; Frenkel 1993), although the structural limitations of unions (Deyo 1989), the level of industrialisation (Sharma 1991) and the relative timing of the development process are subthemes (Dore 1979; Vogel 1991).

After 1961 the purpose of the state's dominant economic role in Korea was rapid growth in volume through export-led, low-cost competition. By directional intervention, referred to as 'traffic control', the state determined the growth strategy of the *chaebol* (i.e. by exploiting the economies of large-scale operations). This strategy's purpose was achieved, first, by the *chaebol* extensively diversifying their businesses, horizontally and vertically, within and across industries (called the 'octopus-tentacle style'); and second, by the *chaebol* exploiting their assigned monopolistic positions in the market (Lee 1985:122–36; Chung 1988).

The most obvious role of the state is as a labour legislator, and since the end of the 1950s—as in the other NIEs, although far less so in Hong Kong—labour legislation in Korea has sought to regulate industrial relations to promote export-led industrialisation.[2] Statutes promulgated under the AMG were essentially labour protection, and those passed at the cessation of the Korean War under the First Republic—the Labour Union Act, the Labour Dispute Adjustment Act, the Labour Relations Commission Act and the Labour Standards Act— were replicas of the pluralist labour legislation imposed on Japan by the Occupation Authority after 1945 and incompatible with the unitarist approach of Korean governments. Consequently, they were amended:

in 1962 and 1963 by the Park Chung-hee government when the scope of collective activities, including political activities, was restricted, but protection for individual workers was tightened in 1967 when there was legislation to promote vocational training.

Although the labour law revision of the early 1960s has been challenged as unconstitutional, it in fact caused few problems because of the state of the labour market at that time. In 1970, foreign-owned firms were substantially excluded from unionisation. (The Act providing for this exclusion was repealed in 1981.) The 'Yushin' constitution of 1972 and the 1.14 State Emergency Act Concerning Economic Affairs, following the first world-wide oil-price hike in 1973, were the preludes to further revisions of labour law in the 1970s. The revisions were part of a repression of labour that also involved the police and the Korean CIA. However, in recognition of the need to obtain employee commitment to the government's development plans, some of the legislation aimed at improvements in worker welfare. This included extending the provisions of the Labour Standards Act to companies with five or more employees and extending the coverage of state industrial accident insurance.

While the government pursued worker welfare improvements paternalistically, the official union peak body, the FKTU, and the state failed to meet workers' concerns for better working conditions. Disenchantment with the FKTU spawned an underground labour movement led by intellectuals, human rights activists and religious leaders. Repression did not prevent about 100 labour disputes occurring each year. It was such a dispute that was the catalyst for the political crisis, the 'Seoul Spring', in 1979 and 1980 following the assassination of President Park.

The 'Seoul Spring' included 407 labour disputes. It ended in May 1980 with the military coup of General Chun Doo-hwan and the establishment of the Fifth Republic. The labour laws were amended, unions restructured and union leaders suspended, and the Labour–Management Council Act was passed with the intention of weakening unions at the workplace and making labour–management relations non-confrontational. On the welfare side, the Industrial Safety and Health Act and the Minimum Wage Act were passed and the scope of the Industrial Accident Compensation Insurance Act was extended.

In spite of repressive laws, in the 1980s the underground labour movement was active and growing. It drew much of its leadership from university students who took jobs in factories as 'disguised workers' and mobilised the unions at workplaces to strike in 1984 and 1985. They became particularly active in 1987 and 1988 following the '6.29 [June 29] Democratisation Declaration'. Partly as a result some minor amendments were made to the labour laws, including those to the Labour Dispute Adjustment Law to facilitate the use of official conciliation and legal procedures by unions.

Since 1987 the government in one way or another has sought to exercise a national incomes policy for the private sector. Its applications have been variously named the 'one digit policy', the 'total wage system' and the 'social accord between the FKTU and the KEF'. Attempts have been made to regulate pay settlements within central guidelines to avoid wage explosions, but this has not been easy to attain because of the *de facto* deregulation of unions. Thus, wage increases in Korea for the five years 1989 to 1993 inclusive were 21.1, 18.8, 17.7, 15.2 and 12.2 per cent respectively, way outside the guidelines, and in contrast to pre-1987 when wage increases were suppressed by the government. Wage restraint has been more easily attained in the public sector than in the private sector (Park 1996).

The main processes

Collective bargaining and disputation

Collective bargaining in Korea is regulated by the Trade Union Act. The representatives of a union (or others appropriately authorised) may negotiate a collective agreement or other matters concerning employees with an employer or employers' organisation. A union may also entrust to a federation of unions with which it is affiliated the authority to negotiate on its behalf, and the law allows multi-employer bargaining to be conducted at enterprise and industry levels. Most collective bargaining takes place at the enterprise or plant level, but multi-employer regional and national wage bargaining is conducted in transport and textiles, where firm size is relatively small, and in mining, where the number of employers is few.

Since 1987, collective bargaining has become a more important means of regulating industrial relations. However, in only a few small-sized enterprises are industrial relations regulated by a collective agreement—only 3 per cent of establishments employing 99 workers or less in 1990—and in only about 7 per cent of them are labour–management councils (see below) established. More than 90 per cent of small establishments have no collective arrangements.

Disputation peaked in 1987 and remained relatively high in 1988 and 1989—3749, 1873 and 1616 strikes, respectively. After 1989 the number substantially declined, to as few as 322 in 1990 and less than 100 in 1995 (Table 11.2). The decline was due to four factors. First, the Korean economy went into a recession in 1989 and as a result public sympathy for militant unionism declined. Second, union activists continued to be harassed and imprisoned. Third, strikes, although fewer, tended to be longer. Employers and unions were less inclined to use the strike or lockout as a weapon in collective bargaining other than

Table 11.2   Industrial disputes in Korea

	Number of strikes and lockouts	Workers involved ('000)	Working days lost ('000)	Incidence (days per 1000 paid workers)
1970	4	1	9	2.4
1975	52	10	14	2.9
1980	407	49	61	9.5
1985	265	29	64	7.9
1986	276	47	72	8.5
1987	3749	1262	6947	755.8
1988	1873	294	5401	562.0
1989	1616	409	6351	611.3
1990	322	134	4487	409.8
1991	234	175	3271	288.2
1992	235	105	1528	132.1
1993	144	109	1308	111.3
1994	121	104	1484	120.7
1995	88	50	393	30.9

Source: Korea Labor Institute.

as a last resort. Fourth, the government became more assertive in insisting on orderly workplaces and compliance with established procedures.

Labour–management councils

The Labour–Management Council Act 1980 stipulated that a labour management council (LMC) should be created and meet four times a year in any establishment employing 50 or more persons. The council is required to consult with employee representatives on productivity increases, employee welfare, education and training, and grievance handling. Firms are required to submit the rules of their LMCs to the Minister of Labour, who has the authority to dissolve them or order the reselection of their members (Kim 1984:123). Before 1987, the LMCs were largely the means by which the government and the *chaebol* sought to legitimise their power over workforces and in many cases they remained more symbolic than consultative. However, after 1987 the LMCs began to take on a more active industrial relations role. Although by the legislation LMCs were not required to include wages and welfare on their agenda, in practice they do so, and in non-unionised establishments they negotiate wages.

Where there is a union presence and an LMC, it has become usual for union leaders to be the workers' representatives on the LMC. Nevertheless, Korean unions generally regard LMCs as inhibiting unionism and there were calls for the 1980 Act to be amended or repealed. On the other hand, employers and the government were inclined to favour the retention of LMCs as agencies for handling non-collective bargaining matters. As part of the 1997 labour law amendments, the Labour–Management Council Act was renamed the Act for Participation and Cooperation Promotion, and its scope was expanded to include establishments with as few as 30 employees.

Dispute settlement

Mechanisms for resolving labour disputes have long been formalised in Korea. In 1953, legislation established a Labour Relations Commission (LRC) to provide for the conciliation, mediation and arbitration of disputes. Besides the Central LRC and Regional LRCs, which come under the Ministry of Labour, there are nine Special LRCs, which are under the Ministry of Transport. When they cannot reach a collective agreement and the union intends taking industrial action, under the Labour Dispute Adjustment Act 1953 both parties are required to notify the appropriate LRC of their intentions at least ten days before commencing industrial action—for essential services the notice period is 15 days—and during this period industrial action is prohibited. Meanwhile the LRC commences mediation by forming a tripartite (labour, employer and public) mediation committee. Following unsuccessful mediation, one or both disputing parties (depending on the terms of the collective agreement) may request arbitration by the LRC, which appoints a neutral arbitration panel. An arbitration award may be appealed against but otherwise it is binding on the parties. In cases where the public interest is involved, or the economy or the daily lives of the public are deemed to be threatened, the Minister of Labour may request the Central LRC to undertake emergency adjustment, during which a cooling-off period applies and the mediation and arbitration processes are followed. Disputes in an 'essential public enterprise' require longer cooling-off periods and compulsory arbitration. (The designation of an 'essential public enterprise' was extended by the December 1996 legislation.) The regulations for 'major defence industries' are such that a legal strike by their employees is virtually impossible.[3]

Current issues

Labour law reform

Calls by the National Assembly in 1989 to reform Korea's labour laws were directed at lifting the ban on 'third parties', such as lawyers and employment relations specialists (but often representatives from non-recognised union federations) from participating in labour disputes; at legalising unions' political activities; and at extending labour rights to civil servants. But such changes were vetoed by the President. In 1992 the government planned labour law amendments that would constrain union activity, including that of the FKTU, but was forced to withdraw its proposal. Instead, later that year, it set up a tripartite Labour Law Study Committee to find an acceptable set of amendments. External pressure for reform has come from the ILO, which Korea joined in 1991 and to which complaints about violations of the right to freedom of association in Korea have been made. Anticipation of possible opposition, perhaps from the USA, to Korea joining the OECD in 1996, also made the government sensitive to external pressures for labour law reform.

With the election of a civilian President, Kim Young-sam, early in 1993 there was some expectation that labour law amendments would be proposed in the National Assembly later that year. The expectation was fuelled by the new Minister of Labour's revised labour–management relations guidelines which were more favourable to labour than hitherto, but such expectations were frustrated when the government postponed any amendments until 1994.

The independent KCTU was again frustrated when, in December 1996, the government in amending the Trade Union Act failed to meet its demands for recognition and freedom of association. While the amended labour legislation permitted unions to engage in politics, the Electoral Law forbids participation by any organisation unless it is a registered political party. The possibility of multi-unionism in workplaces was deferred until the year 2003, and recognition of federations, other than the official FKTU, until 2000; and then third party involvement was to be confined to people 'officially' linked with unions and/or management. The rights of teachers to form a union and take industrial relations action is still denied and collective relations in education were confined to joint consultation. However, what prompted the largest outcry, including from the FKTU, was a reduction in the restrictions on employers laying off workers to increase productivity.

When confronted by a combination of the public outcry, a well-organised series of strikes by the KCTU and the corruption exposed by the collapse of the Hanbo Steel Company, the government postponed the new industrial relations legislation. According to President Kim Young-sam, who came into office pledging to sever the traditional link between government and the *chaebol*, 'The Hanbo case showed the shocking fact that corruption and the collusive link between politics and business remain deeply rooted in some parts of our society' (Garran 1997:23).

In March 1997 the National Assembly passed a revised set of amendments to the labour legislation which allowed for the recognition of a rival national union federation and delayed the relaxation of restrictions on layoffs, but this still did not meet the demands of the KCTU.

The state and the chaebol

The abandonment of repressive intervention by the state government has altered the role of the state in employment relations. The primary responsibility for resolving industrial conflict is shared by the unions and employers at the workplace as recently emphasised by the government. However, the government's policy on wage determination seems similar to the past: it has continued to intervene in the private sector while constraining the workers' right to select their own representatives.

Because of the monopolistic nature of Korea's industrial structure, it is expected that the government should be involved in *chaebol* employment relations to some degree. Despite increased union influence, substantial wage increases, the importance of non-performance factors in pay determination, and relative job security, *chaebol* employees have not been satisfied with the outcomes over the past few years. Some observers see a need for the state to become more proactive in getting the workers and their unions, together with the *chaebol* managements, to overcome the employment relations inertia and focus on ways of increasing productivity instead of complacently accepting the status quo. They advocate the government completing the process of democratising the labour market and allowing workers their chosen union representation (Park 1995; Park & Lee 1996).

The public sector

With some exceptions—such as manual workers in certain government enterprises who belonged to unions before becoming public sector employees—civil servants do not have a legal right to belong to a union. Their wages and conditions of employment are determined unilaterally by the government.

Since 1987, employees in the public sector where unions are legal, have enjoyed the same rights as those in the private sector, and trade union membership increased to 296 000 with a density of eligible workers of 92 per cent in 1991. Being the first target of incomes policies by the government, public sector workers' unions have abandoned their 'moderate' stances and emphasised their solidarity by forming *Kongdodae* (Council of Representatives of Public Sector Unions), which is affiliated neither to the FKTU nor to the KCTU. Teachers, on the other hand, are banned from joining or forming a trade union by the Education Act. This caused confrontations between the government and teachers in the late 1980s, and although they may discuss their employment conditions with the Minister of Education, teachers are deprived of the right of freedom of association. While the IRRC reviewed the labour rights of civil servants and teachers and the ILO and OECD recommended to the Korean government that they be granted the right to unionise, the December 1996 amended legislation did not address the laws relating to unions of teachers and civil servants.

Labour market flexibility

Also reviewed by the IRRC was legislation concerning the protection of the individual at work, including the Labour Standards Act 1953. Employers claimed that some of the protective legislation made labour as a human resource inflexible and thereby undermined Korean companies' competitiveness in international markets when other countries are increasing the flexibility of their labour markets, through deregulation. They argued that both the conditions under which the courts would permit layoffs resulting from restructuring, and the Ministry of Labour's guidelines, were too tight, and that more flexible rules should apply.

As mentioned, in December 1996 the government's amendment to the legislation to supply more flexible rules for collective dismissals resulted in protests that in turn led to a withdrawal of the amendment. With the revitalisation of unionism, the conditions surrounding collective dismissals have become more the subject of collective bargaining and the content of collective agreements than of legislated management prerogatives.

Employers have also sought to reduce labour costs and increase human resource flexibility by employing contract labour known as 'dispatched workers'. The contract is with the job agencies that employ the 'dispatched workers' and which, therefore, are responsible for their employment costs, such as welfare provisions. Employment of dispatched workers is technically an illegal practice, but the employers argue that it should be legalised and government-regulated. The unions are opposed to the legalisation of 'dispatched workers', fearing that they will undermine the bargaining power of their members.

Other reforms advocated by employers and opposed by the unions— the FKTU and the KCTU—are the rationalisation of paid holidays (they claim there are too many) and the reintroduction of the pre-1987 rules for the calculation of paid overtime rates (to prevent overtime rates being paid for hours worked within an averaged 44-hour week). The latter was included in the December 1996 amendments and was particularly provocative to Korean workers as their relatively high wages depend substantially on overtime payments (Asian Monitor Research Centre 1996:8).

Foreign labour

As with the other Asian NIEs, a tight labour market has led to Korea employing migrant workers, mostly unskilled, especially in the labour-intensive industries of textiles, fabricated metal and machinery, electrical and electronics, and rubber and chemical products. This phenomenon is relatively recent; it grew in the 1990s and represents a reversal of the situation when Korea was a major exporter of labour. Legal labour immigration is restricted to those engaged in reporting, technology transfer, business, capital investment, education and research, entertainment or employment approved by a government minister, and had amounted to 10 557 people by 1996. Unskilled foreign workers however are admitted only as 'trainees', and in 1996 these totalled 58 810. Originally, foreign 'trainees' were just that—they were in Korea to upgrade their skills; but intensified labour shortages have led to abuse of the scheme in order to meet the shortfalls. Thus, of the total 'trainees', 16 385 were brought in by firms with a foreign affiliation and 42 425 were admitted as unskilled labour. The Peoples' Republic of China, the Philippines, Vietnam and Indonesia are the source countries for more than half of the 'trainees', but there are also workers from the Indian subcontinent, notably Nepal, and elsewhere.

The number of illegal migrant workers is probably around 100 000. They comprise former 'trainees' who have overstayed their visas and foreign nationals, including some of Korean ancestry, who entered Korea on tourist visas. Because of their illegal status, such foreign workers are vulnerable to employer exploitation and tend to live and work in substandard conditions. Government policy remains ambiguous. While the need for foreign workers is recognised as a means of containing labour costs, there are concerns that a straightforward employment-pass system for foreign workers (and increases in migrant labour) could lead to long-term economic and social problems.

Conclusions

The historical circumstances in which Korea's industrial relations institutions emerged, and the unique significance of the *chaebol*, in part explain the contemporary, if uncertain, patterns of employment relations in this country.

With the industrialisation of East and South-East Asian countries since the 1960s, there have developed distinctive national features of employment relations, which have tended to be overlooked in the literature. Researchers, bent on finding common features, may have given less attention and attributed less importance to national differences than subsequent observation warrants. While some of the characteristics of contemporary Korean employment relations have their antecedents in the Japanese colonial period and in the situation under the immediate post-1945 AMG, the most important period has been that since the end of the Korean War and during the drive under several governments—particularly those of Presidents Park Chung-hee and Chun Doo-hwan—for industrialisation.

The industrialisation of Korea has unique characteristics because of the importance of the *chaebol* in the progress of economic development, and particularly because of the relationship between the state and *chaebol*. With the *chaebol* chosen as the agency for industrialisation, the unions were required to be compliant—and the state saw to this. However, with successful industrialisation, the legitimacy of the authoritarian state has been challenged and, in a climate of democratisation, workers' rights and trade union rights have become part of the agenda for reform.

Most observers concur that in all four of the Asian NIEs (Korea, Taiwan, Hong Kong and Singapore) the union movement has been subordinated in one way or another to state-initiated economic development priorities. However, in Korea—and Taiwan also—there has been a renaissance of independent trade unionism. The structure of unions in Korea partly reflects the ownership structure of industry, and the new unions aspire to free collective bargaining with the *chaebol* employers. They also seek greater freedom of association (from the state) and the restoration of full rights of recognition (from the employers). Because of the extent of *chaebol* employment, particularly significant employment relations issues include *chaebol* unionisation and the levels at which collective bargaining takes place. Confrontation is exacerbated by the rival union federation, recently restructured as the KCTU. While having legitimacy for many workers, it was not legal in the eyes of the government until 1997.

A chronology of Korean employment relations

1876	Japan forcefully opened up feudal Chosun.
1888	First organised strike, by goldminers.
1898	Korea's first union, Seongjin Stevedores' Union, formed.
1898	Chosun mining strike.
1910	Japan occupied Korea. Three–One National Independence Movement.
1920	The first national organisation, *Chosun Nodongkongjeahoe* (Chosun Labour Fraternal Association), was initiated by the liberal intelligentsia.

1922	The socialist-oriented *Chosun Nodongyeonmeainghoe* (Chosun Labour Confederation) was formed.
1924	*Chosun Nonong Chongyeonmeaing* (Chosun Labour and Farmer Confederation) was formed.
1925	Law and Order Maintenance Act repressed national trade unionism.
1929	First general strike, in Wonsan.
1938	Unions were prohibited with the onset of the China–Japan war.
1945	Korea was liberated from the Japanese, and the United States Army Military Government in Korea (USAMGIK), known as the AMG, was established in South Korea. National and Provincial Mediation Boards were set up. *Chun Pyung* (General Council of Korean Trade Unions) was formed.
1946	The Child Labour Law and the Basic Labour Law were enacted. The Labour Department was established. The 'September National Strikes' were called. *Daehan Dogrib Chockseong Nodong Chongyeonmyeng* (General Federation of Korean Trade Unions, GFKTU) was formed.
1947	*Chun Pyung* was banned by the AMG.
1948	Syngman Rhee was elected President of the First Republic of Korea. Five Year Economic Rehabilitation Plan established which aimed for economic independence from consumption aid.
1950–53	Korean War.
1953	The Trade Union Act, the Labour Standards Act, the Labour Dispute Adjustment Act and the Labour Relations Commission Act were enacted.
1957	The Chosun Textile Company dispute in Pusan in December split the FKTU.
1959	*Cheonkuk Nodongjohab Hyeobuiehyo* (National Council of Trade Unions or NCTU) was formed.
1960	The 'Four Nineteen Revolution' of 19 April deposed Syngman Rhee. The Chang Myeon government was elected. The FKTU and the NCTU merged to form a new national centre known as *Cheonnohyeob*.
1961	General Park Chung-hee took power in a military coup in May. The FKTU was restructured into 12 industrial union associations. GFKTU was renamed and became the *Daehan Nochong*.
1963	Park Chung-hee was elected President of the Third Republic of Korea. Labour laws were revised.

1970	Restrictions placed on unionism in foreign-owned firms.
1971	Law Concerning the Special Measures for Safeguarding National Security (LCSMSNS) gave Park Chung-hee lifetime presidency. Compulsory arbitration was extended to all industries. Korea Employers' Federation (KEF) was established.
1975	Labour Standards Act was extended to companies with five to 15 employees.
1979	Park Chung-hee was assassinated.
1980	Successful military coup by General Chun Doo-hwan.
1981	Labour–Management Council Act, the Industrial Safety and Health Act and the Minimum Wage Act passed, and the scope of the Industrial Accident Insurance and Compensation Act was extended.
1987	29 June Democratisation Declaration.
1991	*Cheonnohyeob*, the Korea Trade Union Congress (KTUC), was formed. Korea joined the ILO.
1995	*Minju Nochong*, the Korea Confederation of Trade Unions (KCTU) was formed.
1996	The Presidential Industrial Relations Reform Commission (IRRC) was formed.
1996	December amendments to the labour laws provoked a public outcry.
1997	Wave of strikes organised by the KCTU was followed by the postponement and revision of the amended labour legislation, including official recognition of the KCTU. Serious economic recessions in Asia-Pacific countries, including Korea, which experienced corporate collapses. An International Monetary Fund (IMF) aid package was accepted by the Korean government, which involved the acceptance of IMF conditions. Election of Kim Dae-jun as President.

12 Conclusions: Towards a synthesis of international and comparative experience in employment relations

Oliver Clarke,
Greg J. Bamber and
Russell D. Lansbury

Preceding chapters have focused on the differing experiences of ten industrialised market economies (IMEs). This chapter attempts to review and synthesise the development of employment relations in these countries—with occasional references to the experience of other countries—and to identify some important trends during the decades since the Second World War.

Post-war employment relations systems

It is useful to start by noting some of the factors that helped shape the different employment relations systems after the Second World War. The war itself was obviously of key importance. War-devastated Germany and Japan had to make a new start. In Italy and France, where free unions had led a shadowy underground existence during the war, some elements of the pre-Fascist, pre-war pattern carried forward but with significant new features (see chs 6 and 7). In the United States (USA) the exigencies of war production induced practitioners and public policy makers to refine the Wagner Act procedures. Although the strike wave of 1946 led to what unions saw as the repressive Taft-Hartley Act of 1947, there was not a strong lobby to replace the New Deal system (see ch. 3).

Canada had only recently adopted arrangements deriving from the US New Deal model and was building on them (see ch. 4). In Britain, where the employment relations system was then seen as generally effective, neither the industrial relations parties nor the government saw a need to effect major changes (see ch. 2). In Australia, though employment relations often proved turbulent in the 1940s, the parties were not moved to seek major changes (see ch. 5). Sweden did not participate in the Second World War. It had laid a new foundation for its employment relations in the late 1930s. During the war and its aftermath the parties ensured that its employment relations system was well adapted to the post-war world (see ch. 9). It was then that the active labour market and solidaristic wage policies were designed, that centralised collective bargaining developed, and that the Swedes conducted a fruitful debate on the relationship between wages and full employment. Korea's current approaches to employment relations have been developed since the end of the Korean War in 1953. The influence of the *chaebol* represents a continuity with the pre-war period (see ch. 11).

An important feature of the post-war employment relations systems in nearly all of the countries was the new prominence of unions. Although some of them had already had a continuous life of nearly a century, the unions had 'come of age' during the war. Their contribution to the war effort in the victorious countries as well as their role in resistance movements in occupied countries and as a potential democratic force in defeated countries, generally seemed to ensure their place in the post-war polity. They had become valued partners of governments.

In rebuilding their economies, the continental Western European countries showed some similarities in their approach to employment relations. The model chosen was broadly one in which pay and working conditions were determined by collective bargaining at the industry level, whether nationally or regionally, while matters of shared interest to employers and workers were dealt with by works councils or works committees. Such committees became compulsory for all but small firms, either by law or by central collective agreement, in Germany, France, Italy and Sweden (and in Belgium, Denmark, the Netherlands and Norway). By this role differentiation, collective industrial conflict was largely—though not, of course, entirely—steered away from individual enterprises. Interestingly, the types of institutions constructed did not adopt the format of the (voluntary) joint consultative or joint production committees that attracted so much attention in Britain in the 1940s, but accorded specific rights to the representative committee in relation to managerial decisions.

Challenges to the post-war orthodoxy

By 1952, the post-war systems of employment relations in our sample of countries (apart from Korea) were broadly in place, in forms that would remain essentially unchanged for around two decades in some cases—and on a continuing basis in others. Until the early 1970s there were insufficient pressures to induce fundamental change in employment relations structures. However, their operation was notably influenced by two factors: the changing attitudes of workers and their consequent expression in their unions; and a growing conflict between the outcome of pay-determination processes and the needs of economies as perceived by governments.

First, a new generation of workers came into the labour force: better—and less conservatively—educated; more confident of their bargaining power in a situation (in most countries) of unprecedentedly low unemployment; and confident that thanks to apparently endless economic growth they could count on regular improvements in wages and working conditions without extra effort on their part. The acceptance of a subservient role which had characterised earlier generations of workers was replaced by a growing militancy, a demand for more say in decisions within the enterprise, and less willingness to accept boring, repetitive or otherwise unpleasant jobs. Workers protested in manifestations that seemed to herald a new era—the French 'events' of 1968, the 'hot autumn' of 1969 in Italy, the wildcat strikes in Germany, Belgium and Sweden in 1969–70, and the Lordstown strike at General Motors in 1971 in the USA. In Britain, in 1969, unions forced a Labour government to withdraw its own industrial relations reform proposals and, in 1974, a miners' strike precipitated the end of Heath's Conservative government and its Industrial Relations Act 1971 (see ch. 2).

A major factor associated with the change in attitudes and in the economic environment was the new propensity, at least in peace-time, for pay increases to outstrip what employers could afford from higher productivity and any improvement in the terms of trade. This added to inflationary pressures. The severity of the tendency varied considerably. In Germany and Japan (as well as Austria and Switzerland) it was rarely a serious political or economic problem; but it often became such a problem in Britain, Italy and Sweden and occasionally in the USA, Australia and Canada. Where the problem became troublesome, governments placed increasing reliance on monetary and fiscal policies. As alternative strategies, however, some governments also tried the remedies of what came to be known as incomes policies, which could be statutory or voluntary, bilateral, multilateral or unilateral. Where the need for checking the growth of wages was immediate and obvious, a temporary wage freeze might be acceptable; otherwise pay moderation tended to become a factor that unions would seek to trade off against government promises to adjust their policies in other fields to take more account of union aspirations. The advantage of an incomes policy was that if excessive pay increases could be restrained, monetary policies could be less harsh, thereby avoiding consequential reduction in business activity and hence increased unemployment. There were successful incomes policies, but they were few and mainly short-lived. The chief disadvantages were that it was difficult to ensure continued compliance; that the price of union cooperation tended to be condemned by governments as too high; that it was difficult to ensure that the policy bore equitably on different groups of the working population; and that such advantage as might be gained could be lost in the free-for-all that tended to follow an incomes policy.

The impact of recessions

The late 1960s and early 1970s, then, constituted a period of worker militancy in many IMEs which seemed set to continue, at least in some of the countries under discussion. Nonetheless, in the early 1970s the economic environment deteriorated sharply, following the collapse of the Bretton Woods monetary stabilisation arrangements (1971) and after the massive increase in oil prices by the Organisation of Petroleum Exporting Countries (OPEC) and the subsequent recycling of 'petro-dollars' (1973). That increase was in effect a supply-side shock which dramatically increased prices in non-oil-producing countries. If recompensed by equivalent pay increases, these would add to inflation. In the event, the behaviour of the collective bargaining partners varied between countries. In Germany relatively little inflation ensued. In Japan there was major inflation, but only for one year. In Britain and Australia pay increases were generally seen by economic policy makers as unjustifiably high. Both the USA and Canada tried incomes policies in the 1970s. In Italy, and in other countries where indexation of wages on prices was an important component of wage-fixing machinery, there was no avoiding the inflationary effects.

It took time for the industrial relations parties to adjust to the new and tougher economic environment, and some of them had not fully done so at the end of the 1970s when the Islamic revolution in Iran induced the second large rise in oil prices. By then, however, although the impact on the parties again varied between countries, the government of the United Kingdom (UK) and those of several other countries were determined to rely to a greater extent on non-accommodating monetary policies—stronger measures that would make it more difficult for employers to concede wage increases—to lessen wage pressures. These policies proved effective, though they also had a discouraging effect on industrial activity in a world that was already moving into the 1980–82 recession (the worst recession since the 1930s).

This recession was not just a cyclical phenomenon but rather marked a shift in the world economy. The long-term competitive advantage of the old IMEs had been increasingly challenged in the post-war years. Multinational enterprises (MNEs) were globalising production to expand markets and to make use of low labour costs in some countries. Some of the newly industrialising economies (NIEs), notably Korea (Republic of Korea, see ch. 11), Taiwan, Singapore and Hong Kong were outperforming the old IMEs. Also, the adoption of new technologies was facilitating the internationalisation of production.

For several of the countries this recession also heralded a new phase in employment relations. A phase of union growth (in most countries), of relatively full employment, of moves towards industrial democracy, and of regular annual improvements in pay and working conditions, was giving way to a phase of difficulty for unions, of much higher levels of unemployment, and of concession bargaining (discussed later). How the industrial relations parties fared after the recession of the early 1980s is the subject of the next part of this chapter.

The unions

The immediate evidence of the changing fortunes of the unions is to be found in membership data.[1] Across our ten countries the development has been uneven, though in almost all cases membership density failed to keep pace with the growth of the labour force. In the USA membership *density* has declined almost continuously since 1955, though *absolute membership numbers* peaked as late as 1979, since which time they too have declined. In Japan, density declined slowly but steadily from 1975. Australian union density dropped from 51 per cent in 1976 to 33 per cent in 1995 while union density in the UK fell from 45 per cent in 1985 to some 29 per cent in 1995. Membership density also fell substantially in France. On the other hand, Swedish membership density increased steadily from the 1960s until the 1990s (when it decreased slightly), density in Canada held up relatively well, German density remained fairly steady, while that in Korea increased rapidly in the late 1980s, before declining in the early 1990s (see Appendix).

That unionisation should fall in the conditions of the 1980s and 1990s is hardly surprising. Unemployment rose in most countries—and unemployed workers are more likely to drop out of than join unions. Union membership was generally strong in the old manufacturing and extractive industries, but these industries were among those most severely hit in the recessions of the early 1980s and early 1990s. Most employment growth during this period was in the service sector, much of which is hard to organise. Unionisation tends to be relatively easy to achieve in large establishments with a stable full-time (male) workforce; however, the size of establishments has been tending to fall and there has been a considerable influx of women workers and workers on atypical conditions—part-time, temporary and fixed-term workers—with a lower propensity to unionise. Also, in the more competitive product markets of the 1980s and 1990s, unions were less able to attract members by achieving large improvements in pay and working conditions.

What accounts for the considerable differences in the fortunes of unions between countries? Which common elements emerge, for instance, when one looks at the countries where membership has held up well or even improved? (For example Germany, Sweden and Korea in this book, to which could be added Belgium, Luxembourg, and some of the other Nordic countries.) It is difficult to see any factors common to these countries, but there are some elements that seem relevant. Except in Korea, unions in these countries are deeply involved in day-to-day public affairs. In some they are concerned with the administration of social security, though as the French experience shows, this by no means guarantees maintenance of membership.

Comparisons between the US and Canadian experiences are particularly interesting (see chs 3 and 4). The two countries have comparable labour legislation and most of their bargaining is at enterprise level. Further, despite some defections, in 1988, a total of 33 per cent of Canadian unionised workers were still affiliated to US unions (Chaykowski & Verma 1992:21). Whereas in 1965 membership density was a little higher in the USA than in Canada, by 1995 a unionisation rate of 15 per cent in the USA was less than half of the Canadian rate (35 per cent). The explanation would seem to lie in the more favourable union-recognition procedures of Canadian legislation, the more union-accommodating stance of Canadian employers (who have no 'Sun Belt' in the south to escape to), and the more vigorous strategies of Canadian unions including, Lipsig-Mumme (1989:254) suggests, their political strategies.

The substantial drop in membership density in the UK is easier to explain. Aggressive union behaviour in the 1970s, culminating in the 'winter of discontent' of 1978–79, harmed the public image of unions, thereby reducing the propensity to join. Also, the drastic decline of the unions' traditional heartlands of steel, engineering, coalmining, the docks and rail transport lost many members. The series of laws bearing on unions and their activities enacted by the post-1979 Conservative governments also had a negative impact on union membership (see ch. 2).

There was a similar drop in union density in Australia even though there were federal Labor governments from 1983 to 1996 which were sympathetic to unions' interests (see ch. 5). This is partly explained by significant structural changes in the economy, including a sharp decline in the proportion of the workforce in manufacturing (Peetz 1990).

Unions' political influence

Where membership declined (coupled with the tougher economic climate and high unemployment in several countries), bargaining power in relation to employers was reduced and, to some extent, influence on governments lessened. Unions' political activities and influence do, of course, vary across our countries. Most US union leaders prefer political power to be in the hands of the Democrats; nonetheless, most US unions formally maintain a neutral stance, while applying the electoral test of 'reward your friends and punish your enemies'. After years of Republican administrations the unions were heartened by the election, and in 1996 the re-election, of President Clinton, but given his political stance and the size of the Republican Party in the Senate and the House of Representatives, most union objectives did not receive legislative support.

In our sample of countries, the British unions suffered the worst reverses of political influence. Under the Labour governments of 1974–79 union influence on government policies reached a higher level than ever before, but it vanished with the accession to power of Margaret Thatcher's Conservative government in 1979. Closely linked with the Labour Party—as the British Trades Union Congress and most of its large constituent unions were—the unions were associated with Labour's electoral policies which lost four successive general elections. Unions, however, continued to play a part in Britain's quasi-autonomous non-government organisations, and their influence in local government continues. Following the significant election win of Britain's (New) Labour Party in 1997, some of the sharp edges of the Conservative anti-union legislation may be blunted. However, Labour's Prime Minister Mr Blair has indicated that he will retain most of the Conservatives' labour laws. We would not anticipate a dramatic revival in the membership density of most British unions.

The French unions, long divided into factions of differing political viewpoints, fared unevenly, though all of the central confederations tended to lose ground as measured by such indicators as elections to enterprise committees. The CGT, though still the biggest union centre, was weighed down by its close association with the increasingly unpopular Communist Party. In the earlier part of the 1980s the CFDT suffered from identification with the governing Socialist Party at a time when the government was forced to adopt austerity measures. The FO's 'business unionism', however, retained popularity (though the FO has since become more militant). But even after the advent of right-wing President Jacques Chirac in 1995, despite their fall in membership, the French unions' political influence to some extent endured, even though it was less than in some former periods. Indeed, the unions can take some credit for the convincing victory by the French Socialist Party in the French general election of June 1997, which had been called by President Chirac earlier than required.

The Italian unions also continued to wield influence, as evidenced by their relative success in persuading successive governments to modify their social policies.

In Sweden, though strains developed in its relationship with the employers' confederation, the manual-workers' union centre, LO, has retained a powerful influence on the Social Democratic Party, which, except for 1976–82 and 1991–94, has governed since 1932. In the 1970s, LO persuaded the party to adopt the electorally unpopular wage-earner funds proposal, and through the 1980s and early 1990s the unions, despite government pleas for moderation, successfully secured pay increases which were often difficult for the government to reconcile with price stability.

If the Swedish experience is an example of the durability of union influence, Australia shows a remarkable transformation. Australian unions have long had a political role, but during the 1983–96 Accord the ACTU—hitherto a relatively weak confederation in comparison with, for example, its Swedish and German equivalents—came to have a strong influence on a broad range of Australian economic and social policies, an influence that continued until the Labor government lost office in 1996. Furthermore, some observers argued that the defeat of the Labor government could be attributed partly to perceptions among the electorate that the ACTU had exerted undue influence on both the Hawke and Keating governments.

The employers

From the period of post-war reconstruction until the end of the 1970s, in most of the countries it was the active pressure of workers and their unions that led to a majority of initiatives in the structure and operation of employment relations systems. Employers and their organisations found it difficult to cope with workers' demands and claims for improvements in pay and conditions at the level of the enterprise, and with legislative moves to strengthen workers' rights. Nevertheless, they generally devoted little priority in this period to seeking reform of employment relations systems. When they were faced with a choice between making concessions and resisting a strike, their market position, in the years of sustained economic growth, often inclined them to concede. The economically rational behaviour of employers then came into conflict with the efforts of governments to ensure price stability; pay increases achieved by workers and unions were also inflationary increases in labour costs on the part of employers. Employers were also expected to shoulder much of the mounting cost of social security and various advances in worker protection in the form of payroll taxes and strengthened legislative requirements.

After the early 1980s' recession, employers in the IMEs were faced with new challenges and new opportunities. Many industries had to restructure and competition became increasingly fierce; hence, there was a greater need to ensure efficient working and to restrain labour costs. Governments saw that industries' struggle for survival precluded adding to their cost burdens and sought to lighten their load. At the same time, growing unemployment sapped the bargaining strength of workers and their unions. Thus there was a tendency in most countries for employers to take a tougher stance both in collective bargaining and in trying to increase the efficiency of working practices. Employers made more use of human resource management (HRM) techniques, some of which discouraged unionisation. There were, however, interesting differences in employers' policies between countries.

In the USA, union gains in the prosperous years and widespread cost-of-living clauses induced a substantial number of employers to take aggressive action to lower their labour costs. Moreover, in a political climate favourable to them, employers' resistance to union recognition intensified. Particularly notable in the early 1980s, the attack took the form of 'concession bargaining', involving some mixture of pay reductions, reduction of holidays, and cutbacks in fringe benefits and, in some cases, the introduction of 'two-tier' structures with new workers being engaged on terms less favourable than those applied to existing employees. A substantial number of US employers moved to parts of the south where unionisation was low (see ch. 3). Interestingly, Canadian employers were much less aggressive than US employers, despite the prevalence of US-owned firms and the many similarities between the employment relations systems of the two countries.

Of all our sample of countries it was particularly in the USA that a large number of employers took an overtly anti-union stance. In many other countries, by contrast, employers tended to pursue cost reduction by improving productivity, reducing employment levels and enhancing operational flexibility rather than attacking pay, working conditions and unionisation. Perhaps the key factor dictating the tougher stance of US employers was the extent to which pay levels, particularly in the unionised sector, had overtaken those in other US sectors and in other countries. Such differences had been supportable when American industrial and technological superiority had been almost unchallenged, but as other IMEs and the NIEs moved towards American levels of efficiency it was more difficult for US enterprises to sustain such high labour costs.

Until the early 1990s economic growth was more rapid in Japan and Korea than in any other of the countries under discussion. There is little evidence of aggressive anti-unionism being adopted by employers in Japan, even where their enterprise was confronting difficult times. Some Japanese enterprises responded to the changed market conditions by expanding their labour-intensive operations in low-labour-cost countries, but in Japan they continued to pursue efficiency coupled with workplace harmony. Unemployment, though a little higher than it used to be, has continued at lower levels than in any of the other countries except Korea. By contrast, with the support of the government, Korean employers were generally successful in opposing the growth of independent unions, until the success of the democratisation movement in 1987 and widespread strikes in 1996–97 (see ch. 11).

In Australia some employers aligned themselves with the New Right (e.g. Rio Tinto, formerly CRA, an MNE in the mining industry), but in general the major focus of interest of employers was in making the best of the Australian Industrial Relations Commission's arbitrated awards, during the successive stages of the 1983–96 Accord (which by the 1990s were placing increasing emphasis on enterprise bargaining; see ch. 5). The employers' organisations were disadvantaged in the face of the strong union–government partnership. Their disadvantage was magnified by their multiplicity—the Australian Chamber of Commerce and Industry, the Business Council of Australia, the important, independent-minded Metal Trades Industry Association and the National Farmers' Federation, among others, all represented different viewpoints. After the ALP lost the 1996 general election, however, it was the unions that were increasingly disadvantaged as the conservative coalition government sought to reform the labour market.

In continental Europe many employers strengthened their resistance to union claims and their insistence on more efficient working, but there were few attacks on unions; employers generally still saw their relationship with unions as a continuing one, to be fostered. Though some lost members, there was not a general change in the role of the employers' associations or the extent of their influence on governments. Nor was there a substantial shift in their policies, except in Sweden. There, under new leadership, SAF—the central organisation of private sector employers—abandoned its bargaining role and moved away from the centralised tripartism that had characterised Swedish industrial relations for so long (see ch. 9).

Developments elsewhere in continental Europe were broadly similar, but there were some differences. Unionised employees achieved a position in British manufacturing workplaces that some employers claimed was more powerful than in any other country considered here. Especially after the British legislation of 1974–76, in few countries did unions have so much bargaining power and such a strong legal position. However, in Britain the early 1980s' recession coincided with the advent of a Conservative government that saw the unions as a major cause of the country's industrial malaise and which, through a series of laws, weakened the ability of unions to resist change—though the high level of pay increases through the 1980s and into the early 1990s suggests that, in some contexts, they retained considerable bargaining power. Since 1979 British employers have implemented more reform of workplace practices than those of most of the other countries (arguably they had more incentive to do so). Nevertheless, though there were some cases of withdrawal of union recognition and more determination in beating strikes, most employers were less strongly anti-union than their US counterparts. When faced with problems where they could have used the new legislation against the unions, most British employers preferred not to go beyond merely drawing workers' attention to the current legal position.

In Britain, as in continental Europe, pay and working conditions in the early post-war years were mainly determined by industry-wide collective bargaining. But though there was some erosion of such bargaining in several European countries, only in Britain was it largely superseded by enterprise or workplace bargaining. This clearly reduced the bargaining role of the British employers' associations. Significantly, early in 1990 the Engineering Employers' Federation, long regarded as the most important of the industry associations, announced that it would discontinue industry-level bargaining on wages and working conditions, thereby ending 92 years of negotiations at industry level. (Admittedly, such bargaining in the engineering industry had been decreasing in importance for more than 20 years.)

Collective bargaining

In all of the countries covered here except Australia and Korea, collective bargaining has long been the officially preferred way of determining pay and working conditions, though Conservative governments in the UK dropped this preference in the early 1990s. In the post-war years until the 1980s, collective bargaining was used increasingly, extending to cover more white-collar and public service workers. It is difficult to assess recent changes in coverage, but one authoritative study concluded that 'the extent to which workers are covered by collective agreements has been fairly stable over the last decade' (OECD 1994a:187). The same study noted that in 12 out of 17 OECD countries covered, at least two-thirds of workers with bargaining rights were covered by some form of collective agreement, the lowest coverage being in countries characterised by single-enterprise bargaining (1994a:172).

There is no uniformity of the level at which collective bargaining is customarily conducted. In North America, multi-employer bargaining is only a minority practice with enterprise or workplace (plant) bargaining the norm (see chs 3 and 4). In Japan too, bargaining is mainly at the enterprise level (see ch. 10): at the national level, the *Shunto* establishes union objectives and influences bargaining strategy, but the outcome is determined within the enterprise. German collective bargaining remains basically at the national or regional industry level, although workplace negotiation has been increasing over the years and was given further impetus by the important metal industry agreements in 1984 which required several aspects of working time to be determined at the workplace. Moreover, the works councils also play an important role in Germany (see ch. 8). French bargaining levels, traditionally at national or regional industry level, were affected by the law of November 1982 requiring unionised enterprises to negotiate each year on pay and working hours—though it did not require them to reach agreement. The law has certainly shifted collective bargaining towards the enterprise but has not fundamentally changed workplace relations in France (see ch. 7).

Bargaining levels have long been an issue in Sweden. In the 1950s collective bargaining between SAF and LO, the peak private sector employer and manual worker union bodies, began to be conducted centrally (i.e. for all industries) though there was controlled flexibility in the application of the central agreement in different industries and firms. The flexibility was not, however, considered sufficient in the important metals sector and, in 1983, that sector opted out of the central negotiations. In the next year's bargaining round, decentralisation was general and, though there were subsequent central agreements, there was uncertainty at each round about which level would prevail. As mentioned above, SAF has relinquished its bargaining role and favours adoption of enterprise-level bargaining, but this has not been achieved (see ch. 9).

Despite the arbitration system—which to an increasing extent incorporates collective bargaining—in Australia there have also always been direct negotiations (see ch. 5). For a few years after the advent of the Accord in 1983, direct negotiations on pay and working conditions were less important in comparison with the general adjustments awarded by the Australian Industrial Relations Commission. But as the Accord continued there was an increasing amount of flexibility in its successive stages. Commission awards in the late 1980s and early 1990s provided for significant adjustments to be negotiated at enterprise level, having regard to productivity and other issues, a process characterised as 'managed decentralism'. With the legal changes of 1993, enterprise negotiation became increasingly important. Then, following the advent of the Liberal–National Party coalition government in 1996, and its Workplace Relations Act, the pattern of Australian pay determination continued to evolve, with enhanced possibilities for determination by enterprises and a reduced role for the Commission (Kitay & Lansbury 1997).

Internationally, the most clearly defined shift in the level at which pay is determined has been from industry-wide to enterprise or workplace. But there has also been a perceptible shift in some countries to national discussions, if not bargaining, involving governments. Australia was a clear example of this, with the key post-1983 negotiations between the former

Labor government and the ACTU. In Sweden, where the traditional model required the government to keep out of collective bargaining, governments in the late 1980s were increasingly having to confront economic difficulties such as high inflation. In Italy, governments have been embroiled with the unions and employers on several issues. In Japan, discussions take place between government, unions, employers and independents within the framework of the Labour–Management Round Table, though such discussions should not be described as bargaining and are a continuing process of creating understanding and accommodation, rather than specific negotiations.

Most of these bargaining shifts result from increased international competition, which induces demands for more flexible and efficient workplace practices. This draws negotiation to the enterprise or workplace. At the same time, the continued tendency in some countries for the level of increases in labour costs to be of concern to the government sometimes induces state intervention (Bamber, Córdova & Sheldon 1998). Then, too, the ever-growing costs of social security provision have caused governments to seek union acquiescence in cost-limitation programs. And in some European countries government behaviour is influenced by the prospect of the single European currency. This has led them to adopt strict economic management so as to satisfy the onerous criteria for admission. In some cases this has led to strong union resistance.

Industrial conflict

In all the countries where collective bargaining is established, strikes and lockouts are usually accepted as the logical continuation of a dispute when bargaining fails. There have been few major national changes in the conduct or treatment of strikes in the countries considered here, except for the British legislation after 1979 which substantially limited the wide immunities granted to the unions by the Trade Disputes Act 1906 (see ch. 2), and the restrictions embodied in the Australian Workplace Relations Act 1997 (see ch. 5).

Some countries mediate their industrial conflicts much more successfully than others (though it does not follow that a high-strike country is necessarily a country with 'bad' employment relations). The incidence of working days lost through disputes fell in most countries in the 1980s, and by the early 1990s the losses were much less than in the period of militancy that marked the late 1960s. This is what we would expect in the prevailing economic circumstances. But, as shown in the Appendix, there is a great deal of variation in the experience of different countries. Using average data for the decade 1986–95 as a whole, Germany and Japan appeared to lose relatively few working days, while Korea, Canada, Italy and Australia were relatively strike-prone, with France, Sweden, the UK and the USA occupying inter-mediate positions (see Appendix Figure A.1).

Relative positions in any such league table of disputes may vary from one year to another, but generally in the medium term there is stability in the relative position of most countries. In the longer term, though, the order can change. Thus, in the 1950s there were more working days lost per 1000 employees in Japan than in Britain. Yet later Japan became a low-strike country. Also, in the early 1950s France was more strike-prone than Australia, while Sweden was one of the most strike-prone countries before its long period of Social Democratic government beginning in the 1930s. Major industrial con-flicts erupted in the public sector, in particular, during the period 1986–1995 as Sweden moved towards a more decentralised bargaining system. Differences between countries can be very large. In 1993 Switzerland had no recorded strikes, a feat matched by Austria in 1994. The corresponding figures for Italy in those years—admittedly a much larger country—were about 3.4 million days lost in 1993 and in 1994 (ILO 1996).

Labour–management cooperation and industrial democracy

Relationships between labour and management contain elements of conflict and cooperation. In the mid-1960s and the 1970s, there was much debate about workers' participation and industrial democracy—often seen in terms of giving workers or unions seats on the board of directors of enterprises, or strengthening works councils. In Canada there was considerable interest in the late 1960s and early 1970s in improving cooperation (though it did not appear to have much lasting impact). The movement peaked with Sweden's Board Representation Act 1972 and Co-determination at Work Act 1976; the German Works Constitution Act 1972 and Co-determination Act 1976; and legislation in, for instance, Austria, Denmark, Ireland's public sector, the Nether-lands and Norway. In Britain the ambitious proposals of the Bullock Committee on Industrial Democracy, 1977, met with little support and tough opposition; after the Callaghan Labour government left office in 1979 the subject was no longer discussed by policy makers, at least not in terms of institutional change. In Australia, the 1973–75 Whitlam Labor government became interested in industrial democracy, though little was achieved before the government lost office. Labour–manage-ment councils (LMCs) have existed in Korea since 1980 but have taken a more active industrial relations role since 1987. Many unions have a negative attitude towards LMCs while employers and government tend to favour them. However, where unions are well organised within the enterprise, they are usually able to exert influence through the LMC.

There were minor legislative reforms during the 1980s (e.g. the Swedish amendment of 1987 extending the possibilities for board representatives, the German works council legislation of December 1988, and the more substantial Auroux laws in France in 1982), but the movement to enhance workers' participation by statutory means appeared to wane. Nevertheless, there has been continued interest in enhancing the involvement of workers in their enterprises at the shop-floor level. In several countries, as part of HRM strategies, employers are adopting schemes to elicit higher degrees of employee commitment, at least in relation to their core workforce. The apparent success of Japanese MNEs has been linked by many with Japan's consensual pattern of enterprise labour–management relations. This has led to many attempts at emulation. In the USA the well-known car plant innovations, such as Saturn and NUMMI, are worthy of note (Kochan et al. 1997). Although it was not formally implemented, the main thrust of the Dunlop Report on 'The Future of Worker–Management Relations' was the desirability of building cooperative structures and attitudes at the workplace. The Hawke Labor government in Australia produced a governmental statement (there was also a joint employer–union statement) on increasing industrial democracy, but stressed employee involvement rather than institutional changes (Davis & Lansbury 1996). In forms of cooperation, as in bargaining, the enterprise level has become more important in all the countries studied. This is due to the increased need for enterprise competitiveness and collaboration between management and workers to maximise productive use of capital and labour.

Parallel with the interest in industrial democracy came an increase in critical attitudes towards work which, often accompanied by shortage of labour, led to a reconsideration of work organisation. It was found that many jobs could be made more satisfying to workers and that operating efficiency might even gain thereby. A series of major enterprises, like Volvo and Saab-Scania in Sweden, Olivetti in Italy, and ICI and Shell in Britain and Australia, led the way in reorganising work, and much was done—and still is being done—through diffusion by public or private agencies and programs which sprang up in several of the countries in the 1970s. Examples include the Humanisation of Work Programme in Germany, the National Agency for the Improvement of Working Conditions in France, the Centre for Working Life in Sweden, the Work Organisation Branch of the Department of Industrial Relations in Australia and the Work in America Institute in the USA. (The earlier work by the Tavistock Institute in Britain and the Work Research Institutes in Norway was also particularly notable in promoting new thinking about work.)

The role of the government and the legal framework

In the aftermath of the Second World War, governments almost every-where took on an unprecedentedly active role in regard to employment relations. The role of governments in employment relations may be categorised in terms of at least five components: maintaining protective standards; establishing the rules for the interaction between the parties; ensuring that the results of that interaction are consistent with the apparent needs of the economy; providing services for labour and management; and as a major employer.

During the years of economic growth all of these roles were extended. Protective legislation became more detailed, adding appre-ciably to unit labour costs. The volume of legislation concerned with the relations of the parties increased too, though less so than protective legislation and in different ways and at various times in different countries. Services to employers and workers expanded—notably in the field of work organisation and the quality of working life in the 1970s. In several countries the conflict between collective bargaining outcomes and economic policies caused government intervention. There was widespread extension of the right of public service workers to organise and to have what sometimes amounted to collective bar-gaining rights.

From the early 1980s there was a clear shift in these functions. Governments became cautious about extending protection, and some even started to review existing protection—assessing if the need still justified the costs. France abolished the need for administrative author-isation for dismissals, and several countries relaxed rigid rules about working time and the rules about the employment of women on night work. There were some attempts to change employment relations rules through legislation. First, in Britain Conservative governments sought, through a series of new laws, to reduce the volume of unofficial strikes and to strengthen the members' control of unions. Some argue that the legislation has helped fundamentally to change British employment relations; it has certainly made workers and their unions more hesitant about going on strike (see ch. 2). Second, in France the Auroux reforms of 1982 sought to establish more cooperative labour–management re-lations at the workplace. Though that legislation effected a number of changes, it did not transform French workplace relations to a great extent (see ch. 7). A third case of change is Australia. From 1987, the several revisions of the Accord placed increasing emphasis on employ-ment relations at the enterprise level, while the sweeping changes of the post-1996 coalition government's Workplace Relations Act further decentralised employment relations (see ch. 5). Fourth, though New Zealand is outside our sample of countries, it is worth noting that until the 1980s it had a century-old centralised arbitration system. However, vast changes to individual and enterprise bargaining were introduced by the Employment Contracts Act 1991 (Rasmussen 1997).

In the 1980s and early 1990s there was little appreciable change in the provision of public conciliation, mediation and arbitration services or of the newer advisory services concerning work organisation. With stronger international competition, the pursuit of non-accommodating monetary policies and the high level of unemployment in most of our sample of countries, the tendency for the outcome of collective bargaining to create problems for economic policy makers generally decreased, though it did not disappear. Italy abolished its long-established indexation system in 1992. Germany had problems managing the integration of its new eastern States (e.g. with regard to pay levels) following unification in 1990.

In their role as employers, governments had tended to follow practices equivalent to those of recognised 'good' private employers, but were subsequently faced with rapidly rising costs and restricted income. Hence they found it necessary to cut their labour costs, by reducing numbers and by limiting pay increases. Margaret Thatcher in Britain initiated the privatisation of publicly owned industries and enterprises, which took workers out of the public and into the private sector. A series of other countries followed this path, including Australia, even under a Labor government. A perceived need to restrain public sector pay and the number of public employees continued to be widespread in the 1990s.

Korea represents an interesting case in which government has played a significant but changing role in employment relations through its domination of political and economic affairs. Since the 1987 'Democratisation Declaration', the Korean government has permitted collective bargaining to become a more important means of regulating employment relations. When amendments to the Trade Union Act in December 1996 met with widespread public opposition, the government was forced to further relax its control over aspects of employment relations. Concessions included permitting unions to engage in politics, recognition of a rival national union federation and maintaining restrictions on employers' scope to lay off employees. However, unions have demanded that the government permit greater freedom of association and rights to employees in the future.

International aspects of employment relations

As they have been touched on in relation to several countries, it is appropriate to discuss the international institutions concerned with employment relations. In the past, international activity rarely impinged in an obvious way on workplace industrial relations or on much national legislation. An exception is the standard-setting work undertaken by the International Labour Organisation (ILO), but otherwise, in government, employer (except multinational employer) and union circles, international affairs were usually marginal.

However, the World Bank Report 1995, *Workers in an Integrating World*, noted that in today's world of fast-moving capital markets, workers often bear the brunt of financial crises, in the form of high inflation, higher taxes and unemployment. According to the United Nations, global economic trends have proceeded at a more rapid pace than the capacity of international agencies to develop supporting norms and institutions. The impact of globalisation on labour and labour market institutions is complex. Campbell (1992) has argued that the internationalisation of markets and globalisation have rendered national institutions that govern labour markets less effective, thereby creating a 'regulatory deficit' (see also ILO 1997).

Multinational enterprises

The 'engine' of globalisation is the MNE, which results in far-reaching organisational changes both within and between firms. Growth of world trade and finance has facilitated the spread of MNEs which have, in turn, contributed to market globalisation via foreign direct investments (UNCTAD 1993). The growth of MNEs has eroded the significance of national boundaries and weakened the ability of governments, local firms and unions in a single country to insulate themselves from external influences. MNEs have often played an important role in 'exporting', or trying to transfer, HRM policies and practices from one country to another, especially from their home country to various host countries in which they operate (Dowling, Schuler & Welch 1994; Shadur, Rodwell & Bamber 1995).

A global firm is one whose products are sold in all key markets of the world and whose world-wide activities are integrated across national markets (Porter 1990). There is no single model of the global firm, and thoroughly globally integrated industries are rather few in number. Some large MNEs, such as the Swedish–Swiss conglomerate Asea-Brown Boveri (ABB), aims to be 'multidomestic' rather than global in the markets in which it operates (Björkman 1993). Similarly, the Japanese company Sony pursues a strategy of 'global localisation' (Ohmae 1990). Nevertheless, these firms employ globally coordinated strategies in areas such as product planning and component sourcing, which have important implications for employment relations. Hence, the process of globalisation has eroded the significance of national boundaries, and employment relations systems have been required to adjust to market conditions that are increasingly outside their ambit of control. Despite attempts by international trade union secretariats to develop coordinated strategies, they have not been able to keep pace with the speed and extent of globalisation.

In some countries, particularly those that are competing for capital investment by providing cheap labour, employment laws may be relaxed, and tax privileges granted, to attract MNEs. Although it is often argued that MNEs provide good pay and working conditions for their employees in less-developed economies (LDEs) and NIEs, many of these firms have used 'offshore' manufacturing locations to avoid the higher pay and stricter regulation of working conditions that have been achieved by unions in their home country. There are, of course, considerable differences in the degree to which a multinational can impose its will on a host country. As Blanpain (1998) notes: 'the entities of a multinational enterprise located in various countries are subject to the laws of these countries . . . (and have to) manage their business within the framework of law, regulations and prevailing labour relations and employment practices, in each of the countries in which they operate'. Thus, there is a two-way influence between a firm and the countries in which it operates. A multinational must adapt to the local laws and practices, yet it may also use its influence to change these in accordance with its own self-interest.

By investing in NIEs and using relatively cheap labour to gain a competitive advantage in labour-intensive industries, many MNEs have closed some or all of their labour-intensive manufacturing operations in the IMEs. The increased competition from offshore production has led to a scaling down of labour-intensive manufacturing in the IMEs, with local companies experiencing increasing difficulties competing with cheaper imports. This has led to problems of structural unemployment—employees having skills no longer relevant to the local labour market (Campbell 1994).

By the 1970s, the post-war growth of multinational enterprises led governments—only partly on the urging of unions—to establish, through the OECD (1976; 1994b) and the ILO (1977), international codes (instruments) concerning the operations of such enterprises, including guidelines regarding employment and industrial relations.[2] The guidelines were voluntary and there was no provision for possible individual transgressions to be judged. Consultation facilities were provided for the international organisations of unions and employers. Since the promulgation of the instruments, the unions have pressed for the guidelines to have more force and have submitted cases of alleged infringement to the relevant authorities in the OECD and the ILO. The unions' representations had some impact, particularly in the early days, but the results fell far short of their hopes. The employers' organisations, for their part, have made efforts to promote voluntary adherence to the guidelines but have argued against their strengthening. In recent years governments have shown little enthusiasm for any tightening or extension of the guidelines.

Globalisation and unions

In most IMEs, globalisation has had a negative effect on unions' bargaining power and political influence, and weakened Keynesian-style economic strategies. Jacoby (1995) noted that competition from lower cost producers, especially in LDEs, has exerted downward pressure on wages and employment in many unionised industries, from steel to apparel. In IMEs, many employers have shifted towards the production of more technology-intensive goods and services in order to secure a competitive advantage further up the value chain, thereby reducing the demand for less-skilled labour. International currency speculation has also inhibited nations from pursuing labourist economic strategies. Governments have been less willing to use deficit financing to take up slack in the labour market in case this triggers an anticipatory run against the nation's currency.

Yet globalisation cannot be blamed for all of the problems that confront organised labour. Disparities in union growth rates have always existed. Unions with the highest density levels in the 1950s, such as those in Nordic countries, have *continued* to have among the highest levels of density. Conversely, those unions with the lowest density levels have experienced the greatest losses. Countries whose density levels have remained robust in recent decades have tended to have corporatist industrial relations systems where bargaining has been more centralised, where governments have consulted unions regarding national economic policies and where there have been strong national organisations representing the union movement (Crouch 1985).

Campbell (1992) has highlighted the many effects of globalisation on unions and labour market institutions, which have both positive and negative consequences. On the negative side, globalisation appears to be associated with a widening of the gap between 'core' and 'peripheral' workers in internal labour markets. Those on the periphery of the labour market often work under temporary or part-time contracts and are difficult for unions to organise. Furthermore, the blurring of boundaries between globally organised firms makes it more difficult for governments or unions to regulate their internal labour markets. Additionally, there have emerged 'company-centred' models of organisation which emphasise employee commitment to managerial goals and which discourage or exclude union affiliation among employees. However, these developments are not exclusively associated with globalisation even though such trends may be accentuated in MNEs. Furthermore, other labour market implications of globalisation are ambiguous. The 'vertical disintegration' of MNEs into small entrepreneurially driven firms can create opportunities for former employees to become independent, self-employed contractors, although there is no guarantee of such a positive outcome. The implications of the development of global networks between firms are also difficult to predict. Employees and their unions at the local level may experience a loss of autonomy and control or, conversely, they may be able to exercise greater leverage on the employer depending on their bargaining position. Indeed, national unions may be able to pool their experience and coordinate their actions when dealing with MNEs, thereby developing effective bargaining strategies. To maximise the benefits of globalisation and minimise the costs, however, it may be necessary for governments and trade unions to coordinate their strategies for dealing with MNEs. The ILO's *World Employment Report* noted that 'the increased footlooseness of MNEs, combined with pressures to attract and retain foreign investment, could lead to a debasement of labour standards' (ILO 1995:10). For this reason the ILO has urged that fresh impetus should be given to cooperative international action to protect labour standards.

International union organisations

Since the nineteenth century unions have built links across national boundaries in an attempt to counter the influence of international capital. Since the decline, after 1989, of the World Federation of Trade Unions (WFTU), whose clientele was mainly provided by the unions in the communist countries, there are two main international union confederations: the International Confederation of Free Trade Unions (ICFTU) and the much smaller World Confederation of Labour (WCL). The difference between them is mainly ideological.

The American Federation of Labor–Congress of Industrial Organizations (AFL–CIO) rejoined the ICFTU in 1981 after an absence of 12 years. Nearly all of the main union confederations in the countries discussed in this book belong to the ICFTU, which plays a major role in organising the workers' group at the ILO. In 1997 it claimed 124 million members, represented by 195 union affiliates from 137 countries and territories. Most ICFTU activities fall into one of three categories. First, in its representational activities, the ICFTU calls attention to injustices committed by governments or employers. Second, its services, and especially its organisational activities, are largely directed to LDEs and NIEs where unionism is weak. Third, the ICFTU has fairly self-sufficient regional organisations for Asia and for North and South America and since the 1970s has become rather stronger in Africa than it was formerly.

The WCL now has few major members among unions in the Western market economies and is much smaller than the ICFTU. Formerly it had a Christian identity, but it now has a secular radical socialist ideology. The *Confédération française démocratique du travail*

(CFDT), the second-largest French confederation, used to be a major constituent, but it no longer belongs to the WCL.

On a regional basis the biggest union grouping is the European Trade Union Confederation (ETUC), which coordinates union activity relative to the European Union (EU) and meets with its employer counterpart, the Union of Industrial and Employers' Confederations of Europe (UNICE). The ETUC, founded in 1973, has never confined its membership to member countries of the EU but rather has included other European movement centres. In 1997 there were 61 confederations from 28 countries and 14 European Trade Union Federations affiliated to the ETUC; covering some 57 million workers. A complementary grouping with the same membership is the European Trade Union Institute (ETUI), which conducts research on subjects of union concern.

Covering a wider field geographically is the Trade Union Advisory Committee to the OECD (TUAC), which ensures that the OECD has a union viewpoint on its work. A notable activity of the ICFTU and particularly of TUAC has been to formulate views on the desirable form of international economic and social policies, which they have then put before heads of government at their various summit meetings. The union officials involved in this work come from a variety of national and international collectivities—for instance, an official from one of the Swedish union centres might also be active in the Nordic Trade Union Council, the ICFTU, the ETUC, TUAC and the workers' group in the ILO and, indeed, other bodies. The international unions have consultative rights with a range of international organisations as well as with those mentioned.

There have been international trade (union) secretariats (ITSs) for particular crafts, occupations or industries since 1889 (Northrup & Rowan 1979). The ITSs bring together individual national unions, in particular sectors of industry. They are sometimes referred to as the 'industrial internationals', since they focus on particular industries or occupations and concentrate on sectors or major companies rather than on wider political issues. For instance, they coordinate research on health and safety hazards and technological change in their sectors. They also aim to gather information and to maintain international union solidarity in relation to certain large MNEs (e.g. Ford, Philips, Shell and Nestlé). The latter is an almost impossible task, as workers' interests in one country may seem to conflict with those in another (e.g. if an MNE aims to retrench in one country but expand to another). The ITSs are autonomous organisations, but most of them generally follow the ICFTU on broad policy issues. Mergers and recruitment have considerably increased the size of the main ITSs in recent years; they have also increased their activity, particularly as a response to the growth of MNEs and the internationalisation of production. The largest ITS is Education International, covering some 20 million teachers. The second-largest is the International Metalworkers' Federation (IMF) with 140 affiliated unions in 70 countries, covering around 16 million workers. The IMF has established 'world councils', mirroring particular major MNEs, to provide a forum for representatives of workers employed by those firms in different countries. Other large ITSs include the Commercial and Clerical Workers (FIET), the Public Service Employees, the Chemical Workers, the Textile Workers, and the Transport Workers. A General Conference of ITSs meets about once a year to review common problems and interests (see Windmuller 1995).

There is also another small confederation in Europe—the *Confédération internationale des cadres* (CIC), which aims to represent executive and professional staffs as a 'third force' between capital and labour (Bamber 1986).

The moves towards market-based economies in Eastern Europe have significant implications for the international trade union movement; the ICFTU, the ETUC and several of the ITSs have forged links with the new unions in Eastern Europe. Although this has extended the movement's coverage, it has strained resources as many of these unions do not pay full affiliation fees.

In spite of the activities of these and many other international union organisations, the labour movement has found it extremely difficult to exercise much influence over the activities of multinationals. However, most unions are concerned about the growing power of multinationals, and consequently their international activities are increasing.

International employers' associations

International employers' organisations corresponding to the general and regional international union bodies—mainly the International Organisation of Employers (IOE) in Geneva, *Union des Industries de la Communauté Européenne* (UNICE) in Brussels, and the Business and Industry Advisory Committee to the OECD (BIAC) in Paris—have also been increasingly busy in recent years. Unlike many employers' organisations at the national level, those at the international level began less as a response to the growth of unions and more as a reaction to the growth of supranational governmental agencies (Oechslin 1993). Hence most international employers' organisations have a shorter history and play a less general role than their union counterparts.

The origins of the IOE, the most comprehensive employers' group concerned with labour matters, can be traced back to the first ILO Conference in 1919. The IOE's role has grown since the Second World War, although its main activities are still focused on representing employers' interests at the ILO (Windmuller & Gladstone 1984; Upham 1990).

As a parallel to the situation in many countries, another employers' confederation places more emphasis on trade and economic matters:

the International Chamber of Commerce (ICC). There is a broad division of responsibilities between the IOE and ICC, with the former concentrating on industrial relations issues; however, the division is not always clear. Both the IOE and ICC, for example, are concerned about the various attempts to constrain MNEs by unions, governments and international agencies. Unlike the unions, the employers are rarely divided in terms of political ideology; but, in the post-1945 period, and until the collapse of communism, the IOE did not admit members from Eastern Europe.

International governmental and tripartite organisations

The ILO is the major forum for international industrial relations activities by governments, employers and unions (Servais 1996). It was founded in 1919 under the First World War peace treaty and was associated with the League of Nations. Unlike the League, it survived the Second World War and became associated with the United Nations. By 1997, the ILO had 174 member states; its structure is illustrated in Figure 12.1.

The ILO has been an important agency for the development of word-wide labour standards since its inception. As the major source of international labour law and of data on international and comparative employment relations, it has adopted over 181 conventions and around 188 recommendations, which have had more than 6433 ratifications.

These instruments deal with a wide range of issues, including: (1) fundamental human rights such as freedom of association, equality of treatment and abolition of forced labour; (2) occupational health and safety; (3) working conditions; (4) social security and workers' compensation; (5) labour administration; (6) migrant workers and (7) the specific needs or circumstances of particular occupational groups. Collectively, these standards are referred to as the 'International Labour Code'.

The ILO is also an important source of information on HRM policies and practices throughout the world (Galenson 1981). Although it constitutes 'a gigantic exercise in transplantation' (Kahn-Freund 1976), like most other international agencies the ILO is cautious about offending its members, and so its recommendations are drafted carefully. It is significant that many of the ILO's conventions and recommendations relate to issues that are seen as not directly impinging upon the power relations between labour, capital and the state, such as protective standards, discrimination in employment and general conditions of work. The ILO cannot compel its members to adhere to particular standards and it is left to governments to decide which ones they will ratify. Conventions may also be renounced (e.g. Britain, see ch. 2).[3]

Figure 12.1   The structure of the International Labour Organisation

Source: Adapted from Smith (1984:23).

The ILO suffers from severe budgetary constraints. It has been criticised as being over-bureaucratic and conservative. But as Creighton puts it:

> . . . there is abundant evidence to suggest that the ILO can and does play an important role in protecting basic human rights and in combating the exploitation of the economically and socially disadvantaged.
>
> It is, for example, widely recognised that the ILO played a major part in protecting union rights in Poland in the 1980s, when the authorities in that country were intent upon suppressing the Solidarity union. It is now very actively involved in helping the emerging democracies of Eastern Europe, Africa and Latin America to adopt labour laws and systems of labour administration which conform to accepted international standards. (Creighton 1992:39)

Moreover, the ILO can have a considerable impact; for instance, through its freedom of association standards (especially in relation to the right to strike and to engage in autonomous collective bargaining). Furthermore, these are standards that cannot be avoided simply by non-ratification. Respect for the principles of freedom of association is an obligation associated with ILO membership.

With the growth of the global economy, international trade has an increasing relevance to industrial relations. As recently as the 1960s, advanced IMEs, like many of those considered in this book, had little competition for their products and services from the rest of the world. That is no longer the case, with the rise of the NIEs and of former communist countries, and the greater propensity of developing countries to compete in world markets. Since their pay and working conditions tend to be much superior to those elsewhere, the developed countries are finding it increasingly difficult to compete in a range of products and services. Inevitably, this fuels protectionist views among interest groups in IMEs, including unions, as was shown by the opposition by American unions to the North American Free Trade Agreement (NAFTA): the unions feared that US firms would move across the border to Mexico, to take advantage of its much lower labour costs.

Given the widespread acceptance of the notion of free trade (at least in theory), it is difficult to criticise competition—for example, based on lower pay or longer working hours—still less, greater efficiency. If, however, competition is based on forced or child labour, or on a workforce that is not allowed to unionise, bargain collectively or strike, or which has inadequate health and safety protection, many would consider it to be unfair. It was with this in mind that, early in 1994, in the final negotiations of the Uruguay Round of the General Agreement on Tariffs and Trade (GATT), the USA, with support from France, called for a clause to be inserted in trade agreements requiring the parties to observe some of the more fundamental labour conditions. The move met strong resistance from developing countries (who saw it as protectionist) and lukewarm or critical responses from others. Although the proposal for a social clause was not accepted, the idea remains on the international agenda. The idea has been around for a long time (see Caire 1994) but it has been dormant for some years. However, principles apart, the practicalities of pursuing a social clause are not simple. The ILO already has conventions and recommendations covering the kind of basic conditions that might gain international support in the World Trade Organisation (WTO), and there would be little point in duplicating what has been done in the past. But the ILO standards are not as forceful, nor as effectively policed, as advocates of the social clause would like. Trade is the responsibility of the WTO and the United Nations Commission on Trade and Development (UNCTAD) rather than the ILO; but such trade organisations are not expert in labour matters. And, if agreement could be reached on what constitutes fair standards, how should alleged defaulters be dealt with?

If it is decided to pursue the possibility of a social clause, there is still much work to do to make it operational.

An organisation that has played an increasingly significant role in recent years is the EU. The Treaty of Rome 1957, which set up the earlier European Community (EC), contained generalised references to promoting improved working conditions and living standards for workers. Among the binding commitments were freedom of movement for workers; equal pay for equal work; and the establishment of a European Social Fund to facilitate employment and labour mobility. The EC was provided with an Economic and Social Committee to be consulted on relevant matters. It established consultative arrangements with the union confederation, the ETUC; the private employers' confederation, the UNICE; and the European Centre for Public Enterprises (CEEP). Nonetheless, the EU provides an example of the limits to transferability of employment relations regulations and processes, as the member countries have generally preserved their separate approaches to industrial relations, despite their attempts to move towards joint policies in other spheres.

The European Commission, the EU's executive arm, has always monitored employment relations developments and has promoted directives concerning, for instance, collective redundancies (1975); the rights of workers when the enterprise is transferred to another owner (1977); protection of workers in cases of insolvency (1980); and working time (1993). It has also been interested, without much impact so far, in the possibilities for international collective bargaining.

From the mid-1960s, the Commission drafted proposals concerning, first, the creation of a European Company; second, the harmonisation of company law; and third, informative and consultative arrangements in large national firms and MNEs. Of these, the first two failed to gain acceptance largely due to the ambiguous position of workers in company structures, with the Commission insisting on some measure of co-determination and consultation on an international basis. All three proposals met determined opposition from the employers and some governments. They were effectively put aside until a more propitious time, but some of the features of the third found their way into a directive of 1994, requiring the establishment of European Works Councils.

In 1986 the Single European Act set the target of a 'free movement of goods, persons, services and capital' in a more closely integrated Europe by the end of 1992. The single European market is removing the barriers between national labour markets, but perhaps more importantly it is precipitating greater competition in product markets, which also has implications for labour markets. Both developments are of considerable concern to unions.

The new Europe should also, it was considered, have a 'social dimension'. In 1988 the European Company proposal was brought forward again, this time in a much more flexible form (revised yet again in 1997). In 1989 the Commission presented a Draft Charter of Fundamental Social Rights which, at the Strasbourg summit, became the subject of a 'solemn declaration' by 11 of the then 12 member states, Britain dissenting.

The Commission and most EU national governments (with the notable exception of Britain before 1997) appeared to be determined to legislate on industrial relations and working conditions. This led the UNICE to the view that it might be better off seeking understandings with the unions on an international basis, so as to discourage European legislation—a departure from the longstanding conviction among most employers that workplace matters should never be dealt with internationally. The Commission has long favoured such employer–union dialogue at European level and this was allowed for in the Single European Act of 1986, which incorporated the possibility in a new Article (118B) inserted in the EC Treaty, and the Maastricht Treaty.

In the Maastricht Conference of 1991 the British refusal to accept a stronger EU social policy that the other members wanted led to an unprecedented agreement that the 11 member states other than Britain might have recourse to the EU institutions and procedures to pursue certain social objectives with widened provisions for the use of qualified majority voting in the Council, without British participation. Britain was not to be bound by instruments adopted under this procedure, thus opening up a prospect of some uniform arrangements applying in the other member countries with different arrangements being operative in Britain. This procedure was followed in the case of the European Works Council Directive of 1994. The Maastricht Agreement also opened up further possibilities for substituting international employer–union agreements for European legislation, or for such agreements to be carried forward into European legislation. This was the case with an agreement by European employers and unions on parental leave in 1995 which, on the parties so requesting the Commission, became a European directive in 1996. The relevant part of the Maastricht Agreement was known as the 'Social Chapter'. Immediately after its election in May 1997 the new Labour government in Britain signified its intention to end the 'opt-out' negotiated by the Conservatives in 1991. After this has been effected a new union–employer agreement, concerning the rights of part-time workers to equality with those of full-time workers, is likely to be adopted.

Later in 1997 the Commission proposed the setting up of information and consultation committees in enterprises on a national basis. Whatever the outcome of these varied developments, there are going to be significant developments in the European dimensions of industrial relations. Although transnational bargaining on wages and working conditions is still on the remote horizon, the European Works Councils Directive has been implemented. This requires MNEs to establish Europe-wide councils in which worker representatives are informed and consulted.

International migration of labour and capital

International migration of labour has steadily become more important since the 1950s for most of the countries discussed here. The USA, Canada and Australia have long welcomed immigration, but the number of immigrants in France, Germany and Britain—where they are mainly Commonwealth and Irish immigrants—has risen until there are now several million in each. In Germany the position of immigrants—mainly from Turkey and South-East Europe, but recently from former communist countries—has been complicated by the problems of industry in the eastern States. Italy, formerly a labour-exporting country, has recently attracted many African and Albanian immigrants. Within the EU, free movement of labour was provided in the Treaty of Rome 1957, but movement between the EU member states has been less than might have been expected. Even in Japan, one of the world's most ethnically homogeneous nations, there has been an influx of labour from Korea and other Asian countries. Although the level of Japan's immigration has been small by Western standards, it has become a matter of public debate. Though it has often been associated with social problems and has changed the composition of the labour force, in most countries immigration has not had a dramatic impact on industrial relations.

Capital migration also increased, particularly into the EU, as non-EU firms sought to ensure a European base in view of the prospect of a 'Fortress Europe' built by the EU. The influx of Japanese capital—not only into Europe—was particularly marked and Japanese management achieved some notable successes in building good and productive employment relations in the European, North American and Australian plants of Japanese companies (Oliver & Wilkinson 1992; Grant 1994; Shadur, Rodwell & Bamber 1995).

Eastern Europe[4]

The sudden collapse of the communist regimes of Eastern Europe was very significant for employment relations as for other things. The ensuing unification of Germany, for most practical purposes, appeared to spread the former West German system of employment relations, including the union structure, to the whole of Germany (see ch. 8). Unification did not change the West German system fundamentally, but it did precipitate problems in reconciling different levels of productivity and different levels of wages in East and West Germany. These problems led to serious unemployment in what used to be East Germany, though by the late 1990s that situation was improving.

Developments in the other former communist countries are beyond the scope of this book. Suffice it to say that their employment relations systems are still evolving. The results are unlikely to have much impact on the structures of West European employment relations. However, these new market economies can be expected to provide increased competition, as well as markets, thereby in due course affecting employment and pay levels elsewhere. As their unions and employers become more closely linked with those of the West, there may be some convergence between patterns of industrial relations in Eastern and Western Europe (cf. Bamber & Peschanski 1996).

Further challenges for international and comparative employment relations

The main challenges faced by employment relations decision makers in IMEs (and some NIEs like Korea) in the 1990s sprang from the need to adjust to a changing political, economic and industrial environment and an increasing rate of organisational and technological change; the two are, of course, interrelated. Technological change of itself was readily accommodated in all of the countries (Bamber & Lansbury 1989); there have been few cases of serious opposition. Many workers realised that the enterprises for which they worked had to use the latest technology to stay in business and welcomed the feeling of being in the front line of technological advance. But of course there were winners and losers; understandably the latter were less inclined to cooperate. In any case, reduced union bargaining power has impaired their ability to resist, even had they wished to do so.

The changing political, economic and industrial context poses more difficult problems. The redistribution of world production and trade and the accompanying substantial contraction of industries like steel, shipbuilding and textiles, together with technological change and the shift from manufacturing to services, add up to a considerable loss of jobs and change in skill requirements. Although a significant number of new jobs have been created, there have been many cases where a large number of jobs have disappeared in areas in which there was little alternative employment available. There have been some major upsets—such as the long strike against the pit closures by the British mineworkers' union in 1984–85—but in most cases, closures and reductions have been effected without much industrial conflict. In part, of course, workers—and their union leaders in particular—recognise the inevitability of such closures. In most countries the laws, social policies and collective agreements of the post-war period have helped to cushion the severity of redundancy.

Different countries have dealt with job security in different ways.

The USA, where there has long existed the principle of 'employment-at-will', reluctantly enacted the fairly mild Worker Adjustment and Retraining Notification Act 1988. The ease of dismissal in the USA is matched by that nation's capacity for creating new jobs and the mobility of much of its working population. In Japan, great efforts are made to help workers whose services are no longer required. In Germany, and some other European countries, the law requires that a 'social plan' be drawn up where sizeable reductions of the workforce are involved, making provision for helping displaced workers. France has similar arrangements; help includes extended notice, redundancy payments, facilitated early retirement, training and retraining arrangements, and relocation allowances. In Britain, legislation originating in the 1960s provides for extended notice of dismissal and for redundancy payments. In Italy laid-off workers can be helped through the *Cassa Integrazione Guadagni*, a public fund guaranteeing up to 80 per cent of pay during layoff. Sweden, with the help of its Active Manpower Policy and the Labour Market Board, experienced remarkably little difficulty in running down its shipyards in the 1960s (Stråth 1987), but has experienced problems in the 1990s as unemployment has accelerated. And in Canada, federal law requires employers planning to terminate the jobs of 50 or more workers to establish a joint planning committee, which attempts to make the best of the situation. In Australia, until recently, the notion of federal laws on redundancy was seen as unconstitutional, but many industrial awards try to regulate redundancies. The widespread strikes that greeted the Korean government's amendments to the Trade Union Act in December 1996 were in large part fuelled by workers' concerns that employers would be granted greater freedom to lay off employees. This coincided with an economic recession (albeit mild by Western European standards) which eroded workers' sense of job security. Following much protest, the government postponed its proposed industrial relations legislation (see Bamber, Park, Lee & Ross: forthcoming).

The changes discussed in this section have had another effect, which is only slowly making itself felt. Before the 1970s, workplaces typically experienced less change than is commonly the case in the 1990s, and usually had a more stable employment structure. There were managers, supervisors, technicians, clerical and administrative staff, skilled, semi-skilled and so-called unskilled manual workers, nearly all employed on the basis of a full working week. However, several of the divisions between these groups have become blurred, not least the distinction between manual and non-manual workers. The need for workforce flexibility—to deal with rapid product changes and fluctuating order books—coupled with new technologies has often led to a gradually increasing segmentation of the enterprise labour force: a core group of functionally flexible, skilled workers enjoying good pay, regular conditions and a relatively high job security; and a secondary labour force of less-skilled and less-advantaged workers, often part-time, fixed-term, or temporary workers, who have become much more numerous in recent years (cf. Curson 1986; Sarfati & Kobrin 1988; Gladstone & Wheeler 1992).

Conclusion

In summary, it is useful to consider the evolution of post-war employment relations by reference to 1960, 1980 and the late 1990s. Comparing employment relations in 1980 with those in 1960 for countries in this book, there are few significant structural changes to note, other than legislation to strengthen industrial democracy in Germany and Sweden, the Italian Workers' Charter of 1970, and the failed British Industrial Relations Act 1971. (The subsequent Labour government's legislation in Britain, though it also strengthened the position of unions and workers, was essentially concerned with restoring the framework to its pre-1971 position.) Union membership had declined steadily in the USA and had started to decline in France and Japan, but in other countries it had increased or remained steady. There were few significant comparable changes on the employers' side, although their activities had declined at the central level as bargaining had become more decentralised.

Various forms of collective bargaining continued to be the most widespread way of regulating pay and working conditions in most of the countries, but the level at which it was conducted was generally shifting from the industry to the enterprise in Britain, and there was an increase in workplace negotiation in some other countries. Several countries had problems in reconciling the results of collective bargaining with their economic policies and some of them had responded with incomes policies (which had mostly been found to be only minimally effective). Real wages and working conditions had shown steady improvement. Industrial disputes had increased over the period but were starting to decline. Unionisation had increased in the public sector; the USA, Sweden and Canada had strengthened the rights of public employees.

Interest in promoting industrial democracy had grown, peaked and largely been dissipated. Mainly that interest was concerned with expanding workers' and union rights institutionally, by such means as putting workers' representatives on company boards and strengthening works councils. There had been little change in the traditional organisation of work, though Japanese innovations were already attracting attention and a few enterprises had experimented with semi-autonomous work groups. In several countries regulations had been introduced that made dismissals more difficult and expensive for the employer.

The contrast between the late 1990s and 1980 is much more marked. Britain has made substantial changes in its legal framework; France has had the Auroux laws of 1982; Italy the significant changes of the early 1990s; and Sweden the decline of the traditional 'Swedish model'. Australia experienced, first, the government–union Accord of 1983, then the gradual decentralism until the Accord ended in 1996, after which the incoming Liberal–National Party coalition government sought further to decentralise and deregulate the industrial relations system. Korea announced major and controversial changes to its labour laws in late 1996. Otherwise, systematic changes were not great. More widespread in the 1980s and 1990s were changes in the balance between employers and unions within the systems, reflecting higher unemployment and a more difficult economic environment than was usual before the early 1970s.

Subsequent to 1980, union membership decreased in most countries, but not in Sweden. Employers were induced by increased international competition to press more strongly for efficient working practices and to limit labour costs. National–central (rare) and national–industrial levels of collective bargaining remained but enterprise negotiations became more important. The volume of strikes fell significantly in nearly all of the countries.

Despite high unemployment, pay and working conditions continued to improve in most countries, albeit more slowly than before; however, pay differentials, which earlier had tended to narrow, subsequently tended to widen. Working time was cut in several countries, partly as a government-favoured response to high unemployment. Interest in institutional forms of industrial democracy was still generally low, but managements increasingly discussed ways of promoting more worker involvement, often as part of HRM programs. Managements also experimented with new methods of production and adopted increasingly varied patterns of employment. In the public sector—which had shrunk significantly due to privatisation programs—financially straitened governments became more resistant to pay claims.

For the European countries, the increased involvement of the EU in the labour field added to the volume of regulation. This was despite arguments that, in comparison with the USA, the costs of such regulation in Europe were a cause of the higher and more obdurate unemployment from which most European countries suffered. The implementation of European Works Councils (EWCs) within the EU, after decades of debate, has occurred at a time when interest in this area may be said to have declined. Yet as EWCs become established the importance of worker representation at the enterprise level may increase and the role of works councils may expand. Another aspect of industrial democracy is the movement to give workers more say in shop floor decisions and to make jobs more interesting. Such moves were fuelled, especially at times of labour shortages, by some employer opinion leaders who believed that these moves would facilitate the recruitment and retention of workers.

The forces underlying the changes in employment relations systems in IMEs in recent years are interrelated and readily apparent. Economically they are the global redistribution of industry consequent on the entry into international markets of NIEs and even LDEs; the impact of new technologies; the growth of MNEs, facilitated by the free movement of capital; and lower real transport and communications costs; and the removal of barriers to international trade.

For several countries changes in prevailing attitudes also influence employment relations; thus, beliefs in collectivism, public ownership, state planning and regulation of working arrangements have faded in favour of individualism, privatisation, the working of the market and flexible use of labour. These beliefs seem set to continue.[5] But though they may bring forth similar responses from countries, there is little to suggest that they are inducing convergence in employment relations systems. Rather, this suggests the continuation of a process of 'converging divergences' (as suggested by Darbishire & Katz 1997). Of course, the systems will continue to adapt and they will continue to be imperfect—there will always be conflict and the need for further adjustment at places of work. Will there be significant further structural change in employment relations systems in the near future? Reforms would probably require political changes as well as greater motivation to change among employers and union leaders. The most successful enterprises and employment relations systems will be those that, while preserving a degree of equity between management and workers, and building on their human resources, prove most adaptable to the external challenges, not least in terms of increasing their efficiency and effectiveness.

Appendix
Employment, economics and industrial relations: Comparative statistics

Peter Ross,
Greg J. Bamber and
Gillian Whitehouse

The collection of international statistics presented in this Appendix[1] provides a context for the themes covered throughout the book. It helps to meet the increasing demand for cross-nationally comparable statistics from researchers and practitioners in employment relations and related fields. The aim is to display and review selected data for the ten countries covered in the preceding chapters over a time period that allows patterns of continuity and change to be demonstrated.

There are many difficulties associated with this task. For example, methods of collecting data and definitions used may vary a great deal between countries. While some of our tables are based on hitherto unpublished statistics, we rely, wherever possible, on the standardised data published by agencies such as the International Labour Organisation (ILO), Eurostat—the statistical office of the European Union (EU), the Organisation for Economic Co-operation and Development (OECD)[2] or the US Department of Labor's Bureau of Labor Statistics (BLS). Each of these organisations attempts to some extent to standardise data from individual countries. The ILO, for example, sets standards through the International Conference of Labour Statisticians. Although there is a time lag before such data become available, they are generally more reliable for cross-national comparison than most national sources. Since most agencies have started publishing on the World Wide Web (WWW), a great deal of data have become available more quickly than was previously the case when we had to wait for the publication of 'hard copies'. In this edition we have drawn on WWW sources wherever possible, and examples of such sources are located at the end of the reference section for this Appendix. Where national sources have been used this is noted in the tables. National sources have been most often used for our data on Korea, which did not become a member of the OECD until 1996.

Where our data are inconsistent with national sources, it is usually due to our use of standardised figures. However, the quality of such data depends on the collection and processing of figures at national level, where there is always some risk that political expediency might interfere with the procedures; for example, where rates of unemployment, inflation or industrial stoppages are being reported. In several countries, including Australia, the government statistical offices follow international standards and have statutory independence so that politicians should not be involved in changing the definitions or publication dates of statistics.

As most tables cover a lengthy period of time, another problem encountered is series breaks in data sets. The United Kingdom (UK), United States (USA), Canada and other countries have breaks in important data series. Furthermore, there is a delay before time series reflect major political changes such as the reunification of Germany. While the former German Democratic Republic (East Germany) joined the Federal Republic of Germany in 1990, it is only recently that most available data for Germany have included the former East Germany. Where possible, data for unified Germany have been used, and the tables note which part of Germany the data refer to where applicable. In the tables presented here, we do not attempt to correct for major series breaks, but note where they occur. Allowing for such breaks, in most tables time-series data are reasonably reliable for comparisons within a country—but despite the attempts at standardisation, comparisons between countries generally have less reliability, due to major international differences of definition and methods of calculation.

Any work in this field dates, but the data are used here to draw broad comparisons over time and between countries, rather than to focus on the very latest statistics. We cite details of our sources so that readers can update such data and analyse them further. To simplify this Appendix, we do not include full definitions. For precise definitions, which vary slightly over time and between the various agencies, see the official ILO, OECD and BLS source publications (e.g. ILOa; OECDb; US BLS 1996a). In the following pages the data chronicle the broad context for each of the countries discussed in this book; for example, in terms of population, patterns of employment and unemployment, and the structure of the economy. We then turn to more specific employment relations issues such as unionism and disputes. Our goals are to illuminate broad trends and cross-national contrasts and to highlight some of the difficulties of measurement and interpretation of the data.

Total labour force and civilian employment

Table A.1 shows changes in population and total labour force over three decades in the ten countries. With the exception of Sweden and Italy—where there have been, respectively, a slight decrease (Sweden) and no change (Italy) in the size of the total labour force over the decade from 1985–95—steady increases in total labour force accompany those in population. In most of the ten countries, however, increases in total labour force are well in excess of increases in population over the three decades. This implies an increasing participation rate (see Table A.2).

To illustrate the importance of definitions, note that Table A.1 cites data on the total labour force, while Table A.4 refers to civilian employment. The relationship between these two concepts is as follows:

Total labour force = civilian employment + unemployment + armed forces

Civilian employment includes all those above a specified age in self-employment (own account), as well as employees in paid employment. Also included are unpaid family members and those temporarily absent due to factors such as illness, holidays, bad weather or industrial disputes. Thus many part-time workers are included; however, US employment data omit unpaid family workers working fewer than 15 hours in the reference week.

Labour force participation

Participation rates for each country are shown in Table A.2. The

Table A.1   Population and labour force[3]

	Population (millions)				Total labour force (millions)			
	1965	1975	1985	1995	1965	1975	1985	1995
Australia	11	14	16	18	4.7	6.2	7.4	9
Canada	20	23	25	30	7.3	10	13	15
France	49	53	55	58	20	22	24	25
Germany[b]	59	62	61	82	27	27	29	39
Italy	52	55	57	57	20	21	23	23
Japan	96	112	121	125	48	53	60	67
Korea	27[a]	35	41	45	8.0[a]	12	15	20
Sweden	8	8.2	8.3	8.8	3.7	4.1	4.4	4.3
UK	54	56	57	59	26	26	28	29
USA	194	216	238	263	77	95	117	134

Notes: a   1963 data.

b   Data after 1990 are for united Germany.

Sources: OECDb, c (various years), d; Korean National Statistical Office (NSO).

Table A.2   Labour force participation

	Men (%)				Women (%)				Total (%)			
	1965	1975	1985	1995[a]	1965	1975	1985	1995[a]	1965	1975	1985	1995[a]
Australia	94	89	86	85	40	50	55	64	68	70	71	75
Canada	89	86	85	83	36	50	63	68	63	68	74	76
France	87[d]	84	77	74	47[d]	51	55	60	67[d]	68	66	67
Germany[b]	94	87	82	80	49	51	53	61[b]	71	69	68	71[b]
Italy	87	85[e]	79	74	31	34[e]	41	43	58	59[e]	60	58
Japan	89	90	88	91	56	52	57	62	72	70	72	77
Korea	NA	NA	NA	82	NA	NA	NA	54	NA	NA	NA	68
Sweden	91	89	86	82	54	68	78	77	73	79	82	80
UK	97	92	89	86	51	55	61	68	74	74	75	77
USA	89	86	84	87	44	53	64	72	66	69	74	79

Notes: a   Total employment divided by the working age population.
        b   Former West Germany only.
        c   1963 data.
        d   1968 data.
        e   1974 data.
        NA   Not available.
Sources: OECDa, b (various years).

participation, or activity, rate is the total labour force divided by the population of working age. In most countries working age is considered to be 15–64 years of age, but in some countries there is no upper limit.

In all of the countries for which data are available, except Japan, the long-term trend is towards a lower participation rate for men. This reflects the expansion of tertiary education and the increasing levels of incomes and pensions which enable men to retire earlier. The decade 1985–95, however, has seen a slowing down in this process, with participation rates for men levelling off in Australia and increasing in Japan and the USA.

By contrast, the long-term trend is towards higher participation rates for women, although this has slowed in some countries in recent years. This trend has been more uneven in Japan, where, although many young women enter the labour market, fewer take up permanent jobs. Italy and Korea appear to have comparatively low female participation rates, though the long-term trend for Italy still exhibits increasing participation levels.

The longer years of schooling and increasing levels of incomes and pensions, leading to earlier retirements, also influence women's participation levels, but the influence of these factors has been overridden by the increasing role of women in the world of paid work. Decreasing birth rates, changing social attitudes and structural changes in labour markets are factors conducive to the higher participation rates of women.

Table A.3   Part-time employment

	Part-time employment as a % of:									Women's % share of part-time employment		
	Total employment			Male employment			Female employment					
	1973	1985	1995	1973	1985	1995	1973	1985	1995	1973	1985	1995
Australia	12	18	25	3.7	6.2	11	28	37	43	79	79	74
Canada	10	17	19	4.7	8.8	11	19	28	28	68	70	69
France	5.9	11	16	1.7	3.2	5.0	13	22	29	82	83	82
Germany	10[c]	13[c]	16	1.8[c]	2.0[c]	3.6	24[c]	30[c]	34	89[c]	91[c]	87
Italy	6.4	5.3	6.4	3.7	3.0	2.9	14	10	13	58	62	71
Japan	14	17	20	6.8	7.5	10	25	30	35	70	73	70
Korea	NA	NA	NA	NA	NA	NA	NA	NA	NA	NA	NA	NA
Sweden[a]	18	24	24	3.7	6.1	9.4	39	44	40	88	87	80
UK	16	21	24	2.3	4.4	7.7	39	45	44	91	88	82
USA[b]	16	17	19	8.6	10	11	27	27	27	66	68	68

Notes: a   Break in series after 1986 and 1992.

b   Break in series after 1993.

c   Former West Germany only.

NA   Not available.

Sources: OECDa, d.

Table A.2 shows an increasing disparity in the participation rate for men, which now varies from around 74 per cent for France and Italy, to 91 per cent for Japan. However, the differing total participation rates largely reflect the differing levels of female participation in each country. These vary quite markedly across countries, ranging from 43 per cent for Italy to 77 per cent for Sweden. Sweden's high female participation rates can be attributed partly to the high proportion of part-time workers, most of whom are women (see Table A.3), and the widespread availability of childcare. However, the most recent figures show a slight decline in women's participation rates in Sweden. The low rate in Italy may reflect the relatively large 'informal' economy of 'clandestine' employment there. It is possible that people may be 'discouraged' from engaging in 'active search for work' and it can be difficult for the authorities to measure the size of the labour force accurately, particularly in the large rural sector in southern European countries like Italy. The existence of these 'informal' economies means that the number of women in the workforce tends to be underestimated because of the higher percentage of women who are likely to be involved, for instance, as farm workers or looking after other parents' children for pay (ILO 1995:14).

Although we do not present participation rate data analysed by age, it is worth noting that there are significant differences between the participation rates of people in different age categories. For example, in 1966, the male participation rate in Australia was 96 per cent for the 45–54 age group, but only 79 per cent for the 60–64 age group. Such differences tend to be magnified in periods of economic recession. By 1979, the rate was 92 per cent for the 45–55 age group, but it had fallen to 54 per cent for the older age group. This suggests that such groups may become 'discouraged job-seekers' and take up the option of early retirement particularly when there are fewer jobs available (Carter & Gregory 1981; ILOa and OECDb, which include detailed data on labour force participation by age; see also OECDa 1992, which includes a chapter on the participation of older workers).

Part-time employment

Part-time employment has grown in most of the countries in recent years. This is shown in Table A.3. The definition of part-time working varies greatly between countries, so inter-country comparisons are difficult. Nevertheless, we can infer from Table A.3 that part-time working is much more usual in Australia than in Italy. However, it seems likely that there are also many part-timers in the 'informal' economy in Italy.

In all the countries, a large majority of part-timers are women. In Europe and Japan part-time work is predominantly associated with the life-cycle phase when women are most likely to be involved in bearing and caring for children. In Canada and the USA, however, part-timers tend to be younger than full-timers and are often single people who are combining employment with education.

Besides such supply-side factors, there has been a change in demand. The shift towards labour-intensive services, with weekly and daily peak demands, has tended to increase the demand for part-timers. Many employers are seeking increased labour market flexibility through greater reliance on casual and part-time employment; however, this is not the only way in which increased working-time flexibility is sought. Alternatives include the use of overtime for full-time employees to avoid incurring the overhead costs of taking on additional workers, and increasing the spread of hours worked. The main risk associated with the pursuit of working-time flexibility is that it may exacerbate labour market divisions, and affect women in particular. Part-timers often are not covered by the same degree of labour market regulation nor are they necessarily entitled to as many fringe benefits. As such, they may be easier to dismiss and cost proportionately less than full-timers (Thurman & Trah 1989:5). Casual workers are usually the least protected, even when, as in many Australian awards, hourly rates are increased in lieu of forgone leave and other entitlements.

Structure of employment

Table A.4 displays structural shifts in employment in the ten countries over three decades. The common pattern is a consistent decrease in agricultural and industrial employment, with an increase in service sector employment. Some clarification of categories is necessary in interpreting these data, however. The conventional division into the three broad categories of agriculture (including hunting, forestry and fishing), industry (including manufacturing, mining and construction) and services is based on United Nations definitions established in the 1970s (UN 1971). These distinctions are becoming outdated, however, especially as the agricultural and industrial categories are tending to contract, while services are expanding. The services category is now extremely heterogeneous as it includes all the industries that do not fit one of the first two categories, including public administration, finance, property and business services, community services, recreation, and personal and other services. Therefore, some commentators suggest that it would be appropriate to subdivide services into further categories such as tertiary, consisting of tangible economic services; quaternary, comprising data processing; and quinary, covering unpaid work and homework where pay is secondary, and professional services of a quasi-domestic nature (e.g. Jones 1995). However, as yet the authorities do not provide a sufficiently comprehensive set of such data, nor do we have a sufficiently well-developed conceptual framework within which to gather and analyse data.

As an additional complication, the distinctions between categories are not always precise due to classification difficulties and because some people work in more than one sector. Moreover, the trend towards subcontracting and the growth of employment agencies have tended to distort the data and so have exaggerated the growth of services.

Unemployment

The unemployed comprise all people above a specified age who during the reference period were: (a) without work, that is were not in paid employment or self-employment; (b) currently available for work, that is were available for paid employment or self-employment; and (c) seeking work, that is had taken specific active steps to seek paid employment or self-employment (OECDb). With regard to comparative measures of unemployment, the OECD generally uses standardised unemployment rates. On a national basis most countries discussed use unemployment statistics measured directly through the monthly labour force survey, which uses international concepts and standards. However, in some countries, including Germany and the UK, unemployment

335

able A.4   Civilian employment by sector

	Civilian employment (millions)				Agriculture (% of civilian employment)				Industry (% of civilian employment)				Services (% of civilian employment)			
	1965	1975	1985	1995	1965	1975	1985	1995	1965	1975	1985	1995	1965	1975	1985	1995
ustralia	4.6	5.8	6.7	8.2	9.9	6.9	6.1	5.0	40	34	2.8	23	50	59	66	72
anada	6.8	9.2	11	14	10	6.1	5.1	4.1	34	29	25	23	56	65	70	73
ance	20	21	21	22	18	10	7.6	4.7	39	39	32	26	43	51	60	69
ermany[c]	27	26	26	36	11	6.8	4.6	3.3	50	45	41	38	39	48	54	59
aly[b]	19	21	23	20	26	17	11	7.5	41	39	34	32	33	44	55	60
apan	47	52	58	65	24	13	9	5.7	32	36	35	34	44	52	57	61
orea	7.6[a]	12	15	20	63[a]	46	25	13	NA	NA	30	33	NA	NA	46	54
weden	3.7	4.0	4.3	4	11	6.4	4.8	3.1	43	37	30	26	46	57	65	71
K	25	25	24	26	3.3	2.8	2.5	2.0	48	40	32	27	49	57	66	70
SA	71	86	107	125	6.1	4.1	3.1	2.9	33	31	25	24	61	65	69	73

otes: a   1963 data.
          b   Data after 1980 have been revised.
          c   1995 are for united Germany.
urces: OECDb, c (various issues), d; Korean NSO.

statistics are compiled as an administrative byproduct of a system for registration for unemployment benefits or job-placement assistance, which will be affected over time by changes in legislation and eligibility criteria.

Comparisons of different methods of collecting unemployment statistics show contrasting results, as can be seen in Table A.5. In 1994 the survey data were higher than the registration data in the UK, while the reverse held true for France. In developing and transitional economies the registration figures are usually much lower than the survey results, as can be seen in the case of Russia and Turkey (ILO 1995:19).

Unemployment levels are a crucial influence on the relative bargaining power of workers and employers. Table A.6 shows that unemployment rates have generally been lower in Japan, Korea and Sweden than in the other countries and that Japan and Sweden maintained low levels of unemployment throughout the recessions of the 1970s and 1980s, in marked contrast to most other countries. Before the 1970s, Australia and Germany also had comparatively low rates. The 1973 oil crisis was a turning point that was associated with an increase in unemployment in most countries. Unemployment generally fell in the mid-1980s, but did not return to the relatively low levels that prevailed in the 1950s and 1960s. In the 1990s the trend was for unemployment to remain high; however, significant cross-national differences were still evident, with Sweden no longer retaining its status as a country with low levels of unemployment. Though rising, unemployment in Japan

Table A.5 Comparisons of alternative measures of unemployment

	Survey unemployment ('000)	Registered job-seekers ('000)	Difference ('000)
France[a]	3115	3327	−208
UK[b]	2650	2620	+30
Russia[c]	3955	780	+3175
Turkey[c]	1659	618	+1041

Notes: a   March 1994.
              b   1994.
              c   1993.
Source: ILO (1995).

is still comparatively low, while unemployment in Korea has fallen consistently, giving it the lowest unemployment rate of the ten countries. The USA has also reduced its unemployment rate to a low level compared with Australia, Canada and most European countries.

Gross domestic product

Gross domestic product (GDP) is a measure of the total sum of final goods and services produced by an economy at market prices. GDP includes the cost of capital goods consumed in production processes. Intermediate products are not counted separately, as their value is already included in the prices of final goods and services. Income from abroad is excluded; hence the term gross *domestic* product. Gross *national* product (GNP) equals GDP plus net property income arising from foreign investments and possessions.

Like most of the other indicators we discuss, measuring GDP is fraught with difficulties. Apart from the inherent limitations of such measures of national output and income as indications of a country's economic well-being (e.g. see Waring 1988; Clark 1989:36; Ball & McCulloch 1996:46), there is also a degree of variation between countries in how GDP is measured. For instance, Italy includes an estimate of GDP from its 'underground economy'—its informal sector—but such estimates are inevitably crude. Nevertheless, most national authorities use internationally agreed conventions, which include a notion of the 'economically active population' and define GDP in a narrow economic sense. Although far from perfect, it is the best available indicator of relative economic prosperity because it is measurable and comparable. We need to keep in mind its limitations, however, and must also refer to other complementary measures such as those developed by the OECD and United Nations Development Programs (see also Anderson 1991).

Table A.6 Unemployment

Year	Australia	Canada	France	Germany[c]	Italy	Japan	Korea	Sweden	UK	USA
1960	1.4	6.4	1.4	1.0	5.5	1.7	4.8	1.7	1.3	5.4
1965	1.5	3.6	1.2	0.5	5.3	1.2	7.4	1.2	1.2	4.4
1970	1.6	5.6	2.4	0.6	5.3	1.1	4.1	1.5	2.2	4.8
1975	4.8	6.9	4.0	4.0	5.8	1.9	4.1	1.6	3.2	8.3
1980	6.0	7.5	6.2	2.9	7.5	2.0	5.2	2.0	6.4	7.0
1981	5.7	7.5	7.4	4.2	7.8	2.2	4.5	2.5	9.8	7.5
1982	7.1	10.9	8.1	5.9	8.4	2.4	4.4	3.5	11.3	9.5
1983	9.9	11.9	8.3	7.7	8.8	2.6	4.1	3.9	12.4	9.5
1984	8.9	11.2	9.7	7.1	9.4	2.7	3.8	3.4	11.7	7.4
1985	8.2	10.5	10.2	7.1	9.6	2.6	4.0	3.0	11.2	7.1
1986	8.0	9.5	10.4	6.4	10.5	2.8	3.8	2.8	11.2	6.9
1987	8.0	8.8	10.5	6.2	10.9	2.8	3.1	2.3	10.3[a]	6.1
1988	7.2	7.7	10.0	6.2	11.0	2.5	2.5	1.9	8.6	5.4
1989	6.1	7.5	9.4	5.6	10.9	2.3	2.6	1.6	7.2	5.2
1990	6.9	8.1	8.9	4.8	10.3	2.1	2.4	1.8	6.9[b]	5.6
1991	9.5	10.3	9.4	4.2	9.9	2.1	2.3	3.3	8.8	6.8
1992	10.7	11.3	10.3	4.6	10.5	2.2	2.4	5.8	10.1	7.5
1993	10.8	11.2	11.7	7.9	10.2	2.5	2.8	9.5	10.4	6.9
1994	9.8	10.4	12.3	8.4	11.4	2.9	2.4	9.8	9.6	6.1
1995	8.6	9.5	11.6	8.2	11.9	3.1	2.0	9.2	8.8	5.6
1996	8.6	9.7	12.3	9.0	12.0	3.4	2.0	10.0	8.2	5.4

Notes: a Series break 1986–87.

          b New series based on EU labour force surveys.

          c Up to and including 1992 data concerning former West Germany only.

Sources: OECDa, OECDc; Korean NSO.

Table A.7, columns 3 and 4, show that Korea had the highest annual rate of GDP growth between 1985 and 1996. This is in keeping with the rapid economic growth of many newly industrialising economies (NIEs) in the Asia–Pacific region. Japan had the second-highest rate of growth during this period; however its growth rates have declined substantially since its economy matured. Column 5 shows that in nominal terms, using nominal current prices and exchange rates, Japan has the highest GDP per capita. This reflects an upward movement in dollar prices inside Japan relative to actual US prices and does not necessarily mean that Japanese citizens are richer than US citizens.

To make more realistic comparisons of productivity or living standards, an attempt should be made to eliminate price differences between countries. In view of the vagaries of currency exchange rates, various organisations attempt to calculate purchasing power parities (PPPs). These are alternative rates of conversion which try to equalise the purchasing power of different currencies so that it is theoretically possible to buy the same basket of products everywhere. To calculate PPPs, detailed comparisons are made between the prices of individual

Table A.7 Gross domestic product per capita and by sector

| | GDP^n (billion $US) | | Average annual GDP change^a % | | GDP per capita ($US '000) | | Sectoral % contributions to GDP by: | | | | | |
| | | | | | | | Agriculture | | Industry | | Services | |
	1996^j	1995	1995 –96^j	1985 –95	1995^n	1995^p	1995	1985	1995	1985	1995	1985
Australia	392	349	4.1	3.0	19	19	2.9^d	4.0	28^{d,h}	34^h	70^{d,h}	62^h
Canada	578	560	1.5	2.2	19	21	2.1^c	2.8	26^c	32	72^c	66
France	1545	1538	1.3	2.0	26	20	2.4	3.9	27	31	71	65
Germany	2354	2413	1.1	2.3	30	20	1.1	1.4^g	31	35^g	68	64^g
Italy	1204	1087	0.8	2.0	19	19	2.9	4.5	32	35	66	60
Japan	4578	5114	3.6	3.0	41	22	2.1^d	3.2	38	41	60^d	56
Korea	NA	456	9.0^b	8.7	10	NA	6.6	13	44	41	50	47
Sweden	253	231	1.7	1.3	26	19	2.0^d	3.3	28^d	31	71^d	66
UK	1140	1101	2.4	2.2	19	18	1.7^d	1.7	27^{d,f}	35^f	71^{d,f}	63^f
USA	7263	6955	2.4	2.5	26	26	1.7^e	2.1	26^{e,h}	31^h	72^{e,h,i}	67^{h,i}

Notes:
a Average annual percentage change from previous period.
b 1995–94.
c 1992.
d 1994.
e 1993.
f Repair services of consumer durables other than clothing included under services.
g 1991.
h Sanitary and similar services included under services.
i Includes government enterprises.
j National submissions and Secretariat estimates.
n Nominal—at current prices and exchange rates.
p Based on purchasing power parities (PPPs).
NA Not available.

Sources: OECD *National Accounts*, Vol. 1 (March 1997); OECDd.

goods and services in different countries. Special price surveys have been conducted for this purpose by the OECD and Eurostat. Some results are shown in Table A.7, column 6 (see also Tables A.8 and A.12).

Conversions of GDP figures by means of PPPs, as in Table A.7, column 6, show that in *real* terms the US per capita GDP continues to be ahead of that of the other countries. Japan has the second-highest PPP, being approximately 85 per cent of the US level.

Comparisons of PPPs are more valid between similar countries but there are some circumstances when PPPs may give a misleading indication of comparative standards. If taxes are high, purchasing power is low; but this ignores the fact that there may be commensurately high

Table A.8   Exchange rates

	Official exchange rates per $US					% adjustment of the exchange rate required for wage comparisons to reflect purchasing power in 1994–95[a]
	1980	1985	1990	1995	1996	
Australia	0.88	1.40	1.30	1.35	1.28	+ 38.0%
Canada	1.20	1.40	1.20	1.37	1.36	+ 47.0%
France	4.20	9.00	5.40	5.00	5.10	+ 1.2%
Germany[c]	1.80	2.90	1.60	1.43	1.51	—
Italy	855.00	1909.00	1198.00	1629.00	1543.00	+ 12.0%
Japan	226.00	238.00	145.00	94.00	109.00	− 50.0%
Korea	607.00	870.00	708.00	771.00	829.00[b]	NA
Sweden	4.20	8.60	5.90	7.10	6.70	+ 9.7%
UK	0.43	0.77	0.56	0.63	0.64	+ 23.0%
USA	1.00	1.00	1.00	1.00	1.00	+ 5.9%
(Switzerland)	1.68	2.45	1.39	1.18	1.24	− 23%

Notes: a   Former West Germany (FRG) is the reference country purchasing power is being compared with.

   b   October 1996.

   c   Former West Germany only.

   —   As other countries are being compared with West Germany, no percentage wage adjustment is required.

   NA   Not available.

Sources: US BLS (1991) for columns 1–3; OECDh (February 1997) for columns 4–5; IMF (1996:89), using German data for column 6; The Bank of Korea; IMF, *International Financial Statistics*, selected years.

public provision of non-traded (free) *services*. So the rankings change dramatically depending on whether nominal exchange rates or PPPs are used. For example, Sweden and the USA rank equally under the former measure; however, Sweden's ranking drops substantially under the latter.

Exchange rates and purchasing power parities

Official annual average market exchange rates are summarised in Table A.8. Unlike the other tables, this one also includes Switzerland for reference, as Swiss francs are sometimes used as a basis for international comparisons. Note how exchange rates fluctuate considerably, even when averaged over a whole year. On a daily basis these rates are much more volatile. There has been greater stability among those countries that have joined the European Exchange Rate Mechanism (ERM), though it has suffered periods of considerable strain—in 1992 intense speculation on the pound caused the UK to withdraw from the ERM.

PPPs may differ significantly from the official exchange rates, as noted above. Table A.8, column 6, shows the percentage adjustment of the official exchange rate for comparisons of *pay* based on purchasing power. This column indicates whether the cost of living in the country concerned is higher (a negative figure) or lower (a positive figure) compared with Germany. This adjustment is based on an analysis of differing national consumption patterns conducted by the German Federal Statistics Office. The analysis embraces some 350 goods and services, but reflects merely consumer expenditure, excluding direct taxation and employees' contributions to social insurance (IMF 1996:88).

Hourly labour (remuneration/compensation) costs

Hourly labour costs vary a great deal between countries. Table A.9 presents an index of the relative costs per hour of production work in manufacturing, compared with those in the USA. These compensation costs include pay for time worked; other direct pay; levies for insurance, pension, contractual and other benefits; and for some countries, labour taxes. The index implies that, in comparison with the USA, these total costs were significantly lower, in 1995, in the UK, Australia and Korea. Marked contrasts in pay levels between countries can be inferred from Tables A.9 and A.10. Such comparisons should be undertaken with caution due to the vagaries of nominal exchange rates. For

Table A.9   Hourly labour costs[a]

| | Hourly labour costs (index USA = 100) | | | | |
	1975	1980	1985	1990	1995
Australia	88	86	63	88	84
Canada	94	88	84	106	93
France	71	91	58	102	112
Germany[b]	100	125	74	147	185
Italy	73	83	59	119	96
Japan	47	56	49	86	138
Korea	5	10	9	25	43
Sweden	113	127	74	140	124
UK	53	77	48	85	80
USA	100	100	100	100	100

Notes: a   These data relate to production workers in manufacturing. Costs are converted from national currency to $US at prevailing annual average exchange rates, as in Table A.8.

   b   Former West Germany only.

Source: US BLS (1996a).

Table A.10   Changes in labour costs in the business sector[a]

	Compensation (remuneration) per employee (annual % change)			Unit labour costs[d] (annual % change)		
	1984–94	1995	1996	1984–94	1995	1996
Australia	5.0	2.7	5.7	3.8	3.3	2.7
Canada	4.2	1.0	3.7	3.2	0.6	3.6
France	4.2	2.8	2.8	1.8	1.3	0.8
Germany	4.3[b]	3.2	2.4	1.9[b]	0.9	−0.3
Italy	7.3	5.9	4.9	4.7	2.0	4.3
Japan	2.8	1.3	0.9	0.4	0.1	−2.4
Korea	12.6	10.2	12.3	6.6	3.4	7.0
Sweden	7.4	2.8	7.0	5.1	0.9	5.0
UK	6.8	3.1	3.4	4.9	1.9	1.8
USA	4.0	2.7	3.5	3.2	3.1	2.9
EU	5.8	3.4	3.5	3.5	1.4	1.8
Total OECD[c]	4.7	2.8	3.3	2.9	1.9	1.7

Notes: a Aggregates are computed on the basis of 1991 GDP weights expressed in 1991 purchasing power parities.
   b Average growth rate has been calculated by chaining on data for the whole of Germany to the corresponding data for West Germany prior to 1992.
   c Excluding high inflation countries (i.e. annual inflation of 10% or more).
   NA Not available.
Sources: OECDa.

example, it might be inferred that Japanese wages were lower than those in the USA in 1990, but higher in 1995. But this apparent change of relativities is largely an exchange rate phenomenon which reflects the rapid rise of the yen (*endaka*) in the early 1990s, rather than an enormous increase in Japanese wages since 1990.

Hourly labour costs can be divided into two broad components: pay for time worked; and all the other above-mentioned costs. In most countries, these other compensation costs have increased more rapidly over the long term than has pay for time worked, though such increases have tended to level out during the last decade. There was an exception to the long-term trend in Italy, where social insurance rates were partially subsidised in 1977. Although Korea is the only NIE cited in Table A.9, in the NIEs of Hong Kong, Singapore and Taiwan compensation cost levels in 1995 ranged between 30 and 40 per cent of US levels (US BLS 1996a).

Table A.11   Output and labour productivity levels

	GDP per person engaged (OECD = 100)	GDP per hour worked (OECD = 100)
Australia	94	90
Canada	103	97
France	114	118
Germany	105	109
Italy	121	130
Japan	92	80
Korea	NA	NA
Sweden	89	90
UK	92	97
USA	123	122

Note: NA   Not available.

Sources: Pilat (1996) based on OECD National Accounts; OECD Analytical Database; and OECDa using 1994 data.

Changes in labour costs

Changes in labour costs are particularly significant in labour-intensive industries. But compensation per employee (Table A.10, columns 1–3) is less significant than *unit labour costs* (columns 4–6). *Unit labour costs* reflect changes in productivity as well as hourly labour costs. Table A.10 summarises some comparative unit labour cost data on a US dollar basis. It shows that unit labour costs rose most in Korea and least in Japan during the 1984–94 period, with a decrease in Japanese unit labour costs in 1996. Korea also had the highest growth in wages and unit labour costs in 1996.

Increases in labour costs tend to be associated with low or falling rates of unemployment. This is one basis for economic forecasting on such issues conducted by international organisations. While unemployment remained high across many of the OECD countries during the late 1990s, the underlying conditions for growth, such as low inflation and low interest rates, were seen as favourable. Economic activity was, therefore, forecast to rise with an improvement in domestic demand. As illustrated in Table A.10, employees in all the listed countries received a rise in remuneration in 1996.

The OECD expected moderate increases in employment growth in the late 1990s, to be accompanied by increases in labour productivity across the OECD, but anticipated that large differences in unemployment rates would remain between countries (OECDa 1996).

Output

Output can be measured in terms of GDP per employed person and GDP per hour worked. Although these measures relate output to the number of people employed and the number of hours worked, they do not measure the specific contribution of labour as a single factor of production. Rather, they reflect a range of other influences, including the use of new technologies, capital investment, capacity utilisation, energy efficiency, and the skills and efforts of managers as well as workers. Like many of the other indicators, this one is only an approximation, because the type, quantity and quality of the output vary greatly from one country to another, and between industries and firms (Smith et al. 1982). While countries may be highly productive in one sector, they may be comparatively inefficient in another (see Pilat 1996).

The first column in Table A.11 shows that variations in productivity (GDP per person engaged) are quite large, being highest in the USA and lowest in Sweden. However, the second column, which adjusts the figures in terms of GDP per hour worked, changes some of these cross-country comparisons. Those countries that work comparatively fewer annual hours, such as France and Germany, record higher rates for GDP per hour worked compared with GDP per person engaged. The rate for Japan, where annual hours of work are comparatively long (see Table A.14), drops quite substantially when considered in terms of GDP per hour worked.

Purchasing power

Comparative purchasing power calculations provide a way of overcoming some of the problems in comparing living standards. Such calculations aim to evaluate the relative purchasing power of workers' pay in different countries, as discussed with reference to GDP per capita at purchasing power parities (see Tables A.7 and A.8).

The International Metalworkers' Federation (IMF) publishes surveys of metalworkers' purchasing power, based on average hourly net wages (i.e. after deduction of workers' social security contributions), expressed in working time required for the purchase of selected consumer items. In an attempt to obtain comparable data, the price levels used are for medium-quality goods in a major industrial town. One of the IMF's objectives in undertaking a regular international comparison of net earnings is to determine approximate differences in standards of living between workers performing the same quantity and quality of work. These differences result from gaps in the purchasing power of their incomes: 'Using the method of purchasing power parities, therefore, makes it possible to obtain a comparison of earnings which

Table A.12   The purchasing power of working time

	Bread (per kg)	Coffee (per kg)		Men's shoes (per pair)		1 litre petrol (Super)	Rent 4 rooms[a]		Colour TV (50 cm screen)		Income tax[b] (annual)		Net earning (hour in 199.
	mins	hrs	mins	hrs	mins	mins	hrs	mins	hrs	mins	hrs	mins	$US
Australia	6.5	2	11.0	4	10.0	2.5	26	47.5	22	34.0	265	30.5	12.5
Canada[c]	6.5	—	47.5	3	4.5	1.5	28	32.0	14	16.0	481	3.0	16.7
France[c]	11.5	—	25.0	9	59.0	6.0	59	43.5	51	11.5	119[d]	26.5[d]	10.1
Germany[f]	5.0	—	20.0	2	38.0	2.0	15	25.5	35	—	135	42.0	27.0
Italy	10.0	—	42.5	4	56.0	5.5	54	46.0	43	49.0	260	35.5	13.8
Japan	12.5	4	1.5	6	—	4.5	78	41.5	32	48.5	82	23.5	18.3
Korea	18.0	4	15.5	10	8.0	7.5	69	46.0[e]	101	20.0	95	11.5	6.1
Sweden	12.0	—	34.5	4	12.5	4.5	52	17.5	72	34.0	974	29.5	12.6
UK	6.0	—	55.0	3	3.0	5.5	91	26.5	38	6.0	345	16.5	10.0
USA	3.5	—	36.5	4	56.5	1.0	54	56.5	16	29.0	122	24.0	18.2

Notes: a   Four rooms including kitchen.
　　　　 b   Metalworkers' family of four with one income.
　　　　 c   1994 data.
　　　　 d   Unmarried metalworker.
　　　　 e   Three rooms including kitchen.
　　　　 f   Former West Germany only.
Source: IMF (1996) using 1995 data.

is closer to reality than does a simple comparison based on official rates of exchange' (IMF 1996:88).

Table A.12 presents such an analysis for the automobile industry. This table is reproduced to illustrate a different approach. We do not necessarily endorse the IMF data as reliable, for these calculations are particularly difficult. As such, they do not always accurately reflect reality even though most of the data are derived from the German Federal Statistics Office. This office aims to take into account the cost of living and the different patterns of consumption in the various countries. Nevertheless, these data show that there are wide differences in the cost of living, earnings and tax between countries.

Consumer prices

Cost of living increases are a major influence on pay settlements, union growth and other aspects of human resources management (HRM) and industrial relations. In the USA, income tax brackets are indexed to the

Table A.13   Consumer prices[a]

	% average annual increase		% average annual change			CPI index 1996[b]
	1975–84	1984–93	1994	1995	1996	1990 = 100
Australia	9.7	5.8	1.9	4.6	2.6	117
Canada	8.5	3.9	0.2	2.2	1.6	115
France	10.5	3.2	1.7	1.7	2.0	114
Germany	4.2[c]	2.4[c]	2.7	1.8	1.5	121
Italy	16.2	5.9	3.9	5.4	3.8	133
Japan	5.0	1.7	0.7	–0.1	0.1	107
Korea	NA	5.9	6.2	NA	5.0	143
Sweden	10.0	6.2	2.4	2.9	0.8	122
UK	11.2	5.2	2.5	3.4	2.4	122
USA	7.6	3.7	2.6	2.8	2.9	121

Notes: a Percentage changes from previous period, not seasonally adjusted.
         b December 1996.
         c Former West Germany only.
         NA Not available.
Sources: OECD *Press Release*, SG/COM/NEWS(97)31 (16 April1997); OECD *Hot File*, *Key Economic Indicators* (1997); OECDd; Korean NSO.

consumer price index (CPI), making it an important determinant of take-home pay. Table A.13 shows that Italy, France, Sweden and the UK all experienced 'double digit' rates of increase in their cost of living, CPI, in the 1975–84 period. By contrast, the rate was 5 per cent and below in Japan and Germany. In all the countries for which data are available, the inflation rate was less during the 1984–93 period than in the preceding decade. Inflation remained low during the mid-1990s with some countries still experiencing recessionary influences. The 1996 index (column 6) shows that during the first half of the 1990s, Korea experienced the highest rate of inflation of the ten countries, while Japan recorded the lowest rate.

Hours of work

Hours of work are also difficult to compare between countries because the data are not consistent, but generally include part-time workers. In brief, some countries collect data on average hours *actually worked*, while others collect data on average *hours paid for*. Hours actually worked include normal hours of work, overtime, stand-by hours at place of work, and short rest periods at the workplace including tea or coffee breaks. Hours paid for comprise hours actually worked and, depending on national practices, may also include factors such as paid annual leave, paid public holidays, paid sick leave, meal breaks and time spent on travel from home to work and vice versa. These broad differences are indicated by the summary notes against each country in Table A.14. Apart from the USA, in most countries in the post-1945 period there has been a general reduction in the number of hours worked per year. The reduction largely reflects an increase in holiday entitlements, as well as a fall in the length of the basic working week.

Table A.14 illustrates, nevertheless, that the general long-term trend towards a reduction in the average working week in manufacturing was not sustained in all countries during the 1985–95 period; however, this may not necessarily reflect the trends in other sectors. There were increases in hours per week during the decade in Australia and the USA, while for many other countries the rate remained fairly stable. Significant falls occurred in Korea, Japan and Germany. One explanation as to why labour hours are no longer falling in many countries is that, for men, the trend towards a reduction in formal hours worked may be being counteracted by an increase in overtime. The average hours for women have decreased in some countries, but increased in Australia and Sweden. The difference between hours of paid work for men and women remains marked in most countries for which a gender breakdown is available, and increased during the 1985–95 period in Australia and Japan.

In 1995, among the countries for which we have reasonably comparable data relating to manufacturing industry (total), the Swedish and Japanese appeared to work on average the least hours *per week*, while the Koreans, Americans and British appeared to work the most. However, if we look at the annual hours worked, Japan ranks third after Korea and the USA. This paradox can be explained through the Japanese having comparatively few holidays and by the propensity of Japanese workers to forgo part of their holiday entitlement (column 7). Relatively long annual hours in the USA are due mainly to annual leave entitlements which are nearly three weeks shorter than the European average, combined with a relatively low level of absence from work (ILO 1987:29). This illustrates that it is often more appropriate to compare working hours on an annual, rather than on a weekly, basis.

On an annual basis, we can infer from Table A.14 (column 9) that Korean, Japanese, American and Australian industrial employees are contracted to work significantly longer than their counterparts in Europe. For example, in the late 1980s, based on a notional 40-hour week, Japanese workers had contractual hours that represented the equivalent of an additional 11.5 weeks per year compared with those in Germany (Blyton 1989:134). However, the hours for Japanese workers, which traditionally have been among the highest in the OECD, appear to have been falling.

Table A.14   Hours of work

	Men[d]		Women[d]		Total[d]			Annual hours of work[e]	
	1985	1995	1985	1995	1985	1995	Holidays[g]	1985	1995
Australia[a]	38.4	40.8[n]	32.7	33.1[n]	36.9	38.7[n]	31[h]	1852[j,l]	1876[j]
Canada[b]	NA	NA	NA	NA	38.6	38.5	NA	1746[j]	1737[j]
France[a]	NA	NA	NA	NA	38.6	38.7[d]	35	1541[k]	1520[k]
Germany[b,c]	41.1	38.6	39.5	37.2	40.7	38.3	42	1639[k]	1499[k]
Italy	NA	NA	NA	NA	NA	NA	39[j]	1736[j]	1682[k]
Japan[a]	42.9	39.3	38.4	34.7	41.5	37.8	22	2083[j,m]	1898[j,d]
Korea[a]	53.5	49.5	54.2	48.6	53.8	49.2	NA	2339[f]	2166[f]
Sweden	39.9	39.0[n]	33.5	34.0[n]	38.3	37.8[n]	36	1459[j]	1544[j]
UK[b]	44.6	43.0	40.0	39.3	43.7	42.1	35	1719[j]	1735[j]
USA	NA	NA	NA	NA	40.5	41.6	22	1760[k]	1953[k]

Notes: a   Hours actually worked.
  b   Hours paid for.
  c   Former West Germany only.
  d   Manufacturing.
  e   Total number of hours worked over the year divided by the average number of people in employment; all sectors; includes part-time employment.
  f   Estimated from *Monthly Labor Survey.*
  g   Annual leave, extra holidays (averages) and public holidays.
  h   *Workplace: The ACTU magazine,* Summer, 1992, p. 29.
  i   Includes average reduction of working time by 100 hours.
  j   Total employment.
  k   Dependant employment.
  l   1983.
  m   1986.
  n   1994.
  NA Not available.
Sources: ILOa; OECDa; Korea *Monthly Labor Survey* (various issues); Blyton (1989).

Like absence from work, overtime varies considerably among countries, industries and occupations. In the mid-1980s, levels of overtime in manufacturing included 2.9 per cent of hours worked in Sweden, 3.3 per cent in Italy, 4.1 per cent in Germany, 7 to 8 per cent in Japan, 8 per cent in the USA, 8.8 per cent in the UK and 16 per cent in Korea.

Besides the weekly or annual basis, hours of work can also be measured on a lifetime basis. The typical age of entry into the labour force varies. Also, there are considerable international differences in periods of withdrawal from employment in the formal labour market. Furthermore, normal retirement ages vary between 55 and 65 in the ten countries. However, more people are retiring earlier, especially those who experience ill health. Also, on average, women still retire earlier than men. Early retirement tends to be more prevalent in economic recessions. A trend in Australia and Europe is towards a lower retirement age, a trend associated with relatively high levels of unemployment. By contrast, in Japan, there is a trend towards the retirement age moving up from 55 to 60; in the USA, the formal retirement age has been abolished. In most countries there is a move towards a more flexible retirement age.

Women's earnings

The objective of equal pay for women is included in the ILO constitution adopted in 1919 and 1946, and its 1951 Equal Remuneration Convention (no.100), which has been ratified by well over 100 member countries. The notion of equal pay is also endorsed by many other national and international authorities, including the EU's Treaty of Rome. Nevertheless, women's earnings remain significantly below those of men. Table A.15 shows the substantial gap between the earnings of men and women in manufacturing, despite a widespread narrowing of the gap since 1970. As Table A.15 shows, this narrowing was most marked during the 1970s, particularly in Australia, Sweden and the UK, with improvements occurring more recently in the USA and Canada. Japan has been an exception to the trend. Table A.15 also highlights considerable cross-national variation in pay equity. For all years presented, the gap is narrowest in Sweden and widest in Japan. While many factors contribute to the variation, recent analyses have emphasised the importance of institutional factors such as the centralisation of wage bargaining in aiding our understanding of cross-national differences (Whitehouse 1992).

Table A.15 presents *hourly* earnings for most of the countries, apart from Canada, the USA and Japan, so the fact that women on average work fewer hours than men does not contribute directly to the earnings gap identified. The differences shown do, however, reflect factors such as the likelihood that more men will engage in paid overtime and receive bonuses. This is particularly relevant in Japan, where twice-yearly bonuses make up a large proportion of a worker's pay. Furthermore, a major cause of the earnings gap is thought to be the segregation of women into low-status jobs within industries and occupations. This segregation is often explained as a consequence of women still shouldering most of the home-making responsibilities, which means they are more likely than men to have broken career patterns. But processes within the labour market also contribute to the persistence of this pattern (see Walby 1988).

While Table A.15 shows Japanese women workers receiving less than half the earnings of male workers, these figures are calculated on

Table A.15 Women's earnings

	Women's earnings as a % of men's (hourly earnings in manufacturing)					
	1970	1975	1980	1985	1990	1995
Australia	64	79	79	79	82[e]	81[d]
Canada[f]	60	60	64	65	68	70[d]
France	77[a]	76	77	79	79	79[c]
Germany[j]	70	72	73	73	73	74
Italy	NA	NA	NA	NA	NA	NA
Japan[g]	45	48	44	42	41	44[b](56)[h]
Korea	NA	NA	NA	47	50	54
Sweden	80	85	90	90	89	90
UK	58	67	69	68	68	71
USA[f]	62	62	63	68	72	75[i]

Notes:
a 1971.
b 1992.
c 1993.
d 1994.
e Series break in 1990.
f Data for most countries are based on hourly earnings in manufacturing. However, data for Canada refer to average annual earnings for full-time, full-year workers; data for USA refer to median weekly earnings for full-time wages and salary workers. These data are, therefore, not directly comparable with each other, or with figures from the other countries.
g Data for Japan are based on monthly, rather than hourly, earnings in manufacturing. Some differences will be apparent from figures used in earlier editions of this book for which OECD manipulation of Japan's monthly figures into approximate hourly data had been used (see OECDa 1988). These were only available up to 1986, however—hence all figures for Japan are now based on ILO monthly figures.
h 1995 figures based on new series begun in 1994 that includes only establishments with ten or more regular employees and regular cash earnings.
i 1995 figure uses BLS data using same definitions as earlier US Department of Commerce data (as explained in note f).
j Former West Germany only.
NA Not available.

Sources: ILOa; Statistics Canada, Catalogue 13–217; US Department of Commerce; US BLS (1997).

average monthly earnings, without taking into account the number of hours worked. As a large number of women in Japanese manufacturing industries work part-time, counting only the number of workers without considering the number of hours worked has helped contribute to the comparatively low figure for Japanese women (ILO 1995:27). However, previous studies and surveys (e.g. OECDa 1988) suggest that the hourly earnings gap between Japanese men and women is quite large.

Segregation and unemployment of women

The segregation of men and women into different occupations and industries is difficult to measure for the purposes of cross-national comparison. Differences in occupation and industry classification schemes, as well as work organisation practices, hinder effective comparison. Furthermore, there has been extensive debate over the indices used to measure segregation (see Blackburn et al. 1993, and the ensuing debates in *Work, Employment, and Society*; also Rubery et al. 1996:99ff). For example, the most frequently used measure, the dissimilarity index, has been criticised as an indicator of change over time as it may be affected by changes in occupational structure as well as by changes in the proportion of men and women in particular areas of employment. Nevertheless, studies utilising a range of indices suggest that in many countries there has been little change in the degree of occupational segregation over recent decades (see OECDa 1988:209; Rubery et al. 1996:103). Hence, increased participation of women in the labour force does not appear to be associated with a trend towards convergence in the employment distributions of men and women.

Levels of occupational segregation appear to differ consistently between countries. Among the countries covered in this book, Japan and Italy have tended to record comparatively low levels of occupational segregation, while levels in Australia have been comparatively high (OECDa 1988:209). However, these differences need to be interpreted with caution as they may reflect different occupational structures, and they give no indication of the degree of vertical segregation *within* occupations—that is, the extent to which high-status jobs in an occupation may be occupied primarily by men or women. In Japan, for example, few women are recruited into management, and low participation rates of married women indicate that short working careers are common (OECDa 1988:214).

Table A.16 shows that there are considerable variations among countries when comparing unemployment rates between women and men. In 1996 in Italy unemployment among women was nearly twice that among men; however, in the UK unemployment among men was considerably higher than among women. Studies (e.g. ILO 1995) suggest these data understate the real number of unemployed women, because more women than men are generally 'discouraged' from 'active search for work' or from registering as unemployed. Also, much female unemployment is 'hidden' in part-time working. Although some women choose to work part-time, many part-timers would prefer to work full-time. One study found that, in the USA, there was a total of at least 6.5 million non-agricultural workers involuntarily on part-time schedules (ILO 1985:216; see also Table A.3).

While unemployment rates for women in previous decades have

Table A.16   Unemployment by gender

	Women: unemployment rate (%)		Men: unemployment rate (%)	
	1986	1996	1986	1996
Australia	8.6	8.3	7.6	8.7
Canada	9.8	9.4	9.2	9.8
France	13.1	14.8[a]	8.4	10.7[a]
Germany	9.0	10.2[b]	6.8	8.1[b]
Italy	17.6	16.7	7.3	9.3
Japan	2.8	3.4	2.7	3.3
Korea	2.1	1.7[a]	4.9	2.3[a]
Sweden	2.7	7.5	2.7	8.5
UK	8.9	6.8[a]	13.5	10.0[a]
USA	7.1	5.6	6.8	5.5

Notes: a   1995.
            b   Data after 1990 are for united Germany.
Sources: OECDc, e.

been higher than those for men in many countries (one exception being the UK, where there have been definitional changes that may have excluded more women from being counted as unemployed), the figures in Table A.16 suggest this situation is changing in some countries. Two processes may have contributed to such a trend: the impact of recession, which has resulted in many women withdrawing from the labour market altogether; and structural changes, which have led to greater job losses occurring in traditional areas of male employment, particularly heavy industries.

Training

Training, development and skill formation are increasingly recognised as vital issues, not least as sources of competitive advantage. Australia, for instance, has conducted surveys of training expenditure and of how workers get their training. International agencies are increasingly focusing on training issues. Yet, regrettably, systematic international and comparative data are scarce and unreliable (cf. US GAO 1990). This is unfortunate, as debates about product and process flexibility and the impact of training on individuals' pay and labour market careers (see OECDa 1991:141ff) could be advanced through comparative analysis.

   The *output* of competencies and skills is a most important indicator. However, most countries define and measure skills in different ways and training institutions vary greatly between countries. Moreover, most of the available data relate to the training *input*: for example,

Table A.17   Public expenditure on labour market programs as a percentage of GDP

	Adult training		Youth training	
	Training for unemployed adults	Training for employed adults	Measures for unemployed and disadvantaged youth	Support of apprenticeship and related training
	1994–95	1994–95	1994–95	1994–95
Australia	0.16	0.01	0.04	0.03
Canada	0.29[b]	0.03[b]	0.01[b]	–
France	0.43[c]	–	0.06[c]	0.08[c]
Germany	0.38[c]	–	0.05[c]	0.01[c]
Italy	0.02[a]	–	0.28[a]	0.55[a]
Japan	0.03	–	–	–
Korea	–	–	–	–
Sweden	0.75	0.02	–	–
UK	0.12	0.01	0.14	0.13
USA	0.04	–	–	–

Notes: a   1992.
        b   1995–96.
        c   1995.
        –   Nil (or negligible).
Source: OECDa (1996).

expenditure by governments, enterprises or individuals; or time expended by employees (such time may be either on-the-job or off-the-job; pre-employment, during employment or between employment; structured or unstructured). Therefore, the OECD has made a preliminary effort to collect comparative data on training (see Table A.17) which summarise public expenditure on labour market programs.

Table A.17 should be interpreted with caution. As an example, while expenditure in Japan appears low, other sources also infer that Japanese employers conduct much training, both on-the-job and off-the-job (Dore & Sako 1989; JIL 1991:65; Koike 1996). Hence although the publicly funded provision that is measured may be less than in most other countries, the total provision may be more than elsewhere. In Japan, on-the-job training in particular is part of the well-established processes of induction, work organisation, teamworking and supervision.

Public sector

In the post-1945 period, one of the most notable trends was the expansion of the public sector in almost all modern societies. This

Table A.18   Public sector

	Government employment[a] (% of total employment) 1995	Current general government expenditure (% of GDP) 1995	Government final consumption expenditure (% of GDP in 1995)		
			Total	Education	Social security and welfare
Australia	17[d]	36[d]	18[d]	3.7[d]	1.0[d]
Canada	20	47[d]	NA	NA	NA
France	25	51	20[c]	5.2[c]	1.5[c]
Germany	16	47	20[b]	3.7[b]	2.7[b]
Italy	16	50	17[d]	4.5[d]	0.7[d]
Japan	6.0[d]	27[d]	9.6[d]	3.2[d]	0.6[d]
Korea	NA	15[d]	11[d]	2.7d	0.6[d]
Sweden	32	66[d]	28[c]	5.4[c]	6.1[c]
UK	14	42[d]	22[d]	4.5[d]	1.9[d]
USA	14[d]	36[c]	17[c]	NA	NA

Notes: a   Producers of government services, except for Australia, Canada and France which are general government.

b   1992.

c   1993.

d   1994.

NA   Not available.

Source: OECDd.

expansion occurred in numbers employed in the public sector and in levels of public expenditure. Table A.18 shows, however, that there are significant differences between countries. Government employment as a percentage of total employment ranges from 6 per cent in Japan to 32 per cent in Sweden. Large variations are also evident in expenditure levels, with general government expenditure accounting for 15 per cent of GDP in Korea, compared with 66 per cent in Sweden.

Expenditure on social welfare is also highest in Sweden. Table A.18 presents just a part of the picture, however, as it refers only to government expenditure, while in some countries private schemes such as company pension funds and insurance play an important role in welfare. The total government final consumption expenditure included in column 3 of Table A.18 also embraces expenditure on health. This again varies considerably between countries. For instance, the USA does not have a comprehensive public medical care scheme, though it does have schemes for the aged and particular needy groups; Australia reintroduced a universal health insurance scheme in 1984; and the UK has had a National Health Service since the late 1940s.

Cross-national differences in public expenditure on education are not as marked among the countries as differences on other measures

Table A.19   Taxation[a]

| | Total tax receipts as a % of GDP | | Tax structure as a % of total tax receipts | | | | | |
| | | | Personal income tax | | Corporate income tax | | Taxes on goods and services | |
	1985	1994	1985	1994	1985	1994	1985	1994
Australia	30	30	45	40	9.4	14	33	30
Canada	33	36	35	37	8.2	6.6	32	26
France	45	44	13	14	4.5	3.7	30	27
Germany	38[d]	39	29[d]	27	6.1[d]	2.9	26[d]	29
Italy	35	42	27	25	9.2	8.9	25	28
Japan	28	28	25	23	21	15	14	16
Korea	17[b]	20	14[b]	17[c]	11[b]	11[c]	45[b]	37[c]
Sweden	50	51	39	37	3.5	5.4	27	26
UK	38	34	27	28	12.5	8.0	31	35
USA	26	28	38	36	7.5	8.9	19	18

Notes: a   These columns do not add to 100 per cent as miscellaneous taxes and social security contributions by employers and employees are not included.

b   1986.

c   1993.

d   Former West Germany only.

Sources: OECDg; Korean NSO.

reported in Table A.18. Korea spends least, at 2.7 per cent of GDP, and Sweden spends most, at 5.4 per cent of GDP. Once again, the data refer only to government expenditure and do not account for contributions to education and training from private sources.

Public expenditure and taxation

International comparisons in levels of public expenditure reflect different levels of taxation. The relative balance in provision of services between the public and private sectors in areas like health, education, welfare and post-retirement income are relevant factors that affect levels of taxation.

While it is difficult to compare rates of taxation between countries, given the range of means by which taxes are collected, Table A.19 shows that in 1994 total tax receipts as a percentage of GDP varied from 20 per cent in Korea to 51 per cent in Sweden. While the table illustrates that some change has occurred over the period illustrated, Korea, the USA, Australia and Japan have consistently had the lowest levels of tax receipts among the ten countries. While still comparatively low, the level of tax receipts in Korea is steadily rising (see Korea NSO

1997). The contribution of personal income tax to total tax receipts was highest in Australia and lowest in France, while taxes on goods and services were highest in Korea and the UK and lowest in Japan and the USA.

International trade

Exporting, importing and the pattern of world trade do not tend to change dramatically from year to year, but there have been major changes during the post-1945 period. These changes are particularly due to the emergence of the NIEs and the growing importance of the oil trade. For example, when Britain became a substantial oil producer after 1975, oil became an 'import substitute'. The decline in its oil imports tended to mask the increase in its imports of manufactured goods.

In absolute terms, the USA was by far the biggest exporter in 1953, even though Europe had largely recovered from the Second World War. By the 1980s, however, the USA was no longer so dominant. Germany and Japan, in particular, had greatly expanded their exports. Of the top 20 exporting countries in 1953, only 14 were still in the list in 1984. Australia was among the departures. The newcomers were led by Saudi Arabia, Taiwan and South Korea (see *Economist* 18 January 1986:91; see also *Economist* 1991:28). By the late 1990s the USA, Germany and Japan were still the three largest exporters of merchandise goods in the world; however, countries in the Asia–Pacific region had increased their exports dramatically, with Hong Kong, China and Korea ranked ninth, eleventh and twelfth respectively (WTO 1997). Interestingly, those countries that are among the top exporters of merchandise goods are also the world's largest importers. This partly reflects the global division of labour, with multinational enterprises (MNEs) sourcing inputs for manufactured goods from the cheapest sources available (see *Far Eastern Economic Review* 10 October 1996:10).

International trade is proportionately more important in some countries than others. Table A.20 shows that, as a percentage of GDP, of the countries listed, imports and exports are greatest for Sweden and least for the USA and Japan. These differences reflect the small home market in Sweden and the huge ones in the USA and Japan. Nevertheless, international trade is vital for all the ten countries. Exporting and importing of goods and services and overseas investment may be reflected in the traffic of employment and industrial relations policies and practices.

International trade includes commodities, goods and services. Tourism is an increasingly important form of international trade. Column 6 in Table A.20 shows that international tourism was least significant as

Table A.20   International trade and tourism

	International trade in goods and services				International tourism	
	Imports		Exports			
	As a % of GDP (current prices & exchange rate) 1995	Annual average % volume change 1990–95	As a % of GDP (current prices & exchange rate) 1995	Annual average % volume change 1990–95	Expenditure as a % of imports (goods & services)	Expenditure as a % of exports (goods & services)
Australia	21	6.9	20	7.5	6.2	10
Canada	35	7.5	38	9.1	5.2	3.8
France	21	2.5	24	3.9	5.0	7.6
Germany	23	3.8	24	1.0	9.2	2.8
Italy	23	3.4	28	7.6	4.9	9.2
Japan	7.9	3.5	9.4	4.2	9.1	0.7
Korea	25[a]	12[b]	25[a]	13[b]	4.6[a]	4.3[a]
Sweden	35	3.2	41	6.7	6.8	3.7
UK	29	2.7	29	4.6	7.7	6.1
USA	13	9.0	11	7.5	5.1	7.7

Notes: a   1993.

        b   Annual average volume change 1983–93.

Sources: OECD Main Economic Indicators, April 1997; OECDd; Korean NSO.

a source of export income for Japan and Germany, but was comparatively important for Australia, Italy and the USA. In 1993 tourism was Australia's largest source of foreign currency earnings, having overtaken Australia's traditionally dominant exports of such commodities as wool and coal. Therefore, there has been a growing public policy focus on employment relations and other aspects of the Australian tourism industry (Australia Dept of Tourism 1993).

Competitiveness

A recurring theme among governments and business leaders in IMEs has been the need to become more competitive in an increasingly global marketplace. In its *World Competitiveness Yearbook*, the Institute for Management Development (IMD) sees the globalisation of the world economy as causing countries to compete along similar strategies (Garelli et al. 1997). This has had important repercussions for employment relations, as perceived links between employment practices and productivity are often cited as reasons driving industrial relations and human resources change. Evidence for this can be found in the Workplace Relations Act 1997, in Australia, and the controversial industrial

Table A.21   World competitiveness

Country	Score[a] (for 1997)	Rankings				
		1997	1996	1995	1994	1993
Australia	59	18	21	16	16	20
Canada	68	10	12	13	20	17
France	58	19	20	19	13	15
Germany	64	14	10	6	6	5
Italy	35	34	28	29	28	27
Japan	69	9	4	4	3	2
Korea	40	30	27	26	32	28
Sweden	60	16	14	12	9	9
UK	67	11	19	15	14	16
USA	100	1	1	1	1	1

Note: a   Highest score = 100.
Source: Garelli et al. (1997).

relations legislation introduced by the Korean government in 1996. While very different, both pieces of legislation sought to introduce more flexibility into the workplace.

The *World Competitiveness Yearbook* for 1997 released rankings for countries based on the following criteria: domestic economy; internationalisation; government; finance; infrastructure; management; science and technology; and people. The results for the ten countries are shown in Table A.21. While much caution should be exercised in any such attempt to compare countries across such a broad array of data, and while we do not endorse the rankings, they do attract the attention of governments, employers' interests and other prominent groups. Nevertheless it is difficult to see how Canada could really move from twentieth to tenth position in a period of just three years!

The figures imply that countries such as Germany and Japan, which have been world leaders in competitiveness, are slipping down the rankings, while a country such as the UK, which struggled to keep up with other IMEs for much of the post-1945 period, appears to be on the way up.

Union membership

Union membership is a crucial variable for practitioners and students of employment relations. In some countries it can be more appropriate to consider the coverage of collective bargaining agreements or arbitration awards, which can be estimated more accurately. However, it is more usual to consider comparative union membership (density) data, though perhaps there are even more limitations with these than with most other comparative data. Union density is given by the formula:

$$\frac{\text{Actual union menbership}}{\text{Potential union membership}} \times 100$$

The numerator may be based on survey data or on membership figures supplied by the unions themselves. Unions may simply report estimates, as they do not collect precise membership details centrally. Some include unemployed and retired members. For various purposes, moreover, they may wish either to exaggerate or to understate their membership. The numerator also depends on the working definition of a union. Does it include employee associations, as in the USA, staff associations, as in the UK, or professional organisations of doctors and lawyers that may have some union functions? The USA has also seen the growth of 'associate unions', which provide services to their members at reduced prices but are not traditional labour unions (see Stern 1997).

The denominator depends on the definition of potential union membership. This raises many questions. Several countries have more than one series of union density data. For instance, certain series are based on population surveys that may be limited to civilian employment, which excludes the armed forces, but such surveys also tend to show lower density in comparison with those based on union returns. Some series exclude other groups who rarely belong to unions, such as employers, the self-employed, the retired, the unemployed and those employed in agriculture, forestry and fishing in most countries. In Australia in 1996, for instance, according to the series based on union data (ABS 1996a), there was a 40 per cent total union density (though only a 35 per cent density of paid-up 'financial' members); but according to household survey data (ABS 1996b) there was only a 31 per cent total density of employees in their main job (see also Pocock & Wright 1997). While these sources report differing levels of union density, the trend movements over time between these measures have generally been consistent. In some countries, the aggregate union density data can conceal large variations between men and women, and between different occupations and sectors (see Bain & Price 1980; Visser 1990; ABS 1996b).

Bain and Price (1980) is an authoritative source; unfortunately, however, it covers only six of our countries and has little post-1976 data. Walsh (1985) is a good source on our four EU member countries, and for useful discussions the reader should see ILO (1985:5ff) and Chang and Sorrentino (1991). One of the most active researchers in the field has been Visser (see OECDa 1991:98ff; OECDa 1994:184–7). Table A.22 primarily draws on ILO data. This table displays union density in the listed countries over the period 1985–95, and shows that it has remained lowest in France, Korea and

Table A.22   Union membership

	Union density (%)		Union density growth (%)	Rank order of union density[c]	
	1985	1995	1985–95	1985	1995
Australia[d]	46	33	−28	2	4
Canada[e]	35	35	0	6	3
France[d]	15	11	−27	9	10
Germany[e]	36[a]	30	−16	5	5
Italy[d]	42	38	−10	4	2
Japan[d]	29	24	−18	7	7
Korea	12	14	+2	10	9
Sweden[e]	86	83	−2	1	1
UK[d]	45	29	−35	3	6
USA[f]	18	15[b]	−12	8	8

Notes: a   1991.
           b   1993.
           c   Rank order of union density of the ten countries listed.
           d   Replies by governments.
           e   Replies by workers' organisations.
           f   Adjusted density rate.
Sources: ILO unpublished data (1996); Australia ABS Cat. No. 6325.0; Korean NSO.

the USA, and highest in Sweden. During the 1985–95 period there were significant declines in union density in many of the countries, with the UK registering the most severe decline. The rank order of the ten countries remained reasonably consistent over the decade. Explanations for the diminution of union density usually refer, in part, to sectoral changes in employment away from traditionally highly unionised areas, though other factors are also important. Some authors (e.g. Bain & Elsheik 1976) explain the rise and fall of union membership in terms of the business cycle. However, widespread decline or stagnation in union density since the 1970s raises serious questions about such earlier explanations. Peetz (forthcoming) places great emphasis on institutional changes such as the strategies of employers and unions towards governments (see also Price & Bain 1989). Some researchers also focus on patterns of centralisation or decentralisation in wage fixing and union organisation (see Blanchflower & Freeman 1992; Western 1993). For an explanation of union density in Britain, derived from the theory of social selection, which draws from 'Marxian' and 'industrial relations' schools, see Runciman (1991:697–712).

Industrial stoppages

Industrial stoppages include strikes and lockouts. What is the relative incidence of industrial stoppages ('dispute-proneness') in the listed

Table A.23   Labour disputes: comparisons of coverage and methodology

	Minimum criteria for inclusion in statistics	Are political stoppages included?	Indirectly affected workers included?	Sources and notes
Australia	Ten or more workdays not worked.	Yes	Yes	Bureau of Statistics surveys firms identified through press reports and contacts with the IR parties and government departments.
Canada	At least half-a-day in duration plus at least ten workdays not worked.	Yes	No	Manpower Centres, provincial Labour Departments, conciliation services and press.
France	At least one workday not worked; however, agriculture and public sector excluded.	Yes	Yes	Labour inspectors.
Germany	More than ten workers involved and of at least one day in duration or more than 100 workdays lost.	Yes	No	Compulsory notification by employers to local employment offices.
Italy	No restrictions on size.	Yes	No	No information.
Korea	NA	NA	NA	NA
Japan	No restrictions on size, excluding unofficial reports.	Yes	No	Legal requirement to report to Labour Relations Commission.
Sweden	At least one workday not worked.	Yes	No	Information gathered following press reports.
UK	Ten workers involved and one day in duration unless 100 or more workdays are lost.	No	Yes	Employment Service Jobcentres make reports for Office of National Statistics which also checks press, unions and large employers.
USA	More than one day or one shift in duration and more than 1000 workers involved.	No	Yes	Reports from press, employers, unions and agencies.

Note: NA   Not available.
Source: Sweeney & Davies (1997), using ILO data.

countries? Given that studying industrial stoppages is so central to the field, we offer more comment on these data than in the earlier sections. We should be particularly cautious about making international comparisons, however, in view of the many idiosyncracies in national definitional distinctions, which are not adopted consistently across any two of the countries, let alone across all of them (see Table A.23; also Fisher 1973; Sweeney & Davies 1997).

Canada, Germany, Italy, Japan and Sweden, for example, do not take into account the working days 'lost' by workers not directly involved in the dispute. In some countries, such as the UK and the USA, a distinction is made between stoppages about 'industrial' issues and those that arise over 'political' or 'non-industrial' matters. When attempting to make comparisons, such distinctions constitute more traps for the unwary. Before 1975, Italy did not count days lost due to political strikes, while France excludes certain industries from its statistics. Australia, on the other hand, includes stoppages that may last for only a few hours, as long as a total of ten working days are lost. Thus Australia counts stoppages that would not be counted either in the UK or the USA. For such reasons, Shalev (1978) cautions against 'lies, damned lies and strike statistics'. Moreover, in 1981, the USA increased the minimum size threshold for inclusion in its strike statistics to at least a full shift and from five workers to 1000. In 1987, Canada followed suit in an attempt to counter the criticism that it was more strike-prone than the USA. Hence international comparisons became even more difficult (Edwards 1983:392). However, Canada subsequently resumed the publication of data on the pre-1987 basis (ten working days lost) and we have used this threshold in Table A.24. Nevertheless such distinctions make it very difficult to compare the patterns of work stoppages between countries (see ch. 12).

Work stoppages are only one form of sanction, of course. There are many others, including working to rule, working without enthusiasm and bans on working overtime, but there are no comparative data available on such forms of collective sanction. Nor are there comparable data available on the many forms of individual sanction such as apathy, industrial sabotage and quitting.

There are various indicators of dispute-proneness, including the number of working days lost in stoppages per 1000 employees (which are reflected in Figure A.1), number of stoppages per 100 000 employees, number of workers involved per 1000 employees, and the average stoppage duration (Creigh et al. 1982). However, these indicators are not standardised. While the above indicators can be calculated across all sectors, the production and construction industries tend to account for a large proportion of the working days lost in many countries. Furthermore, stoppages in these industries may have a particularly serious impact on an economy. Therefore the ILO also has a series of

Figure A.1   Working days lost per 1000 employees[a] in all industries and services[b]

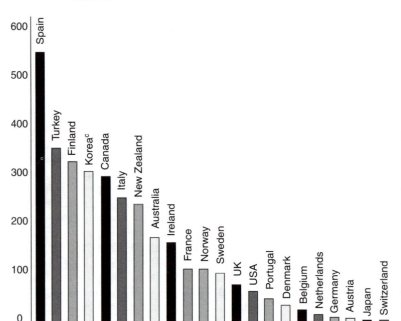

Notes: a   Employees in employment; some figures have been estimated.
          b   Annual averages 1986–95.
          c   Annual averages for Korea are for 1985–94.

Sources: Sweeney & Davies (1997) using ILO, Statistical Office of the European Communities (SOEC) and OECD data; Korea Labor Institute (1995).

international comparisons based on these sectors which reduce the effect of national differences in industrial structure. The number of working days lost in stoppages per 1000 employees in these sectors are a useful international measure of dispute-proneness, and probably the best of a rather dubious bunch of strike activity measures. Therefore they are illustrated in Table A.24.

There are trends in some IMEs towards increasing militancy in other sectors, for instance banking, education and health. In certain cases these have become relatively more prominent in terms of their propensity for industrial action. Also, in most IMEs the service sector has become increasingly important for employment, therefore labour disputes in this sector are shown in Table A.25. It is worth comparing these tables with Figure A.1, which includes an overview of industrial disputes across all industries and services.

Table A.24   Working days not worked per 1000 employees:[a] selected industries[b]

	1986	1987	1988	1989	1990	1991	1992	1993	1994	1995	Average[c] 1986 –90	1991 –95	1986 –95
Australia	674	601	732	415	594	756	313	243	216	NA	602	(383)	(509)
Canada	NA	NA	NA	548	1378	264	464	244	260	325	(956)	311	(511)
France	74	67	134	114	46	56	46	62	77	NA	87	(49)	(68)
Germany[d]	2	3	4	6	11	10	30	41	12	19	5	22	15
Italy	368	441	263	288	630	310	281	356	278	NA	398	(306)	(358)
Japan	8	6	4	3	2	2	2	2	2	NA	5	(2)	(3)
Korea	NA	NA	NA	NA	NA	NA	NA	NA	NA	NA	NA	NA	NA
Sweden	3	11	949	40	8	14	0	183	29	14	201	46	122
UK	195	133	297	149	189	47	25	27	13	15	193	26	117
USA	269	108	96	138	28	60	74	112	109	185	127	109	118
OECD	206	186	211	188	266	151	117	108	91	185	212	127	169

Notes: a   Employees in employment; some figures have been estimated.
b   Production and construction industries.
c   Annual averages for those years within each period for which data are available, weighted for employment.
d   From 1993 data cover united Germany; earlier data represented West Germany only.
( )   Brackets indicate averages based on incomplete data.
NA   Not available.

Source: Sweeney & Davies (1997) using ILO, Statistical Office of the European Communities (SOEC) and OECD data.

There appear to be large differences in dispute-proneness between countries. Shalev (1980) considers three types of explanation for such differences: institutional; infrastructural; and political.[4]

Institutional explanations

Institutional explanations focus on the structure of union movements and bargaining machinery, as well as on links between unions and political parties. Ross and Hartman's classic study, for example, argued that 'the existence of a labour party with close trade union affiliations is perhaps the greatest deterrent to the use of the strike' (1960:68). They also argued on the basis of 1900–56 data that the use of strikes was 'withering away'. Both arguments have subsequently been refuted. Australia and the UK have labour parties and have in the past been comparatively dispute-prone. While there has been a reduction in strikes in both countries over the past decade, strikes have hardly withered away.

    In an attempt to explain why the USA once appeared to be more dispute-prone than five other countries, Clegg (1976) uses three explanatory

Table A.25 Working days not worked per 1000 employees:[a] service industries

	1986	1987	1988	1989	1990	1991	1992	1993	1994	1995	Average[b] 1986 –90	1991 –95	1986 –95
Australia	77	81	95	104	80	96	99	55	34	NA	88	(71)	(80)
Canada	196	256	372	220	96	202	97	99	100	70	225	113	166
France	98	78	85	203	63	30	23	41	24	NA	105	(24)	(62)
Germany[c]	0	0	0	3	17	1	61	3	4	1	4	14	10
Italy	422	239	177	315	174	101	112	149	208	NA	264	(142)	(208)
Japan	4	5	4	6	4	2	6	2	2	NA	4	(3)	(4)
Korea	NA	NA	NA	NA	NA	NA	NA	NA	NA	NA	NA	NA	NA
Sweden	254	1	2	143	275	2	10	9	10	244	135	53	95
UK	46	181	116	199	44	30	24	32	13	20	117	24	69
USA	68	21	21	152	62	38	25	12	24	6	65	21	43
OECD	94	138	82	161	136	61	46	29	29	25	123	38	80

Notes: a Employees in employment; some figures have been estimated.
  b Annual averages for those years within each period for which data are available, weighted for employment.
  c From 1993 data cover united Germany; earlier data represented West Germany only.
  ( ) Brackets indicate averages based on incomplete data.
  NA Not available.
Source: Sweeney & Davies (1997) using ILO, Statistical Office of the European Communities (SOEC) and OECD data.

variables: the level of bargaining; the presence of disputes procedures; and the indirect effect of the level of bargaining through factional bargaining. He argues that the American-style decentralised (plant) bargaining structure promotes factionalism within the unions and hence recourse to unofficial strikes for internal political reasons. Moreover, American unions can call official strikes at particular plants at far less cost to themselves, in contrast with unions in countries that generally engage in industry- or regional-level bargaining.

However, 'collective bargaining arrangements are reflections of the distribution of power and the outcomes of conflicts between labour movements (unions and parties), employers and the state at the time these arrangements came into being' (Shalev 1980:29). Shalev admits that such institutions may subsequently acquire a degree of 'functional autonomy'. Nonetheless, they are no more than intervening variables in comparative theories.

Infrastructural explanations

The focus on the economic infrastructure in some Marxist theories attempts to move beyond an institutional framework. For instance,

Ingham (1974), in his comparative study of strikes in Sweden and Britain, seeks explanations in the influence of industrial concentration, technological complexity and product differentiation on the development of industrial relations systems. He concentrates on how these infrastructural factors influence the structure and strategies of employer organisations, and argues that in Sweden the powerful and cohesive employers' confederation negotiated centralised regulatory procedures with a similarly potent union confederation. This provided a means of settling disputes and a way of exerting control on both sides of industry.

Ingham's analysis, however, attributes too much importance to the employers in the formation of industrial relations institutions. It is more realistic 'to conceive of the development of worker and employer organisations dialectically, that is, as an ongoing process of challenge and response' (Shalev 1980:30). Also, examination of infrastructure alone cannot adequately explain differences in strike propensity between a wider range of countries, nor does it explain the dramatic change in the pattern of Swedish industrial disputes in the late 1930s.

Political explanations

Another school of thought, associated with notions of 'corporatism', offers an explanation in terms of political exchange. Thus in Sweden, the employers were faced with a highly unionised workforce holding a firm grip on political power in the late 1930s. This induced the employers to a policy of accommodation with the labour movement (Korpi 1981).

The fundamental difference between the earlier 'institutional' approaches and this political approach is that the latter emphasises that strikes are merely one working-class strategy, while political action is another. Thus political economists see the role of governments and labour political action as important independent variables. Since the unions have had a powerful position in the polity in Sweden, this provides an alternative to action in the industrial arena. This explanation appears also to apply to Germany, Austria and Norway, which lose a relatively low number of working days. It could also apply to Italy, Canada and the USA, which have been dispute-prone (although disputes have decreased markedly in the USA). In these three countries the unions have relatively little power in the political arena, though arguably the unions have had some influence on governments in Italy and Canada (see ch. 12). It is less easy to explain in these terms the relatively low number of days lost in France and Japan in most recent years. The unions have not consistently been powerful in the polity in these countries.

These summaries of competing explanations of variations in 'dispute-proneness' between countries highlight the complexity of the issues at stake and the need to look beyond mono-causal explanations.

Concluding comment

In any country, the current institutions, infrastructure and working-class representation in the polity reflect a mixture of economic, social and political variables. Therefore, as Creigh et al. point out, 'it is not perhaps surprising that any attempt to relate developments to two or three explanatory variables can be faulted' (1982:20).

Although there are substantial difficulties in acquiring reliable cross-country comparable information, attempting to formulate comparative explanations is still worthwhile as a way of beginning to understand the complex differences between national patterns of employment relations.

For many, the notion of convergence has been an especially attractive theory (see ch. 1); however, the pattern of industrial disputes and other indicators in the countries discussed in this book hardly lend support to the notion of convergence. If anything, they imply that there is a continuing divergence between these countries. For example, some countries are dispute-prone and others much less so. As a whole, this Appendix has summarised a wide range of indicators that relate to the ten countries. These data illustrate a considerable and continuing diversity between them.

Contributors

Greg J. Bamber is Professor and Director of the Graduate School of Management, Griffith University, Brisbane and the Gold Coast, Queensland, Australia. He was formerly Director of the Australian (Key) Centre in Strategic Management, Queensland University of Technology. Prior to that he worked at the University of Queensland, and at Durham University Business School (UK); he also was an independent mediator/arbitrator for the British Advisory, Conciliation and Arbitration Service. His (joint) books include *Managing Managers*, Blackwell; *Organisational Change Strategies: Case Studies of Human Resource and Industrial Relations Issues*, Longman; *Militant Managers?*, Gower; and *New Technology: International Perspectives on Human Resources and Industrial Relations*, Allen & Unwin/Routledge. His publications have been translated into several languages including French, German, Spanish, Italian, Russian, Chinese, Indonesian, Korean and Japanese. He researches and consults with international organisations, governments, employers and unions. His current research includes studies of changing human resources/industrial relations and organisational strategies and structures in car manufacturing and telecommunications. Professor Bamber has been involved in management education and research for 25 years in Europe as well as in Australia, and he is a past President and a Fellow of the Australian & New Zealand Academy of Management.

John R. Berridge is Senior Lecturer in Personnel Policy and Director of International Management Programmes at the Manchester School of Management (UMIST), UK, where he has also been Course Director for the Masters Programme in Personnel Management and Industrial Relations. He has taught widely in Europe and North America, and is the author of six books and more than 40 articles. Since 1991 he has been editor of the international journal *Employee Relations*.

Oliver Clarke is a Visiting Professor at Michigan State University's School of Labor and Industrial Relations, USA. He has also had visiting assignments at the Universities of British Columbia, Wisconsin-Madison, Western Australia, New South Wales, South Australia and Leuven, at Curtin University of Technology, Perth, at the American Graduate School of International Management, Glendale, Arizona, and the Chinese Culture University, Taipei. After working in industry, where he trained in engineering, he became Secretary of a major British employers' association. Then, after a period spent as Research Fellow at the London School of Economics and as a management consultant, he served for 18 years in the Organisation for Economic Co-operation and Development in Paris, where he coordinated its work on industrial relations.

Edward M. Davis is Professor of Management, Director of the Labour–Management Studies Foundation and Deputy Director at the Macquarie Graduate School of Management, Australia. He is joint editor of the *Economic and Labour Relations Review* and author and co-editor of several books. His most recent books are *Making the Link: Affirmative Action and Industrial Relations* No.7, AGPS and *Managing Together: Consultation and Participation at Work*, Longman. The first was co-edited with Catherine Harris and the second with Russell Lansbury. Professor Davis has acted as a consultant on industrial relations to employers, unions and government and he has also undertaken assignments for the International Labor Organisation.

Friedrich Fürstenberg After receiving a doctorate in Economics at Tübingen University, Germany (1953), Professor Fürstenberg did research work at the New York State School of Industrial and Labor Relations, Cornell University (1953–54) and the London School of Economics and Political Science (1956–57). After working as Superintendent of the Central Training Department at Daimler-Benz AG in Stuttgart and as Managing Director of the Research Institute for Cooperatives in Erlangen, he was appointed as a full Professor at the Technical University in Clausthal in 1963. From 1966 until 1981 he was a Professor at Linz University, Austria, and Head of the Sociological Division of the Austrian Institute for Labour Market Research. From 1981 until 1986 he was a Professor at Bochum University, Germany. In 1986 he became a Professor of Sociology at Bonn University, and in 1995 he was made a Professor Emeritus. He was President of the International Industrial Relations Association 1983–86. In 1991 he was awarded an honorary doctorate by Soka University, Tokyo, and published 'Structure and Strategy in Industrial Relations' as a special issue of the *Bulletin of Comparative Labour Relations*, no. 21.

Janine Goetschy is a senior researcher at the *Centre National de la Recherche Scientifique* (CNRS), Paris. Her publications are in the fields of comparative industrial relations and industrial sociology with special reference to industrial democracy and neo-corporatist aspects. She also lectures at several French universities. In recent years she has been conducting research in Brussels on the 'social' dimensions of the European Union and on industrial relations developments in the Nordic countries.

John Goodman CBE is Frank Thomas Professor of Industrial Relations in the Manchester School of Management, at the University of Manchester Institute of Science and Technology (UMIST), UK. A graduate of the London School of Economics, prior to taking up his present appointment in 1975 he worked as a personnel officer in the motor industry, as an industrial relations adviser at the National Board of Prices and Incomes and as a Lecturer/Senior Lecturer at the University of Nottingham (where he received his doctorate) and the University of Manchester. He has held visiting appointments at the Universities of Western Australia, McMaster and Auckland. An experienced arbitrator and mediator, he has been an independent member of the governing Council of the Advisory Conciliation and Arbitration Service since 1987, and of the Economic and Social Research Council since 1993. The author or co-author of eight books and over 60 journal articles/book chapters, he has a wide range of research interests, including workplace industrial relations, collective bargaining, dispute resolution processes, employee participation and the impact of legislative change.

Olle Hammarström received an MBA from Gothenburg School of Economics and Business Administration, Sweden, in 1967, and worked as a consultant in personnel administration before joining the Sociology Department of Gothenburg University. He worked as a researcher and change-agent during the first generation of industrial democracy experiments in Sweden, from 1969 to 1974. He later joined the Ministry of Labour as a policy adviser in the field of industrial democracy and work environment, and as a liaison officer with labour market organisations. He joined the *Arbetslivcentrum* (Swedish Centre for Working Life) as a Research Director in 1978. From 1981 to 1995 he was a senior official with the Swedish Union of Clerical and Technical Employees in Industry (SIF). He has published several books and articles on industrial democracy and industrial relations. In 1976–77, he worked at the Australian Department of Employment and Industrial Relations and the Australian Department of Productivity. He was a Visiting Research Fellow with the Department of Industrial Relations at the University of Sydney in 1990–91. This research was funded by the Swedish Work Environment Fund and included a comparative study of labour market policies in each country (with Rut Hammarström). He now works as a consultant.

Annette Jobert is a senior researcher at the *Centre National de la Recherche Scientifique* (CNRS), Paris, where she specialises in the sociology of work and industrial relations. Her current projects include studies of the development of collective bargaining, ways of classifying jobs and qualifications, and the development of consultation in European multinational enterprises. Her publications include *Les Classifications dans l'Entreprise: Production des Hiérarchies Professionnelles et Salariales* (jointly with F. Eyraud, P. Rozenblatt and M. Tallard), La Documentation Française; 'La négociation collective dans les entreprises multinationales en Europe' in G. Devin ed. *Syndicalisme: Dimension Internationale*, Editions Européennes Erasme; and *Education and Work in Great Britain, Germany and Italy* (jointly with C. Marry and L. Tanguy), Routledge.

Thomas A. Kochan is the George M. Bunker Professor of Management, Sloan School of Management, Massachusetts Institute of Technology, USA. He was President of the International Industrial Relations Association from 1992 to 1995. He is the author and co-author of many articles and books on employment relations including *Introduction to Collective Bargaining and Industrial Relations*, McGraw-Hill; *The Transformation of American Industrial Relations*, Basic Books; *The Mutual Gains Enterprise*, Harvard Business School Press; *Employment Relations in a Changing World Economy*, MIT Press; and *Employment Relations in the Growing Asian Economies*, Routledge.

Yasuo Kuwahara is a Professor of Economics and Director of the International Centre at Dokkyo University, and a Visiting Professor of the University of the Air, Japan. He is a member of the board of trustees of the Japan Industrial Relations Association (JIRA) and is in charge of the programming committee of the International Industrial Relations Association's World Congress, to be held in Tokyo in the year 2000. He is a graduate of Keio University, and Tokyo, and the New York State School of Industrial and Labor Relations, Cornell University, USA. He has worked at Nippon Light Metal Co. and at the Organisation for Economic Co-operation and Development as a consultant and adviser. He has been a Visiting Lecturer at Yokohama National University, St Paul University and Hosei University, and is a member of the Central Commission on Minimum Wages, and Tokyo Metropolitan Government's Commission on Occupational Stability. He has published over 100 papers and books on technological change, foreign direct investment, equal employment opportunities, foreign workers and industrial relations.

Russell D. Lansbury is Professor and Head of the Department of Industrial Relations at the University of Sydney, Australia. He holds degrees in Psychology and Political Science from the University of

Melbourne and a doctorate from the London School of Economics. Professor Lansbury has worked for British Airways in London and has taught at a number of universities in Europe, North America and Asia. He has been a Senior Fulbright Scholar at both MIT and Harvard University in the United States. In addition to undertaking assignments for the International Labour Organisation and the Organisation for Economic Co-operation and Development he has been a consultant to industry, government and trade unions. He has been a Visiting Research Fellow at the International Institute for Labour Studies at the International Labour Organisation, Geneva, and at the *Arbetslivsinstitutet* (Swedish Centre for Working Life) in Stockholm. Professor Lansbury's publications cover a wide range of subjects including organisational change, work design, comparative industrial relations and human resource management. His recent books include *Changing Employment Relations in Australia* (with Jim Kitay), Oxford University Press; and *After Lean Production: Evolving Employment Practices in the World Auto Industry* (with Tom Kochan and John Paul MacDuffie), Cornell University Press.

Chris Leggett is Professor and Head of School of Management, University of South Australia, and was formerly Professor and Co-Director of the Asia–Pacific Research Centre at Central Queensland University. Before joining Central Queensland University he was Acting Head of the School of Industrial Relations and Organisational Behaviour at the University of New South Wales (UNSW). He is the editor of the UNSW 'Studies in Human Resource Management and Industrial Relations in Asia' monograph series. Professor Leggett has taught and researched industrial relations in the United Kingdom, Africa and the Asia–Pacific region, and has published widely on the region.

John A. McClendon is Associate Professor of Human Resource Administration in the School of Business and Management at Temple University, USA, where he teaches labour–management relations and human resource management. He received his PhD from the University of South Carolina in 1989. His current research interests include industrial disputes, union organising, union restructuring and worker militancy. Since 1993 he has published articles in *Industrial and Labor Relations Review, Journal of Labor Research, Employee Rights and Responsibilities Journal, Relations Industrielles* and *Personnel Psychology*.

Mick Marchington is Professor of Human Resource Management and Dean of Management Studies at the Manchester School of Management. His first degree is in Chemical Engineering and he has a Masters degree and a doctorate in employment relations. Before moving to UMIST in 1986, he worked at the Universities of Aston and Central Lancashire, and he has also been a Visiting Fellow at the University of Sydney. He has written a number of books, including *Changing Patterns of Employee Relations*, Harvester Wheatsheaf; and *Core Personnel and Development*, Institute of Personnel and Development; as well as many articles in refereed journals. His current research activities centre around studies of employee involvement, total quality management and human resource management, employment relations in retailing, and the role of grievance and disciplinary procedures in settling workplace disputes.

Tommy Nilsson has a PhD in Sociology from the University of Lund, Sweden, and is an Associate Professor in Sociology at Stockholm University. He now works at the Swedish National Institute for Working Life in Stockholm. His research is mainly in the fields of work organisation, modern production systems, wage formation and industrial relations. He has taken part in case studies at Saab and Volvo (in the International Motor Vehicle Program of MIT) on new forms of work organisation in the Swedish car industry. Currently he is engaged in research programs about development processes in organisations and how these relate to networking.

Young-bum Park is a Professor of Economics and Business at Hansung University in Seoul, Republic of Korea, and teaches labor economics and industrial relations. He holds a PhD in Economics from Cornell University. From 1988 until May 1997 he was a Senior Research Fellow at the Korea Labor Institute (KLI)—a government-sponsored research institute examining industrial relations issues—and during 1995–96 was a Visiting Research Fellow at the East–West Centre in Hawaii, USA. Professor Park has published extensively on industrial relations, economics and related fields in Korea and Asia; his publications include *Public Sector Industrial Relations*, KLI Press; and 'Korea', in *Telecommunications: Restructuring Work and Employment Relations Worldwide*, Cornell University Press.

Claudio Pellegrini graduated from the University of Rome and obtained a PhD in Industrial Relations from the University of Wisconsin at Madison, USA. He is currently at the University of Rome and has also taught at the University Paris 1, Pantheon, Sorbonne. He has published articles on industrial relations in the construction industry, on collective bargaining, vocational training, and on management and union rights. He co-edited with R. Blanpain and C. Engels the volume *Contractual Policies Concerning Continued Vocational Training in the European Community Member States*, Peeters.

Peter Ross is a PhD candidate and researcher at the Graduate School of Management, Griffith University, Queensland, Australia. In 1994 he graduated with an honours degree in International Business from Griffith University. He has specialised in comparative human resource (HR) and industrial relations (IR) practices and is particularly interested in the issue of the transferability of Japanese 'participatory' HR/IR practices to Australian enterprises. Prior to this he worked as an industrial officer with the Queensland State Government. He is currently working on a number of projects in the comparative IR field.

Ed Snape teaches in the Department of Human Resource Management at the University of Strathclyde, Scotland. Prior to that he spent four years as Associate Professor in the Department of Management at the Hong Kong Polytechnic University. He has published widely in the human resource management and industrial relations field and has particular interests in performance management, trade union development and the industrial relations of Hong Kong. He received his PhD from the University of Durham, UK.

Mark Thompson is the William M. Hamilton Professor of Industrial Relations, University of British Columbia, Canada. He received his PhD from the School of Industrial and Labor Relations, Cornell University, USA. He has taught at McMaster University, and has been a member of the International Institute for Labour Studies and of the International Labour Organisation (ILO), Geneva. Professor Thompson has been a visiting scholar at the University of Texas, El Colegio de Mexico, Cornell University, University of Warwick, University of New South Wales and University of Sydney. He is a member of the ILO–UNESCO Committee of Experts on the application of the Recommendation Concerning the Status of Teachers. In addition to being a past President of the Canadian Industrial Relations Association he was a Governor of the Workers' Compensation Board of British Columbia representing the public interest. He was appointed as a Commissioner to review employment standards in British Columbia and issued a report in 1994. Professor Thompson served on the board of governors of the National Academy of Arbitrators and the executive of the Industrial Relations Research Association. His research interests include public sector industrial relations, the role of management in Canadian industrial relations, and industrial relations and free trade. He is the editor of *Collective Bargaining in the Public Sector: Beginning of the End or End of the Beginning?*; *Conflict or Compromise: The Future of Public Sector Industrial Relations*; and *Industrial Relations in a Decade of Economic Change*. He has published articles in *Relations Industrielles, British Journal of Industrial Relations, Industrial Relations, Industrial and Labor Relations Review* and *International Labour Review*.

Hoyt N. Wheeler became a full Professor in 1981 at the College of Business Administration, University of South Carolina, Columbia, USA, where he helped to establish a new graduate program in employment relations. After obtaining a BA in Political Science at Marshall

University and a law degree from the University of Virginia, he practised labor law as a partner in a law firm from 1961 to 1970. He received his PhD in 1974 from the University of Wisconsin. He taught at the University of Wyoming from 1973 to 1976; during this time he became an active labour arbitrator. From 1976 to 1981, he taught at the University of Minnesota. He is a member of the National Academy of Arbitrators and past President of the Industrial Relations Research Association. His publications include *Industrial Conflict: An Integrative Theory*, University of South Carolina Press; and *Workplace Justice: Employment Obligations in International Perspective* (co-edited with Jacques Rojot), University of South Carolina Press; as well as numerous publications in scholarly and practitioner journals.

Gillian Whitehouse teaches in the Department of Government at the University of Queensland, Brisbane, Australia, where she was also an undergraduate and post-graduate student. She is currently involved in research focusing on studies of work and employment equity in Australia, and in Organisation for Economic Co-operation and Development and Asia–Pacific nations. Her recent publications include articles in the areas of casual and part-time work and homeworking.

Abbreviations

ACAS	Advisory, Conciliation and Arbitration Service (UK)
ACCI	Australian Chamber of Commerce and Industry
ACSPA	Australian Council of Salaried and Professional Associations
ACTU	Australian Council of Trade Unions
ACTWU	Amalgamated Clothing and Textile Workers Union (USA)
ADGB	*Allgemeiner Deutscher Gewerkschaftsbund* (General Federation of German Trade Unions)
AEU	Amalgamated Engineering Union (merged in 1992 to form Amalgamated Engineering and Electrical Union) (UK)
AFAP	Australian Federation of Air Pilots
AFL	American Federation of Labor
AFL–CIO	American Federation of Labor–Congress of Industrial Organizations
AIRC	Australian Industrial Relations Commission
ALP	Australian Labor Party
AMG	American Military Government (Korea)
AMS	*Arbetsmarknadsstyrelsen* (Labour Market Board) (Sweden)
AN	*Alleanza Nazionale* (National Alliance) (Italy)
ARAN	*Agenzia per la rappresentanza negoziale delle pubbliche amministrazione* (Agency for bargaining in the public administration) (Italy)
ASAP	*Associazione Sindacale Aziende Petrolchimiche* (Employers' Association of Petrochemical Firms) (Italy)

ASEAN	Association of South East Asian Nations
Assicredito	*Associazione Italiana Credito* (Italian Association of Employers in Credit)
ATP	*Allmän tilläggspension* (Swedish old age pension scheme)
AWA	Australian workplace agreement
AWIRS	Australian Workplace Industrial Relations Survey
BCA	Business Council of Australia
BDA	*Bundesvereinigung der Deutschen Arbeitgeberverbände* (Confederation of German Employers' Associations)
BIAC	Business and Industry Advisory Committee to the OECD
BLS	Bureau of Labor Statistics of the US Department of Labor
BNA	Bureau of National Affairs Inc (USA)
CAGEO	Council of Australian Government Employee Organisations
CAI	Confederation of Australian Industry (merged in 1992 to form ACCI)
CBI	Confederation of British Industry
CDU	Christian Democratic Union (Germany)
CEEP	*Centre Européen des Entreprises Publiques* (European Centre for Public Enterprises)
CF	*Civilingenjörsförbundet* (Association of Graduate Engineers) (Sweden)
CFDT	*Confédération française démocratique du travail* (French Democratic Confederation of Labour)
CFE–CGC	*Confédération française de l'encadrement– Confédération générale des cadres* (French Confederation of Executive Staffs, the successor to the CGC)
CFTC	*Confédération française des travailleurs chrétiens* (French Confederation of Christian Workers)
CGB	*Christlicher Gewerkschaftsbund Deutschlands* (Confederation of Christian Trade Unions of Germany)
CGC	*Confédération générale des cadres* (General Confederation of Executive Staffs) (France)
CGIL	*Confederazione Italiana Generale del Lavoro* (Italian General Confederation of Labour)
CGPME	*Confédération générale des petites et moyennes entreprises* (Confederation of small and medium sized enterprises) (France)
CGT	*Confédération générale du travail* (General Confederation of Labour) (France)
CIA	Central Intelligence Agency (USA)

CIC	*Confédération internationale des cadres* (International Confederation of Executive Staffs)
CIDA	*Confederazione Italiana Dirigenti di Azienda* (Italian Confederation of Enterprise Managers)
CIG	*Cassa Integrazione Guadagni* (Wages Integration Funds) (Italy)
CIO	Congress of Industrial Organizations (USA)
CISAL	*Confederazione Italiana Sindacati Lavoratori Autonomi* (Italian Confederation of Unions of Autonomous Workers)
CISAS	*Confederazione Italiana Sindacati Addetti ai Servizi* (Italian Confederation of Unions in the Service Sector)
CISL	*Confederazione Italiana Sindacati Lavoratori* (Italian Confederation of Workers' Unions)
CISNAL	*Confederazione Italiana Sindacati Nazionali Lavoratori* (Italian Confederation of National Unions of Workers)
CLC	Canadian Labour Congress
CNPF	*Conseil national du patronat français* (National Council of French Employers)
CNTU	Confederation of National Trade Unions (Canada)
COLA	Cost of living (pay) adjustment (USA)
Confagricoltura	*Confederazione Generale dell'Agricoltura* (General Confederation of [Employers in] Agriculture) (Italy)
Confapi	*Confederazione Italiana della Piccola e Media Industria* (Italian Confederation of Small and Medium Enterprises)
Confcommercio	*Confederazione Generale del Commercio* (General Confederation of [Employers in] Commerce) (Italy)
Confindustria	*Confederazione Generale dell'Industria Italiana* (General Confederation of Italian Industry)
CONFSAL	*Confederazione Sindacati Autonomi Lavoratori* (Confederation of Unions of Autonomous Workers) (Italy)
COPE	Committee on Political Education (USA)
CSU	Christian Social Union (Germany)
CWA	Communication Workers of America
DAG	*Deutsche Angestelltengewerkschaft* (German Salaried Employees' Union)
DBB	*Deutscher Beamtenbund* (Confederation of German Civil Service Officials)
DC	*Democrazia Cristiana* (Christian Democratic Party) (Italy)
DGB	*Deutscher Gewerkschaftsbund* (German Trade Union Federation)

Domei	Japanese Confederation of Labour
DSP	Democratic Socialist Party (Japan)
EC	European Community
EETPU	Electrical, Electronic, Telecommunication and Plumbing Union (merged in 1992 with Amalgamated Engineering Union) (UK)
EFA	Enterprise flexibility agreement (Australia)
EMU	European monetary union
ENI	*Ente Nazionale Idrocarburi* (National Institute for Hydrocarbons) (Italy)
ERM	Exchange rate mechanism (of EU)
ETUC	European Trade Union Confederation
EU	European Union
FDGB	*Freier Deutscher Gewerkschaftsbund* (Free German Trade Union Federation) (in the former German Democratic Republic)
FDP	Free Democratic Party (Germany)
Federazione	CGIL–CISL–UIL (Italian Inter-union Federation)
FEN	*Fédération de l'éducation nationale* (National Federation of Education) (France)
FIET	*Fédération internationale des employés techniciens et cadres* (International Federation of Commercial, Clerical, Professional and Technical Employees)
FKI	Federation of Korean Industries
FKTU	Federation of Korean Trade Unions
FO	*Force ouvrière* (Workers' Force; also known as CGT–FO) (France)
Forza Italia	Go on Italy political party
FSU	*Fédération syndicale unitaire de l'enseignement de la recherche et de la culture* (Left-wing union federation) (France)
FTA	Free Trade Agreement
GATT	General Agreement on Tariffs and Trade
GCHQ	Government Communications Headquarters (UK)
GDP	Gross domestic product
GFKTU	*Daehan Nochong* (General Federation of Korean Trade Unions)
GHQ	General Headquarters of the Allied Powers (Japan)
GNP	Gross national product
HR	Human resources
HRM	Human resource management
IBT	International Brotherhood of Teamsters (USA)
ICC	International Chamber of Commerce
ICFTU	International Confederation of Free Trade Unions

IG Chemie-Papier-Keramik	Union of Chemical, Paper and Ceramics Industry Workers (Germany)
IG Metall	Union of Metal Industry Workers (Germany)
ILO	International Labour Organisation
IMEs	Industrialised market economies
IMF	International Metalworkers' Federation
IMF–JC	Japan Council of Metalworkers' Unions
IOE	International Organisation of Employers
IRI	*Istituto per la Ricostruzione Industriale* (Institute for Industrial Reconstruction) (Italy)
IRRC	Industrial Relations Reform Commission (Korea)
ITSs	International trade (union) secretariats
IWW	Industrial Workers of the World (USA and Canada)
JCP	Japan Communist Party
JSP	Japan Socialist Party
KCCI	Korean Chamber of Commerce and Industry
KCTU	Korea Confederation of Trade Unions
KEF	Korean Employers' Federation
KFTA	Korean Foreign Trade Association
KLI	Korea Labor Institute
KTUC	Korea Trade Union Congress
LDEs	Less-developed economies
LDP	Liberal Democratic Party (Japan)
Ledarna	Association of Management and Professional Staff (Sweden)
LMC	Labour–management council (Korea))
LO	*Landsorganisationen i Sverige* (Swedish Trade Union Confederation)
LRC	Labour Relations Commission (Korea)
MBL	*Medbestämmandelagen* (Act on Co-determination at Work) (Sweden)
MNE	Multinational enterprise
MSI	*Movimento Sociale Italiano* (Italy)
MTIA	Metal Trades Industry Association (Australia)
NA	Not available
NAFTA	North American Free Trade Agreement
NCIR	New Conception of Industrial Relations (Korea)
NDP	New Democratic Party (Canada)
NIEs	Newly industrialising economies
Nikkeiren	Japan Federation of Employers' Associations
NLRA	National Labor Relations Act (USA)
NUM	National Union of Mineworkers (UK)
NUMM	New United Motor Manufacturing–Toyota-General Motors joint venture (USA)

OECD	Organisation for Economic Co-operation and Development
OPEC	Organisation of Petroleum Exporting Countries
OSHA	Occupational Safety and Health Act, 1970 (USA)
PCI	*Partito Comunista Italiano* (Italian Communist Party)
PDS	*Partito Democratico della Sinistra* (Democratic Party of the Left) (Italy)
PDS	Party of Democratic Socialism (Germany)
PGEU	Plumbers and Gasfitters Employees' Union (Australia)
PLI	*Partito Liberale Italiano* (Italian Liberal Party)
PPPs	Purchasing power parities
PRI	*Partito Repubblicano Italiano* (Italian Republican Party)
PSDI	*Partito Socialista Democratico Italiano* (Italian Social Democratic Party)
PSI	*Partito Socialista Italiano* (Italian Socialist Party)
PTK	*Privattjänstemannakartellen* (Federation of Salaried Employees in Industry and Services) (Sweden)
QCC	Quality control circles
QWL	Quality of working life
Rengo	Japan Trade Union Confederation (JTUC)
Rodosho	Ministry of Labour (Japan)
RSA	*Rappresentanza Sindacale Aziendale* (Firm Union Representative) (Italy)
RSU	*Rappresentanza Sindacale Unitaria* (Unitary Union Representative at Firm Level) (Italy)
SACO	*Sveriges Akademikers Centralorganisation* (Swedish Confederation of Professional Associations; also known as SACO/SR)
SAF	*Svenska Arbetsgivareföreningen* (Swedish Employers' Confederation)
SAP	*Socialdemokratiska Arbetarpartiet* (Social Democratic Labour Party) (Sweden)
SAV	*Statens Arbetsgivarverk* (National Agency for Government Employers) (Sweden)
Scala Mobile	Wage indexation (Italy)
SDP	Social Democratic Party (Japan)
SED	*Sozialistische Einheitspartei Deutschlands* (East German Communist Party, in the former FDR)
Shunto	Spring labour offensive (Japan)
SIF	*Svenska Industritjänstemannaförbundet* (Swedish Union of Clerical and Technical Employees in Industry)

SKTF	*Svenska Kommunaltjänstemannaförbundet* (Swedish Union of Local Government Officers)
SLD	Social and Liberal Democrats (UK)
SMEs	Small and medium-sized enterprises
SMIC	*Salaire Minimum Interprofessionnel de Croissance* (national minimum wage) (France)
SNCF	*Société Nationale des Chemins de Fer* (National Railways) (France)
SNECMA	*Société Nationale d'Etude et de Construction de Moteurs d'Aviation* (French Aerospace)
SNUI	*Syndicat National Unitaire des Impots* (National and United Unions of Tax Collectors) (France)
Sohyo	General Council of Trade Unions (Japan)
Somucho	Management and Coordination Agency (Japan)
SPD	*Sozialdemokratische Partei Deutschlands* (Social Democratic Party of Germany)
SUD–PTT	*Solidaire Unitaire Démocratique–Poste, Télégraphe, Téléphone* (United and democratic union of the post) (France)
TCO	*Tjänstemännens Centralorganisation* (Confederation of Salaried Employees) (Sweden)
TCO–OF	*TCOs förhandlingsråd för offentliganställda* (Confederation of Salaried Employees, Public Sector Negotiation Council) (Sweden)
TDL	*Tarifgemeinschaft der Deutschen Länder* (German State Government Employers' Association)
TGWU	Transport and General Workers' Union (UK)
THC	Trades Hall Council (Australia)
TLC	Trades and Labor Council (Australia)
TQC	Total quality control
TQM	Total quality management
TUAC	Trade Union Advisory Committee to the OECD
TUC	Trades Union Congress (UK)
UAW	United Automobile Workers (USA)
UCC	*Union confédérale des ingénieurs et cadres* (Confederated Union of Engineers and Executive Staffs of CFDT) (France)
UCI	*Union des cadres et ingénieurs* (Union of Executive Staffs and Engineers of FO) (France)
UCR	*Union confédérale de retraités* (Union of Pensioners of CGT) (France)
UGICA	*Union générale des ingénieurs et cadres* (General Union of Engineers, Executive staffs and Technicians of CFTC) (France)
UGICT	*Union générale des ingénieurs, cadres et techniciens*

	(General Union of Engineers, Executive Staffs and Technicians of CGT) (France)
UIL	*Unione Italiana del Lavoro* (Italian Union of Labour)
ULA	*Union der Leitenden Angestellten* (Union of Senior Managers) (Germany)
UMW	United Mine Workers of America
UNCTAD	United Nations Commission on Trade and Development
UNICE	*Union des Industries de la Communauté Européenne* (Union of Industrial and Employers' Confederations of Europe)
USWA	United Steelworkers of America
VKA	*Vereinigung der Kommunalen Arbeitgeberverbände* (Federation of Local Government Employers' Associations) (Germany)
WARN	Worker Adjustment and Retraining Notification Act (USA)
WCL	World Confederation of Labour
WFTU	World Federation of Trade Unions
WIRS	Workplace Industrial Relations Survey (UK)
WTO	World Trade Organisation
Zaibatsu	Group of holding companies based on a group's commercial bank (Japan)
Zenkoun	All Japan Council of Traffic and Transport Workers' Unions
Zenminrokyo	Japanese Private Sector Union Council

Endnotes

Chapter 1   An introduction to international and comparative employment relations

1   For further reading, see the many relevant publications of the International Labour Organisation (ILO), its International Institute for Labour Studies and the International Industrial Relations Association. Also, there is a range of books that provide valuable sources of references, including Bennett & Fawcett (1985); Poole (1986); Bray (1991); Ferner & Hyman (1992); Dowling, Schuler & Welch (1994); Locke et al. (1995a, b); Verma et al. (1995); Gardner & Palmer (1997); and Kitay & Lansbury (1997). The European Foundation for the Improvement of Living and Working Conditions has initiated a useful series, *European Employment and Industrial Relations Glossaries,* general editor Tiziano Treu (e.g. see Terry & Dickens 1991 in References: ch. 2).
2   The term employment relations is increasingly used in the literature to reflect the growing interconnectedness of labour–management relations, industrial relations (IR) and human resource management (HRM) (see Locke et al. 1995b; Kochan et al. 1997; Gardner & Palmer 1997; Kitay & Lansbury 1997; Darbishire & Katz 1997).
3   There are *comparative* studies that focus, say, on two industries or establishments within one country. Although such studies can be very insightful, they do not have an *internationally* comparative dimension.

Chapter 2   Employment relations in Britain

1   Britain includes England, Scotland and Wales, while the UK includes Britain and Northern Ireland. Although Northern Ireland has much in common with Britain, some important elements of industrial relations

are different. This chapter concentrates on Britain, although some of the cited statistics here and in the Appendix refer to the UK as a whole.

2   *Labour Market Trends*, February 1997:39.

3   *Labour Market Trends*, June 1997:231. The union density data in this paragraph are based on a question in the Labour Force Survey of individuals, and so are not strictly comparable with earlier data that were based on union sources. According to WIRS, which excludes establishments with fewer than 25 employees, union density among manual workers fell from 58 per cent in 1984 to 48 per cent in 1990 (Millward et al. 1992).

4   British unions usually have unpaid union representatives at the workplace, often referred to as shop stewards or staff representatives. Some employers allow them time off work to represent fellow union members in the workplace (see Goodman & Whittingham 1969; Terry & Dickens 1991).

5   Membership of the Institute of Directors is based on individuals, and tends to reflect the views of directors in small and medium-sized companies. By contrast, membership of the CBI is on a corporate basis, giving greater influence to larger companies.

6   An unofficial strike takes place without the official approval of the union hierarchy.

Chapter 6   Employment relations in Italy

1   In Italy, it is possible to obtain a referendum for abolishing a piece, or part, of legislation, when a minimum of 500 000 citizens sign a petition and the Constitutional Court approves the request. The most important referendums on union matters were held in 1984, when the popular vote upheld the government decision on wage indexation, and in 1995, when legislation relating to check-off and representation matters was submitted to the popular vote. In practical terms, in the latter case, the consequences have not been great, because these issues were also agreed upon in collective agreements, but the changes in legislation have created a series of inconsistencies and contradictions in the legislation that will make overall reform necessary.

Chapter 7   Employment relations in France

1   We acknowledge that this is a revised version of the chapter that was written by Janine Goetschy and Jacques Rojot for the first 1987 edition of this book.

Chapter 10   Employment relations in Japan

1   The total number of disputes including those without industrial action was recorded at a peak of 8435 cases (in terms of people participating,

10 261 209) in 1975. The figure dramatically decreased to 1136 (1 321 087 in terms of people participating) in 1994. The number of disputes with industrial action (e.g. strikes, lockouts and sabotage) was recorded at a peak of 7574 (4 613 962 in terms of people participating) in 1975. This figure also decreased, to 628 (263 035 in terms of people participating) in 1994 (Rodosho 1995).

2   The current unemployment ratio by definition does not include those who retired from the labour market early because they were discouraged by the unfavourable economic climate. Women workers, particularly, tend to take this option when unemployed. Many of those 'discouraged' workers are ready to return to the labour force quickly if jobs become available.

3   In 1995, 184 240 part-time workers were unionised, a figure that represents 0.01 per cent of the total union members. They belonged to 111 330 unit unions (*tan-i sosiki kumiai*) (Rododaijin Kambo Seisaku Chousabu 1996).

4   Another major employers' organisation, *Keidanren*, the Japan Federation of Economic Organisations, was established in 1946. It is the major employers' organisation, which exerts great influence on policy setting in various fields, including responses to international trade disputes.

5   The ratio of female workers among 'short-hour' workers differs by definition. Among those who work less than 35 hours a week as employees, the female ratio was 73 per cent in 1995. Among those who are usually called part-timers, 95 per cent were female in 1995 (Somucho 1995).

Chapter 11   Employment relations in Korea

1   Except in cases where the usage has long been otherwise, for example 'Syngman Rhee', Korean names are represented according to Korean convention, that is family name first followed by two hyphenated given names, the second with a lower case initial. In the references and where necessary in the text the second initial is retained unhyphenated (and in upper case) for consistency in this volume and to facilitate the distinction of authors with common family names.

2   A helpful account of Korea's labour legislation, which includes a tabular summary, is provided by Park & Lee (1996).

3   For a more detailed account of labour-dispute settlement machinery in Korea, see Park (1993:153–7).

Chapter 12   Conclusions

1   See Appendix (Table A.22); in addition this section draws on Visser (1989); also his work as summarised in OECD (1991).

2   On the OECD, see Appendix, note 2.
3   ILO conventions can be renounced only 'within the year following the expiration of ten years from the date upon which the convention first comes into force', and during every tenth year thereafter. Ratification remains operative even following withdrawal from the ILO, unless and until renounced in an appropriate year. (South Africa continued to report on ratified conventions even though it withdrew from the ILO in the early 1960s.)
4   On employment relations in other former communist countries see, for example, Hegewisch et al. (1996); Bamber & Peschanski (1996).
5   For a discussion of change in employment relations see Clarke & Niland (1991).

Appendix

1   This appendix is a point of departure, and we encourage readers to send us suggestions for improvement. For a longer though less up-to-date point of departure, see Bean (1989). We acknowledge that an earlier version of most of our tables was published in the *International Journal of Human Resource Management*.
2   Both the EU and the OECD conduct research and hold conferences on employment relations issues that are relevant to their member countries, which are all IMEs. (However, the OECD has phased down its industrial relations work.) Five of the ten countries belong to the EU. Each of our ten countries belongs to the OECD, which includes 29 IMEs in total; this organisation publishes useful data sets, projections and appraisals. The OECD was formed in 1960; it was based on an earlier group of 18 European countries set up in 1948 to coordinate the distribution of Marshall aid after the Second World War. The OECD's aims include:

> to achieve the highest sustainable economic growth and employment and a rising standard of living in member countries, while maintaining financial stability, and thus to contribute to the development of the world economy; to contribute to sound economic expansion in member as well as non-member countries in the process of economic development. (OECDa:ii).

In comparison with the United Nations, ILO, World Bank and other large international bureaucracies, the EU and OECD have an advantage insofar as their members have much more homogeneous economies and embrace fewer different cultures and languages, though as they both gain new members this homogeneity is decreasing. Unlike the EU, the OECD has no formal power over its members. It is not a supranational organisation but a forum where economic policy makers discuss problems and experiences. It does not have the authority to impose policies; rather, its power lies in its capacity to disseminate ideas. The work of the OECD in respect of employment relations, which is on a small scale, tends to be primarily concerned with those aspects of the subject that are most relevant to the major concerns of the organisation, such as economic and employment policies. Unlike the ILO, the OECD does not establish rules or conventions relating to the rights of labour that member countries are expected to follow. As indicated above, it is primarily an organisation where governments can discuss common problems, and policy options for dealing with them (Clarke 1987).

3   In tables, when citing data that relate to a particular year, we are usually referring to an average for that calendar year. In most cases, numbers less than ten are rounded to one decimal place; numbers greater than ten are rounded to the nearest whole number, which is appropriate in view of the imprecision of many of them.

4   For other points of departure, see Batstone (1985) and Jackson (1987).

References

Preface

Adams, R.J. (1991) 'An international survey of courses in comparative industrial relations' in M. Bray ed. *Teaching Comparative Industrial Relations* Sydney: Australian Centre for Industrial Relations Research and Teaching, University of Sydney

Chapter 1   An introduction to international and comparative employment relations

Adams, R. (1981) 'A theory of employer attitudes and behaviour towards trade unions in Western Europe and North America' in G. Dlugos and K. Weiermair in collaboration with W. Dorow eds *Management under Differing Value Systems* Berlin: de Gruyter, pp. 277–93
——(1988) 'Desperately seeking industrial relations theory' *International Journal of Comparative Labour Law and Industrial Relations* 4, 1, pp. 1–10
Albeda, W. (1984) 'European industrial relations in a time of crisis' in P. Drenth et al. eds *Handbook of Work and Organisational Psychology*, New York: John Wiley
Bain, G.S. & Clegg, H.A. (1974) 'A strategy for industrial relations research in Great Britain' *British Journal of Industrial Relations* 12, 1, pp. 91–113
Bamber, G.J. (1986) *Militant Managers? Managerial Unionism and Industrial Relations* Aldershot: Gower
——(1990) 'Flexible work organisation: Inferences from Britain and Australia' *Asia-Pacific Human Resource Management* (Journal of the Institute of Personnel Management Australia) Melbourne 28, 3, pp. 28–44

Bamber, G.J., Boreham, P. & Harley, B. (1992) 'Economic and industrial relations outcomes of different forms of flexibility in Australian industry: An analysis of the Australian Workplace Industrial Relations Survey' in *Exploring Industrial Relations: Further Analysis of AWIRS* Canberra: Department of Industrial Relations, Industrial Relations Research Series, No. 4, pp. 1–70

Bamber, G.J. & Lansbury, R.D. eds (1989) *New Technology: International Perspectives on Human Resources and Industrial Relations* London: Unwin Hyman

Bamber, G.J., Shadur, M.A. & Howell, F. (1992) 'The international transferability of Japanese management strategies: An Australian perspective' *Employee Relations* 14, 3, pp. 3–19

Barbash, J. & Barbash, K. eds (1989) *Theories and Concepts in Comparative Industrial Relations* Columbia: University of South Carolina Press

Bean R. (1994) *Comparative Industrial Relations: An Introduction to Cross-National Perspectives* London: Routledge

Bendix, R. (1970) *Embattled Reason* New York: Oxford University Press

Bennett, J. & Fawcett, J. eds (1985) *Industrial Relations: An International and Comparative Bibliography* London: Mansell/British Universities Industrial Relations Association

Björkman, T. (1993) 'ABB: Performance Improvement in a multidomestic corporation' in K. North *Improving Enterprise Performance: International Transfer of Approaches* Geneva: International Labour Organisation

Blain, A.N. & Gennard, J. (1970) 'Industrial relations theory: A critical review' *British Journal of Industrial Relations* 8, 3, pp. 389–407

Blanchflower, D.G. & Freeman, R.B. (1989) 'Going different ways: Unionism in the United States and other OECD countries' Mimeo. August

Blanpain, R. (1998) 'Comparativism in labour law and industrial relations' in R. Blanpain et al. *Comparative Labour Law and Industrialised Relations in Industrialised Market Economies* 6th edn, Deventer: Kluwer, pp. 3–22

Blanpain, R. et al. ed. (1998) *Comparative Labour Law and Industrial Relations in Industrialised Market Economies* 6th edn, Deventer: Kluwer

Bray, M. ed. (1991) *Teaching Comparative Industrial Relations* Sydney: Australian Centre for Industrial Relations Research and Teaching, University of Sydney

Brown, D. & Harrison, M.J. (1978) *A Sociology of Industrialisation* London: Macmillan

Brulin, G. & Nilsson, T. (1997) 'Sweden: The Volvo and Saab road beyond lean production' in T.A. Kochan, R.D. Lansbury & J.P. MacDuffie eds *After Lean Production: Evolving Employment Practices in the World Auto Industry* Ithaca, New York: Cornell University Press

Calmfors, L. (1993) 'Centralisation of wage bargaining and macroeconomic performance: A survey' Working Paper No. 131 Paris: Organisation for Economic Co-operation and Development (Economics Department)

Calmfors, L. & Driffill, J. (1988) 'Bargaining structure, corporatism and macroeconomic performance' *Economic Policy* 6, pp. 13–61

Campbell, D. (1992) 'The globalizing firm and labour institutions' in P. Bailey et al. eds *Multinationals and Employment: The Global Economy of the 1990s* Geneva: International Labour Organisation

Campbell, D. & Vickery, G. (1991) *Managing Manpower for Advanced Manufacturing Technology* Paris: Organisation for Economic Co-operation and Development

Camuffo, A. & Micelli, S. (1997) 'Spain, France and Italy: Mediterranean lean production' in T.A. Kochan, R.D. Lansbury & J.P. MacDuffie eds *After Lean Production: Evolving Employment Practices in the World Auto Industry* Ithaca, New York: Cornell University Press

Chalmers, N.J. (1989) *Industrial Relations in Japan: The Peripheral Workforce* London: Routledge

Chamberlain, N.W. (1961) Book review of Kerr et al. (1960) *Industrialism and Industrial Man* Harvard: Harvard University Press in *American Economic Review* 51, 3, pp. 475–80

Clarke, R.O. (1990) 'Industrial restructuring and industrial relations in continental European countries' *Bulletin of Comparative Labour Relations* 20, pp. 19–38

Clegg, H.A. (1976) *Trade Unionism Under Collective Bargaining: A Theory Based on Comparisons of Six Countries* Oxford: Blackwell

Cochrane, J.L. (1976) 'Industrialism and industrial man in retrospect: A preliminary analysis' in J.L. Stern & B.D. Dennis eds (1977) *Proceedings of the Twenty-ninth Annual Winter Meetings, Industrial Relations Research Association* Series Madison, Wisconsin: Industrial Relations Research Association, pp. 274–87

Craig, A. (1975) 'The framework for the analysis of industrial relations systems' in B. Barrett et al. eds *Industrial Relations and the Wider Society* London: Collier Macmillan, pp. 8–20

Crouch, C. (1985) 'Conditions for trade union wage restraint' in L. Lindberg & C. Maier eds *The Politics of Inflation and Economic Stagnation* Washington DC: Brookings

Darbishire, O. & Katz, H. (1997) *Converging Divergences: Worldwide Changes in Employment Relations* Manuscript, New York School of Industrial and Labor Relations, Cornell University

Dell'Aringa, C. & Samek Lodovici, M. (1992) 'Industrial relations and economic performance' in T. Treu ed. *Participation in Public Policy Making: the Role of Trade Unions and Employer Associations* Deventer: de Gruyter, pp. 26–58

Deyo, F. (1981) *Dependent Development and Industrial Order: An Asian Case Study* New York: Praeger

Doeringer, P.B. (1981) 'Industrial relations research in international perspective' in P.B. Doeringer et al. eds *Industrial Relations in International Perspective: Essays on Research and Policy* London: Macmillan, pp. 1–21

Dore, R. (1973) *British Factory, Japanese Factory: The Origins of National Diversity in Industrial Relations* London: Allen & Unwin

Dowling, P., Schuler, R.S. & Welch, D.E. (1994) *International Dimensions of Human Resource Management* 2nd edn, Belmont, California: Wadsworth

Dunlop, J.T. (1958) *Industrial Relations Systems* New York: Holt, Rinehart & Winston

Ferner, A. & Hyman, R. eds (1992) *Industrial Relations in the New Europe* Oxford: Blackwell Business

Flanders, A. (1970) *Management and Unions: The Theory and Reform of Industrial Relations* London: Faber

Freeman, R.B. (1988) 'Labor markets, institutions, constraints and performance' National Bureau of Economic Research Working Paper No. 2560 Cambridge: National Bureau of Economic Research

——(1989) 'On the divergence in unionism among developed countries' Discussion Paper No. 2817 Cambridge: National Bureau of Economic Research

Fucini, J. & Fucini, S. (1990) *Working for the Japanese: Inside Mazda's American Auto Plant*, London: Macmillan

Gardner, M. & Palmer, G. (1997) *Employment relations* 2nd edn, Melbourne: Macmillan

Giles, A. (1989) 'Industrial relations theory, the state and politics' in J. Barbash & K. Barbash eds *Theories and Concepts in Comparative Industrial Relations* Columbia: University of South Carolina Press pp. 123–54

Giles, A. & Murray, G. (1988) 'Towards an historical understanding of industrial relations theory in Canada' *Relations Industrielles* 43, 4, pp. 780–810

Gill, C. & Krieger, H. (1992) 'The diffusion of participation in new information technology in Europe: Survey results' *Economic and Industrial Democracy* 13, 3, pp. 331–58

Gill, J. (1969) 'One approach to the teaching of industrial relations' *British Journal of Industrial Relations* 7, 2, pp. 265–72

Goldthorpe, J.H. (1984) 'The end of convergence: Corporatist and dualist tendencies in modern western societies' in J.H. Goldthorpe ed. *Order and Conflict in Contemporary Capitalism: Studies in the Political Economy of Western European Nations* Oxford: Clarendon, pp. 315–44

Gould, W.B. (1984) *Japan's Reshaping of American Labor Law* Cambridge, Mass.: MIT Press

Gourevitch, P. et al. (1984a) 'Industrial relations and politics: Some reflections' in P.B. Doeringer et al. eds (1981) *Industrial Relations in International Perspective: Essays on Research and Policy* London: Macmillan, pp. 401–16

Gourevitch, P. et al. (1984b) *Unions and Economic Crisis: Britain, West Germany and Sweden* London: Allen & Unwin

Hyman, R. (1975) *Industrial Relations: A Marxist Introduction* London: Macmillan

——(1980) 'Theory in industrial relations: Towards a materialist analysis' in P. Boreham & G. Dow eds *Work and Inequality Vol 2: Ideology and Control in the Labour Process* Melbourne: Macmillan, pp. 38–59

——(1987) 'Strategy or structure? Capital, labour and control' *Work, Employment and Society* 1, 1, pp. 25–53

ILO (International Labour Organisation) (1994) *World Employment Report*, Geneva: ILO

Jacoby, S.M. (1995) 'Social dimensions of global economic integration' in S.M. Jacoby ed. *The Workers of Nations: Industrial Relations in a Global Economy*, New York: Oxford University Press, pp. 3–30

Kahn-Freund, O. (1974) 'On uses and misuses of comparative law' *The Modern Law Review* 37, 1, pp. 1–27

——(1976) 'The European Social Charter' in F.G. Jacobs ed. *European Law and the Individual* Amsterdam: North Holland, pp. 181–211

——(1979) *Labour Relations: Heritage and Adjustment* Oxford: Oxford University Press

Katz, H.C. (1993) 'The decentralization of collective bargaining: A literature review and comparative analysis' *International and Labor Relations Review* 47, 1, pp. 1–22

——(1997) *Telecommunications* Ithaca, NY: Cornell University Press

Kerr, C. (1983) *The Future of Industrial Societies: Convergence or Continuing Diversity?* Cambridge, Mass.: Harvard University Press

Kerr, C., Dunlop, J.T., Harbison, F.H. & Myers, C.A. (1973) *Industrialism and Industrial Man: The Problems of Labour and Management in Economic Growth* 2nd edn, London: Penguin (first published in 1960)

Kim, Dong-heon (1997) 'Works councils in Korea and Taiwan: A comparative perspective' *Working Paper* Champaign: Institute of Labour and Industrial Relations, University of Illinois

Kitay, J. & Lansbury, R.D. eds (1997) *Changing Employment Relations in Australia* Melbourne: Oxford University Press

Kochan, T. A., Lansbury, R. D. & MacDuffie, J. P. eds (1997) *After Lean Production: Evolving Employment Practices in the World Auto Industry* Ithaca, New York: Cornell University Press

Kochan, T.A., Locke, R. & Piore, M. (1992) 'Introduction: Employment relations in a changing world economy' Mimeo. Cambridge, Mass.: Massachusetts Institute of Technology, Sloan School of Management

Kochan, T.A., McKersie, R. & Cappelli, P. (1984) 'Strategic choice and industrial relations theory' *Industrial Relations* 23, 1 Winter, pp. 16–39

Korpi, W. (1981) 'Sweden: Conflict, power and politics in industrial relations' in P.B. Doeringer et al. eds (1981) *Industrial Relations in International Perspective: Essays on Research and Policy* London: Macmillan, pp. 185–217

Kume, I. (1997) *Disparaged Success: Labor Politics in Postwar Japan* Ithaca, New York: Cornell University Press

Lange, P., Ross, G., Vannicelli, M. & Harvard University Center for European Studies (1982) *Unions, Change and Crisis: French and Italian Unions and the Political Economy, 1945–1980* London: Allen & Unwin

Lansbury, R.D., Sandkull, B. & Hammarström, O. (1992) 'Industrial relations and productivity: Evidence from Sweden and Australia' *Economic and Industrial Democracy* 13, 3, pp. 295–330

Layard, R., Nickell, S. & Jackman, R. (1992) *Unemployment, Macroeconomic Performance and the Labour Market* Oxford: Oxford University Press

Littler, C. (1982) *The Development of the Labour Process in Capitalist Societies: A Comparative Study of the Transformation of Work Organisation in Britain, Japan and the USA* London: Heinemann

Locke, R.M. (1992) 'The decline of the national union in Italy: Lessons for comparative industrial relations theory' *Industrial and Labor Relations Review* 45, 2, pp. 229–49

Locke, R.M., Kochan, T.A. & Piore, M. (1995) *Employment Relations in a Changing World Economy* Cambridge, Mass.: MIT Press

Locke, R.M., Piore, M. & Kochan, T.A. (1995) 'Reconceptualising comparative industrial relations: Lessons from international research' *International Labour Review* 134, 2, pp. 139–61

Mandel, E. (1969) *A Socialist Strategy for Europe* Institute for Workers' Control Pamphlet No. 10 Nottingham: Institute for Workers' Control

Mayo, E. (1949) *The Social Problems of an Industrial Civilization* London: Routledge

Mills, C. Wright (1959) *The Sociological Imagination* New York: Oxford University Press

Nevile, J.W. (1996) 'Minimum wages, equity and unemployment' *Economic and Labour Relations Review* 7, 2, pp. 198–212

OECD (Organisation for Economic Co-operation and Development) (1994) *Jobs Study*, Paris: OECD

Ohmae, K. (1990) *The Borderless World: Power and Strategy in the Interlinked Economy* New York: Harper

Oswald, A.J. (1985) 'The economic theory of trade unions: An introductory survey' *Scandinavian Journal of Economics* 87, pp. 160–93

——(1987) 'New research on the economics of trade unions and labor contracts' *Industrial Relations* 26, 1, Winter, pp. 30–45

Parker, M. & Slaughter, J. (1988) *Choosing Sides: Unions and the Team Concept* Boston: South End Press

Peetz, D., Preston, A. & Docherty, J. eds (1992) *Workplace Bargaining in the International Context* Canberra: Australian Government Publishing Service

Piore, M.J. (1981) 'Convergence in industrial relations? The case of France and the United States' Working Paper No. 286, Department of Economics, Cambridge: Massachusetts Institute of Technology

Piore, M.J. & Sabel, C. (1984) *The Second Industrial Divide: Possibilities for Prosperity* New York: Harper & Row

Poole, M. (1986) *Industrial Relations: Origins and Patterns of National Diversity* London: Routledge

——(1992) 'Industrial relations: Theorising for a global perspective' in R.J. Adams & N. Meltz eds *Industrial Relations Theory, Its Nature, Scope and Pedagogy* Metuchen, NJ: Scarecrow

Porter, M.E. (1990) *The Competitive Advantage of Nations* London: Macmillan

Purcell, J. (1989) 'The impact of corporate strategy on human resource management' in J. Storey ed. *New Perspectives on Human Resource Management* London: Routledge, pp. 67–91

Rogers, J. & Streeck, W. (1995) *Works Councils: Consultation, Representation and Cooperation in Industrial Relations* Chicago, Illinois: University of Chicago Press

Ross, A.M. & Hartman, P.T. (1960) *Changing Patterns of Industrial Conflict* New York: Wiley

Schregle, J. (1981) 'Comparative industrial relations: Pitfalls and potential' *International Labour Review* 120, 1 Jan.–Feb., pp. 15–30

Servais, J.M. (1989) 'The social clause in trade agreements: Wishful thinking or an instrument of social progress?' *International Labour Review* 128, 4, pp. 423–32

Shalev, M. (1978) 'Lies, damned lies and strike statistics: The measurement of trends in industrial conflict' in C. Crouch & A. Pizzorno eds *The Resurgence of Class Conflict in Western Europe Since 1968, Vol 1: National Studies* London: Macmillan, pp. 1–20

——(1980) 'Industrial relations theory and the comparative study of industrial relations and industrial conflict' *British Journal of Industrial Relations* 18, 1, pp. 26–43

Shirai, T. ed. (1983) *Contemporary Industrial Relations in Japan* Madison: University of Wisconsin Press

Sisson, K. (1987) *The Management of Collective Bargaining: An International Comparison* Oxford: Blackwell

——(1994) *Personnel Management* 2nd edn, Oxford: Blackwell

Soskice, D. (1990) 'Wage determination: The changing role of institutions in advanced economies' *Oxford Review of Economic Policy* 6, 4, Winter, pp. 36–61

Storper, M. (1995) 'Boundaries, compartments and markets: Paradoxes of industrial relations in growth pole regions of France, Italy and the United States' in S.M. Jacoby ed. *The Workers of Nations: Industrial Relations in a Global Economy* New York: Oxford University Press, pp. 155–81

Strauss, G. (1992) 'Creeping toward a field of comparative industrial relations' in H. Katz ed. *The Future of Industrial Relations* Ithaca, New York: Cornell University Press

Streeck, W. (1987) 'The uncertainties of management and the management of uncertainty: Employers, labor relations and industrial relations in the 1980s' *Work, Employment and Society* 1, 3, pp. 281–308

——(1988) 'Change in industrial relations: Strategy and structure' *Proceedings of an International Symposium on New Systems in Industrial Relations* 13–14 September, Tokyo: Japan Institute of Labour

——(1997) 'Neither European nor works councils' *Economic and Industrial Democracy* 18, 2, pp. 325–38

Thurley, K. & Wood, S. (1983) *Industrial Relations and Management Strategy* London: Cambridge University Press

Van Liemt, G. (1989) 'Minimum labour standards and international trade: Would a social clause work?' *International Labour Review* 128, 4, pp. 433–48

Verma, A., Kochan, T.A. & Lansbury, R.D. eds (1995) *Employment Relations in the Changing Asian Economies* London: Routledge

Walker, K.F. (1967) 'The comparative study of industrial relations' *Bulletin of the International Institute for Labour Studies* 3, pp. 105–32

Walton, R.E. & McKersie, R.B. (1991) *A Behavioral Theory of Labor Negotiations: An Analysis of a Social Interaction System* 2nd edn, Ithaca, New York: ILR Press

Womack, J., Jones, D. & Roos, D. (1990) *The Machine that Changed the World* New York: Rawson-Macmillan

World Bank (1995) *World Development Report 1995: Workers in an Integrating World* New York: Oxford University Press

Chapter 2   Employment relations in Britain

ACAS (Advisory Conciliation and Arbitration Service) *Annual Report* London: ACAS, Her Majesty's Stationery Office (annually)

Ackers, P., Smith, C. & Smith P. (1996) 'Against all odds: British trade unions in the new workplace' in P. Ackers, C. Smith & P. Smith eds *The New Workplace and Trade Unionism* London: Routledge

Atkinson, J. (1984) 'Manpower strategies for flexible organisations' *Personnel Management* August, pp. 28–31

Bacon, N. & Storey, J. (1993) 'Individualisation of the employment relationship, and the implications for trade unions' *Employee Relations* 15, 1, pp. 5–17

Bain, G.S. & Price, R.J. (1983) 'Union growth in Britain: Retrospect and prospect' *British Journal of Industrial Relations* 11, 1, pp. 46–68

Bamber, G.J. & Snape, E.J. (1986) 'British routes to employee involvement' in E.M. Davis & R.D. Lansbury eds *Democracy and Control in the Workplace* Melbourne: Longman Cheshire

Bassett, P. (1986) *Strike Free: New Industrial Relations in Britain* London: Macmillan

Beaumont, P.B. (1987) *The Decline of the Trade Union Organisation* London: Croom Helm

——(1992) *Public Sector Industrial Relations* London: Routledge

Berridge, J.R. (1992) 'Human resource management in Britain' *Employee Relations* 14, 5, pp. 62–92

——(1995) 'United Kingdom' in I. Brunstein ed. *Human Resource Management in Western Europe* Berlin: de Gruyter

Booth, A. (1994) *The Economics of the Trade Union* Cambridge: Cambridge University Press

Brown, W. (1981) *The Changing Contours of British Industrial Relations* Oxford: Blackwell

——(1993) 'The contraction of collective bargaining in Britain' *British Journal of Industrial Relations* 31, 2, pp. 189–200

Brown, W., Marginson, P. & Walsh, J. (1995) 'Management: Pay determination and collective bargaining' in P. Edwards ed. *Industrial Relations: Theory and Practice in Britain* Oxford: Blackwell

Burke, R.J. (1988) 'Sources of managerial and professional stress in large organisations' in C.L. Cooper & R. Payne eds *Causes, Coping and Consequences of Stress at Work* Chichester: Wiley

Casey, B. (1991) 'Survey evidence on trends in non-standard employment' in A. Pollert ed. *Farewell to Flexibility?* Oxford: Blackwell

Certification Office *Annual Report of the Certification Officer for Trade Unions and Employers' Associations* London: Certification Office for Trade Unions and Employers' Associations (annually)

Claydon, T. (1989) 'Union derecognition in Britain in the 1980s' *British Journal of Industrial Relations* 27, 2, pp. 214–24

Department of Employment *Employment Gazette* London: Her Majesty's Stationery Office (monthly) (In 1995 this monthly publication was re-titled *Labour Market Trends,* and is published by the Central Statistical Office)

Donovan, T.N. (1968) *Royal Commission on Trade Unions and Employers' Associations: Report* Cmnd 3623, London: Her Majesty's Stationery Office

Dunn, S. & Gennard, J. (1984) *The Closed Shop in British Industry* London: Macmillan

Edwards, P. (1995) 'Strikes and industrial conflict' in P. Edwards ed. *Industrial Relations: Theory and Practice in Britain* Oxford: Blackwell

Foulkes, F. (1980) *Personnel Policies in Large Non-union Companies,* Englewood Cliffs, NJ: Prentice Hall

Fox, A. (1985) *History and Heritage: The Social Origins of the British Industrial Relations System* London: Allen & Unwin

Gall, G. (1993) 'Harmony around a single table' *Labour Research* June
——(1994) 'The rise of single table bargaining in Britain' *Employee Relations* 16, 4, pp. 62–71

Gall, G. & McKay, S. (1994) 'Trade Union De-Recognition in Britain 1988–94' *British Journal of Industrial Relations,* 32, 3, pp. 433–48

Goodman, J.F.B. (1984) *Employment Relations in Industrial Society* Oxford: Philip Allan
——(1994) 'The United Kingdom' in *Towards Social Dialogue: Tripartite Co-operation in National Economic and Social Policy-Making* Geneva: International Labour Organisation, pp. 273–96

Goodman, J.F.B. & Earnshaw, J. (1995) 'New industrial rights and wrongs: The changed framework of British employment law' *New Zealand Journal of Industrial Relations* 19, 3, pp. 305–21

Goodman, J.F.B. & Whittingham, T.G. (1969) *Shop Stewards in British Industry* London: McGraw-Hill

Gospel, H.F. & Littler, C.R. (1983) *Managerial Strategies and Industrial Relations: An Historical and Comparative Study* London: Heinemann

Green, F. (1992) 'Recent trends in trade union density' *British Journal of Industrial Relations* 30, 3, pp. 445–58

Guardian (1995) 'Edmonds and CBI clash on "shameful" opt-out', attributed to Adair Turner, Director-General of the CBI, 4 December

Guest, D. (1995) 'Human resource management, trade unions and industrial relations' in J. Storey ed. *Human Resource Management: A Critical Text* London: Routledge, pp. 110–41

Guest, D. & Hoque, K. (1994) 'The good, the bad and the ugly: Employment relations in new non-union workplaces' *Human Resource Management Journal* 5, 1, pp. 1–14

Hall, M., Carley, M., Gold, M., Marginson, P. & Sisson, K. (1995) *European Works Councils: Planning for the Directive,* London/Coventry: Eclipse Group/Industrial Relations Research Unit

Hart, T.J. (1993) 'Human resource management—Time to exorcise the militant tendency' *Employee Relations* 15, 3, pp. 29–36

IRS (Industrial Relations Service) (1995) 'Single table bargaining: An idea whose time is yet to come' *IRS Employment Trends* 577, February, pp. 10–16, London: IRS

Jackson, M., Leopold, J. & Tuck, K. (1992) 'Decentralisation of collective bargaining: The case of the retail food industry' *Human Resource Management Journal* 2, 2, pp. 29–45

James, P. (1994) 'Worker representation and consultation: The impact of European requirements' *Employee Relations* 16, 7, pp. 32–42

Joseph Rowntree Foundation (1995) *Income and Wealth* York: Joseph Rowntree Foundation

Kelly, J. (1982) *Scientific Management, Job Redesign and Work Performance* London: Academic Press

Kessler, S. & Bayliss, F. (1995) *Contemporary British Industrial Relations* 2nd edn, London: Macmillan

Labour Market Trends Central Statistical Office, London: Her Majesty's Stationery Office (monthly)

Legge, K. (1995) *Human Resource Management: Rhetorics and Realities* Basingstoke: Macmillan

LRD (Labour Research Department) (1995) *Human Resource Management: A Trade Unionists' Guide,* London: LRD

McCarthy, W.E.J. (1964) *The Closed Shop in Britain* Oxford: Blackwell

McIlroy, J. (1995) *Trade Unions in Britain Today* 2nd edn, Manchester: Manchester University Press

MacInnes, J. (1987) *Thatcherism at Work: Industrial Relations and Economic Change* Milton Keynes: Open University Press

McLoughlin, I. & Gourlay, S. (1994) *Enterprise Without Unions: Industrial Relations in the Non-union Firm* Buckingham: Open University Press

Marchington, M. (1995a) 'Employee relations' in S. Tyson ed. *Strategic Prospects for Human Resource Management* London: Institute of Personnel and Development, pp. 81–111

——(1995b) 'Fairy tales and magic wands: New employment practices in perspective' *Employee Relations* 17, 1, pp. 51–66

Marchington, M., Goodman, J., Wilkinson, A. & Ackers, P. (1992) *Recent Developments in Employee Involvement* Employment Department Research Series No. 2 London: Her Majesty's Stationery Office

Marchington, M. & Parker, P. (1990) *Changing Patterns of Employee Relations* Hemel Hempstead: Harvester Wheatsheaf

Marginson, P. (1992) 'European integration and transnational management-union relations in the enterprise' *British Journal of Industrial Relations* 30, 4, pp. 529–45

Marginson, P., Edwards, P.K., Martin, R., Purcell, J. & Sisson, K. (1988) *Beyond the Workplace: Managing Industrial Relations in the Multi-Establishment Enterprise* Oxford: Blackwell

Millward, N. (1994) *The New Industrial Relations?* London: Policy Studies Institute

Millward, N. & Stevens, M. (1986) *British Workplace Industrial Relations 1980–1984: The DE/ESRC/PSI/ACAS Surveys* Aldershot: Gower

Millward, N., Stevens, M., Smart, D. & Hawes, W. (1992) *Workplace Industrial Relations in Transition* Aldershot: Dartmouth Publishing

OECD (Organisation for Economic Co-operation and Development) (1991) *OECD Employment Outlook* Paris: OECD

——(1997) *Implementing the OECD Job Strategy: Lessons from Member Countries' Experience* Paris: OECD

Oliver, N. & Wilkinson, B. (1992) *The Japanization of British Industry*, Oxford: Blackwell

Pollert, A. ed. (1991) *Farewell to Flexibility?* Oxford: Blackwell

Purcell, J. (1981) *Good Industrial Relations: Theory and Practice* London: Macmillan

——(1987) 'Mapping management styles in employee relations' *Journal of Management Studies*, 24, 5, pp. 533–48

Ramsay, H. (1977) 'Cycles of control: Worker participation in sociological and historical perspective' *Sociology*, 11, 3, pp. 481–506

Sisson, K.F. (1987) *The Management of Collective Bargaining: An International Comparison* Oxford: Blackwell

——(1992) 'Change and continuity in UK industrial relations: "Strategic choice" or "muddling through"?' Paper presented to the International IR/HR Project, Paris: Organisation for Economic Co-operation and Development/Cambridge, Mass.: Massachusetts Institute of Technology

——(1993) 'In search of human resource management' *British Journal of Industrial Relations* 31, 2, pp. 201–10

——(1994) *Personnel Management* 2nd edn, Oxford: Blackwell Publishers

Snape, E.J. & Bamber, G.J. (1989) 'Managerial and professional employees: Conceptualising union strategies and structures' *British Journal of Industrial Relations* 27, 1, pp. 93–111

Stevens, M., Millward, N. & Smart, D. (1989) 'Trade union membership and the closed shop in 1989' *Employment Gazette* November, pp. 615–23

Stewart, J. & Walsh, K. (1992) 'Change in the management of public services' *Public Administration* 70, 4, pp. 499–518

Storey, J. (1992) *Developments in the Management of Human Resources: An Analytical Review* Oxford: Blackwell

——(1995) 'Human resource management: Still marching on, or marching out?' in J. Storey ed. *Human Resource Management: a Critical Text* London: Routledge

Terry, M. & Dickens, L. eds (1991) *European Employment and Industrial Relations Glossary: United Kingdom* London: Sweet and Maxwell/Luxembourg: Office for Official Publications of the European Communities

Towers, B. (1997) *The Representation Gap* Oxford: Oxford University Press

TUC (Trades Union Congress) (1991) *Unions in Europe in the 1990s* London: TUC

——(1994) *HRM: a Trade Union Response* London: TUC

——(1995) *Your Voice at Work* London: TUC

Turner, H.A. (1962) *Trade Union Growth, Structure and Policy: A Comparative Study of the Cotton Unions* London: Allen and Unwin

Tyson, S. ed. (1995) *Strategic Prospects for HRM* London: Institute of Personnel and Development

Walsh, J. (1993) 'Internalisation versus decentralisation: An analysis of recent developments in pay bargaining' *British Journal of Industrial Relations* 31, 3, pp. 409–32

Welch, R. (1994) 'European works councils and their implications: The potential impact on employer practices and trade unions' *Employee Relations* 16, 4, pp. 48–61

Willman, P., Morris, T. & Aston, B. (1992) *Union Business: Trade Union Organisation and Financial Reform in the Thatcher Years* Cambridge: Cambridge University Press

Winchester, D. & Bach, S. (1995) 'The state: The public sector' in P. Edwards ed. *Industrial Relations: Theory and Practice in Britain* Oxford: Blackwell

Chapter 3 Employment relations in the United States

Adams, R.J. (1980) *Industrial Relations Systems in Europe and North America* Hamilton, Ontario: McMaster University

Allen, R.E. & Keaveny, T.J. (1988) *Contemporary Labor Relations* 2nd edn, Reading, Mass.: Addison-Wesley Publishing Co.

Applebaum, E. & Batt, R. (1994) *The New American Workplace* Ithaca, New York: ILR Press

Barbash, J. (1967) *American Unions: Structure, Government and Politics* New York: Random House

——(1981) 'Values in industrial relations: The case of the adversary principle' *Proceedings of the Thirty-third Annual Meeting, Industrial Relations Research Association* Madison, Wisconsin: Industrial Relations Research Association, pp. 1–7

Bauman, A. (1989) 'Union membership in 1988' *Current Wage Developments, February, 1989* Washington: Government Printing Office

Bernstein, I. (1970) *The Turbulent Years* Boston: Houghton Mifflin

Bureau of National Affairs (1995) *Collective Bargaining Negotiations and Contracts* Washington: Bureau of National Affairs

Bureau of the Census (1989) *National Data Book and Guide to Sources, Statistical Abstracts of the United States* 109th edn, Washington: Government Printing Office

Commerce Clearing House (1987) *Unemployment Insurance Reports* Chicago: Commerce Clearing House

Commons, J.R. (1913) 'American shoemakers, 1648–1895' *Labor and Administration* New York: Macmillan

Cooper, W.J. & Terrill, T.E. (1991) *The American South: A History* New York: Alfred A. Knopf

Eaton, A. & Kriesky, J. (1994) 'Collective bargaining in the paper industry: Developments since 1979' in P. Voos ed. *Contemporary Collective Bargaining* Madison, Wisconsin: Industrial Relations Research Association

Feuille, P. & Wheeler, H.N. (1981) 'Will the real industrial conflict please stand up?' in J. Stieber, R.B. McKersie & D.Q. Mills eds *US Industrial Relations 1950–1980: A Critical Assessment* Madison, Wisconsin: Industrial Relations Research Association, pp. 255–95

Foner, P.S. (1947) *History of the Labor Movement in the United States* vol. 1 New York: International Publishers

Gifford, C.D. (1992) *Directory of U.S. Labor Organizations* Washington: Bureau of National Affairs

Gomez-Mejia, L.R., Balkin, D.B. & Cardy, R.L. (1995) *Managing Human Resources* Englewood Cliffs, NJ: Prentice Hall

Gompers, S. (1919) *Labor and the Common Welfare* New York: Dutton

Heneman, H.G. III, Schwab, D.P., Fossum, J.A. & Dyer, L.D. (1980) *Personnel/Human Resource Management* Homewood, Illinois: Richard D. Irwin

Hession, C.H. & Sardy, H. (1969) *Ascent to Affluence: A History of American Economic Development* Boston: Allyn & Bacon

Hutchison, J. (1972) *The Imperfect Unions* New York: E.P. Dutton

Johnston, W.B. & Packer, A.E. (1987) *Workforce 2000* Indianapolis: Hudson Institute

Kassalow, E.M. (1974) 'The development of western labor movements: Some comparative considerations' in L.G. Reynolds, S.A. Masters & C. Moser eds *Readings in Labor Economics and Labor Relations* Engelwood Cliffs, NJ: Prentice Hall

Katz, H.C. (1993) 'The decentralization of collective bargaining: A literature review and comparative analysis' *Industrial and Labor Relations Review* 47, 1, pp. 3–22

Kempski, A. (1989) 'Bargaining '89' *AFL-CIO Reviews the Issues* Issue No. 31 Washington: AFL–CIO

Kochan, T.A. (1980) *Collective Bargaining and Industrial Relations* Homewood, Illinois: Richard D. Irwin

Kochan, T.A., Katz, H.C. & McKersie, R.B. (1986) *The Transformation of American Industrial Relations* New York: Basic Books

Lebergott, S. (1984) *The Americans: An Economic Record* New York: W.W. Norton

Ledvinka, J. & Scarpello, V.G. (1991) *Federal Regulation of Personnel and Human Resource Management* 2nd edn, Belmont, California: Kent

McClendon, J.A., Kriesky, J. & Eaton, A. (1995) 'Member support for union mergers: An analysis of an affiliation referendum' *Journal of Labor Research* 16, 1, pp. 9–23

Mitchell, D.J.B. (1983) 'The 1982 union wage concessions: A turning point for collective bargaining?' *California Management Review* 25, 4, pp. 78–92

OECD (Organisation for Economic Co-operation and Development) (1997) *OECD in Figures: Statistics on the Member Countries* Paris: OECD (set of summary tables published as a supplement to the mid-year issue of the *OECD Observer*)

Perlman, S. (1970) *The Theory of the Labor Movement* New York: Augustus M. Kelly

Sexton, Patricia Cayo (1991) *The War Against Labor and the Left* Boulder, CO.: Westview Press

Stieber, J. (1980) 'Protection against unfair dismissal: A comparative view' *Comparative Labor Law* 3, 3, pp. 229–40

Sturmthal, A. (1973) 'Industrial relations strategies' in A. Sturmthal & J. Scoville eds *The International Labor Movement in Transition* Urbana, Illinois: University of Illinois Press

Taft, P. (1964) *Organized Labor in American History* New York: Harper & Row

Taylor, F.W. (1964) *Scientific Management* New York: Harper & Row

Taylor, G.R. (1951) *The Transportation Revolution* New York: Rinehart

United States Department of Commerce, Bureau of Economic Analysis (1995) 'Survey of Current Business' Washington: United States Department of Commerce

US BLS (United States Bureau of Labor Statistics) (1997) 'Union members in 1996' *Bureau of Labour Statistics* Internet WWW page at <ftp://stats.bls.gov/pub/news.release/union2.txt> (released on 31 January 1997)

Voos, P. (1994) 'An economic perspective on contemporary trends in collective bargaining' in Paula Voos ed. *Contemporary Collective Bargaining* Madison, Wisconsin: Industrial Relations Research Association

Wheeler, H.N. (1985) *Industrial Conflict: An Integrative Theory* Columbia: University of South Carolina Press

Chapter 4   Employment relations in Canada

Adams, G. (1995) *Canadian Labour Law* 2nd edn, Aurora, Ont.: Canada Law Book

Betcherman, G., McMullen, K., Leckie, N. & Caren, C. (1994) *The Canadian Workplace in Transition* Kingston, Ont.: IRC Press, Queen's University

Brown, D.J.M. & Beatty, D.M. (1995) *Canadian Labour Arbitration* 3rd edn, Agincourt, Ont.: Canada Law Book

Chaykowski, R. & Verma, A. (1992) *Industrial Relations in Canadian Industry* Toronto: Holt, Rinehart & Winston

Craig, A.W.J. & Solomon, N. (1993) *The System of Industrial Relations in Canada* 4th edn, Scarborough, Ont.: Prentice Hall

Craven, P. (1980*) 'An Impartial Umpire': Industrial Relations and the Canadian State* Toronto: University of Toronto Press

Drache, D. & Glasbeeck, H. (1992) *The Changing Workplace: Reshaping Canada's Industrial Relations System* Toronto: James Lorimer

Finkelman, J. & Goldenberg, S. (1983) *Collective Bargaining in the Public Service: The Federal Experience in Canada* 2 vols, Montreal: The Institute for Research on Public Policy

Godard, J. (1994) *Industrial Relations: The Economy and Society* Toronto: McGraw-Hill Ryerson

Gunderson, M. & Ponak, A. (1995) *Union-Management Relations in Canada* 3rd edn, Toronto: Addison-Wesley

Hébert, G., Jain, H.C. & Meltz, N.M. eds (1989) *The State of the Art in Industrial Relations* Kingston: Industrial Relations Centre, Queen's University and Centre for Industrial Relations, University of Toronto

Kumar, P. (1993) *From Uniformity to Divergence: Industrial Relations in Canada and the United States* Kingston, Ont.: IRC Press, Queen's University

Maslove, A.M. & Swimmer, G. (1980) *Wage Controls in Canada, 1975–1978: A Study of Public Decision Making* Montreal: The Institute for Research on Public Policy

Ministry of Supply and Services (1994) *Annual Report of the Minister of Supply and Services Under the Corporations and Labour Unions Reporting Act, Part II* Ottawa: Ministry of Supply and Services

OECD (Organisation for Economic Co-operation and Development) (1996) *OECD Economic Surveys 1995–1996: Canada* Paris: OECD

Palmer, B.D. (1983) *Working class experience: the rise and reconstitution of Canadian labour, 1800–1980* Toronto: Butterworths

Panitch, L. & Swartz, D. (1993) *The Assault on Trade Union Freedoms: From Wage Controls to Social Contract* Toronto: Garamond Press

Riddell, C.W. (1986) *Canadian Labour Relations* Toronto: University of Toronto Press

Rose, J.B. (1980) *Public Policy, Bargaining Structure and the Construction Industry* Toronto: Butterworths

Sethi, A. ed. (1989) *Collective Bargaining in Canada* Scarborough, Ont.: Nelson Canada

Sims, A.C.L., Blouin, R. & Knopf, P. (1995) *Seeking a Balance: Canada Labour Code Review Part 1* Ottawa: Minister of Public Works and Government Services

Statistics Canada (1997) 'Effective wage increases in new collective agreements' Internet www page at http://www.statcan.ca/english/Pgdb/People/Labour/Labour.htm>

Swimmer, G. & Thompson, M. eds (1995) *Public Sector Collective Bargaining in Canada: The End of the Beginning or the Beginning of the End?* Kingston, Ont.: IRC Press, Queen's University

Weiler, P. (1980) *Reconcilable Differences* Toronto: Carswell

White, J. (1993) *Sisters and Solidarity: Women and Unions in Canada* Toronto: Thomson Educational Publishing

Woods, H.D., Carruthers, A.W.R., Crispo, J.H.G. & Dion, G. (1969) *Canadian Industrial Relations* Ottawa: Information Canada

Chapter 5   Employment relations in Australia

ABS (Australian Bureau of Statistics) (1995) *The Labour Force Australia*, Canberra: ABS, Catalogue No. 6203.0, May, pp. 73–83

——(1996) *Trade Union Members Australia*, Canberra: ABS, Catalogue No. 6325.0, August, p. 5

ACCIRT (Australian Centre for Industrial Relations Research and Training) (1995) *Agreements Data Base and Monitor* No. 7, Sydney: ACIRRT

ACTU/DU (Australian Council of Trade Unions/Trade Development Council) (1987) *Australia Reconstructed* Canberra: Australian Government Publishing Service

ALP/ACTU (Australian Labor Party/Australian Council of Trade Unions) (1983) *Statement of Accord by ALP and ACTU Regarding Economic Policy* Melbourne: ALP–ACTU

AMC (Australian Manufacturing Council) (1990) *The Global Challenge: Australian Manufacturing in the 1990s* Melbourne: AMC

Automotive Industry Council (1990) *Labour Turnover and Absenteeism* Melbourne: Automotive Industry Council

BCA (Business Council of Australia) (1989) *Enterprise-based Bargaining Units: A Better Way of Working* Melbourne: BCA

——(1991) *Avoiding Industrial Action* Melbourne: BCA

Beggs, J.J. & Chapman, B.J. (1987) 'Australian strike activity in an international context: 1964–1985' *Journal of Industrial Relations* 29, 2, pp. 137–49

Bennett, L. (1994) *Making Labour Law in Australia: Industrial Relations, Policies and Law* Melbourne: Law Book Company

Callus, R., Moorehead, A., Cully, M. & Buchanan, J. (1991) *Industrial Relations at Work: The Australian Workplace Industrial Relations Survey* Canberra: Australian Government Publishing Service

Coelli, M., Fahrer, J. & Lindsay, H. (1994) 'Wage dispersion and labour market institutions: A cross country study' *Reserve Bank Economic Research Discussion Paper* No. 9404 Sydney: Reserve Bank

Committee of Review into Australian Industrial Relations Law and Systems (1985) *Report* Canberra: Australian Government Publishing Service

Confederation of Australia Industry and Australian Council of Trade Unions (1988) *Joint Statement on Participative Practices* Canberra: Australian Government Publishing Service

Cook, P. (1991) 'Address at the Launch of Industrial Relations at Work' in K. Nash ed. *Designing the Future: Workplace Reform in Australia* Melbourne: Workplace Australia, pp. 102–3

Creigh, S.W. & Makeham, P. (1982) 'Strike incidence in industrial countries: An analysis' *Australian Bulletin of Labour* 8, 3, pp. 139–55

Dabscheck, B. (1989) *Australian Industrial Relations in the 1980s* Melbourne: Oxford University Press

——(1990) 'Industrial relations and the irresistible magic wand' in M. Easson & J. Shaw eds *Transforming Industrial Relations* Sydney: Pluto, pp. 117–30

——(1991) 'A decade of striking figures' *Economic and Labour Relations Review* 2, 1, pp. 172–96

——(1995) *The Struggle for Australian Industrial Relations* Melbourne: Oxford University Press

Davis, E.M. (1996) 'The 1995 ACTU congress: Recruitment and retention *Economic and Labour Relations Review* 7, 1, pp. 165–81

Davis, E.M. & Harris, C. eds (1996) *Making the Link: Affirmative Action and Industrial Relations*, vol. 7, Canberra: Australian Government Publishing Service, pp. 61–3

Davis, E.M. & Lansbury, R.D. eds (1986) *Democracy and Control in the Workplace* Melbourne: Longman Cheshire

Davis, E.M. & Lansbury, R.D. (1996) *Managing Together: Consultation and Participation in the Workplace* Melbourne: Longman

Davis, E.M. & Pratt, V. eds (1990) *Making the Link: Affirmative Action and Industrial Relations* Canberra: Australian Government Publishing Service

Department of Employment and Industrial Relations (1986) *Industrial Democracy and Employee Participation* Canberra: Australian Government Publishing Service

Eccles, S. (1982) 'The role of women in the Australian labour market' *Journal of Industrial Relations* 24, 3, pp. 315–36

Evans, A.C. (1989) 'Managed decentralism in Australia's industrial relations' Eleventh Sir Richard Kirby Lecture, University of Wollongong

Ford, G.W., Hearn, J. & Lansbury, R.D. eds (1980) *Australian Labour Relations: Readings*, Melbourne: Macmillan

Frenkel, S. (1990) 'Australian trade unionism and the new social structure of accumulation' Paper presented to the Asian Regional Conference, International Industrial Relations Association, Manila

Frenkel, S. & Peetz, D. (1990) 'Enterprise bargaining: The BCA's report on industrial relations reform' *Journal of Industrial Relations* 32, 1, pp. 69–99

Gerritsen, R. (1994) 'Microeconomic reform' in S. Bell & B. Head eds *State, Economy and Public Policy* Melbourne: Oxford University Press

Howard, W.A. (1977) 'Australian trade unions in the context of union theory' *Journal of Industrial Relations* 19, 3, pp. 255–73

Hyman, R. (1989) *Strikes* 4th edn, London: Macmillan

Isaac, J.E. (1977) 'Wage determination and economic policy' The Giblin Memorial Lecture, University of Melbourne

Karpin, D. (1995) *Enterprising Nation*, Report of the Industry Task Force on Leadership and Management Skills, Canberra: Australian Government Publishing Service

Keating, P.J. (1993) Speech to Institute of Directors luncheon, Melbourne, 21 April

Lansbury, R.D. (1978) 'The return to arbitration: Recent trends in dispute settlement and wages policy in Australia' *International Labour Review* 117, 5, pp. 611–24

——(1980) *Democracy in the Workplace* Melbourne: Longman Cheshire

——(1985) 'The Accord: A new experiment in Australian industrial relations' *Labour and Society* 10, 2, pp. 223–35

——(1994) 'Changing patterns of industrial relations and human resources in the Australian automotive industry: Towards transformation?' *International Journal of Employment Studies* 2, 1, pp. 3–40

Lansbury, R.D. & Davis, E.M. (1990) 'Employee involvement and workers' participation in management: The Australian experience' *Advances in Industrial and Labor Relations* 5, pp. 33–57

Lansbury, R.D. & Macdonald, D. eds (1992) *Workplace Industrial Relations: Australian Case Studies* Melbourne: Oxford University Press

Lansbury, R.D. & Niland, J.R. (1995) 'Managed decentralization? Recent trends in Australian industrial relations and human resource policies' in R. Locke, T.A. Kochan & M. Piore eds *Employment Relations in a Changing World Economy* Cambridge, Mass.: MIT Press, pp. 59–90

Ludeke, J. (1993) 'The public interest and the Australian industrial relations commission' *Journal of Industrial Relations* 34, 4, pp. 593–604

McCallum, R. & Ronfeldt, P. (1994) 'Our changing labour law' in P. Ronfeldt & R. McCallum eds *Enterprise Bargaining, Trade Unions and the Law* Sydney: Federation Press

MacDermott, T. (1994) 'The changing role of the safety net: The Australian Industrial Relations Commission's S150A Review' in P. Ronfeldt & R. McCallum eds *Enterprise Bargaining, Trade Unions and the Law* Sydney: Federation Press

McDonald, T. & Rimmer, M. (1989) 'Award restructuring and wages policy' *Growth* CEDA, 37, pp. 111–34

MacIntyre, S. & Mitchell, R. eds (1989) *Foundations of Arbitration* Melbourne: Oxford University Press

McKinnon, B. (1996) 'The struggle for managerial prerogative: Ramifications of the CRA Weipa dispute' in R. Fells & T. Todd eds *Current Research in Industrial Relations* Perth: Association of Industrial Relations Academics of Australia and New Zealand

Moorehead, A., Steel, M., Alexander, M., Stephen, K. & Duffin, L. (1997) *Changes at Work: The 1995 Australian Workplace Industrial Relations Survey*, Melbourne: Longman

National Wage Case March 1987 Dec 110/87 M Print G6800

National Wage Case August 1988 Dec 640/88 M Print H4000

National Wage Case August 1989 Dec 530/89 M Print H9100

Niland, J.R. (1976) *Collective Bargaining in the Context of Compulsory Arbitration* Sydney: New South Wales University Press

——(1989) *Transforming Industrial Relations in New South Wales: A Green Paper* Vols 1 & 2 Sydney: NSW Government Printer

Peetz, D. (1990) 'Declining union density' *Journal of Industrial Relations* 32, 2, pp. 197–223

Pittard, M. (1994) 'International labor standards in Australia: Wages, equal pay, leave and termination of employment' *Australian Journal of Labour Law* 7, 2, pp. 170–98

Plowman, D. (1989) *Holding the Line: Compulsory Arbitration and National Employer Coordination in Australia* Melbourne: Cambridge University Press

Quinlan, M. (1996) 'The reform of Australian industrial relations: Contemporary trends and issues' *Asian Pacific Journal of Human Resources* 34, 2, pp. 3–27

Sheehan, B.I. & Worland, D. eds (1986) *Glossary of Industrial Relations Terms* 3rd edn, Melbourne: Industrial Relations Society of Victoria

Wailes, N. & Lansbury, R.D. (1997) 'Flexibility versus collective bargaining? Patterns of industrial relations reform in Australia in the 1980s and 1990s' *ACIRRT Working Paper* no. 49, University of Sydney

Willis, R. (1997) 'Productive employment and sustainable livelihoods' Address to the Commission for Social Development, New York: United Nations

Yerbury, D. (1980) 'Collective negotiations, wage indexation and the return to arbitration: Some institutional and legal developments during the Whitlam era' in Ford, Hearn & Lansbury (1980), *op cit*, pp. 462–503

Yerbury, D. & Isaac, J.E. (1971) 'Recent trends in collective bargaining in Australia' *International Labour Review* 110, pp. 421–52

Chapter 6   Employment relations in Italy

Accornero, A. (1989) 'Recent trends and features in youth unemployment' *Labour: Review of Labour Economics and Industrial Relations* 3, 1, pp. 127–47

Altieri, G. et al. (1983) *La Vertenza sul Costo del Lavoro e le Relazioni Industriali* Milano: F. Angeli

Baglioni, G. (1991) 'An Italian mosaic: Collective bargaining patterns in the 1980s' *International Labour Review* 130, 1, pp. 81–93

Banca D'Italia (1997) *Relazione del Governatore sull'esercizio 1996* Assemblea generale ordinaria dei partecipanti Roma 31 maggio 1997

Barbadoro, I. (1973) *Storia del Sindacalismo Italiano* vol. 2 Firenze: La Nuova Italia

Beccalli, B. (1972) 'The rebirth of Italian trade unionism 1943–54' in S.J. Woolf *The Rebirth of Italy, 1943–50* London: Longman, pp. 181–211

Bordogna, L. (1989) 'The COBAS fragmentation of trade union representation and conflict' in R. Leonardi and P. Corbetta eds *Italian Politics: A review* vol. 3 London: Pinter, pp. 50–65

Brusco, S. (1982) 'The Emilian model: Productive decentralization and social integration' *Cambridge Journal of Economics* 6, pp. 167–89

——(1986) 'Small firms and industrial districts: The experience of Italy' in D. Keeble & E. Weber eds *New Firms and Regional Development in Europe* London: Croom Helm

Cagiano de Azevedo, R. & Musumeci, L. (1989) 'The new immigration in Italy' in R. Leonardi & P. Corbetta eds *Italian Politics: A Review* vol. 3 London: Pinter, pp. 66–78

Cella, G.P. & Treu, T. (1986) 'Collective and political bargaining' in O. Jacobi et al. eds *Economic Crisis, Trade Unions and the State* London: Croom Helm, pp. 171–90

——(1989) *Relazioni Industriali: Manuale per l'analisi dell'esperienza Italiana* Bologna: Mulino

——(1995) 'Between conflict and institutionalisation: Italian industrial relations in the 1980s and early 1990s' *European Journal of Industrial Relations* 1, 3 pp. 385–404

Compston, H. (1995) 'Union participation in economic policy making in France, Italy, Germany and Britain, 1970–1993' *West European Politics* 18 April, pp. 314–39

Dal Co, M. & Perulli, P. (1986) 'The trilateral agreement of 1983: Social pact or political truce' in O. Jacobi et al. eds *Economic Crisis, Trade Unions and the State* London: Croom Helm, pp. 157–70

Dell'Aringa, C. & Lodovici, M.S. (1990) 'Industrial relations and economic performance' *Review of Economic Conditions in Italy* 1, Jan.–Apr., pp. 55–83

Economist Intelligence Unit (1991) *Italy: Country Report No.1* London: Business International Limited

Ferner, A. & Hyman, R. (1992) 'Italy: Between political exchange and micro-corporatism' in A. Ferner & R. Hyman eds *Industrial Relations in the New Europe* Oxford: Blackwell, pp. 524–96

Flanagan, R.J. et al. (1984) *Unionism, Economic Stabilization, and Income Policy: European Experience* Washington DC: Brookings Institution

Franzosi, R. (1995) *The Puzzle of Strikes: Class and State Strategies in Postwar Italy* Cambridge: Cambridge University Press

Garonna, P. & Pisani, E. (1986) 'Italian unions in transition: The crisis of political unionism' in R. Edwards, P. Garonna & F. Todling eds *Unions in Crisis and Beyond: Perspectives from Six Countries* Dover, Mass.: Auburn House, pp. 114–72

Ginsborg, P. (1990) *A History of Contemporary Italy: Society and Politics* Harmondsworth: Penguin

Giugni, G. (1972) 'Recent trends in collective bargaining in Italy' in ILO (International Labour Organisation) *Collective Bargaining in Industrialised Market Economies* Geneva: ILO

——(1973) *Il Sindacato fra Contratti e Riforme 1969–1973* Bari: De Donato

——(1984) 'Recent trends in collective bargaining in Italy' originally published in *International Labour Review* 123, 5, pp. 559–614. Reprinted in J.P. Windmuller *Collective Bargaining in Industrialised Market Economies: A Reappraisal* Geneva: International Labour Organisation, pp. 225–40

Golden, M. (1988) *Labor Divided: Austerity and Working-Class Politics in Contemporary Italy* Ithaca, New York: Cornell University Press

Horowitz, D.L. (1963) *The Italian Labor Movement* Cambridge, Mass.: Harvard University Press

Jemolo, A.C. (1963) *Chiesa e Stato in Italia negli ultimi cento anni Roma*, quoted in D.L. Horowitz (1963) *The Italian Labor Movement* Cambridge, Mass.: Harvard University Press, p. 96

Katz, H.C. (1993) 'The decentralization of collective barganing: A literature review and comparative analysis' *Industrial and Labor Relations Review* 47, 1, pp. 3–22

Lange, P. (1977) *Studies on Italy 1943–1975: Selected Bibliography of American and British Materials in Political Science, Economics, Sociology and Anthropology* Torino: Fondazione Agnelli

Lange, P. et al. (1982) *Unions, Change and Crisis: French and Italian Union Strategy and the Political Economy, 1945–1980* London: Allen & Unwin

Lange, P. & Vannicelli, M. (1982) 'Strategy under stress: The Italian union movement and the Italian crisis in developmental perspective' in Lange et al. *Unions, Change and Crisis* London: Allen & Unwin

Lanzalaco, L. (1990) 'Pininfarina, president of the confederation of industry, and the problems of business interest associations' in R. Nanetti & R. Catanzaro eds *Italian Politics Review* vol. 4 London: Pinter, pp. 102–23

Locke, R.M. (1990) 'The resurgence of the local union: industrial restructuring and industrial relations in Italy' *Politics and Society* 18, Summer, pp. 347–79

——(1992) 'The decline of the national union in Italy: Lessons for comparative industrial relations theory' *Industrial and Labor Relations Review* 45, 2, pp. 229–49

Martinelli, A. & Treu, T. (1984) 'Employers' associations in Italy' in J.P. Windmuller & A. Gladstone eds *Employers' Associations and Industrial Relations: A Comparative Study* Oxford: Clarendon Press

Negrelli, S. & Santi, E. (1990) 'Industrial relations in Italy' in S. Baglioni & C. Crouch eds *European Industrial Relations: The Challenge of Flexibility* London: Sage, pp. 154–98

OECD (Organisation for Economic Co-operation and Development) (1991) *Historical Statistics 1960–1989* Paris: OECD

——(1995a) 'The public employment service in Denmark, Finland and Italy' in *Employment Outlook* July 1995 Paris: OECD

——(1995b) *Economic Surveys Italy* Paris: OECD

Pellegrini, C. (1983) 'Technological change and industrial relations in Italy' *Bulletin of Comparative Labour Relations* 12, pp. 93–209

——(1989) 'Italy' in M.J. Roomkin ed. *Managers as Employees: An International Comparison of the Changing Character of Managerial Employment* Oxford: Oxford University Press, pp. 228–52

——(1994) 'Italy' in R. Blanpain, C. Engels & C. Pellegrini eds *Contractual Policies Concerning Continued Vocational Training* Peeters: Leuven pp. 215–43

——(1995) 'La contrattazione aziendale' in G. Baglioni, S. Negrelli & D. Paparella eds *Le relazioni sindacali in Italia* Roma: Edizioni Lavoro, pp. 183–90

Perulli, P. (1991) 'Industrial flexibility and small firm districts: The Italian case' *Economic and Industrial Democracy* 11, 3, pp. 337–53

Piore, M. & Sabel, C. (1984) *The Second Industrial Divide: Possibilities for Prosperity* New York: Basic Books

Pyke, F., Beccattini, G. & Sengenberger, W. eds (1990) *Industrial Districts and Inter-firm Cooperation in Italy* Geneva: International Institute for Labour Studies, International Labour Organisation

Regalia, I. et al. (1978) 'Labour conflicts and industrial relations in Italy' in C. Crouch & A. Pizzorno eds *The Resurgence of Class Conflict in Europe* London: Macmillan, pp. 101–58

Regalia, I. & Regini, M. (1995) 'Between voluntarism and industrialization: Industrial relations and human resource practice in Italy' in R. Locke, T. Kochan & M. Piore eds *Employment Relations in a Changing World Economy* Cambridge, Mass.: MIT Press, pp. 131–63

Regini, M. (1987) 'Social pacts in Italy' in I. Scholten ed. *Political Stability and Neo-corporatism* London: Sage

Regini, M. & Regalia, I. (1997) 'Employers, unions and the state: The resurgence of concertation in Italy?' *West European Politics* 20, 1; in M. Bell & M. Rhodes eds Special Issue on 'Crisis and Transition in Italian Politics' pp. 210–30

Reyneri, E. (1989) 'The Italian labor market: between state control and social regulation' in P. Lange & M. Regini *State, Market, and Social Regulation* Cambridge: Cambridge University Press

——(1994) 'Italy: A long wait in the shelter of the family and of safeguards from the state' in O. Benoit-Guibot & D. Gallie eds *Long Term Unemployment* London: Pinter

Sabel, C.F. (1982) *Work and Politics: The Division of Labor in Industry* Cambridge, Mass.: Cambridge University Press

Salvati, M. (1985) 'The Italian inflation' in L.N. Lindberg & C.S. Mayer eds *The Politics of Inflation and Economic Stagnation* Washington DC: Brookings Institution

Santi, E. (1988) 'Ten years of unionization in Italy 77–86' *Labour: Review of Labour Economics and Industrial Relations* 2, 1, pp. 153–82

Sciarra, S. (1977) 'The rise of the Italian shop steward' in *Industrial Law Journal* 6, 1, March, pp. 35–44

Sforzi, F. (1990) 'The quantitative importance of Marshallian industrial districts in the Italian economy' in F. Pyke, G. Beccattini & W. Sengenberger eds *Industrial Districts and Inter-firm Cooperation in*

Italy Geneva: International Institute for Labour Studies, International Labour Organisation, pp. 75–107

Sirianni, C.A. (1992) 'Human resource management in Italy' *Employee Relations* 14, 55, pp. 23–38

Solinas, G. (1987) 'Labour market segmentation and workers' careers: The case of the Italian knitwear industry' in R. Tarling ed. *Flexibility in Labour Markets* London: Academic Press, pp. 271–305

Treu, T. (1981) 'Italy' in R. Blanpain ed. *International Encyclopedia for Labour Law and Industrial Relations* vol. 6 Deventer: Kluver

——(1983) 'Collective bargaining and union participation in economic policies: The case of Italy' in C. Crouch & F. Heller eds *Organizational Democracy and Political Processes* New York: Wiley

——(1987) 'Centralization and decentralization in collective bargaining' *Labour: Review of Labour Economics and Industrial Relations* 1, 1, pp. 147–75

Treu, T. & Roccella, M. (1979) *Sindacalisti nelle Istituzioni* Roma: Edizioni Lavoro

Veneziani, B. (1972) *La mediazione dei pubblici poteri nei conflitti colletivi di lavoro* Bologna: Il Mulino

Weitz, P. (1975) 'The CGIL and the PCI: From subordination to independent political force' in D. Blackmer & S. Tarrow eds *Communism in Italy and France* Princeton: Princeton University Press

Chapter 7   Employment relations in France

Adam, G. (1983) *Le pouvoir syndical en France* Paris: Dunod

Ardagh, J. (1982) *France in the 1980s: The Definite Book* London: Penguin

Auroux, J. (1981) *Report on the Right of Workers* Paris: Ministère du Travail

Bélier, G. (1990) *Report on employee representation* Paris: Ministère du Travail

Bevort, A. & Labbé, D. (1992) *La CFDT: organisation et audience depuis 1945* Paris: La Documentation Française

Bibes, G. & Mouriaux, R. eds (1990) *Les syndicats européens à l'épreuve* Paris: FNSP

Bridgford, J. & Sterling, J. (1994) *Employee Relations in Europe* Oxford: Blackwell

Bunel, J. & Saglio, J. (1984) 'Employers' associations in France' in J.P. Windmuller & A. Gladstone eds *Employers' Associations and Industrial Relations: a Comparative Study* Oxford: Clarendon Press

Caire, G. (1992) *La négociation collective* Paris: PUF

Coffineau, M. (1993) 'Report to the French Prime Minister on the Auroux Laws Ten Years After' in *Liaisons sociales* 29

Crouch, C. (1993) *Industrial Relations and European State Traditions* Oxford: Clarendon

Crouch, C. & Streeck, W. eds (1996) *Les capitalismes en Europe* Paris: La Découverte

Delamotte, Y. (1988) '*Workers participation and personnel policies in France*' International Labour Review 16, pp. 59–76

Denis, J.M. (1996) *Le groupe des dix* Working document Paris Institut de Recherches Economiques et Sociales IRES

Despax, M. & Rojot, J. (1987) *Labour Law and Industrial Relations in France* Deventer: Kluwer

Fajertag, G. ed. (1996) *Collective Bargaining in Western Europe* Bruxelles: European Trade Union Institute

Ferner, A. & Hyman, R. eds (1992) *Industrial Relations in the New Europe* Oxford: Blackwell

Gallie, D. (1978) *In Search of the New Working Class* Cambridge: Cambridge University Press

Gandois, J. (1993) *Le choix de la performance globale* Paris: La Documentation Française

Goetschy, J. (1983) 'A new future for industrial democracy in France' *Economic and Industrial Democracy* 1, pp. 85–103

——(1991) 'An appraisal of French research on direct participation' in R. Russel & V. Rus eds *International Yearbook of Participation in Organizations* Oxford: Oxford University Press

——(1995) 'Major developments and changes in French industrial relations since 1980s' in M. Mesch, *Sozialpartnershaft und Arbeitsbeziehungen in Europa* Vienna: Manz Verlag

Goetschy, J. & Linhart, D. (1990) *La crise des syndicats en Europe occidentale* Paris: La Documentation Française

Jefferys, S. (1996) 'Down but not out: French unions after Chirac' *Work, Employment and Society* 10, 3, pp. 509–27

Jobert, A. (1990) 'La négociation collective dans les entreprises multinationales en Europe' in G. Devin *Dimensions internationales* Nanterre: Editions Européennes Erasme

Jobert, A., Rozenblatt, P. et al. (1989) *Les classifications dans l'entreprise: production des hiérarchies professionnelles et salariales* Paris: La Documentation Française

Kesselman, M. ed. (1984) *The French Workers' Movement: Economic Crisis and Political Change* London: Allen & Unwin

Labbé, D. (1996) *Syndicats et syndiqués en France* Paris: L'Harmattan

Lallement, M. (1996) *Sociologie des relations professionnelles* Paris: La Découverte

Lane, C. (1989) *Management and Labour in Europe: The industrial enterprise in Germany, Britain and France* Aldershot: Edward Elgar

Lange, P., Martin, A., Ross, G. & Vannicelli, M. (1982) *Unions, Change and Crisis: French and Italian Union Strategy and Political Economy* London: Allen & Unwin

Leysink, P., Van Leemput, J. & Vilrocks, J. (1996) *The Challenge of Trade Unions in Europe* Cheltenham: Edward Elgar

Liaisons sociales (1993) Paris: Législation sociale

Linhart, D. & Malan, A. (1988) 'Individualisme professionnel des jeunes et action collective' *Travail et Emploi* 36–7 (June–Sept.), pp. 9–18

Maurice, M., Sellier, F. & Silvestre, J.J. (1986) *The Social Foundations of Industrial Power. A Comparison of France and Germany* Cambridge, Mass.: MIT Press

Mesh, M. ed. *Sozialpartnerschaft und Arbeitsbeziehungen in Europa* Wien: Manz Verlag

Morville, P. (1985) *Les Nouvelles Politiques Sociales du Patronat* Paris: La Découverte

Moss, B.H (1980) *The Origins of the French Labour Movement 1830–1914: The Socialism of Skilled Workers* Berkeley: University of California Press

——(1988) 'Industrial law reform in an era of retreat: The Auroux laws in France' *Work, Employment and Society* 2, 3, September, pp. 317–34

Mouriaux, R. (1983) *Les Syndicats dans la Société Française* Paris: Fondation Nationale des Sciences Politiques

——(1986) *Le Syndicalisme face à la Crise* Paris: La Découverte

——(1994) *Le syndicalisme en France depuis 1945* Paris: La Découverte

Murray, G., Morin, M.L. & Da Costa, I. eds (1996) *L'Etat des Relations Professionnelles* Québec Octares editions: Les presses de l'université Laval

Reynaud, J.D. (1975) *Les syndicats en France* Paris: La Découverte

Rojot, J. (1983) 'Technological changes and industrial relations' in G.J. Bamber and R.D. Lansbury eds *Technological Change and Industrial Relations: An International Symposium* A special issue of the *Bulletin of Comparative Labour Relations* vol. 12, pp. 175–93.

——(1986) 'The developments of French employers' policy towards trade-unions' *Labour and Society* January, pp. 175–93

——(1988) 'The myth of French exceptionalism' in J. Barbash & K. Barbash eds *Theories and Concepts in Comparative Industrial Relations* Columbia: University of South Carolina Press

Rosanvallon, P. (1986) *La Question Syndicale* Paris: Calmann-Lévy

——(1988) *La Question Syndicale* Paris: Seuil

Segrestin, D. (1990) 'Recent changes in France' in G. Baglioni & C. Crouch eds *European Industrial Relations* London: Sage

Sellier, F. (1984) *La confrontation sociale en France: 1936–1981* Paris: PUF

Shorter, E. & Tilly, C. (1974) *Strikes in France 1830–1968* Cambridge: Cambridge University Press

Smith, R. (1984) 'Dynamics of pluralism in France: the CGT, CFDT and industrial conflict' *British Journal of Industrial Relations* 22, 1 March, pp. 15–33

Touraine, A. et al. (1996) *Le grand refus* Paris: Fayard

Visser, J. (1990) *In Search of Inclusive Unionism* Deventer: Kluwer

Visser, J. & Ruysseveldt, J. (1996) *Industrial Relations in Europe* London: Sage

Chapter 8 Employment relations in Germany

Altmann, N. & Dull, K. (1990) 'Rationalization and participation: Implementation of new technologies and problem of works councils in the FRG' *Economic and Industrial Democracy* 11, 1

Baethge, M. & Wolf, H. (1992) 'The German system of industrial relations in transition?' Paper presented to the MIT/OECD conference on *Recent Trends in Industrial Relations and Human Resource Policies and Practices*, Cambridge: Massachusetts Institute of Technology/Paris: Organisation for Economic Co-operation and Development

Berghahn, V.R. & Karsten, D. (1987) *Industrial Relations in West Germany* Oxford: Berg

Bergmann, J. & Tokunaga, S. (1984) *Industrial Relations in Transition: The Cases of Japan and the Federal Republic of Germany* Tokyo: Tokyo University Press

Boedler, H. & Kaiser, H. (1979) 'Dreissig Jahre Tarifregister' *Bundesarbeitsblatt*, p. 26

Budde, A. et al. (1982) 'Corporate goals, managerial objectives and organisational structures in British and West German companies' *Organisation Studies* 3, 1, pp. 1–32

Bunn, R.F. (1984) 'Employers' associations in the Federal Republic of Germany' in J.P. Windmuller & A. Gladstone eds *Employers' Associations and Industrial Relations: A Comparative Study* Oxford: Clarendon Press, pp. 169–201

Clark, J. (1979) 'Concerted action in the Federal Republic of Germany' *British Journal of Industrial Relations* 17, 2

Clark, J. et al. (1980) *Trade Unions, National Politics and Economic Management: A Comparative Study of the TUC and DGB* London: Anglo-German Foundation

Clasen, L. (1989) 'Tarifverträge' *Bundesarbeitsblatt*, p. 26

Daubler, W. (1989) 'The individual and the collective: No problem for German labor law?' *Comparative Labor Law Journal* 10, 4, Summer

Federal Republic of Germany (1978) *Co-determination in the Federal Republic of Germany* (translations of the Acts of 1952, 1972 & 1976) Bonn: The Federal Minister of Labour and Social Affairs

Florian, M. & Hartmann, H. (1987) 'German trade unions and company information' *Industrial Relations Journal* 18, 4

Fox, A. (1985) *History and Heritage: The Social Origins of the British Industrial Relations System* London: Allen & Unwin

Fürstenberg, F. (1978) *Workers' Participation in Management in the Federal Republic of Germany* Geneva: International Institute for Labour Studies

——(1983) 'Technological change and industrial relations in West Germany' *Bulletin of Comparative Labour Relations* 12, pp. 121–37

——(1984) 'Recent trends in collective bargaining in the Federal Republic of Germany' *International Labour Review* 123, 5, pp. 615–30

——(1985) 'The regulation of working time in the Federal Republic of Germany' *Labour and Society* 10, 2, pp. 133–50

——(1991) *Structure and Strategy in Industrial Relations* Special issue of *Bulletin of Comparative Labour Relations* Deventer: Kluwer

Fürstenberg, F. & Steininger, S. (1984) *Qualification Aspects of Robotisation: Report of an Empirical Study for the OECD* Mimeo. Bochum: Ruhr Universität Bochum

Hart, D. (1996) 'Take-home pay compared: production workers in the UK and the OECD' *Labour Market Trends* 104, 10, October, pp. 453–5

Hartmann, G. et al. (1983) 'Computerised machine tools, manpower consequences and skill utilisation: a study of British and West German manufacturing firms' *British Journal of Industrial Relations* 21, 2, pp. 221–31

Hartmann, H. & Conrad, W. (1981) 'Industrial relations in West Germany' in P.B. Doeringer et al. eds *Industrial Relations in International Perspective: Essays on Research and Policy* London: Macmillan, pp. 218–45

Hassencamp, A. & Bieneck, H.J. (1983) 'Technical and organisational changes and design of working conditions in the Federal Republic of Germany' *Labour and Society* 8, pp. 39–56

Havlovic, S.J. (1990) 'German works councils: A highly evolved institution of industrial democracy' *Labor Studies Journal* 15, 2, Summer

Hutton, S.P. & Lawrence, P.A. (1981) *German Engineers: The Anatomy of a Profession* Oxford: Clarendon

Hyman, R. (1996) 'Institutional transfer: Industrial relations in eastern Germany' *Work, Employment and Society* 10, 4, pp. 601–39

IIRA (International Industrial Relations Association) (1986) *Proceedings of the Seventh World Congress of the International Industrial Relations Association* Geneva: IIRA

Institut der Deutschen Wirtschaft (1996) *Zahlen zur wirtschaftlichen Entwicklung der Bundesrepublik Deutschland* Köln: Deutscher Instituts-Verlag

Jacobi, O. & Müller-Jentsch, W. (1990) 'West Germany: Continuity and structural change' in G. Baglioni & C. Crouch eds *European Industrial Relations: The Challenge of Flexibility* London: Sage, pp. 127–53

Keller, B.K. (1981) 'Determinants of the wage rate in the public sector: The case of civil servants in the Federal Republic of Germany' *British Journal of Industrial Relations* 19, 3, pp. 345–60

Kissler, L. & Sattel, U. (1982) 'Humanization of work and social interests: Description and critical assessment of the state-sponsored program of humanization in the Federal Republic of Germany' *Economic and Industrial Democracy* 3, pp. 221–61

Lapping, A. (1983) *Working Time in Britain and West Germany* London: Anglo-German Foundation

Lawrence, P. (1980) *Managers and management in West Germany* London: Croom Helm

McCathie, A. (1992) 'Germans go into training' *Australian Financial Review* 24 July, p. 16

Maitland, I. (1983) *The Causes of Industrial Disorder: A Comparison of a British and a German Factory* London: Routledge & Kegan Paul

Markovits, A.S. (1986) *The Politics of the West German Trade Unions* Cambridge: Cambridge University Press

Marsh, A. et al. (1981) *Workplace Relations in the Engineering Industry in the UK and the Federal Republic of Germany* London: Anglo-German Foundation

Miller, D. (1978) 'Trade union workplace representation in the Federal Republic of Germany' *British Journal of Industrial Relations* 16, 3, pp. 335–54

——(1982) 'Social partnership and determinants of workplace independence in West Germany' *British Journal of Industrial Relations* 20

Moses, J.A. (1982) *Trade Unionism in Germany from Bismarck to Hitler, Vol. 1, 1869–1918; Vol. 2, 1919–1933* Totowa, NJ: Barnes & Noble

Mueller, F. (1992) 'Designing flexible teamwork: Comparing German and Japanese approaches' *Employee Relations* 14, 1, pp. 5–16

Neal, A.C. (1987) 'Co-determination in the Federal Republic of Germany' *British Journal of Industrial Relations* 25, 2

Niedenhoff, H.U. (1995) *Betriebsrats—und Sprecherausschusswahlen 1994* Köln: Deutscher Instituts-Verlag

OECD (Organisation for Economic Co-operation and Development) (1997) *OECD News Release, Standardised Unemployment Rates* SG/COM/NEWS(97)59, Paris: OECD, June

Owen Smith, E. (1981) 'West Germany' in E. Owen Smith ed. *Trade Unions in the Developed Economies* London: Croom Helm

Pieper, R. ed. (1990) *Human Resource Management: An International Comparison* Berlin: de Gruyter

Projektträger Humanisierung des Arbeitslebens (1981) *Das Programm zur Humanisierung des Arbeitslebens* Frankfurt and New York: Campus

Reichel, H. (1971) 'Recent trends in collective bargaining in the Federal Republic of Germany' *International Labour Review* 104, 6, pp. 253–71

Schregle, J. (1987) 'Workers participation in the Federal Republic of Germany in an international perspective' *International Labour Review* May–June

Seglow, P. et al. (1982) *Rail Unions in Britain and West Germany* London: Policy Studies Institute–Anglo-German Foundation

Sengenberger, W. (1984) 'West German employment policy restoring worker competition' *Industrial Relations* 23, 3, pp. 323–44

Sorge, A. et al. (1983) *Microelectronics and Manpower in Manufacturing: Applications of Computer Numerical Control in Great Britain and West Germany* Berlin: International Institute of Management/Aldershot: Gower

Sorge, A. & Warner, H. (1981) 'Culture, management and manufacturing organisation: A study of British and German firms' *Management International Review* 21, pp. 35–48

Statistisches Bundesamt (1994) '*Datenreport 1994*' *Zahlen und Fakten üeber die Bundesrepublik Deutschland* Bonn: Schriftenreihe der Bundeszentrale für politische Bildung, Bd, 325

Statistisches Jahrbuch (various years) Stuttgart: Metzler-Poeschel

Streeck, W. (1984) *Industrial Relations in West Germany: A Case Study of the Car Industry* London: Heinemann

——(1991) 'More uncertainties: German unions facing 1992' *Industrial Relations* 30, 3, pp. 317–49

Thelen, K. (1992) *Union of Parts: Labor Relations in Post-War Germany* Ithaca, New York: Cornell University Press

Turner, L. (1991) *Democracy at Work* Ithaca, New York: Cornell University Press

Tüselmann, H. (1996) 'Progress towards greater labour flexibility in Germany: The impact of recent reforms' *Employee Relations* 18, 1, pp. 50–67

Wächter, H. & Stengelhofen, T. (1992) 'Human resource management in a unified Germany' *Employee Relations* 14, 4, pp. 21–37

Wiesner, H. (1979) *Rationalisierung* Köln: Bund-Verlag

Wiesner, H. ed. (1983) *Bismarck to Bullock* London: Anglo-German Foundation

Williams, K. (1988) *Industrial Relations and the German Model* Aldershot: Avebury/Gower

Wirtschaft und Statistik (various years) Statistische Monatszahlen, Stuttgart & Mainz: Kohlhammer

Chapter 9   Employment relations in Sweden

Abrahamsson, B. & Broström, A. (1980) *The Rights of Labor* New York: Sage

Ahlén, K. (1989) 'Swedish collective bargaining under pressure' *British Journal of Industrial Relations* 27, 3, November, pp. 330–46

Auer, P. (1985) *Industrial Relations, Work Organisation and New Technology; the Volvo Case* Berlin: Wissenschaftzentrum

Bosworth, B. & Rivlin, A. eds (1987) *The Swedish Economy,* Washington DC: Brookings Institution

Brulin, G. (1995) 'Sweden: Joint councils under strong unionism' in J. Rodgers & W. Streeck eds *Works Councils* Chicago: University of Chicago Press

Brulin, G. & Nilsson, T. (1991): 'From societal to managerial corporatism. New forms of work organization as a transformation vehicle' *Economic and Industrial Democracy* 12, 3, August 1991

Delsen, L. & Van Veen, T. (1992) 'The Swedish model: Relevant for other European countries?' *British Journal of Industrial Relations* 30, 1, March, pp. 83–105

Edlund, S. & Nyström, B. (1988) *Developments in Swedish Labour Law,* Stockholm: The Swedish Institute

Elvander, N. (1990) 'Incomes policies in the Nordic countries' *International Labour Review* 129, 1, pp. 1–21

——(1992) *Labour Market Relations in Sweden and Great Britain: A*

Comparative Study of Local Wage Formation in the Private Sector During the 1980s Uppsala: Economic Studies Institute

Fry, J.A. ed. (1979) *Industrial Democracy and Labour Market Policy in Sweden* Oxford: Pergamon

——(1986) *Towards a Democratic Rationality: Making the Case for Swedish Labour* Aldershot: Gower

Fulcher, J. (1988) 'Trade unionism in Sweden' *Economic and Industrial Democracy* 9, pp. 129–40

——(1991) *Labour Movements, Employers and the State: Conflict and Cooperation in Britain and Sweden* Oxford: Clarendon Press

Graversen, G. & Lansbury, R.D. (1986) *New Technology and Industrial Relations in Scandinavia* Aldershot: Gower

Hammarström, O. (1978a) *Negotiations for Co-determination* Stockholm: Swedish Working Life Centre

——(1978b) *On National Strategies for Industrial Democracy: Some Reflections on Ten Years of Industrial Democracy Development in Sweden,* Stockholm: Swedish Centre for Working Life

Hammarström, O. & Mahon, R. (1994) 'Sweden: At the turning point?' *The Economic and Labour Relations Review* 5, 2, December, pp. 14–27

Hammarström, O. & Piotet, F. (1980) *Evaluation of the Main Trends in Work Organisation within the Context of Economic, Social and Technological Changes* Brussels: European Community

Hanami, T. & Blanpain, R. (1987) *Industrial Conflict Resolution in Market Economies: A Study of Canada, Great Britain and Sweden,* Deventer: Kluwer

Higgins, W. (1996) 'The Swedish municipal workers union: A study in the new political unionism' *Economic and Industrial Democracy* 17, 2, May pp. 167–98

Himmelstrand, U. et al. (1981) *Beyond Welfare Capitalism* London: Heinemann

Industrial Relations Services (1983) 'Sweden: employee investment funds' *European Industrial Relations Review* 199, December, pp. 22–3

Jangenas, B. (1985) *The Swedish Approach to Labour Market Policy* Stockholm: The Swedish Institute

Johannesson, J. & Wadensjö, E. ed. (1995) *Labour Market Policy at the Crossroads* Reports from The Expert Group for Labour Market Policy Evaluation Studies (EFA) no. 34, Stockholm: EFA

Johnston, T.L. (1962) *Collective Bargaining in Sweden* London: George Allen & Unwin

Jones, H.G. (1987) 'Scenarios for industrial relations: Sweden evolves a new consensus' *Long Range Planning* 20, 3, pp. 65–76

Korpi, W. (1978) *The Working Class in Welfare Capitalism: Work, Unions and Politics in Sweden* London: Routledge & Kegan Paul

Lash, S. (1985) 'The end of new-corporatism?: The breakdown of centralised bargaining in Sweden' *British Journal of Industrial Relations* 23, 2, July, pp. 215–39

Lawrence, P. (1986) *Management and Society in Sweden* London: Routledge & Kegan Paul

Meidner, R. (1983) *Strategy for Full Employment* Stockholm: PSI Symposium

Neal, A.C. et al. (1981) *Law and the Weaker Party: An Anglo-Swedish Comparative Study, Vol. 1, The Swedish Experience* Oxfordshire: Professional Books

Nilsson, T. (1996) 'Lean production and white collar work' in *Economic and Industrial Democracy* 17, 3, August

OECD (Organisation for Economic Co-operation and Development) *Quarterly Labour Force Statistics* Paris: OECD (Quarterly)

Olson, G.M. ed. (1988) *Industrial Change and Labour Adjustment in Sweden and Canada* Toronto: Garamond Press

——(1992) *The Struggle for Economic Democracy in Sweden,* Aldershot: Avebury

Olsson, A.S. (1989) *The Swedish Wage Negotiation System* Uppsala Department of Sociology, University of Uppsala

——(1990) *Swedish Wage Negotiation System* Aldershot: Dartmouth

Peterson, R.B. (1987) 'Swedish collective bargaining: A changing scene' *British Journal of Industrial Relations* 25, 1, March, pp. 31–48

Pontusson, J. (1992) *The Limits of Social Democracy: Investment Politics in Sweden* Ithaca: Cornell University Press

Pontusson, J. & Kuruvilla, S. (1992) 'Swedish wage-earner funds: An experiment in economic democracy' *Industrial and Labor Relations Review* 45, 4, July, pp. 779–91

Rehn, G. & Viklund, B. (1990) 'Changes in the Swedish model' in G. Baglioni & C. Crouch eds *European Industrial Relations: The Challenge of Flexibility* London: Sage, pp. 300–25

Rosendahl, M. (1985) *Conflict and Compliance: Class Consciousness among Swedish Workers* London: Coronet Books

Sandberg, Å. et al. (1992) *Technological Change and Co-determination in Sweden* Philadelphia: Temple University Press

Schmidt, F. (1976) *The Democratisation of Working Life in Sweden: A Survey of Agreements, Legislation, Experimental Activities, Research and Development* Stockholm: Tjänstemännens Centralorganisation (TCO)

——(1977) *Law and Industrial Relations in Sweden* Stockholm: Almqvist & Wiksell International

Swenson, P. (1985) *Unions, Pay and Politics in Sweden and West Germany,* Ithaca, New York: Cornell University Press

Tilton, T. (1990) *The Political Theory of Swedish Social Democracy* Oxford: Clarendon

Chapter 10 Employment relations in Japan

Abegglen, J.C. (1958) *The Japanese Factory: Aspects of Its Social Organisation* Glencoe, Ill.: Free Press

——(1973) *Management and Worker: The Japanese Solution* Tokyo: Sophia University Press

Abegglen, J.C. & Stalk, G. Jr (1985) *Kaisha: The Japanese Corporation* New York: Basic Books

Aoki, M. (1988) *Information, Incentives, and Bargaining in the Japanese Economy* Cambridge: Cambridge University Press

Chalmers, N.J. (1989) *Industrial Relations in Japan: The Peripheral Workforce* London: Routledge

Chusho Kigyo Cho (Small and medium-sized enterprise agency) (1983) *Chusho Kigyo Hakusho* White Paper on SMEs Tokyo: Okurasho Insatsukyoku (Ministry of Finance Printing Office)

Clarke, R. (1979) *The Japanese Company* New Haven: Yale University Press

Cole, R.E. (1971) *Japanese Blue Collar: The Changing Tradition* Berkeley: University of California Press

Dore, R. (1979) *British Factory-Japanese Factory: The Origin of National Diversity in Industrial Relations* London: George Allen & Unwin/ Berkeley: University of California Press

——(1987) *Taking Japan Seriously* Stanford: Stanford University Press

Ford, G.W. (1983) 'Japan as a learning society' *Work and People* 9, 1, pp. 3–5

Freeman, R. & Weitzman, M. (1987) 'Bonuses and employment in Japan' *Journal of the Japanese and International Economies* 1, pp. 168–94

Gordon, A. (1985) *The Evolution of Labor Relations in Japan* Cambridge: Council on East Asian Studies, Harvard University

Gould, W.B. (1984) *Japan's Reshaping of American Labor Law* Cambridge, Mass.: MIT Press

Hanami, T. (1979) *Labour Relations in Japan Today* Tokyo: Kodansha-International

Hashimoto, M. (1990) *The Japanese Labor Market in a Comparative Perspective with the United States* Kalamazoo, MI: W.E. Upjohn Institute for Employment Research

JIL (Japan Institute of Labour) (1979–89) *Japanese Industrial Relations Series* 1–12, Tokyo: JIL (Nihon Rodo Kenkyu Kiko)

——(1995) *Japanese Working Life Profile* Tokyo: JIL (Nihon Rodo Kenkyu Kiko)

——*Japan Labor Bulletin* Tokyo: JIL (Nihon Rodo Kenkyu Kiko) (monthly)

JISEA (Japan Institute for Social Economic Affairs) (1984) *Japan 1990: An International Comparison* Tokyo: Keizai Koho Centre

Keizai Kikakucho (Economic Planning Agency) (1996) *Keizai Hakusho* (White Paper on economy) Tokyo: Toyo Keizai Shimpo Sha

——(1997) *Nihon no Keizai Kozo* (Economic Structure of Japan) Tokyo: Toyo Keizai Shimpo Sha

Koike, K. (1988) *Understanding Industrial Relations in Modern Japan* New York: St Martin's Press

Koseisho (Ministry of Health and Welfare) (1989) *Kani Seimei Hyo* (Simplified Life Expectancy Table)

Kuwahara, Y. (1983) 'Technological change and industrial relations in Japan' *Bulletin of Comparative Labour Relations* 12, pp. 32–52

——(1985) 'Labour and management views of and their responses to microelectronics in Japan' Paper presented to the International Symposium on Microelectronics and Labour, Tokyo

——(1989) *Industrial Relations Systems in Japan: A New Interpretation* Tokyo: Japan Institute of Labor

——(1993) 'Untied knots: Labour migration and development in Asia' *International Labour Migration in East Asia* Tokyo: The United Nations University

——(1996) 'The impact of globalization on industrial relations: corporate governance and industrial relations in Japan' *Democratization, Globalization and the Transformation of Industrial Relations in Asian Countries* International Industrial Relations Association, 3rd Asian Regional Congress, Taipei, Taiwan, ROC

——(1997) 'Japan's dilemma: Can international migration be controlled?' in M. Weiner & T. Hanami eds *Temporary Workers or Future Citizens?* New York: Macmillan

Levine, S.B. (1984) 'Employers' associations in Japan' in J.P. Windmuller & A. Gladstone eds *Employers' Associations and Industrial Relations: A Comparative Study* Oxford: Clarendon, pp. 318–56

Marsh, R.M. (1992) 'The difference between participation and power in Japanese factories' *Industrial and Labor Relations Review* 45, 2, January

Ministry of Labour (1997) *White Paper on Labour 1996: Summary* Tokyo: Japan Institute of Labour

Morishima, M. (1992) 'Use of joint consultation committees by large Japanese firms' *British Journal of Industrial Relations* 30, 3, September, pp. 405–23

Mueller, F. (1992) 'Designing flexible teamwork: Comparing German and Japanese approaches' *Employee Relations* 14, 1, pp. 5–16

Nakayama, I. (1975) *Industrialisation and Labor-Management Relations in Japan* Tokyo: Japan Institute of Labour

OECD (Organisation for Economic Co-operation and Development) (1977) *The Development of Industrial Relations Systems: Some Implications of Japanese Experience* Paris: OECD

Olson, M. (1982) *The Rise and Decline of Nations: Economic Growth, Stagflation, and Social Rigidities* New Haven: Yale University Press

Ota, T. (1988) 'Work rules in Japan' *International Labour Review* 127, 5, pp. 627–39

Ozaki, R. (1991) *Human Capitalism* New York: Penguin

Rododaijin Kambo Seisaku Chousabu (Labour Minister's Secretariat) (1996) *Nihon no Rodokumiai no Genjyo* (The Current Situation of Japanese Trade Unions) Tokyo: Okurasho Insatsukyoku

Rodoscho (Ministry of Labour) (1987) *Rodo Hakusho* (White Paper on labour) Tokyo: Nihon Rodo Kenkyu Kiko
——(1991 & 1996) *Rodo Kumiai Kihon Tokei Chosa* (The Basic Survey on Trade Unions) Tokyo: Rodosho
——(1995) *Rodo Sogi Tokei Chosa* (The Survey on Industrial Disputes) Tokyo: Rodosho
Sako, M. (1990) *Women in the Japanese Workplace* London: Hilary Shipman
Sako, M. & Sato, H. eds (1997) *Japanese Labour and Management in Transition: diversity, flexiblity and participation* London and New York: Routledge
Shimada, H. (1994) *Japan's 'Guest Workers': Issues and Public Policies* Tokyo: University of Tokyo Press
Shirai, T. ed. (1983) *Contemporary Industrial Relations in Japan* Madison, Wisconsin: University of Wisconsin Press
Somucho (General Coordination Agency) (1986) *Jigyosho Tokei* (Census of Establishments) Tokyo: Ministry of Finance Printing Office
——(1995) *Rodoryoku Chosa* (Survey on Labour Force) Tokyo: Ministry of Finance Printing Office
Sugeno, K. (1992) *Japanese Labor Law* translated by Leo Kanowitz Tokyo: University of Tokyo Press
Sumiya, M. (1990) *The Japanese Industrial Relations Reconsidered* Tokyo: The Japan Institute of Labour
Ward, B. (1958) 'The firm in Illyria: Market syndicalism' *American Economic Review* 68, pp. 566–89
Weitzman, M.L. (1984) *The Share Economy: Conquering Stagflation* Cambridge: Harvard University Press
White, M. & Trevor, M. (1983) *Under Japanese Management* London: Heinemann
Whittaker, D.H. (1997) *Small firms in the Japanese Economy* Cambridge: Cambridge University Press

Chapter 11 Employment relations in Korea

Asian Monitor Research Centre (1996) 'New versus old labour laws in Korea' *Asian Labour Update*, No. 23, pp. 7–15
Bank of Korea (1990) *Economic Indicators* Seoul: Bank of Korea
Choi, J.J. (1989) *Labor and the Authoritarian State: Labor Unions in South Korean Manufacturing Industries* Seoul: Korea University Press
Chun, B.Y. (1985) 'Hankukjabonjooeuwa Yimnodongeu Kujobyeonhwa' (Korean Capitalism and Structural Changes in Wage Labour) *Sahyeowa Sasang Hankil*, May, pp. 239–70
Chun, K.H. (1989) *Hankuk Nodongkyeoungjearo* (Korean Labour Economics) Seoul: Hankilsa
Chung, K.H. (1988) *Hankukeu Seongjangjeonlyagkwa Kyeoungyeoungkujo*

(Diversification Strategy and Managerial Structure of Korean Firms) Seoul: Korean Chamber of Commerce and Industry

Deyo, F.C. (1989) *Beneath the Miracle: Labor Subordination in the New Asian Industrialism* London: University of California Press

Dore, R. (1979) 'Industrial relations in Japan and elsewhere' in A.M Craig ed. *Japan: A Comparative View* Princeton, NJ: Princeton University Press, pp. 324–70

Dunlop, J.T. (1958) *Industrial Relations Systems* New York: Holt, Rinehart & Winston

Frenkel, S. ed. (1993) *Organized Labor in the Asia-Pacific Region: A Comparative Study of Trade Unionism in Nine Countries* Ithaca, New York: International Labor Relations Press

Garran (1997) 'Korea in transition' *The Australian* 5 March, p. 23

Kim, H.J. (1993) 'The Korean union movement in transition' in S. Frenkel ed. *Organised Labour in the Asia-Pacific: A Comparative Study of Trade Unionism in Nine Countries* Ithaca, New York: International Labour Relations Press, pp. 133–61

Kim, K.C. & Kim, S. (1989) 'Kinship group and patrimonial executives in a developing nation: a case study of Korea' *The Journal of Developing Areas* 24, October, pp. 27–46

Kim, J.N. (1984) 'Kiyeobeu Seongjangkwa Kyeoungjaeryeog' (Growth of the corporation and managerial power) *Monthly Chosun*, February, pp. 116–23

Kong, B.H. (1992) *Chaebol*, Seoul: Yemyung

Korea Labor Institute (1994) *The Profile of Korean Human Assets: Labor Statistics 1994* Seoul: KLI

Korean Chamber of Commerce and Industry (1988) *Hankukeu Kyeoungyeoung Nosakwankyei (Labour–Management Relations in Korea)* Seoul: KCCI

Kuk, M.H. (1987) *The Relationship between Government and Private Companies in the Industrial Development of South Korea, A Study of Korean Way of Development* PhD Thesis Urbana-Champaign: University of Illinois

Kwon, S.H. & Leggett, C.J. (1994) 'Industrial relations and the South Korean Chaebol' *Proceedings of the 8th Association of Industrial Relations Academics of Australia and New Zealand (AIRAANZ)* February 1994 Sydney: AIRAANZ

Lee, J.N. (1985) *Chaebol (The Chaebol)* Seoul: Hyunjae

Moon, C.I. (1994) 'Changing patterns of business–government relations in South Korea' in A. Macintyre ed. *Business and Government in Industrialising Asia* Sydney: Allen & Unwin, pp. 142–61

Ogle, G.E. (1990) *South Korea: Dissent within the Economic Miracle* Washington: Zed Books

Paisley, E. (1994) 'May Day! Spring wage talks threaten South Korean recovery' *Far Eastern Economic Review* 3 February, p. 54

Park, D.J. (1992) 'Industrial relations in Korea' *The International Journal of Human Resource Management* 3, 1, May, pp. 105–23

Park, Y.B. (1995) 'Economic development, globalization, and practices in industrial relations and human resource management in Korea' in A. Verma, T.A. Kochan & R.D. Lansbury eds *Employment Relations in the Growing Asian Economies* London: Routledge, pp. 27–61

——(1996) *Labour Trends in the 1990s in Korea* Seoul Korea Labor Institute

Park, Y.B. & Lee, C.S. (1996) 'Labour standards and economic development in Korea' in J.S. Lee *Labour Standards and Economic Development* Taipei: Chung-Hua Institution for Economic Research, pp. 173–208

Park, Y.K. (1993) 'South Korea' in S.J. Deery & R.J. Mitchell eds *Labour Law and Industrial Relations in Asia* Melbourne: Longman-Cheshire, pp. 137–71

Park, Y.K. & Lee, M.B. (1995) 'Economic development, globalisation and practice in industrial relations and human resource management' in A. Verma et al. eds *Employment Relations in the Growing Asian Economies* London: Routledge, pp. 27–61

Sharma, B. (1991) 'Industrialisation and strategy shifts in industrial relations: a comparative study of South Korea and Singapore' in C. Brewster & S. Tyson eds *International Comparisons in Human Resource Management* London: Pitman, pp. 92–102

Vogel, E.F. (1991) *The Four Little Dragons: The Spread of Industrialization in East Asia* Cambridge: Harvard University Press

Wilkinson, B. (1994) *Labour and Industry in the Asia-Pacific: Lessons from the Newly-Industrialised Countries* Berlin: de Gruyter

Woo, S.H. (1996) 'Approaching the 21st century: Perspectives on Korean industrial relations' *Proceedings of the International Industrial Relations Association 3rd Asian Regional Congress September 30–October 4, 1996, Taipei* vol. 4, pp. 155–76

Chapter 12 Conclusions

Adams, R. ed. (1991) *Comparative Industrial Relations* Contemporary *Research and Theory* London: Harper Collins

Baglioni, G. (1989) 'Industrial relations in Europe in the 1980s' *Labour and Society* 14, 3, July

Baglioni, G. & Crouch, C. eds (1990) *European Industrial Relations: The Challenge of Flexibility* London: Sage

Bamber, G.J. (1986) *Militant Managers? Managerial Unionism and Industrial Relations* Aldershot: Gower

Bamber, G.J., Córdova, E. & Sheldon, P. (1998) 'Collective bargaining' in R. Blanpain & C. Engels *Comparative Labour Law and Industrial Relations in Industrialised Market Economies* 6th edn, Deventer: Kluwer

Bamber, G.J. & Lansbury, R.D. (1989) *New Technology: International*

Perspectives on Human Resources and Industrial Relations London: Unwin-Hyman

Bamber, G.J., Park, F., Lee, C. & Ross, P.K. eds (forthcoming) *Changing Approaches to Industrial Relations in the Asia-Pacific* Sydney: Allen & Unwin

Bamber, G.J. & Peschanski, V.V. (1996) 'Transforming industrial relations in Russia: A case of convergence with industrialised market economies?' *Industrial Relations Journal* 27, 1, pp. 74–8

Beaumont, P. & Harris, R. (1997) 'Trade union membership in the EU' *European Industrial Relations Review* 279, April, pp. 121–3

Björkman, T. (1993) 'ABB: Performance improvement in a multidomestic corporation' in K. North *Improving Enterprise Performance: International Transfer of Approaches* Geneva International Labour Organisation

Blanpain, R. (1998) 'Comparativism in labour law and industrial relations' in R. Blanpain et al. eds *Comparative Labour Law and Industrial Relations* 6th edn, Deventer: Kluwer, pp. 3–22

Blanpain, R. et al. eds (1998) *Comparative Labour Law and Industrial Relations* 6th edn, Deventer: Kluwer

Boyer, R. (1988) *The Search for Labour Market Flexibility. The European Economies in Transition* Oxford: Clarendon

Brewster, C. (1995) 'Towards a "European" model of human resource management' *Journal of International Business Studies* 1st quarter, 26, 1, pp. 1–21

Caire, G. (1994) 'Labour standards and international trade' in W. Sengenberger & D. Campbell eds *International Labour Standards and Economic Interdependence* Geneva: International Institute for Labour Studies

Campbell, D. (1992) 'The globalizing firm and labour institutions' in P. Bailey et al. eds *Multinationals and Employment: The Global Economy of the 1990s* Geneva: International Labour Organisation

——(1994) 'Foreign investment, labour immobility and the quality of employment' *International Labour Review* 133, 2, pp. 185–204

Chaykowski, R.P. & Verma, A. eds (1992) *Industrial Relations in Canadian Industry* Toronto: Dryden

Clarke, O. & Niland, J. eds (1991) *Agenda for Change: An International Analysis of Industrial Relations in Transition* Sydney: Allen & Unwin

Creighton, B. (1992) 'How the ILO works' *Workplace: The Australian Council of Trade Unions Magazine* Summer, pp. 36–9

Crouch, C. (1985) 'Conditions for trade union wage restraint' in L. Lindberg & C. Maier eds *The Politics of Inflation and Economic Stagnation* Washington DC: Brookings

Curson, C. (1986) *Flexible Patterns of Work* London: Institute of Personnel Management

Darbishire, O. & Katz, H. (1997) *Converging Divergences: Worldwide Changes in Employment Relations* Manuscript, New York School of Industrial and Labor Relations, Cornell University

Davis, E.M. & Lansbury, R.D. eds (1996) *Managing Together, Consultation and Participation in the Workplace* Melbourne: Longman

Dowling, P.J., Schuler, R.S. & Welch, D.E. (1994) *International Dimensions of Human Resource Management* 2nd edn, Belmont, California: Wadsworth

Ferner, A. & Hyman, R. eds (1997) *Industrial Relations in the New Europe* 2nd edn, Oxford: Blackwell

Frenkel, S. & Clarke, O. eds 'Economic restructuring and industrial relations in industrialised countries' *Bulletin of Comparative Labour Relations*, 20, Deventer: Kluwer

Galenson, W. (1981) *The International Labor Organization: An American View* Madison: University of Wisconsin Press

Gladstone, A. & Wheeler, H. eds (1992) *Labour Relations in a Changing Environment* New York: de Gruyter

Gold, M. & Hall, M. (1992) *Report on European-level Information and Consultation in Multinational Companies: An Evaluation of Practice* Dublin: European Foundation for the Improvement of Living and Working Conditions

Grant, D. (1994) 'New style agreements at Japanese transplants in the UK' *Employee Relations* 16, 2, pp. 65–83

Hegewisch, A., Brewster, C. & Koubek, J. (1996) 'Different roads: Changes in industrial and employee relations in the Czech Republic and East Germany since 1989' *Industrial Relations Journal* 27, 1, pp. 50–64

Hyman, R. (1996) 'Institutional transfer: Industrial relations in eastern Germany' *Work, Employment and Society* 10, 4, pp. 601–39

ILO (International Labour Organisation) (1977) *Tripartite Declaration of Principles Concerning Multinational Enterprises and Social Policy* Geneva: ILO

——(1995) *World Employment Report* Geneva: ILO

——(1996) *Yearbook of Labour Statistics* Geneva: ILO

——(1997) *World Labour Report* Geneva: ILO

Jacoby, S.M. (1995) 'Social dimensions of global economic integration' in S.M. Jacoby ed. *The Workers of Nations: Industrial Relations in a Global Economy* New York: Oxford University Press, pp. 3–30

Johnston, G.A. (1970) *The International Labour Organisation: Its Work for Social and Economic Progress* London: Europa

Kahn-Freund, O. (1976) 'The European social charter' in F.G. Jacobs ed. *European Law and the Individual* Amsterdam: North Holland, pp. 181–211

Kitay, J. & Lansbury, R.D. eds (1997) *Changing Employment Relations in Australia* Melbourne: Oxford University Press

Kochan, T.A., Lansbury, R.D. & MacDuffie, J.P. eds (1997) *After Lean Production: Evolving Employment Practices in the World Auto Industry* Ithaca, New York: Cornell University Press

Lane, C. (1987) *Management and Labour in Europe: The Industrial Enterprise in Germany and France* Aldershot: Gower

Lipsig-Mumme, C. (1989) 'Canadian and American unions respond to economic crisis' *Journal of Industrial Relations* 31, 2, June, pp. 229–56

Locke, R.M., Kochan, T.A. & Piore, M. (1995) *Employment Relations in a Changing World Economy* Cambridge, Mass.: MIT Press

Moss, B.H. (1988) 'Industrial law reform in an era of retreat: The Auroux Laws in France' *Work, Employment and Society* 2, 3, pp. 317–34

Northrup, H. et al. (1988) 'Multinational union–management consultation in Europe' *International Labour Review* 127, 5

Northrup, H. & Rowan, R.L. (1979) *Multinational Collective Bargaining Attempts: The Records, the Cases and the Prospects* Philadelphia: Industrial Research Unit, The Wharton School, University of Pennsylvania

OECD (Organisation for Economic Co-operation and Development) (1976) *Declaration by the governments of OECD member countries and decisions of the OECD Council on guidelines for multi-national enterprises, national treatment, international investment, incentives and disincentives, consultation procedures* Paris: OECD

——(1979) *Collective Bargaining and Government Policies: the Experience of Ten OECD Countries* Paris: OECD

——(1991) *Employment Outlook* Paris: OECD

——(1994a) 'Collective bargaining: levels and coverage' *Employment Outlook* Paris: OECD

——(1994b) *The OECD Guidelines for Multinational Enterprises* Paris: OECD

Oechslin, J. (1993) 'Employers' organisations' in R. Blanpain et al. eds *Comparative Labour Law and Industrial Relations* 5th edn, Deventer: Kluwer

Ohmae, K. (1990) *The Borderless World: Power and Strategy in the Interlinked Economy* London: Collins

Oliver, N. & Wilkinson, B. (1992) *The Japanization of British Industry* Oxford: Blackwell

Peetz, D. (1990) 'Declining union density' *Journal of Industrial Relations* 32, 2, pp. 197–223

Porter, M.E. (1990) *The Competitive Advantage of Nations* London: Macmillan

Rasmussen, E. (1997) 'Employment relations in New Zealand in the 1990s' Paper presented to the *Comparative Employment Relations Conference*, University of Aalborg, Denmark

Sarfati, H. & Kobrin, C. eds (1988) *Labour market flexibility: A comparative anthology* Aldershot: Gower

Servais, J.M. (1996) 'International Labour Organisation' in R. Blanpain ed. *International Encyclopedia of Laws* The Hague: Kluwer

Shadur, M.A., Rodwell, J.J. & Bamber, G.J. (1995) 'The adoption of international best practices in a western culture: East meets West' *International Journal of Human Resource Management* 6, 3, pp. 735–57

Smith, F. (1984) 'What is the International Labour Organisation?' *International Labour Reports* 6, Nov.–Dec., pp. 23–4

Stråth, B. (1987) *The Politics of De-Industrialisation: The Contraction of the West European Shipbuilding Industry* London: Croom Helm

Sweeney, K. & Davies, J. (1997) 'International comparisons of labor disputes in 1995' *Labour Market Trends* April, pp. 129–33

Trebilcock, A. (1994) *Towards social dialogue: Tripartite cooperation in national economic and social policy* Geneva: International Labour Organisation

UNCTAD (United Nations Commission on Trade and Development) (1993): *World Investment Report 1993: Transnational Corporations and Integrated International Production* New York: United Nations

Upham, M. ed. (1990) *Employers' Organizations of the World* London: Longman

Valticos, N. & Samson, K. (1993) 'International labour law' in R. Blanpain ed. *Comparative Labour Law and Industrial Relations* 5th edn, Deventer: Kluwer

Visser, J. (1989) *European Trade Unions in Figures* Deventer: Kluwer

Windmuller, J.P. (1995) 'International trade union secretariats, the industrial trade union internationals' *Foreign Labor Trends* 47, Washington: US Labor Department, Bureau of International Labor Affairs

Windmuller, J.P. & Gladstone, A. eds (1984) *Employers' Associations and Industrial Relations: A Comparative Study* Oxford: Clarendon Press, International Institute of Labour Studies

Windmuller, J.P. & Pursey, S. (1993) 'The international trade union movement' in R. Blanpain ed. *Comparative Labour Law and Industrial Relations* 5th edn, Deventer: Kluwer, pp. 55–76

World Bank (1995) *World Development Report 1995: Workers in an Integrating World* New York: Oxford University Press

Appendix

Not all of these sources are cited explicitly in the Appendix. The following list includes others as an initial guide to sources of data relevant to the study of international and comparative industrial relations. The ILO and OECD also publish many useful works (including the bi-monthly *International Labour Review* and OECD *Observer*, the OECD annual *Employment Outlook* and half-yearly *Economic Outlook*, and the approximately yearly economic surveys that the OECD makes for each member country). Other useful sources include relevant publications from the World Bank, UN, EU, BLS, JIL, *European Industrial Relations Review, The Economist*, Economist Intelligence Unit and the Korea Labor Institute.

ABS (Australian Bureau of Statistics) (1996a) *Trade Union Statistics, Australia* Canberra: ABS, Catalogue No. 6323.0

——(1996b) *Trade Union Members, Australia* Canberra: ABS, Catalogue No. 6325.0

Adams, L.T. (1985) 'Changing employment patterns of organised workers' *Monthly Labor Review* February, pp. 25–31

Anderson, V. (1991) *Alternative Economic Indicators* London: Routledge

Australia Department of Tourism (1993) *Tourism, Australia's Passport to Growth, A National Tourism Strategy* Department of Tourism Implementation Progress Report No.1 Canberra: Australian Government Publishing Service

Australian Bulletin of Labour Adelaide: National Institute of Labour Studies, Flinders University (quarterly)

Bain, G.S. & Elsheik, F. (1976) *Union Growth and the Business Cycle: An Econometric Analysis* Oxford: Blackwell

Bain, G.S. & Price, R.J. (1980) *Profiles of Union Growth: A Comparative Statistical Portrait of Eight Countries* Oxford: Blackwell

Ball, D. & McCulloch, W. (1996) *International Business, The Challenge of Global Competition* 6th edn, Boston: Irwin

Bamber, G.J. & Whitehouse, G. (1992) 'International data on economic, employment and human resource issues' *International Journal of Human Resource Management* 3, 2, September, pp. 347–70

Batstone, E. (1985) 'International variations in strike activity' *European Sociological Review* 1, 1, May, pp. 47–64

Bean, R. ed. (1989) *International Labour Statistics: A Handbook Guide, and Recent Trends* London: Routledge

Blackburn, R., Jarman, J. & Siltanen, J. (1993) 'The analysis of occupational gender segregation over time and place: consideration of some new measurements' *Work, Employment and Society* 7, 3, pp. 335–62

Blanchflower, D.G. & Freeman, R.B. (1992) 'Unionism in the US and other advanced OECD countries' *Industrial Relations* 31, 1, Winter, pp. 56–79

Blyton, P. (1989) 'Hours of work' *International Labour Statistics: A Handbook Guide, and Recent Trends* London: Routledge, pp. 127–45

Bratt, C. (1996) 'Tables and graphs' *Labour Relations in 18 Countries* 4th edn, Stockholm: Swedish Employers' Confederation (SAF) (intermittently)

Carter, M. & Gregory, R. (1981) 'Government pensions, benefits and the distribution of employment for males during a recession' Working Paper Canberra: Research School of Social Sciences, Australian National University

Chamberlain, N.W., Cullen, D.E. & Lewin, D. (1980) *The Labor Sector* 3rd edn, New York: McGraw-Hill

Chang, C. & Sorrentino, C. (1991) 'Union membership statistics in 12 countries' *Monthly Labor Review* December, pp. 46–52

Clark, D. (1989) 'The problems in measuring GDP' *Australian Financial Review* 12 July, pp. 36–7

Clarke, R.O. (1980) 'Labour–management disputes: A perspective' *British Journal of Industrial Relations* 18, 1, March, pp. 14–25

——(1987) 'The work of the OECD in the labour field' *The International*

Journal of Comparative Labour Law and Industrial Relations 3, 4, Winter, 1987/88

Clegg, H.A. (1976) *Trade Unionism and Collective Bargaining: A Theory Based on Comparisons of Six Countries* Oxford: Blackwell

Creigh, S.W. et al. (1982) 'Differences in strike activity between countries' *International Journal of Manpower* 3, 4, pp. 15–23

Dore, R.P. & Sako, M. (1989) *How the Japanese Learn to Work* London: Routledge

EC (European Community) (1985) *Report on Social Developments Year* Brussels–Luxembourg: European Communities Commission (annually)

Economist 'Economic and financial indicators' London (weekly)

——(1991) *The Economist Pocket World in Figures* London: The Economist Books

Edwards, P.K. (1983) 'The end of American strike statistics' *British Journal of Industrial Relations* 21, 3, pp. 392–4

EU (European Union) *Labour Costs Survey* Brussels: Eurostat (triennially)

Far Eastern Economic Review (1996) 'The cult of the export, there's more to life—and growth—than just exports' Editorial 10 October, p. 10

Fisher, M. (1973) *Measurement of Labour Disputes and their Economic Effects* Paris: Organisation of Economic Co-operation and Development

Garelli, S. et al. (1997) *World Competitiveness Yearbook* Geneva: Institute for Management Development

Hart, R.A. (1984) *Shorter Working Time: A Dilemma for Collective Bargaining* Paris: Organisation for Economic Co-operation and Development

Hussmanns, R., Mehran, F. & Verma V. *Surveys of Economically Active Population, Employment, Unemployment and Underemployment: An ILO Manual on Concepts and Methods* Geneva: International Labour Organisation

ILO (International Labour Organisation) (1976) *International Recommendations on Labour Statistics* Geneva: ILO

——(1984) *World Labour Report Vol. 1: Employment, Incomes, Social Protection, New Information Technology* Geneva: ILO

——(1985) *World Labour Report Vol. 2: Labour Relations, International Labour Standards, Training, Conditions of Work, Women at Work* Geneva: ILO

——(1987) *World Labour Report Vol. 3: Incomes from Work: Between Equity and Efficiency* Geneva: ILO

——(1995) *World Labour Report Vol. 8: Controversies in Labour Statistics* Geneva: ILO

——(1996) 'Union membership rates' Geneva: ILO, unpublished

——a *Yearbook of Labour Statistics* Geneva: ILO (annually)

——b *Bulletin of Labour Statistics* Geneva: ILO (quarterly)

——c *Social and Labour Bulletin* Geneva: ILO (quarterly)

IMF (International Metalworkers' Federation) (1996) *The Purchasing Power of Working Time: An International Comparison 1994–1995* Geneva: IMF (annually)

IMF (International Monetary Fund) *International Financial Statistics* Washington: IMF (annual)

Ingham, G.K. (1974) *Strikes and Industrial Conflict* London: Macmillan

Jackson, M.P. (1987) *Strikes: Industrial Conflict in Britain, USA and Australia* Brighton: Wheatsheaf/Sydney: Allen & Unwin

Japan Institute for Social and Economic Affairs (1992) *Japan 1992: An International Comparison* Tokyo: Keizai Koho Center (annually)

JIL (Japan Institute of Labor) (1991) *Japanese Working Life Profile: Labor Statistics* Tokyo: JIL (annually)

Jones, B. (1995) *Sleepers, Wake! Technology and the Future of Work* 4th edn Melbourne: Oxford University Press

Jonung, C. (1984) 'Patterns of occupational segregation by sex in the labour market' in G. Schmid & R. Weitzel eds *Sex Discrimination and Equal Opportunity: The Labour Market and Employment Policy* New York: St Martin's Press

Kaim-Caudle, P.R. (1973) *Comparative Social Policy and Social Security: A Ten Country Study* London: Martin Robertson

Koike, K. (1996) *The Economics of Work in Japan* Tokyo: LTCB International Library Foundation

Korea Labor Institute (1995) *The Profile of Korean Human Assets: Labor Statistics 1995* Seoul: Korea Labor Institute

Korea NSO (National Statistical Office) (1997) 'Tax burden ratio to GNP', Korea NSO Internet WWW page at <http://www.nso.go.kr/graph/social/picures/gec1b_3.gif>

Korpi, W. (1981) 'Sweden: conflict, power and politics in industrial relations' in P. Doeringer et al. eds *Industrial Relations in International Perspective: Essays on Research and Policy* London: Macmillan

Labour Market Trends Central Statistical Office, London: Her Majesty's Stationery Office (monthly)

Leyland, J. (1990) *Business Comparisons: An Analytical and Statistical Survey of Europe and the USA* London: The Economist Intelligence Unit

Lynch, L. (1992) 'International comparisons of HR/IR practices and labor market outcomes: Evidence from national statistics' Mimeo. Cambridge, Mass.: Massachusetts Institute of Technology, Sloan School of Management

Neef, A. & Kask, C. (1991) 'Manufacturing productivity and labor costs in 14 economies' *Monthly Labor Review* December, pp. 24–37

OECDa (Organisation for Economic Co-operation and Development) *OECD Employment Outlook* Paris: OECD (annually)

——b *Labour Force Statistics* Paris: OECD (annually, with a 20-year historical abstract)

——c *Quarterly Labour Force Statistics* Paris: OECD (quarterly)

——d *OECD in Figures: Statistics on the Member Countries* Paris: OECD (an invaluable set of summary tables, with most data only two years old; it is usually published as a supplement to a mid-year issue of the *OECD Observer*)

——e *Historical Statistics* Paris: OECD (annually; published as a companion volume to the mid-year *Economic Outlook*)

——f *Economic Outlook* Paris: OECD (half-yearly; it includes OECD forecasts based on a review of each OECD member country)

——g *Revenue Statistics of the OECD Member Countries* Paris: OECD (annually)

——h *Main Economic Indicators* Paris: OECD (monthly)

Peetz, D. (forthcoming) *Unions in Decline* Cambridge: Cambridge University Press

Pilat, D. (1996) *Labour Productivity Levels in OECD Countries: Estimates for Manufacturing and Selected Service Sectors* Working Paper No. 169 Paris: Economics Department, Organisation for Economic Co-operation and Development

Pocock, B. & Wright, P. (1997) 'Trade unionism in 1996' *The Journal of Industrial Relations* 39, 1, March 1997

Price, R. & Bain, G.S. (1989) 'The comparative analysis of union growth' in *Recent Trends in Industrial Relations Studies and Theory* Brussels: International Industrial Relations Association, pp. 99–110

Ross, A.M. & Hartman, P.T. (1960) *Changing Patterns of Industrial Conflict* New York: Wiley

Rubery, J., Smith, M. & Fagan, C. in collaboration with Almond, P. & Parker, J. (1996) *Trends and Prospects for Women's Employment in the 1990s* European Network of Experts on the Situation of Women in the Labour Market: Report for the Equal Opportunities Unit, DEV, of the European Commission Manchester: Manchester School of Management, UMIST

Runciman, W.G. (1991) 'Explaining union density in twentieth-century Britain' *Sociology* 25, 4, pp. 697–712

Shalev, M. (1978) 'Lies, damned lies and strike statistics: The measurement of trends in industrial conflict' in C. Crouch & A. Pizzorno eds *The Resurgence of Class Conflict in Western Europe Since 1968* vol. 1 London: Macmillan, pp. 1–20

——(1980) 'Industrial relations theory and the comparative study of industrial relations and industrial conflict' *British Journal of Industrial Relations* 18, 1, March, pp. 26–43

Smith, A.D. et al. (1982) *International Industrial Productivity: A Comparison of Britain, America and Germany* Cambridge: Cambridge University Press, National Institute of Economic and Social Research

Stern, R. (1997) *Organising for Collective Purchasing of Low Cost Services and Political Representation* Ithaca, New York: ILR–Cornell University

Sweeney, K. & Davies J. (1997) 'International comparisons of labour disputes in 1995' *Labour Market Trends* April, pp. 129–33

Thurman, J.E. & Trah, G. (1989) 'Part-time work in international perspective' *Conditions of Work Digest* 8, 1 Geneva: International Labour Organisation, pp. 3–26

Turvey, R. ed. (1989) *Developments in International Labour Statistics* London: Pinter

UK Department of Employment *Employment Gazette* London: Her Majesty's Stationery Office (monthly) (NB This publication has now been incorporated into *Labour Market Trends* London: HMSO)

UN (United Nations) (1971) *Indices to the International Standard Industrial Classification of all Economic Activities* New York: Department of Economic and Social Affairs, United Nations (intermittently)

US BLS (United States Bureau of Labor Statistics) (1985) *Handbook of Labor Statistics* Washington DC: US Bureau of Labor Statistics, Department of Labor (intermittently)

——*Monthly Labor Review* Washington DC: US Department of Labor (monthly)

——*News* Washington DC: Bureau of Labor Statistics Press Releases, US Department of Labor (intermittently)

——*News* Washington DC: US Bureau of Labor Statistics, Department of Labor, April, unpublished (mimeo., intermittently)

——(1991) *International Comparisons of Hourly Compensation Costs for Production Workers in Manufacturing* 1975–90 Report 817 Washington DC: US Bureau of Labor Statistics, Department of Labor

——(1996a) *International Comparisons of Hourly Compensation Costs for Production Workers in Manufacturing, 1975–95* Report 909 Washington DC: US Bureau of Labor Statistics, Department of Labor

——(1996b) *International Comparisons of Manufacturing Productivity and Unit Labor Cost Trends, 1995* Internet WWW page at <http://stats.bls.gov/news.release/prod4.toc.htm> (released on 17 July 1996)

——(1997) *Median usual weekly earnings of full-time wage and salary workers by selected characteristics, annual averages* Internet WWW page at <http://stats.bls.gov/news.release/wkyeng.t06.htm> (released January 1997)

US GAO (United States General Accounting Office) (1990) *Training Strategies: Preparing Noncollege Youth for Employment in the US and Foreign Countries* Washington DC: US General Accounting Office

Visser, J. (1990) 'In search of inclusive unionism' *Bulletin of Comparative Labour Relations* 18, Deventer: Kluwer, pp. 245–78

Walby, S. (1988) *Gender Segregation at Work* Milton Keynes: Open University Press

Walsh, K. (1983) *Strikes in Europe and the United States: Measurement and Incidence* London: Frances Pinter

——(1985) *The Measurement of Trade Union Membership in the European Community* Luxembourg–Brussels: Eurostat

——(1987) *Long-term Unemployment: An International Perspective* London: Macmillan

Walsh, K. & King, A. (1986) *International Manpower Market Comparisons* London: Macmillan

Waring, M. (1988) *Counting for Nothing: What Men Value and What Women are Worth* Wellington: Allen & Unwin/Port Nicholson Press

Western, B. (1993) 'Postwar unionisation in eighteen advanced capitalist countries' *American Sociological Review* 58, April, pp. 266–82

Whitehouse, G. (1992) 'Legislation and labour market gender inequality: An analysis of OECD countries' *Work Employment and Society* 6, 1, pp. 65–86

World Bank (1982) *World Development Report* Washington DC: International Bank for Reconstruction and Development

——*World Bank Atlas* Washington DC: International Bank for Reconstruction and Development (annually)

WTO (1997) 'World Trade Organisation' Internet WWW page at <http://www.wto.org/>

Websites

A large amount of statistical and general information on employment relations issues can now be found on the World Wide Web (WWW). Both country specific data (e.g. the Australian Bureau of Statistics home page) and international/comparative data (e.g. OECD home page) can be readily found. While some sites require a subscription to obtain detailed statistical data, many, such as the OECD's *Frequently Requested Statistics* home page, will supply condensed versions of their statistical publications for no charge. Other organisations, such as the US Bureau of Labor Statistics, will supply large amounts of data at no cost (although much of this information is naturally limited to the United States). Many sites provide edited versions of books, journals and papers on employment relations issues, while industrial relations associations (e.g. the Association of Industrial Relations Academics of Australia and New Zealand, AIRAANZ) also run their own Web pages.

Given the range of material on the WWW it is difficult to compile a comprehensive list of what is available; nonetheless, we have listed below a number of websites that we hope you will find useful as possible starting points. These include the websites for the national statistical offices for all the countries in this book.

However, given the speed with which website addresses change, and indeed how the concept of the WWW itself is changing, we cannot take responsibility for the reader finding information at the sites listed. We would very much appreciate your feedback on the following sites, and would be interested to hear of new sites you find in the comparative employment relations field. Happy net surfing!

Peter Ross
Griffith University Graduate School of Management
Email: <p.ross@gsm.gu.edu.au>

Association of Industrial Relations Academics of Australia and New Zealand (AIRAANZ) <http://www.mngt.waikato.ac.nz/depts/sm&l/airaanz/airaanz.htm>

Australian Council of Trade Unions (ACTU) <http://www.actu.asn.au/>

Australian Bureau of Statistics (ABS) <http://www.statistics.gov.au/>

Canada (Statistics Canada) <http://www.statcan.ca/>

Canadian Industrial Relations Association <http://www.business.mcmaster.ca/cira/>

French National Institute of Statistics and Economics (does not provide online statistical data) <http://www.insee.fr/va/index.htm>

German Federal Statistical Office <http://www.statistik-bund.de/e_home.htm>

Industrial Relations Research Association (IRRA) (USA) <http://www.ilr.cornell.edu/IRRA/>

International Confederation of Free Trade Unions (ICFTU) <http://www.icftu.org/index.html>

International Institute for Management Development (IMD) home page <http://www.imd.ch/imd_home.html>

——Information Resources <http://www.ilo.org/public/english/190bibl/index.htm>

——World Competitiveness On-Line <http://www.imd.ch/wcy_over.html>

International Labour Organisation (ILO) home page <http://www.ilo.org/public/english/index.htm>

International Monetary Fund (IMF) <http://www.imf.org/external/index.htm>

International Organizations, Political Parties, and Labour Unions (Uppsala University, Sweden) <http://www.statsvet.uu.se/parties.htm>

Italian National Statistical Authority <http://www.istat.it/> (English language site at <http://www.istat.it/inglese.html> not available at time of publishing)

Japanese Statistics Bureau and Statistics Centre <http://www.stat.go.jp/>

Korean National Statistical Office (NSO) <http://www.nso.go.kr/eindex.html>

National Statistical Agencies and Offices (links to government agencies worldwide) <http://www.libraries.psu.edu/crsweb/docs/statnats.htm>

Organisation for Economic Co-operation and Development (OECD) home page (Paris) <http://www.OECD.Org./>

——Frequently Requested Statistics <http://www.oecdwash.org/PRESS/CONTENT/frstat.htm>

——Washington Center home page <http://www.oecdwash.org/>

Resource Centre for Access to data on Europe (rcade) <http://rcade.essex.ac.uk/>

Sweden (Statistics Sweden) <http://www.scb.se/indexeng.htm>

Swedish Centre for Working Life <http://www.ralf.se>

UK Office for National Statistics <http://www.emap.com/ons/>

United Nations (UN) home page <http://www.un.org/>

——Social Indicators <http://www.un.org/Depts/unsd/social/main.htm>

——Statistics Division <http://www.un.org/Depts/unsd/statdiv.htm>

US Bureau of Labor Statistics (BLS) home page <http://stats.bls.gov:80/blshome.html>

——Data home page <http://stats.bls.gov:80/blshome.html>

US National Labor Relations Board (NLRB) <http://www.nlrb.gov/>

Workindex (US based) <http://www.workindex.com/>

World Bank <http://www.worldbank.org/html/>

World Trade Organisation <http://www.wto.org/>

Index